Computer Forensics

Computer Forensics

Incident Response Essentials

Warren G. Kruse II
Jay G. Heiser

Addison-Wesley

Boston • San Francisco • New York • Toronto
Montreal • London • Munich • Paris • Madrid • Capetown
Sydney • Tokyo • Singapore • Mexico City

Many of the designations used by manufacturers and sellers to distinguish their products are claimed as trademarks. Where those designations appear in this book, and Addison-Wesley, Inc., was aware of a trademark claim, the designations have been printed in initial capital letters or in all capitals.

The authors and publisher have taken care in the preparation of this book, but make no expressed or implied waranty of any kind and assume no responsibility for errors or omissions. No liability is assumed for incidental or consequential damages in connection with or arising out of the use of the information or programs contained herin.

Screen shots reprinted with permission from Microsoft.

The publisher offers discounts on this book when ordered in quantity for special sales. For more information, please contact:

Pearson Education Corporate Sales Division
201 W. 103rd Street
Indianapolis, IN 46290
(800) 428-5331
corpsales@pearsoned.com

Visit AW on the Web: www.awprofessional.com

Library of Congress Cataloging-in-Publication Data

Kruse, Warren G.
    Computer forensics : incident response essentials / Warren G. Kruse II, Jay G. Heiser.
       p. cm.
    Includes bibliographical references and index.
    ISBN 0-201-70719-5
    1. Computer security. 2. Computer networks—Security measures. 3. Forensic sciences.
    I. Heiser, Jay G. II. Title
   QA76.9.A25 K78 2001
   005.8—dc21   2001034106

Text printed on recycled and acid-free paper.

ISBN 0201707195

1213141516 DOC   08 07

12th Printing   February 2007

CONTENTS

Preface

Billions of dollars are lost annually to crime, and computers are increasingly involved. It is clear that law enforcement agencies need to investigate digital evidence, but does it make sense to encourage a bunch of computer administrators to become junior g-men? Do we really need amateur digital sleuths? In a word, yes. Bad things are happening on computers and to computers, and the organizations responsible for these computers have a need to find out what exactly happened. You probably cannot pick up the phone and bring in law enforcement officials every time something anomalous happens on one of your servers and expect them to send out a team of forensic specialists, and even if you could, your corporate executives may not want that. All major corporations have internal security departments that are quite busy performing internal investigations. However, the security professionals who typically fill this role are accustomed to dealing with theft and safety issues and are often ill-prepared to deal with computer crime.

This book is inspired by the needs of the people who attend the author's seminars on computer forensics. If for no other reason than these sold-out seminars, we know that there is a big demand for greater expertise in digital investigations. System administrators and corporate security staff are the people we've designed the book for. Most of the seminar attendees are fairly skilled in the use and maintenance of Microsoft environments. Some of them are Unix specialists, but many students have expressed a strong desire to learn more about Unix. Once a corporation discovers that they know someone who can investigate Windows incidents, it is assumed that he or she knows everything about computers, and it is usually only a matter of time until this person is pressured into taking a look at a suspect Unix system.

Our students come from a wide variety of backgrounds and have diverse investigatory needs and desires. We try to accommodate these varying agendas in this book, to which we bring our experience in investigation and incident response. Warren Kruse is a former police officer who regularly performs computer forensic examinations inside and outside of Lucent Technologies. Jay Heiser is an information security consultant who has been on the response teams for numerous hacked Internet servers. To the maximum extent possible, this book contains everything useful that we've learned from performing investigations and teaching others to do so for themselves. We know what questions will be asked, and this book is designed to answer them. It is a practical guide to the techniques used by real people to investigate real computer crimes.

How to Read This Book

This book can be read cover to cover, as a complete introductory course in computer forensics. However, it is also meant to serve as a handbook, and we expect many readers to be familiar with some of the subjects we cover. For that reason, each chapter is a complete unit and can be read when convenient or necessary. You probably specialize in one or more of the areas covered in this text. However, we believe that the information presented in this book is at the *minimum* required level of legal and computer literacy, and we urge you to become knowledgeable in all of the areas we cover: legal, procedural, and technical.

A brief description of the information covered in each chapter is provided in the sections that follow.

Introduction to Computer Forensics

Chapter 1 outlines the basic process of evidence collection and analysis, which is the meat of computer forensics. Even those readers with a background in law enforcement will find new techniques in this chapter that are specific to computer forensics.

Tracking an Offender

The Internet is pervasive, and a high percentage of your investigations will involve either incoming or outgoing Internet traffic. The material in Chapter 2 will help you interpret the clues inside of email messages and news postings. It will also start you on the path toward becoming an Internet detective, using standard Internet services to perform remote investigations.

The Basics of Hard Drives and Storage Media

For the computer sleuth, hard drives are the most significant containers of evidence. Chapter 3 provides an understanding of both their logical and their physical configurations. It covers partitions and low-level formatting, filesystems, and hardware drive interfaces.

Encryption and Forensics

Cryptography has become ubiquitous in the virtual world of the Internet. A skilled investigator must have a solid understanding of the technology and goals of modern cryptography. It is relevant both in understanding evidence and, interestingly, in the preservation of evidence. Many investigators lack a necessary level of crypto-literacy, so Chapter 4 provides a broad introduction to encryption with special emphasis on its significance and application in computer forensics. We also discuss common encoding and archiving formats (such as uuencode and PKZIP) that can complicate your keyword searches. As digital signature technology grows in legal significance and finds new uses, forensic investigators will be expected to under-stand its limitations and must have a firm grasp of the ways in which a digital iden-tity can be stolen. The digital timestamping of forensic evidence will soon become standard procedure in digital investigations. If you already have a background in these encryption concepts, then you may wish to skim this chapter.

Data Hiding

Being able to find hidden data is a crucial investigative skill. Even if you are highly crypto-literate, you still may not be aware of steganography (the art of hiding infor-mation by embedding covert messages within other messages) and other data-hiding techniques. Continuing the subject of encryption, Chapter 5 describes the use of specific password-cracking tools that we have successfully used during our inves-tigations. This chapter categorizes and describes the ways that data can be hidden—not just by encryption—and provides practical guidance on how to find and read hidden data.

Hostile Code

Being able to identify and understand the implications of criminal tools is a skill that every investigator needs. Given that hostile code can be arcane and that few readers have a background in it, Chapter 6 provides an introduction to the topic and an overview of the types and capabilities of digital criminal tools that the investiga-tor may encounter. We've included a couple of war stories involving the recent use of "hacker tools" on corporate PCs, which is becoming increasingly common.

Your Electronic Toolkit

Although forensic-specific tools have a certain James Bond–like appeal—and we cover these products—a large percentage of your work will be done with system tools that were not specifically created for the unique needs of forensic investigation. Chapter 7 will introduce you to a wide variety of utility types and specific brand name tools, along with instructions in their use in a digital investigation.

Investigating Windows Computers

Microsoft Windows, in all its various flavors, is the most widely used family of operating systems. While Chapter 8 assumes some background in Windows, you don't need to be a Microsoft Certified Systems Engineer in order to apply the techniques and tricks we discuss. Emphasis is placed on Windows NT 4.0 and Windows 9x, but several important new Windows 2000 features, such as the Encrypting File System, are covered. An experienced investigator soon learns that nothing is too obsolete to be in daily use somewhere, so the chapter concludes with Windows 3.1–specific material.

Introduction to Unix for Forensic Examiners

For those readers with no prior Unix experience, Chapter 9 provides an introduction with special emphasis on Unix characteristics that are most significant for the forensic investigator. Experienced Unix users can skim or skip this chapter.

Compromising a Unix Host

Chapter 10 is intended as background material for the investigation of hacked Internet hosts. It describes the process that Unix attackers typically use and provides an understanding of the goals of typical system hackers.

Investigating a Unix Host

While emphasizing the investigation of hacked Unix hosts, Chapter 11 describes techniques that are applicable to all forms of Unix investigation. It contains a detailed set of Unix-specific techniques and processes that use common Unix utilities for collecting and evaluating evidence. It also contains instructions on using a Unix boot CD to capture information over a network when you can't attach hardware directly to a suspect system.

Introduction to the Criminal Justice System

The final chapter explains what you need to do after you have begun collecting evidence and provides an overview of the criminal justice process. Legal concepts such as affidavits, subpoenas, and warrants are described. You will be a more effective interface between your organization and law enforcement agents if you understand what they do and how both investigations and prosecutions are structured by the legal system.

Appendixes

As in most books, the appendixes in this one contain information that doesn't fit neatly anywhere else. They are standalone guides to specific needs.

Appendix A, Internet Data Center Response Plan, defines a process for handling computer security incidents in Internet Data Centers.

Appendix B, Incident Response Triage, provides a list of general questions that should be asked during the investigation of a computer crime incident.

Appendix C, How to Become a Unix Guru, provides self-study suggestions for forensic examiners who want to improve their ability to investigate Unix hosts.

Appendix D, Exporting a Windows 2000 Personal Certificate, graphically depicts the process of exporting a Personal Certificate from a Windows 2000 computer. Investigators should practice this process to prepare themselves for incidents involving the Encrypted File System.

Appendix E, How to Crowbar Unix Hosts, describes the process of gaining administrative access to a Unix system by booting it from a floppy or CD.

Appendix F, Creating a Linux Boot CD, provides several suggestions on techniques and technology sources that are useful in the creation of bootable Linux CDs that can be used to crowbar Unix or NT systems. Booting from a Linux CD can also provide a trusted environment useful for examining or collecting evidence when it is not feasible to remove the hard drive from a system.

Appendix G, Contents of a Forensic CD, provides a shopping list of useful tools that should be considered the minimum set of forensic utilities that an examiner brings during an incident response.

Acknowledgments

First, we would like to thank the many people who have patiently helped us write this book (not all of whom realized they were doing it at the time): Nate Miller, Geoff Silver, Felix Lindner, Tom Shevock, Tim Lunsford, Dan Farmer, Wietse Venema, Aaron Higbee, Bill Brad, Aaron Kramer, Curt Bryson, Wil Harris, Dave Dittrich, James Holley, Tim O'Neill, Fred Cohen, Lance Spitzner, Gene Spafford, Theresa Ho, Joe Ippolito, Abigail Abraham, Dorsey Morrow, Eoghan Casey, and Robert Weaver.

Our technical reviewers were invaluable for their careful scrutiny and suggestions. They included: Joe Balsama, Steve Rago, Ed Skoudis, Steve Romig, David Rhoades, Vernon Schryver, Peter Gutmann, John Sinteur, Will Morse, John Sebes, Howard Harkness, Chris Kostick, Bruce Schneier, Elizabeth Zinkann, David Weisman, Alain Mayer, John Stewart, Joshua Guttman, and Harlan Carvey.

Mary Hart, Emily Frey, and Patrick Peterson, and the rest of the staff at Addison-Wesley have done a phenomenal job in disciplining us and turning our experience into a real book. We'd especially like to thank our editor, Karen Gettman, who talked us into doing this and saw the project through to the end.

We dedicate this book to our children, Bobby, Caity, and Cassidy Kruse, and Kirk Heiser, and to our wives, Maryann Kruse and Elizabeth Heiser, for their incredible patience over the last two years when we were writing instead of spending time with them.

Now is your time!
W.G.K and J.G.H

Chapter

1

Introduction to Computer Forensics

Whenever we tell people that we work in "computer forensics," they invariably respond "that's interesting" and then ask, "what is that?" Although relatively few people are aware that computers can be examined to learn about human activities, most people are not only aware of more traditional forms of forensics, but are actually quite interested in the subject. This familiarity makes it easy to explain what we do for a living.

What Is Forensics?

During the twentieth century, the coherent application of methodical investigatory techniques to solve crime cases has steadily increased and so has public interest in what detectives do. Not only are Patricia Cornwell novels (starring heroine Kay Scarpetta, a fictional state coroner) a great read, but they also provide a relatively sophisticated understanding of forensic pathology. It isn't surprising that they are among the most popular books at the start of the twenty-first century. Continued public interest in forensic methodology has resulted in a string of morbidly fascinating documentaries on cable television, and the fall 2000 season opened with a drama that explicitly dealt with the adventures of police forensic technicians. Finally the popular media is shifting its focus from the cadaver to the rest of the crime scene. It's apparent that forensics, and computer forensics,[1] are becoming popular subjects. Why? Because it is both fascinating and necessary. Everyone likes a mystery, but interest in crime scene investigation strikes some deeper chord. The application of human skills, high-tech tools, and precise methodology in the fight for justice is a compelling story that is hard to resist.

---

1. Computer forensics involves the preservation, identification, extraction, documentation, and interpretation of computer media for evidentiary and/or root cause analysis. Read on for a more detailed description.

The Growing Problem of Computer Crime

Computer misuse tends to fall into two categories. Either a computer is used to commit a crime, or the computer itself is the target of a crime. Computers are ubiquitous within modern organizations, and it is inevitable that illegal activities will involve computers. Child pornography, threatening letters, fraud, and theft of intellectual property are all crimes that leave digital tracks. Investigations into these types of crimes usually include searching computers that are suspected of being involved in their commission. Such analysis involves sifting through gigabytes of data looking for specific keywords, examining log files to see what happened at certain times, and hopefully providing evidence that a specific person did a specific illegal act—or that a specific person apparently did NOT commit an illegal act.

The other category of crime, when the computer itself is the victim, is commonly referred to as *incident response*. This refers to the examination of systems that have been remotely attacked. During the 1980s, such attacks were carried out over phone lines through modems, but now they originate almost exclusively from the Internet. Remote attacks have become far more common, taking advantage of increasingly complex and vulnerable network services. The ever-growing sophistication and frequency of remote attacks has made the job of the incident response team quite challenging.

Not only is the legal and regulatory environment constantly evolving, but so is the nature of computer crime and the techniques used to investigate it. Computer technology continues to evolve rapidly, new Internet crime tools are constantly appearing, and new security tools are being developed to counter these new threats. In common-law countries like the United States, Canada, and the United Kingdom, legal precedent provides significant guidance in court cases. Computer crime involves many new issues that haven't been subjected to the conservative legal processes that result in precedences that can be referred to in the future. Cyber lawyers have to deal with a greater level of ambiguity than do many other legal specialists. All of this means that the digital sleuth needs to be flexible and continually learning. It is not an appropriate career for the complacent, but it is an exciting and challenging place for someone seeking constant challenge and personal growth.

What Exactly Is Computer Forensics?

Computer forensics involves the preservation, identification, extraction, documentation and interpretation of computer data. It is often more of an art than a science, but as in any discipline, computer forensic specialists follow clear, well-defined methodologies and procedures, and flexibility is expected and encouraged when encountering the unusual.

It is unfortunate that computer forensics is sometimes misunderstood as being somehow different from other types of investigations. For instance, if you were investigating a murder that took place in Times Square, you would photograph the scene, look for evidence, and take samples of the crime scene, including control samples to compare to the evidence. The collection of evidence proceeds similarly in a computer investigation, but for some reason, some people want to recreate the entire system, be it a standalone PC, a server with a terabyte RAID system, or even an entire network. Nobody expects the prosecution to rebuild Times Square in the courtroom, but that is often the expectation in a computer crime case. Admittedly, digital data can be highly volatile. General unfamiliarity not only with computer forensics, but also with computers themselves, makes this field a highly challenging one, but this book can help you prepare for it.

This is a good place to remind ourselves that we have to treat every case as if it will end up in court. Take a minute to think of the consequences; don't start poking around a computer, decide that you have a problem, and then start handling it as evidence. It is easier to regard the computer as evidence from the start, easing up on the evidentiary process if you discover that a crime wasn't committed. The opposite approach is more difficult, if not impossible. However, if you reasonably ("reasonableness" is a key to most laws) believe when you start "looking around" on the computer that it doesn't warrant a forensic analysis and later discover an overtly illicit act was committed, make sure that you fully document what you did and why. Your evidence may still be defensible if explained to a judge and jury that you initially had no reason to suspect that the computer was involved in a criminal act, and subsequently discovered the crime when conducting routine troubleshooting, but only if you fully documented your activities. The key to any investigation, particularly a computer crime investigation, is documentation.

Computer forensics has a brief history. It has been only a few short years since the largest drives available were under 20MB and a zip drive, a DOS disk, and a hex editor were a sufficient forensic toolset. You would be hard-pressed today to find enough zip disks in a computer store to capture the hard drive image of a standard PC, but the highly conservative criminal justice world strongly encourages the continued use of the same techniques we used in the zip drive days. In this book, we share some new techniques appropriate for rapidly changing technology, but remember that basic forensic methodology remains consistent—it doesn't change just because drives get bigger and computers get smaller.

The basic methodology consists of what you can think of as the three As:

1. Acquire the evidence without altering or damaging the original.

2. Authenticate that your recovered evidence is the same as the originally seized data.

3. Analyze the data without modifying it.

We expand on each of these three topics in the sections that follow; they are the framework of every forensic game plan. The details of your specific game plan will depend upon the circumstances and your goals, but the plan will always follow these same three steps.

There are many possible goals other than successful criminal prosecution. Sometimes forensics is conducted to determine the root cause of an event to ensure that it will not happen again. This goal is important—you have to fully understand the extent of your problem before you can be reasonably sure that it will not be exploited again. You also have to fully understand a problem before you know how to respond to it. A friend recently confided a story about unexpectedly finding a high-port telnet daemon. After removing it, he thought that he had removed the intruder and "resecured" his system, but two weeks later, he found the same unauthorized process running. If you do not conduct a complete analysis and find the entire extent of the compromise, it is only a matter of time before you have a bigger problem. It's kind of like termites, but worse—termites don't deliberately retaliate!

In addition to helping us determine what happened, forensics can also address the question of who was responsible. Forensics are used in investigations internal to private organizations and, increasingly, by law enforcement during investigations of all sorts of illegal activity that isn't necessarily characterized as computer crime. Just a few short years ago, as members of an emergency response team, we assisted in a raid on a drug dealer's home. While the detectives were collecting anything that they thought had potential as evidence, we asked if they were going to seize the drug dealer's personal computer. The lead detective replied with certainty that they did not need it. Perhaps they didn't realize how rich a source of information a computer can be about its user's activities. This attitude is much less common today, although the need for law enforcement officers trained for digital investigations still far out-weighs the supply.

Most computer crime cases are not prosecuted, but we should still consider acceptability in a court of law as our standard for investigative practice. We can debate whether or not to pull the plug, or if we should use DOS/Windows or Linux for our analysis, but those are minor details. Our ultimate goal is to conduct our investigation in a manner that will stand up to legal scrutiny. Treat every case like a court case, and you will develop good investigative habits.

If your company has been lucky enough to avoid the need for computer forensics (or so you think), congratulations; it will come soon enough. What do you do when you are asked to investigate an incident, but your management wants the server reloaded and backed up as soon as possible? Do you tell the boss that you need several hours, if not several days, to analyze the system? Instead, you end up performing a watered-down version of forensics, and your results reflect the effort. Even under less-than-ideal circumstances, whatever level of rigor you can apply to the investigation will bear some fruit, and maybe it will convince your boss to give you more leeway during future events.

For the purposes of this chapter, it matters little what operating system, hardware, or software the suspect or victim is using. We discuss examination specifics for both Windows and Unix in Chapters 8 and 11, respectively. For now, let's acquaint ourselves with the three As so that when you are asked to investigate a computer incident, you know what to do.

Step 1: Acquire the Evidence

When it comes to computer forensics, the only thing you can be certain of is uncertainty. We often hear people say "I always do this" or "I always do that" but how can that kind of certainty be possible when there are so many unknowns? A recently published book contains the admonition that an investigator should never directly examine the original storage media. Life should be that easy, but every case is different. In some situations, especially Internet intrusions, the evidence may be found only in RAM, and if you disconnect or turn off the computer before capturing an image of the computer, you will destroy what little evidence exists. (In Chapter 7 we discuss a toolset designed to retrieve evidence off a live system that would otherwise be lost.) It may not be your proudest moment when you explain to your boss that you took down a production server just to avoid examining the original media.

In a perfect world, every computer in need of analysis could be powered off, could boot off a floppy disk, and maybe it would even be mirrored so that all you had to do was remove one of the computer's hard drives and not have to worry about backing up and restoring the evidence on your analysis workstation. But we are not that lucky. The challenge is in encountering unknown elements and thinking fast on your feet. Whatever action you take during an investigation, remember to make sure you act in ways that you can easily explain, and always document all of your actions.

Deciding whether to let a machine continue to run, to pull the power plug from the back of the computer, or to perform the normal administrative shutdown process is one of the longest running arguments in the computer forensics field. Many investigators claim that they always pull the plug, arguing that it is the only way to freeze the computer at its current state. There is precedent for doing this, but it will result in the loss of any data associated with an attack in process, and it may corrupt data on the hard drive. We are not here to tell anyone that immediately pulling the power plug is right or wrong; be flexible, because no two investigations are the same, and there are no cookie-cutter approaches. There are some valid reasons to pull the plug. If you make a mistake on a live system, you can't just click the Undo button—you are stuck with the consequences of your actions. However, if you pull the plug, then you have more time to formulate a game plan and to perform a backup. If you knew for certain that a computer criminal had left behind a software bomb that would destroy all data the next time an administrator logged on, pulling the plug would be a no-brainer, but you will never encounter that level of certainty.

The ideal way to examine a system and maintain the most defensible evidence is to freeze it and examine a copy of the original data. However, this method is not always practical and may be politically unacceptable. Management often refuses to allow the shutdown of a system, especially if the system will be down for an indeterminate length of time. Just remember, you can lower your level of rigor after it is determined that the case will not be prosecuted. Also keep in mind that if the system actually has hostile code (or *malware*) running on it, information associated with that malware will be lost if the system is powered down. Unfortunately, you may not be able to tell whether or not such code is running.

If you do perform an investigation on a live system, you need to be aware that a computer criminal may have anticipated such an investigation and altered some of the system's binaries. This is a long-standing problem on Unix systems (see Chapter 10), and increasingly a problem on Windows systems. You cannot examine a compromised system using the utilities found on that system and have a reasonable expectation that those utilities will accurately report the true state of the system. As summarized in Table 1-1, the examination of a system always involves choosing tradeoffs between quality and convenience.

Handling the Evidence

As stated previously, the first actions a system administrator or investigator takes may make or blow a case. If you don't take care of your evidence, the rest of the investigation will be compromised. All the hard work you do processing evidence will come to naught when the court throws it out because of inadequacies in your process. We will talk about the major events in the life of your evidence, including the initial collection of the evidence and its eventual surrender to law enforcement or the victim. Data handling, especially transportation and storage, is a recurring theme during the entire investigation.

Chain of Custody

While this topic should be second nature for readers experienced in law enforcement, it may be a new concept for others. The goal of carefully maintaining the chain of custody is not only to protect the integrity of your evidence, but also to make it difficult for a defense attorney to successfully argue that the evidence was tampered with while it was in your custody. The chain of custody procedure is a simple yet

Table 1-1 Level of Effort to Protect Evidence and Avoid Hostile Code

Method	Advantages	Disadvantages
Use a dedicated forensic workstation to examine a write-protected hard drive or image of suspect hard drive.	No concern about the validity of either the software or hardware on the suspect host. Produces evidence most easily defended in court.	Inconvenient, time-consuming. May result in loss of volatile information.
Boot the system using a verified, write-protected floppy disk or CD with kernel and tools.	Convenient, quick. Evidence is defensible if suspect drives are mounted as read-only.	Assumes that hardware has not been compromised (which is rare). May result in loss of volatile information.
Build a new system containing an image of the suspect system and examine it.	Completely replicates operational environment of suspect computer, without running the risk of changing its information.	Requires availability of hardware that is identical to suspect computer. May result in loss of volatile information.
Examine the system using external media with verified software on it.	Convenient, quick. Allows examination of volatile information.	If a kernel is compromised, results may be misleading. External media may not have every necessary utility on it.
Verify the software on the suspect system, and then use the verified local software to conduct examination.	Requires minimal preparation. Allows examination of volatile information. Can be performed remotely.	Lack of write-protection for suspect drives makes evidence difficult to defend in court. Finding sources for hash values and verifying the local software requires a minimum of several hours, unless Tripwire was used ahead of time.
Examine the suspect system using the software on the suspect system (without verifying the software).	Requires least amount of preparation. Allows examination of volatile information. Can be performed remotely.	Least reliable method. This is exactly what cyber attackers are hoping you will do. Often a complete waste of time.

effective process of documenting the complete journey of your evidence during the life of the case, including answers to the following questions:

- Who collected it?
- How and where?
- Who took possession of it?
- How was it stored and protected in storage?
- Who took it out of storage and why?

Anyone who has possession of the evidence, the time at which they took and returned possession, and why they were in possession of the evidence must be documented. Be assured that a defense attorney will carefully review the records associated with evidence, cross-referencing it to other documents in an attempt to find discrepancies that can be used to weaken the case against his or her client.

To facilitate record keeping, you can create professional-looking forms or use a spreadsheet program and create a few cells, as shown in Figure 1-1.

You can be creative and include more information, but the table shown in Figure 1-1 will do the trick as long as it is completely filled out.

The fewer people who have access to your evidence room or locker, the better. Defense attorneys love to argue that everyone who had access to the evidence could have altered it. They don't have to prove that the evidence was in fact altered for this tactic to work. They only have to show that the evidence was not adequately safeguarded and hope the jury buys the argument that someone could have planted the evidence.

We don't have to look too far to find a reason why the chain of custody is a crucial aspect of the forensic process. MSNBC reported on June 8, 2000, that the investigation

Item	Date	Time	Location	Name	Reason
Toshiba Tecra 8000 serial # 1234	5/30/2000	9:00 AM	Locked cabinet in room 123	Kruse	Safekeeping
Toshiba Tecra 8000 serial # 1234	5/31/2000	10:53 PM	Removed from locked cabinet	Kruse	Analysis
Toshiba Tecra 8000 serial # 1234	5/31/2000	11:48 PM	Returned to locked cabinet in room 123	Kruse	Safekeeping

Figure 1-1   Example evidence log

of the CD Universe Web site intrusion had "a problem with the preservation of the evidence."[2] Two sources familiar with the investigation were quoted by MSNBC: "the chain of custody was not established properly." MSNBC quoted another source who said, "It's like the O.J. Simpson case, the evidence is tainted. Even if you find whomever is responsible, how do you prosecute it?" Being compared to the O.J. Simpson case should not be one of the goals of your investigation. It is not clear exactly how the evidence was compromised, but MSNBC reported it apparently occurred in the initial investigation in CD Universe's headquarters as FBI agents and employees from three computer security firms worked to determine how the intruder got into the company's network to steal over 300,000 credit card numbers.

Collection

Obviously, you want the evidence collection process to support your case. The complexity of the collection process usually corresponds to the complexity of an incident. When you collect evidence, try to collect everything you can legally get your hands on. This may seem like trivial advice now, but remember this tip when you're in crisis mode in the early stages of incident investigation. Once you leave that data center, there is usually no going back. The computer, backup tape, floppy disk, or scrap of paper that you initially thought was of no evidentiary value will probably be gone when you decide you have to return for additional evidence. This is especially true for log files.

Depending on the computer producing the logs, the data may be overwritten routinely in intervals ranging from a few minutes to a few months. If you are dealing with an Internet service provider (ISP), remember that they are not in the business of storing logs; act quickly or the logs will be long gone. A rule of thumb for most ISPs is 30 days, but because the cost of storing huge log files is high and the business benefit is low, they have little incentive to save huge amounts of data. If you are going to subpoena the logs from an ISP and you want to ensure that the evidence will not be overwritten, you can ask them to preserve the logs while you are going through the legal process. Most ISPs will comply; just try to make sure that your contact at the ISP is not a suspect. We have heard accounts of ISPs being asked to preserve logs, but when the subpoena showed up the data was missing.

Identification

Every single item that comes out of the suspect's or victim's location has to be identified and labeled. Most police departments are skilled in the methodical collection of

---

2. http://www.msnbc.com/news/417406.asp

evidence. In a large investigation, a law enforcement agency assigns a person to be the evidence custodian at the scene. This ensures that a specific individual is responsible for evidence collection instead of everyone walking out of the door with something under his or her arm. You should not collect evidence by yourself; get someone to go with you as a witness. Ask your coworker to document the evidence while you are collecting it.

If you are involved in a large-scale investigation involving numerous computers, an easy way to simplify collection is to position your evidence custodian at the door with a laptop computer, a portable printer, and a label printer such as the Casio Smart Label printer (if such equipment is not available, handwritten labels will do just fine). While your investigators are bringing out hand trucks full of equipment, your evidence custodian can fill out the evidence log online and print labels for the equipment. By creating reports ahead of time that automatically fill in the identical information on sequential reports, labels, and so on, you save a lot of time. Your favorite word processor probably has some of this functionality, but if you want full electronic forms and form flow capability, reasonably priced and easily programmed, check out Jetform.[3] This software makes it easy to create, or re-create, your paper-based forms. You can fill in header information so it automatically appears on every form associated with your case.

You must accurately count and identify the evidence. You can use a label maker for identification, or you can use stickers or tags, as long as they will not easily come off and they are large enough to include

- The case number
- A brief description (in case the label comes off)
- Your signature (on each item)
- The date and time the evidence was collected

You should also photograph the crime scene. Take pictures of the entire scene, gradually getting closer to the suspect computer until you are close enough to take clear photographs of both the front and back while it is still connected to most of its cables. This will help you later if you are questioned about the environment. The reason we say "most of the cables" is because in some cases, you may decide to pull the power cord. If you have reason to believe that destructive code is running and evidence is being destroyed, then the best course of action is to immediately pull the plug. Then photograph the scene as is and document in your reports the condition and state (on, off, screen locked, etc.) of the computer system upon your arrival. If

---

3. http://www.jetform.com

you have no reason to believe that the computer is running anything destructive, your first step should be to take a picture of the screen, followed by a complete photographic documentation of the machine. If you have made the decision to pull the plug, it is best to wait until after you have completed your photographic evidence collection. Obviously do not plug the computer back in just to take a picture. You should try to photograph any serial numbers or other identifying features. It is difficult, but not impossible, to photograph the serial number. You will probably have to use a flash, and because most serial numbers are on a metal or shiny label, the flash creates a glare in the photograph. If you have a digital camera, you can experiment with different angles without wasting film. The camera that we use, manufactured by Sony, enables you to put a 3.5-inch floppy in the camera on which to store photographs. You can print the pictures and store the floppy disk in your file folder. If you do not have a digital camera, store the prints and the negatives too, in case you ever need to have more prints developed.

Your photographs and all the other evidence and reports should be stored in a file folder, also known as a *case folder*, so that all of the information pertaining to this specific incident are stored together. Clearly mark on the front of the folder the same "header" information that we referred to earlier (case or incident number, location, brief description, and so forth). If you are using a label printer, simply print one more label for the front of your case folder. We prefer to use folders that can be closed. Since you may have floppy disks and small scraps of paper in your folder, being able to close it will reduce loss.

Transportation

Keep in mind that your evidence generally is not made to be moved, so be careful when transporting it. Even laptops can be damaged if not handled properly. Hard drives can easily be damaged from the read-write heads coming in contact with the platter. A damaged hard drive is not going to be a happy hard drive, and you might not be a happy camper either if the area of the drive that contains the evidence is damaged and can no longer be read. Remember to use static-free packaging; the grayish plastic is impregnated with graphite dust, making it static-free, and usually pink bubble wrap is static-free.

When the person closing the packaging seals the container, a signature across the seal will indicate that it has not been opened by anyone other than an authorized person. When you do need to open the sealed container, document in your reports that the seal was still intact and why you needed to unseal the package. Once you are finished using the evidence, reseal the container with a new label, preferably in another package, and secure it in a locked evidence locker. By placing the original sealed container or bag inside another sealed bag, you can preserve the original container and label. Your reports must note the person handling the evidence as well as the dates, times, and reason for removing the evidence and the date and time the evidence was returned to the locker.

Storage

Not only is it important to store the evidence in a cool, dry environment appropriate for valuable electronic equipment, but because it is evidence and has legal significance, you need to be even more careful. It has to be in sealed containers, in a secure area with limited access. Controlling access to the evidence is important; the original and still highly popular defense attorney trick is to argue that someone tainted the evidence. When evidence is accessible to everyone and anyone, the defense attorney can argue that any one of the people who had access to the secure storage area could have tainted the evidence. To preemptively strike down that argument, limit the number of persons with access to one primary custodian and one alternate.

Documenting the Investigation

This step may be the most difficult for computer professionals. Most technically adroit people can fix a computer blindfolded, but when you ask them how they did it, they might not be able to tell you. If you fall into this category, it is another good reason to work with a partner. One person works on the computer, and the other person takes notes. You will find that once you start finding evidence, you will be drawn to further exploration and find even more evidence. If you aren't careful, you can become so engrossed in your analysis that you totally forget to take notes. Keep that writing pad handy and don't leave the details to memory.

Document your actions in thorough reports with extensive details including the software and version numbers of your software evidence, collection tools, the methods you used to collect and analyze the computer media, and the explanation of why you did what you did. (Make sure you use only software that you are legally licensed to have. It is embarrassing to be asked in a court of law, with the judge and jury watching, if you were using illegally obtained software.)

Fortunately, the decisions you make in an investigation will not be judged on whether or not you were right or wrong. Your value to the prosecution is usually the "reasonableness" of your actions. If your notes thoroughly document everything you did, they will greatly facilitate your explanation when asked about the incident tomorrow by your boss, next week by your victim, the following month by a union or attorney, and then three years from now when the case goes to trial in either a civil or criminal court. If you believe that your memory alone is sufficient, think back to the last time your computer did not boot properly. What exactly did you do to remedy the problem?

Step 2: Authenticate the Evidence

It is difficult to show that evidence (any kind of evidence) that you've collected is the same as what was left behind by a criminal. Crime scenes age, and computers are no exception. Evidence can be damaged by adverse environmental conditions (for example, mold and dust) and by insects. You can show that the investigator introduced no changes, and that if changes exist, they are due to the nature of computers and don't effect the evidentiary value of the evidence. Computer drives slowly deteriorate, but neither readable text nor pornographic pictures appear at random through the action of digital wear and tear. Any text or pictures found on a computer drive has a deliberate human source. The chain of custody and other evidentiary handling rules assure the jury that no unanticipated or introduced changes occurred and that it is reasonable to extrapolate from the point of collection back to the time of the incident. In the digital world, we even have an advantage in that we can show that the evidence did not change at all after we've collected it. While we cannot show exactly when the evidence was collected, simple techniques enable us to timestamp it, so we can at least show that it was in existence at a specific point in time. Neither of these authentication techniques is possible with other forms of evidence.

Both proof of integrity and timestamping are provided by calculating a value that functions as a sort of electronic fingerprint for an individual file or even an entire floppy or hard drive. This is a cryptographic technique, and the value is called a *hash*. We discuss this concept in Chapter 4, so for now let's say that a hash value is calculated with the use of software, and that all forensic utility suites include such a capability. When you initially collect data, you should create a hash value and record it. After doing so, you can prove that the copies of the data you are using for your examination are identical to what was originally collected.

Two algorithms, MD5 and SHA, are in common use today. If possible, create a hash of the entire drive and the individual files. If you have a program like New Technologies' CRCMD5, use it (it creates both a CRC and an MD5). Increasingly, applications such as Tripwire[4] are using multiple hash algorithms. That way, if a cryptological attack is discovered against a single algorithm in the future, the data from the other algorithm will still be valid. CRC is already obsolete, and we predict that the use of two hash routines will soon become common practice. We also see an advantage in digital timestamping. While this is not yet a usual part of most investigations, we're giving you a leg up on the future by informing you about this simple but effective method of evidence authentication.

---

4. http://www.tripwire.com

Step 3: Analysis

You are now in the home stretch of basic computer forensics and ready for the most gratifying step, the analysis. After you back up the original drive to the Image MASSter (or other hard drive), use your tape drive to create a second copy, using the Image MASSter as the original this time. While you must continue to treat your collected evidence with respect and care during the analysis phase, it is interesting to be actively analyzing the evidence instead of doing paperwork. Remember to include a note in your reports and your chain-of-custody records whenever you obtain and return the original evidence to your secure storage cabinet.

The field of computer forensics has been undergoing a transition from conducting analysis within a command-line environment, such as DOS, to a graphical environment, such as Windows. While image acquisition still must be performed in an environment that does not alter the original evidence, which can mean that you are limited to whatever operating system you can boot from a floppy disk, the analysis can be done in the environment you prefer. Religious wars over operating systems rage, but the fact of the matter is that you should use the one that you are comfortable with.

No matter what operating environment you choose, no single program on it will do everything you require for this phase. You must become proficient with a lot of them. Try to collect a variety of tools to meet unforeseen circumstances.

We discuss platform-specific techniques in Chapters 8 through 11. For now, let's discuss the basic methodology, which is the same on every operating system: "Do no harm!" Whatever else you do, try not to damage your evidence, and never overstep legal boundaries. (We discuss criminal justice regulatory issues in Chapter 12.) Whenever a crime scene investigator lifts a print, he or she destroys the original—or changes it considerably, but the damage is defensible. Computer forensic examiners must develop the same level of standards and acceptable practices that physical investigators adhere to. A little bit of knowledge can be dangerous, so try not to be your own worst enemy and overstep your knowledge. Since we often work at a physical level, it is possible to alter evidence accidentally. Whenever possible, protect your original physical evidence by working with a digital copy so that if you do make a mistake, you can wipe the analysis drive, restore your image once again, and continue your analysis.

We recommend making two backups of the original drive. For the first backup, we use the forensic version of the Image MaSSter, which comes in either a desktop version, which is useful if you are primarily in a lab, or the Solo Forensic unit, which is a portable unit slightly larger than a hard drive.[5] With Image MaSSter you can

---

5. http://www.ics-iq.com

make a drive-to-drive copy that is usually the fastest type of backup. After you back up the original drive, you mount the copy to create an image tape. This tape is useful for both archival purposes and for restoring the image. We prefer an initial drive-to-drive copy instead of a drive-to-tape copy. We try to use the original drive as little as possible, and the drive-to-drive copy is the fastest and most reliable way to collect and secure the original evidence. The fewer steps needed to perform a backup, the fewer things can go wrong, which is especially important when you are dealing with critical original evidence.

Several commercial products are available for drive imaging that are acceptable for use in forensics. A forensic backup is important because you want to make a bit-for-bit (also known as a *bit stream*) clone of the original drive. A "normal" backup doesn't copy deleted files and the other parts of a hard drive that we want to investigate for clues. Hard drives are such a significant part of an examination that we have dedicated an entire chapter to the subject, Chapter 3. Chapter 7 on tools discusses specific utilities that are appropriate for making forensic backups.

Always make an MD5 hash of newly created drive images before doing any analysis. If you are using Unix, don't even mount the filesystem before creating a hash value. You may be tempted to look at a directory listing to take a peek, but hold off until after the MD5 hash is complete. After you have obtained your hash value and recorded it in your notes, you can start your analysis.

With a notepad at your side, you usually start an analysis by looking at the partition table on the suspect drive. Not only is the partition information important to document in your reports, but it is also helpful to know what type of partitions you are dealing with so you know what software tools you can use. For instance, if the partition reports that it is NTFS (Windows NT File System), you can put away Norton Unerase because it doesn't support NTFS.

After you note what partitions the drive has, look at a directory listing, including subdirectories, to get a feel for what you are up against. Send the directory listing to a printer. If you are in DOS and have a local printer attached, the command is:

```
c:\ dir /a /s >lpt1
```

The /a displays files with specified attributes such as hidden files, and the /s recursively searches subdirectories.

If you want to create a file, the syntax is the same except that you replace lpt1 with the filename:

```
dir /s >e:\dirlist.txt
```

e is the drive designation of the external storage device. An Iomega zip drive works well for this purpose, and an Iomega Tool for DOS, the Zip Guest program, recognizes a parallel zip drive from a DOS prompt.

From a UNIX or Linux environment, you redirect the standard output to an external device. In the following example, the data collection device is mounted as /mnt/export:

```
ls -al >/mnt/export/dirlist
```

or

```
find . -ls >/mnt/export/dirlist
```

We prefer to save directory listings in electronic form. After you have your directory listing in a file, you can open it in a spreadsheet, or with a viewer such as Quick View Plus, and use the find capability to access the data you are looking for. Using a spreadsheet also gives you the advantage of being able to sort the data by any field.

You should have developed a sense of your suspect's technical prowess when you were gathering physical evidence. Now you can evaluate your suspect's capabilities by understanding what is on his or her computer. For example, if the suspect appears to have been using standard software, he or she may not be as sophisticated as others you may encounter. Not that you should relax your guard; the suspect's use of standard software simply means that you might not encounter encrypted documents or other schemes to conceal evidence. If your suspect has certain programs such as a steganography utility or password-cracking software, that is a clear sign that you should keep your eyes open for sophisticated attempts to hide data.

You can use a hex editor or a forensic program to view the master boot record and the boot sector. (You should use a hex editor only if you are well versed in its use. For those who have never used a hex editor, at the end of this chapter is a list that provides sources for excellent hands-on training.) For those who are comfortable using a hex editor or forensic program, note the cluster size, and if the evidence drive was using the DOS filesystem, view the File Allocation Table, or FAT, as well. Look for clusters that are marked bad, and then using your hex editor, view the bad clusters as HEX. Check if any data is hidden in the bad blocks. This is especially important if observing your suspect's directory listing and office environment gave you reason to suspect a more advanced user.

If your hex editor or forensic program has a search capability, search for terms related to your case. Avoid overly broad search terms so you don't get too many false positive hits. Because hard drives today have such large capacities, you cannot go through every single sector manually looking for evidence. A powerful forensic program with a sophisticated search capability is essential. Words such as "options," "soft," and "setting," return many false positives. Your analysis should include running searches for key terms but should not be limited to just running string searches. If you are searching for Easton Ave. but unknown to you, your suspect calls the street Eastern Ave., you could miss critical data unless you also conduct a through analysis of individual files. When you notice that your suspect is spelling terms differently or you discover new details that are important to the case, you can, and should, conduct additional searches.

After doing a keyword search, one of the next things you can do is to retrieve deleted files. A thrilling moment in any forensic case is retrieving deleted files and then sliding the recovered files across the table to the suspect during an interview. Files can be recovered manually using a hex editor—if you have a lot of patience. Files stored on a drive are usually fragmented. In order to reconstruct deleted files, you have to chain the clusters together again to make a complete file. When you delete a file in a Windows environment, the first character of the directory entry is changed to a sigma character, the hex value of E5. The operating system recognizes that the sigma indicates that this directory entry should not be displayed because the file has been deleted. The entries in the File Allocation Table assigned to the deleted file are changed to zero, indicating that the sectors they point to are unused and available to the operating system for data storage. The operating system does not do anything to the actual data until another file happens to be saved at the same location, which is why you may be able to find incriminating data that the suspect thought he or she had deleted.

If you are using file retrieval software such as Norton Unerase, it prompts you to change the first character of each recovered file's name to something that the operating system can recognize. When you replace the first character, don't try to guess what the original character was, simply replace the first character with a dash or something that you can say you added to identify it as a retrieved file. Once you are done, presto! Instant heartburn for your suspect. You will have to practice this technique to become proficient at it.

Manual retrieval of deleted files that are fragmented is a complex subject. To study it in detail, we recommend you attend a course in computer forensics or one given by a forensic software vendor. A company that provides excellent instruction is New Technologies Inc. (NTI), which offers a three-day basic forensic class.[6] Guidance Software, the makers of EnCase, a popular forensic program, also offers classes.[7]

After you have retrieved the deleted files, the next step is to check unallocated and slack space for residual data (see Chapter 3 for details and Chapter 7 for programs). Again, the easiest way to check unallocated and slack space is with software tools specifically designed for this purpose. You will be amazed at the amount of data located in these areas.

---

6. The syllabus can be viewed at http://www.forensics-intl.com.

7. Information is available at http://www.encase.com.

As you locate evidence, save copies of it on the hard drive of your analysis work-station. You may also want to clean up the formatting to make the file more legible and for inclusion in your reports. When you save the file to your computer, the file's properties change. You might be thinking "why I am changing any formatting on the evidence?" You are not changing evidence; your evidence is safely locked in your cabinet. The changes are being made only on an electronic transcript of the relevant parts intended for reporting purposes. You are merely presenting a piece of relevant evidence in such a way that it substantiates your case. For example, you might have a file that contains incriminating evidence. If you were to print the entire file, you would have a hundred pages of nothing and one page of data. Instead, copy and paste the relevant text into a file. In your documentation, specify the logical position within the document where the data was found (page, row, paragraph, and so on). If the data is recovered, and the original file is not intact, or cannot be shown as intact, your documentation should include information on exactly where on the drive you recovered that data, including the cylinder, head, and sector of the physical drive. Just saying it was located in the My Documents folder is not adequate.

Depending on your case, this part of the process may be the end of your analysis or just the beginning. After you retrieve all the files, you may have to start unzipping them, searching for and attempting to crack passwords. Don't forget to perform the analysis procedures we have described on all the removable media you have collected. The next chapters in the book will help you in those areas. But for now, let's discuss more basics.

Check This

After a class, we are often asked for a checklist to make it easier to remember all the detailed steps. Checklists can help structure an activity and jog your memory, but we refrain from the use of checklists because the steps we take probably won't be the same in every case. If you had only one list that contained all the possible steps for every single one of your cases, it would be filled with items that are irrelevant to other cases. You could just write "N/A" next to those boxes, but the last thing you want is for a lawyer to ask why you didn't check that area and if exculpatory information could have been located there. Here's another guideline: *Don't encourage the other side to ask a question that you don't want to answer.*

If you want to create a "cheat sheet" of things to look for in order to refresh your memory at 2 a.m., that is perfectly fine. Just don't include checkboxes next to the steps, and as we said previously, keep the list very general without too many specifics like "check cookie file," and "check browsing history." If you want to use a cheat sheet, don't write notes on it, because then it would be a record that has to be included in your case file. You can refer to a list that is as detailed as you want, but as long as you don't put marks or notes on it, it won't be considered as evidence. Remember that if you go to court, anything in your case file can be subpoenaed and could wind up in the defense attorney's hands.

Preservation

The preservation of computer evidence is grunt work. It is tedious, but lack of attention to boring details can blow your case. You must be able to account for the evidence the entire time it is in your custody. If you cannot do this, none of the results of your efforts spent collecting and analyzing data will be admissible in court. Remember to keep a complete chain-of-custody document and store the evidence somewhere where it will not get damaged. The last thing you want to do is have to replace a confiscated computer that was damaged or lose a case because the original evidence is no longer in working order.

Presentation in Court

This is the part that people who are not lawyers dread the most and have the least practice in, but it is one of the most crucial steps in your case. In addition, it keeps us honest—our legal system, for all its faults, has built-in protection mechanisms and works fairly well. If it were not for the potential, slim as it may be, of having to present your evidence in a court of law, what would we use as a gauge to judge ourselves? Continually remind yourself that you may have to explain what you did in front of a judge and jury. If you can articulate what you did, why you did it, and why your actions were reasonable, you should have no problems. We discuss the reasonableness theory and how it pertains to a court of law in Chapter 12.

Some Tips for Courtroom Presentation

Wear appropriate business attire. Even if your normal work attire is "business casual," this is a court of law, not Cape May. Your khakis and polo shirt may be acceptable at a resort, but they are not acceptable in a court of law. A judge works hard to get on the bench, and as the judge in *A Few Good Men* stated, "I deserve some respect; I know I earned it!"

When you are on the stand, if you do not understand a question, ask for it to be repeated. Don't be shy. This is not the place to guess at what you think the lawyer is asking.

During cross-examination, give your attorney a chance to object to every question. If an attorney asks you a question and you answer it right away, you are not giving your attorney enough time to object. Don't waste too much time answering, and don't look to your lawyer for guidance. A brief pause to collect your thoughts will do.

Be honest. If you have an airtight case, the defense is going to attack your credibility. Don't give them any reason to cast doubt on your testimony. If you don't know something, say so. Don't get caught up in any tricks to get you to answer a question incorrectly. Remember, a lawyer never asks a question that he or she doesn't already know the answer to. If the lawyer appears to be asking dumb questions, watch out! He or she may just be setting you up. Some defense attornies may try to act like your buddy before a trial begins. They are looking for an advantage for their client. Be respectful, but don't let them schmooze you.

Don't let a lawyer call you out of the blue and ask you a few quick questions off the top of your head. Make an appointment and have your attorney present. You don't want to let the other side find out that you forgot to mention something, or that the summary has changed from one recount to another. When talking with lawyers, *always use your notes!* When you are testifying, you may not be able to use your notes, so make sure that you know everything on the reports. Dates, times, and locations are important, and you can't get them wrong. If you do, the opposing lawyer will find a way to bring it to the attention of the jury. If you are not sure of an answer, ask to check your notes. Make sure that you thoroughly review your notes before testifying in case you cannot use them while you are testifying. It does not reflect poorly on you to use your notes. After all, a trial can take place months or years after the incident, so don't be afraid to ask. If an attorney starts hooting and hollering that you should not be able to use your notes, just calmly remind him or her that it has been a long time since the events in question occurred, and that you created the notes in the first place so that an accurate record would be available when it was needed in the future. If you can do this as calmly as possible, the jury may think no less of you for admitting that you don't remember, but they might think less of the attorney for pressuring you. As the saying goes, "never let them see you sweat!"

Our final piece of advice on the basics of forensics is "don't take anything for granted." Here are a few things to not take for granted:

- Check every data tape that you find when you are collecting evidence.

- Check every floppy disk. They are a hassle to process, but you never know what they can contain.

- Check CD-ROMs, or DVDs (especially recordable CDs or DVDs).

- Look in books, manuals, Rolodexes, under the keyboard, on the monitor, and so on for passwords or other pertinent information.

- Double-check the analysis. It is surprising what you will find the second time through the evidence. Even better, have someone else look at it. You'd be amazed at what a fresh perspective has on locating evidence. Dealing with computer forensics requires talent, but patience and perseverance make miracles happen.

Conclusion

The meat of computer forensics is the process of acquiring evidence, authenticating evidence, and analyzing that evidence. Successful investigations require both religious adherence to the rigorous standard procedures of evidence collection and custody, while simultaneously being flexible and imaginative in locating and analyzing that evidence. It is a difficult balance between being highly disciplined while also being willing to experiment with new ideas. Depending upon your personal approach, this tension between process and flexibility will be either totally frustrating or highly stimulating. The more knowledge and practice you have, the better prepared you will be to overcome this challenge.

Further Resources

Listserv

Computer Forensic Investigators Digest (CFID) at http://www.infobin.org/cfid

Organizations

High Technology Crime Investigative Association (HTCIA) at http://www.htcia.org

Conferences

HTCIA at http://www.htcia.org

Techno Security at http://www.thetrainingco.com/html/Conferences.html

Formal Training

You can access a list of training and college programs at http://www.ne-htcia.org/training.html.

New Technologies Incorporated (NTI) at http://www.forensics-intl.com

SEARCH at http://www.search.org

Guidance Software at http://www.guidancesoftware.com or http://www.encase.com

Reid Institute—Interviewing and Interrogation http://www.reid.com/training.htm/

Other Web Resources

Best Practices For Seizing Electronic Evidence, http://www.treas.gov/usss/index.htm?electronic_evidence.htm&1>

United States Department of Justice, Computer Crime and Intellectual Property Section (CCIPS), Searching and Seizing Computers Web page, http://www.usdoj.gov/criminal/cybercrime/searching.html

Chapter

2

Tracking an Offender

In this age of pervasive connectivity, it is unrealistic to expect cyber crime incidents to be isolated to a single system. Like characters in a William Gibson novel, cyber sleuths often have to track offenders across the digital matrix. While the techniques of network forensics are still largely undeveloped, it would be a disservice to devote an entire book to *computer* forensics without any discussion of Internet methods that you can use to find leads to suspect computers.

When tracking cyber offenders across the Internet, you use many of the same software tools that system and network administrators use to monitor and test network connectivity. Many of these programs are included in modern operating systems, and you may already be familiar with them. Even if you are already comfortable with the tools we discuss in this chapter, you may not have considered their use during an investigation. Unfortunately, many of our most common Internet application protocols make no provisions for strongly authenticating the transmitter of a communication. Services like email and Usenet are based on simple text-based initiation protocols and basically use the honor system. This complicates investigations because you cannot necessarily trust the identification information contained within Internet messages. The better you understand the underlying protocols and processes, the better you can evaluate the validity of the names and Internet addresses associated with Internet communications.

Internet Fundamentals

This book is intended to be an introduction to computer investigations, not to TCP/IP. If you want to be an effective network tracker, you need a thorough understanding of the Internet protocol suite. Many books are available on this subject. W. Richard Stevens' three-volume set, *TCP/IP Illustrated*, published by Addison-Wesley (1993, 1995, 1996), is considered one of the definitive references. The more comprehensive and detailed your understanding of Internet technology, the greater your skill at investigating network-enabled crime.

The Internet and many private networks run a set of protocols commonly referred to as TCP/IP, which stands for Transmission Control Protocol/Internet Protocol. The label "TCP/IP" is a convenient abbreviation for a set of related network protocols, the development of which effectively started in the late 1960s and is ongoing today. More precisely referred to as "the Internet protocol suite," it is a set of communication conventions that a device must implement in order to participate on the Internet. TCP/IP is not specific to any operating system, programming language, or network hardware. It is an equal opportunity set of standards that enables Macs, Windows, Unix, routers, switches, and a variety of mainframe environments to communicate with each other. It is not specific to network topology, meaning that Ethernet, token ring, and wireless networks can also interoperate. This universal interoperability is a prerequisite to both modern computer crime and investigations.

Plenty of books and essays exhaustively discuss the Open Systems Interconnection (OSI) seven-layer Network Reference model, so we won't spend a great deal of time on it. The model is illustrated in Figure 2-1. The original seven-layer model was conceived as an abstraction that didn't apply to any currently existing technology—especially not the burgeoning suite of Internet protocols—and the exact labeling of Internet services and protocols within this model continues to be a matter of tremendous debate (especially the session and presentation layers). But it is a debate of no consequence because after all, the Internet still functions whatever abstract labels are assigned to its protocols. The important lesson to learn from this model is that certain infrastructural services provide the foundation for the actual file sharing and distributed applications that are the reason the network exists in the first place. These services are stacked on top of each other like Lego building

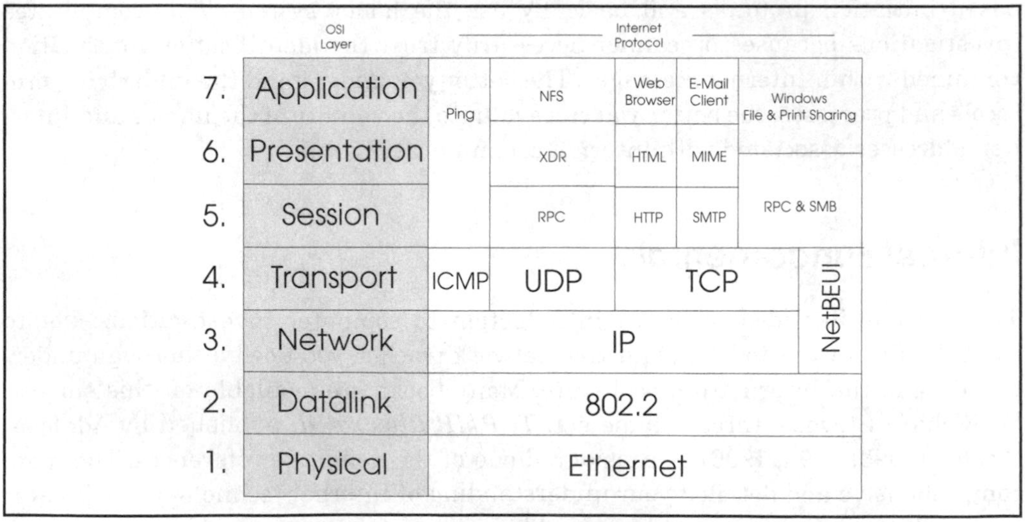

OSI Layer			Internet Protocol				
7.	Application	Ping	NFS	Web Browser	E-Mail Client	Windows File & Print Sharing	NetBEUI
6.	Presentation		XDR	HTML	MIME		
5.	Session		RPC	HTTP	SMTP	RPC & SMB	
4.	Transport	ICMP	UDP	TCP			
3.	Network		IP				
2.	Datalink		802.2				
1.	Physical		Ethernet				

Figure 2-1 OSI seven-layer model

blocks. Its relevance to forensic investigations is that you cannot interpret evidence without understanding its place within the hierarchy of stacked services. Let's look at a concrete example to see how this layering works.

You might not have realized that when you send and receive email, you are dealing with three different addresses, each within a different network layer. (Every network interface has a unique hardware address burned into it at the factory. This address is called the MAC (media access control) address) (We discuss an unusual use Microsoft makes of this address in Chapter 8.) This address enables all of the devices on a LAN segment—those devices that can see each other's network traffic— to refer to each other. At the network layer, devices recognize traffic intended for themselves on the basis of the MAC addresses incorporated within the chunks of data on the network, which are called *packets*. It is entirely impractical for every device on the Internet to refer to devices outside of their LAN segment by this hardware address, so when a computer joins the Internet, it has a numeric IP address assigned to it. An IP address is usually written as a series of four numbers in the range 0–255, separated by dots, such as 192.168.0.55.

Certain IP addresses, or ranges of addresses, are reserved for special purposes. For example, IP addresses that end with 0 denote a network address, such as 192.168.0.0. An IP address that ends with 255 denotes a broadcast address, such as 192.168.0.255. "Private addresses" in the 192.168.0.0 to 192.168.255.255 range may be used on internal networks. These addresses "are intended for intra-enterprise communications, without any intention to ever directly connect to other enterprises or the Internet itself."[1] When tracking offenders, if you locate an address within this range, don't pack your bags for California (the location of the Internet Assigned Numbers Authority[2]); you have to determine the suspects' external IP address to locate them.

An Internet address actually contains two parts. The network portion is unique among all the networks interconnected to the LAN segment (which often means the entire Internet), and the host section is unique among all the devices using the same network portion. The effect is that all IP addresses on the Internet are both unique and identifiable as being within a specific network. Private networks use addressing that is unique within their networks, but any two private networks can use the same "address space" as long as they are not interconnected to each other.

The uniqueness of addresses and the distinction between network and host portions of the address make it practical for routers to know where to route to. Entire books have been written about routing. For our simplified purposes, *routers* are

---

1. From RFC 1918. (For more information on private addresses, see http:// www.isi.edu/in-notes/ rfc1918.txt.)

2. http://www.iana.org

devices that automatically forward your data packets to another network when the destination is not your network. Routers base their decision on where to forward your packet on current conditions and their programmed instructions—routers do whatever is most expedient, which means that the route between any two points can change. This is completely different from the Public Switched Telephone Network (PSTN). When you make a telephone call, the switches within the PSTN sequentially establish a circuit from end to end, and it is maintained throughout the duration of the call. On the Internet, it may often seem as if you are using a circuit, but the actual path taken by each individual packet is dependent upon the whims of the intermediate routers.

The network part of an Internet address is assigned by the Internet Assigned Numbers Authority (IANA) to each network owner, and the host part is assigned to individual hosts and devices by the network owner. The network may be run by an organization (business or government agency), or it may be run by an Internet service provider (ISP) to provide Internet access to its customers. In the latter case, the IP addresses may be used by individuals or multiple organizations. Because IP addresses are used for routing, when a device is moved to a new network, it often requires a new address.

IP address can be statically or dynamically assigned. Computers that are assigned a static IP address always use the same IP address until it is manually changed to a new address, which is becoming increasingly less convenient in a time of constant reorganizations and mobile computers. Dynamic addresses are automatically assigned to a computer when it registers itself on a network using a protocol called Dynamic Host Configuration Protocol (DHCP) or Windows Internet Naming Service (WINS), a Microsoft protocol that is rapidly becoming obsolete. For network administrators, DHCP neatly solves the tedium and confusion of manually assigning constantly moving Internet devices. Virtually all ISPs use DHCP to assign addresses to their dial-up customers, and many permanently connected home users have dynamically assigned addresses that can change whenever their cable modems are powered off and on. Use of DHCP is definitely on the increase, but unfortunately, DHCP makes detective work a little more difficult.

Reading Obfuscated IP Addresses

Those who send spam, unsolicited commercial junk mail, usually try to keep their true identities secret—otherwise, they would be overwhelmed by disgruntled Internet citizens who wish to retaliate. In addition to using a bogus return email address, they often include obfuscated URLs. Instead of having a human-readable name, or the dotted-decimal format such as 135.17.243.191, a URL may appear in 10 Digit Integer Format (base 256), so it appears like this: http://2280853951.

It's fairly easy to convert a number in this format back into the normal quad format so that you can research the ownership of a Web site.

1. Open Windows Calculator in scientific mode (in the Calculator window, choose View | Scientific).
2. Convert 2280853951 to hexadecimal format = 87F311BF.
3. Now convert each pair to decimal notation and add the dots:

```
87 = 135
F3 = 243
11 = 17
BF = 191
135.243.17.191


Dotted Quad to 10 Digit Decimal (base 256):
Dotted Quad format: A.B.C.D = 10 Digit Decimal #
A(256³) + B(256²) + C(256¹) + D =

Example:
185.127.185.152 =
185(256³) + 127(256²) + 185(256¹) + 152 =
3103784960 + 8323072 + 47360 + 152 = 3112155544
```

Or if you hate math like we do, the easiest way to convert is to let ping or traceroute do it for you. Running ping or traceroute on the 10 Digit Decimal Number will resolve its Dotted Decimal notation, showing you the dotted quad format equivalent. For example:

```
C:\>ping 2280853951
Pinging 135.243.17.191 with 32 bytes of data:
```

In case you were worried that we hadn't figured out what to do with media address control (MAC) addresses, don't worry, we still need them. Remember that devices on the same LAN segment are somewhat on a first-name basis. They don't refer to each other by the formal IP addresses used on the Internet. However, the MAC address is used only at the hardware layer, so when a process or application "up the stack" specifies another device on a network segment by IP address, it has to be translated into a MAC address. This is done by looking it up in the ARP table, which is automatically created by the Address Resolution Protocol. ARP is just one of a number of network services that run in the background, invisible to most users but essential to the operation of a network. Networked computers can be quite chatty, constantly comparing notes on routing tables, network conditions, and each other's presence.

There is a common belief that because MAC addresses are burned into the network interface card (NIC), they never can be changed. The MAC address can be changed by using the ifconfig command in Unix. Given that MAC addresses are sometimes used to identify the source of hostile activity, it should also come as no surprise that programs are available that can randomly change a MAC address.[3] Don't automatically assume that a piece of equipment is useless as evidence because its MAC is different than you expected. The MAC you are seeking may have been changed through software, or the NIC may have been changed.

You probably already have used the most common tool for network debugging, ping. (By the way, the name is not an acronym; it is a reference to the underwater echolocation system called SONAR.) ping is a simple, yet greatly valuable program, that uses Internet Control Message Protocol's ECHO_REQUEST datagram. This datagram sends a request to the target machine and listens for an ICMP response. You can use ping to determine when a machine is alive and sometimes the DNS name of the machine. If you want to continuously keep checking for a "live" machine, you can use a program like What's Up Gold. With this program and others, you can input the IP address, and at preset intervals, it automatically checks to ensure that a specific service on a specific host is still reachable. Be aware that ping is a relatively noisy process—it is easily detected by the remote system. Assume that a moderately savvy Internet criminal may be monitoring all forms of connection to his or her host, so don't ping someone when you don't want that person to know about it.

Domain Name Service (DNS)

We expect computers to refer to each other by numbers—not by name. Unfortunately, most humans don't do as well with numbers and prefer to use names that can be easily remembered, spoken, and typed, such as www.cia.gov or www.amazon.com. To accommodate this difference between humans and machine, the Domain Name Service (DNS) was developed. Internet DNS is effectively a huge global database, usable from any point in the Internet and capable of mapping human-readable names such as www.lucent.com to a corresponding numeric IP address. This process is called *domain name resolution*. Use of domain names and associated IP address

---

3. http://galeb.etf.bg.ac.yu/~azdaja/changemac.html

ranges is controlled by the Internet Corporation for Assigned Names and Numbers (ICANN) through accredited registrars.[4] The owner of each domain is responsible for placing all host names and corresponding IP addresses on a name server so that outsiders can resolve their names. Most name servers also support *reverse lookups,* which is the process of providing the human-readable domain name that corresponds to a specific numeric IP address. Many Internet applications perform reverse lookups as a simple security measure, checking to ensure that the IP address associated with an incoming connection attempt is associated with a registered domain name—a weak but useful test.

The domain name server responsible for a particular domain may resolve any query with any IP address. The IP address may not be one within an IP address range assigned to that organization, and that doesn't matter. The owners of a particular domain, such as bubbabbq.com, may choose to host their Web site at someone else's facility. In this case, the specific machine, www.billybob.com, won't have an IP address contiguous with the rest of bubbabbq.com. This provides a great deal of flexibility, allowing organizations to move their machines from network to network, changing Web host service providers or ISPs without having to change their human-readable domain names.

Another type of network tool that will be useful to you in tracking an offender is one that can be manually used to resolve a domain name. The classic tool for this purpose, nslookup, is available on Unix, Windows NT, and Windows 2000. You can use nslookup to perform both forward and reverse lookups, resolving the IP address associated with a specific host name or obtaining the name associated with a numeric address.

In order to use a domain name, the owner must register it with the appropriate authority—a task that is usually facilitated by an ISP or one of several online services. At the time of registration—and ideally whenever it is changed—the owner of the domain is required to include name and contact information for a domain administrator. This person is expected to respond to email messages or telephone calls regarding activities associated with his or her domain. It should come as no surprise that these people are frequently not easy to contact. The whois utility can be used to obtain contact information on a specific domain from a server maintained by the appropriate Internet naming authority. Remember that whois information is furnished by the person who provided the registration information. It isn't really verified for accuracy; either through deliberate deception or an innocent mistake, it is possible to register an address and include inaccurate or totally false contact names, addresses, and phone numbers.

---

4. http://www.icann.org/registrars/accredited-list.html

After pinging a system that we're researching (from a computer that is not going to resolve to our company in case the suspect is watching his or her network), we like to perform a whois just to see what comes up, keeping in mind that the information can be bogus. You don't have to have a whois utility on your workstation because several sites enable you to perform a whois over the Web. One of the most popular is the Sam Spade Web site.[5] Another popular and reliable Web-based whois service is provided by Network Solutions.[6]

After we perform a whois, we like to follow up with an inverse name server lookup to see what it provides and compare the results to the whois output. The inverse lookup can be accomplished on a Unix or Linux machine (or with software such as NetScanTools Pro for Windows) with either the nslookup or the dig –x command, and Sam Spade provides reverse lookup services also. You can use dig on an IP address like this:

```
dig -x 111.222.333.000
```

or

```
dig domainname.com
```

dig is an alternative to nslookup, but we usually run nslookup again just to compare the results to all the previous queries.

After we have obtained contact information using the tools previously described, we usually run traceroute (or tracert) to see what route the packets are taking to get to their destination. Like ping, this handy utility sends your packets to the computer you are examining, so don't use it if you don't want to tip off the suspect that you are watching. We use the results from traceroute to help confirm or question the results of whois (see the example in Figure 2-2). For example, if the site is registered to the Netherlands but traceroute takes a few hops and stops at an ISP in Philadelphia, we might suspect that something is amiss. Be aware that many corporations have their Web sites hosted by an ISP, and not necessarily an ISP in their home town—or even their home country.

---

5. http://samspade.org/.

6. http://networksolutions.com/cgi-bin/whois/whois.

Tracing route to awl.com [204.179.152.52]over a maximum of 30 hops:

```
 1   240 ms   231 ms   220 ms  208.164.95.36
 2   260 ms   230 ms   211 ms  lonukr1-e0.ins.com [208.164.95.1]
 3   330 ms   371 ms   380 ms  svlcar1-s3-30.ins.com [192.168.200.129]
 4   511 ms   491 ms   420 ms  192.168.210.2
 5   460 ms   411 ms   461 ms  svlcar3-fe0.ins.com [192.168.100.3]
 6   451 ms      *      491 ms  charon-inner.ins.com [199.0.207.49]
 7   501 ms   651 ms   510 ms  svlcar6-e0.ins.com [199.0.207.34]
 8   431 ms   450 ms   511 ms  bordercore1-serial5-0-0-13.SanFrancisco.
                               cw.net [166.48.12.53]
 9   420 ms   441 ms   491 ms  corerouter1.SanFrancisco.cw.net
                               [204.70.9.131]
10   510 ms   501 ms   501 ms  corerouter2.WestOrange.cw.net [204.70.9.139]
11   521 ms   511 ms   511 ms  hs-core7-loopback.WestOrange.cw.net
                               [166.49.67.97]
12   501 ms   501 ms   571 ms  savvis-communications-hou.WestOrange.
                               cw.net [166.49.67.106]
13   551 ms   511 ms   561 ms  216.90.236.210
14   581 ms   560 ms   491 ms  204.179.152.52

Trace complete.
```

Figure 2-2 Example traceroute output

Application Addresses

We're almost done with our discussion of Internet addresses—we just have one more layer to discuss: application addresses. Email, Web browsing, ICQ, and Internet Relay Chat (IRC) are just a few of the services that have their own application-specific addressing. When you send email, you know to use a two-part address that includes both a mailbox and a domain, such as wkruse@computer-forensic.com. You can't send email to wkruse, nor can you just send it to computer-forensic.com—you need to specify both in order for a message to reach a destination.

Another ubiquitous form of Internet addressing that includes both domain- and application-specific information is the Universal Resource Locators (URLs) used with Web browsers. For instance, the URL http://www.lucent.com/services provides three types of information. The letters "http://" indicate the application protocol, which in this case is Hypertext Transfer Protocol (HTTP). "www.lucent.com," of course, represents a specific numeric IP address, and "services" points to a specific page.

Stalking the Stalker

When using programs such as ping, and some of the scanning tools, keep in mind that their use may easily tip off even a novice computer crook that he or she is under investigation. In the online world of spy versus spy, you often use the same tools to track an intruder that an intruder uses. Clever attackers are like careful scouts. Those who suspect that they are being tracked will try to cover their tracks (see Chapter 10), and they also sometimes will backtrack to see if someone is following them. Skillful hackers carefully monitor systems they've compromised for signs of unwelcome attention. If your goal is to track and catch your prey, you don't want to be blasting away at the suspect's box—especially from machines that easily resolve back to your company's name. To use the SONAR analogy, there are both passive and active surveillance techniques. ping and traceroute are active and cannot be hidden from the object of the scan. While pings cannot be hidden from the object of the ping, it is easy enough to perform the scans from a system that isn't obviously associated with your organization. You can maintain a few accounts with a dial-up ISP for just this purpose. When it's time to start investigating, unplug the work-station, set it for DHCP, dial your ISP, and you're off the company network. The intruder who has been breaking into CorpNet does not suddenly see CorpNet probing back.

A Dial-Up Session

Now that you have an understanding of some Internetworking basics, let's take a look at how a typical Internet dial-up session works (see Figure 2-3). When you dial to an ISP with a modem, you might use a layer 2 protocol called Point to Point Protocol (PPP). Referring back to Figure 2-1, layer 2 is the datalink layer. Connectivity is not automatic, though. A dial-up session must first be authenticated, and then an IP address is assigned. The modem at the ISP's Point of Presence (POP) is directly connected to—or even a component within—a router that is designed to accommodate PPP connections. When a connection attempt occurs, the dial-up router first prompts the user for a login name and password. A single ISP may have hundreds of POPs spread over an entire continent—it is certainly not practical for each dial-up router to

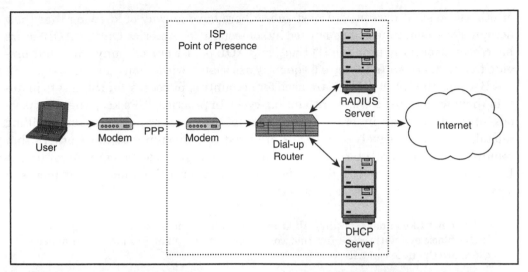

Figure 2-3   Connecting to the Internet through an ISP's dial-up service

maintain a list of all users and their encrypted passwords. A centralized directory contains this list, and the RADIUS protocol is used to support the authentication request between the dial-up routers and the centralized user directory.

After a user is authenticated to the ISP, an IP address is dynamically assigned to that user with DHCP. Although it is possible for individual subscribers to have their own permanently assigned IP addresses, such an inefficient use of valuable IP address space is virtually unheard of. The IP address is almost always associated with a DNS name, allowing reverse lookups. The name will be something generic, such as ppp589.city.isp.com.

RADIUS is used not just for authentication; it is also used for accounting. The RADIUS server is normally the only ISP device that maintains records that can be used to track an offender, so it is very important to your investigation. The server normally maintains records of every login attempt, both successful and unsuccessful, and also every logoff or session end. This information is necessary so the ISP can keep track of subscriber connection time. The information associated with a RADIUS session also includes the IP address assigned to a specific login during a session, and ISPs often use caller ID to keep track of the telephone number used to originate the session. This allows the ISP to determine which login name was using a specific IP address at a specific time, but the association of this login with a specific individual is only as good as the authentication mechanism. Most dial-up accounts authenticate with reusable passwords, and it is common for cyber criminals to guess or otherwise steal passwords (most subscribers have no way of knowing that their accounts are sometimes being abused by someone else). America Online (AOL) users have been especially prone to ID theft, and AOL is just one of many ISPs that provide free trial accounts that are frequently associated with phony names.

Because the RADIUS logs are used for accounting purposes, an ISP has to maintain them for at least a one-month billing cycle. In practice, ISPs keep them for periods of up to a year in order to respond to customer complaints about billing mistakes. Even relatively small ISPs are used to responding to court orders that require providing the Internet equivalent of a trap and trace record. According to Lucent consultant Aaron Higbee, who has worked with the abuse departments of several large Internet service providers:

> ISPs do not like abusers because their mischief affects the bottom line and gives the ISP a black eye within the Internet community. If you want to identify an abuser, these are the necessary steps:
>
> 1. Document the abuse with dates, time, time zone, and logs.
>
> 2. Send the logs as a complaint to abuse@isp.com.
>
> 3. Follow up your email with a phone call. (Do not call a tech support or customer service line.) Ask for the legal department's fax number or ask to speak directly with the abuse/security department.
>
> 4. Fax the same logs to the legal staff and let them know that you will follow up your complaint with a court-ordered subpoena for any and all subscriber information including all captured caller IDs.
>
> You must assume the subscriber information is fraudulent unless the account has a bill payment history and the session in question can be pinpointed as originating in the same calling area as the rest of the subscriber's usage history. If you are lucky, the caller ID will be captured for the session you are interested in. You then subpoena the local phone company for subscriber information for the phone number that was captured in the caller ID. Sometimes reverse telephone lookup sites like http://www.anywho.com/telq.html can give you clues as to who you are tracking, but the definitive answer will come from the subpoenaed subscriber information.

You might think the biggest problem with obtaining information from ISPs would be the result of the terms of service and confidentiality agreements that most service providers have with their customers. But to the contrary, most service providers are willing to assist you because they do not want anyone misusing their system. In a prominent privacy case several years ago, AOL was sued by a subscriber who accused the company of illegally providing sensitive personal information to a law enforcement agency, so ISPs are now very sensitive to the correct legal procedures.

When you obtain the information from the service provider, keep in mind that the subscriber information can be completely bogus. There is little to no authentication for any of the information associated with the subscriber. The value of the information is in determining the telephone number that was used to connect to the ISP. If you can obtain the phone number and the date and time that a session was set up, you are yet another step closer to finding your suspect. You can then start the subpoena process again and try to find other connections originating from that same phone number. This still might not lead directly to your suspect, but you're getting closer and closer to a suspect who thought he or she was well hidden by the free service.

Tracing Email and News Postings

Before heading down the messaging path and looking for tracks in the sand, let's quickly discuss how these messaging services operate. News groups and email are cousins. Descending from original siblings on pre-Internet Unix systems, they have continued to evolve in parallel, with much sharing of genetic material. Both services have the following attributes:

- Simple Internet application protocols that use text commands
- Store-and-forward architecture allowing messages to be shuttled through a series of intermediate systems
- Message body composed entirely of printable characters (7-bit, not 8-bit)
- Human-readable message headers indicating the path between sender and receiver

You'll need the assistance of systems administrators, perhaps on every system the message transited, and they won't be able to help you unless they have logging information on their messaging hosts. If the originator wants to cover his or her tracks, determining the real sender of either bogus news postings or suspicious email can be challenging. News is probably a bit easier, but email is more common today, so let's start with it.

Tracking Email

An email program such as Outlook, Notes, or Eudora is considered a *client* application, which means that it is network-enabled software that is intended to interact with a *server*. In the case of email, it is normal to interact with two different servers: one for outgoing and one for incoming mail. When you want to read email, your client connects to a mail server using one of three different protocols:

- Post Office Protocol (POP, not to be confused with Point of Presence)
- Internet Mail Access Protocol (IMAP)
- Microsoft's Mail API (MAPI)

For the purposes of investigation, the protocol used to gather incoming email from a server is of minimal interest. The most important thing to understand about these different protocols is that their use affects where mail messages are stored (as depicted in Table 2-1). All incoming mail is initially stored on a mail server, sorted by that mail server into individual *mailboxes* for access by the addressee. POP users have the choice of either downloading a copy of their mail from their server, or downloading it and subsequently allowing it to be automatically deleted. Email that has been read or stored for future use is stored on the computer that is running the email client. IMAP and MAPI users have the option of leaving all their mail on their mail server.

There are two major advantages to leaving email stored on the server. First, all of the stored email for an entire organization can be easily backed up from a central location. Second, it provides users the flexibility of accessing their mailboxes from multiple client machines: office, home, through the Web, and so forth. The implica-

Table 2-1   Internet Email Protocols

Post Office Service	Protocol	Relevance to Investigation
Incoming message store only	POP	Must access workstation in order to trace mail.
Storage of all messages (optional)	Open: MAPI Proprietary: Microsoft MAPI Lotus Notes	Copies of both incoming and outgoing messages may be stored on server or workstation (and server/workstation backup tapes).
Web-based: send and receive	HTTP	Incoming and outgoing messages are stored on server, possibly with optional manual download to workstation. Facilitates identity spoofing.

tions of this to the investigator is that POP mail users always use their local machine for their email archives: copies of outgoing mail, mail stored in folders for future reference, deleted mail that hasn't been purged, all are stored on the individual's workstation. Organizations that provide IMAP or MAPI service, or a proprietary service like Lotus Notes, probably store email on the server, although individual users may or may not have the option of storing their email locally.

Outgoing email uses a completely different protocol called Simple Mail Transfer Protocol (SMTP). Unlike the protocols used to retrieve mail from a post office, SMTP doesn't require any authentication—it is much like tossing a message into a mail slot at the post office. Servers that accept mail and relay it to other mail servers are sometimes called mail transfer agents (MTAs), and they also use SMTP. Your ISP will give you the name of the mail server that you should use for outgoing mail, often something along the lines of smtp.bobsisp.com. The SMTP server that the ISP uses relays messages to their destinations. Either the destination server recognizes a message as being addressed to one of its local users, and places it into the appropriate mailbox for that user, or based on a set of rules, it relays the message on further.

SMTP is a very simple protocol. Like many Internet protocols, such as HTTP, it consists of a few simple text-based commands or keywords. One of the first tricks an Internet hacker learns is how to manually send an email message by telneting to port 25, the SMTP port. Not only is it a fun trick to become a human email forwarder, but it also enables you to put any information you want into the headers of the email message you are sending—including fake origination and return addresses. Actually, you needn't do this manually if you want to fake email. When you configure your personal email client, you tell it what return address to put on your outgoing mail. You can always change that configuration, but if you want to send only a single message coming from Pres@whitehouse.gov, it is much easier to use one of several GUI-based hacker tools that enable you to quickly send a message with your choice of return addresses.

SMTP mail has no strong authentication and without using PGP or S/MIME (Secure Multipurpose Internet Mail Extensions) to add a digital signature, the level of trust associated with a mail message is pretty low. The following steps (our input is in boldface) show how incredibly easy it is to fake the return address in an Internet mail message:

```
[root@njektd /root]# telnet localhost 25
Trying 127.0.0.1...
Connected to njektd.com.
Escape character is '^]'.
220 njektd.com ESMTP Sendmail 8.9.3/8.9.3; Tue, 5 Dec 2000 17:37:02 -
0500
```

```
helo
250 OK
mail from: teswt@test.com
250 teswt@test.com... Sender ok
rcpt to: you@domain.com
250 you@domain.com... Recipient ok
data
354
Haha-this is a spoofed mail message!
.
250 RAA25927 Message accepted for delivery
quit
221 njektd.com closing connection
Connection closed by foreign host.
```

The results of this spoofed mail message are shown in Figure 2-4. The test.com domain is just one we made up for demonstration purposes, but the email client reports whatever information it was provided.

As we'll discuss later in this chapter, some identification information is associated with the mail header that is a bit harder to spoof. As recorded in the following mail header, we were indeed logged in as 208.164.95.173:

```
Received: from dhcp-95-173.ins.com ([208.164.95.173]) by
dtctxexchims01.ins.com with SMTP (Microsoft Exchange Internet Mail
Service Version 5.5.2653.13)
      id YM4CM2VP; Sun, 10 Dec 2000 08:46:30 -0600
From: teswt@test.com
Date: Sun, 10 Dec 2000 09:46:46 -0500 (EST)
Message-Id: 200012101446.JAA06830@horh1.emsr.lucent.com
```

When relaying a message from another relay host, current versions of SMTP also keep track of the IP address of the system connecting to them, and they add that IP address to the header of the message. If you want to show that a mail message originated from a specific computer, the best way to do so is to investigate the entire path that appears in the extended header information.

Although SMTP servers won't perform any authentication when receiving mail from the client, most Internet mail servers are configured to accept mail for relay

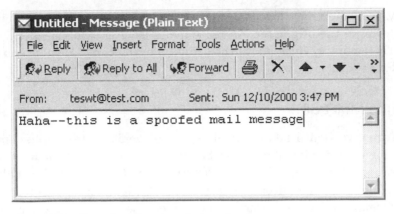

Figure 2-4   Reading the spoofed mail message

only when that mail originates from a specific range of IP addresses. If an ISP does not place any limits on which systems can connect to the ISP's mail server, allowing it to be used as a free relay station, it won't take spammers long to find it. To reduce the amount of spam mail that originates with their mail servers, most ISPs allow relay connections only from IP addresses within the range that they assign to their own subscribers. Authentication based just on IP address is very weak, but for the purposes of preventing unauthorized use of SMTP servers, it is adequate.

It should come as no surprise that Web-based email is not only available, but is becoming increasingly popular. The Internet browser is rapidly becoming the universal front end. Web-based email enables users to access all of their email—both incoming and saved messages—through a Web browser. Not only does this free the user from installing and configuring an email client on his or her workstation, but it also means that the user can easily access email from any workstation virtually anywhere in the world. Undoubtedly, many people are accessing free Web-based email from work for their personal use.

It also shouldn't come as a surprise that free email services are being used by some people to hide their identities. For the novice computer criminal, these services appear to be an easy way to hide their identity, and by adding at least one more server and involving another service provider, it certainly does complicate the association of a mail account with a specific person. The only way to find out who the ISP thinks is using a specific email address is to obtain a subpoena for the account information. If you are working with law enforcement agencies, they can obtain a subpoena to facilitate their investigation, or you can obtain a subpoena from a lawsuit (for more information, see Chapter 12). Fortunately, some providers of free email service are including the originator's IP address in the header information.

Previously, you would have to subpoena the email provider and then the originating ISP to determine the originator. We recommend issuing a subpoena for the email logs from the email provider, but at the same time, you can also subpoena the originating ISP.

Reading the Mail Trail

When you are investigating a case involving email, you have to decipher email headers. If you have never viewed a header before, it might first appear to be gibberish, but once you get the hang of it and understand how SMTP works, it makes sense. The first annoyance you encounter is that most client email programs hide the header information from the user. Depending on the mail client you're using, you may have to do a little bit of digging to get to the header. In most programs, if you click File | Properties, an option to view the header is displayed. If your particular program provides a different way to access header information, consult the Help menu and documentation or try the company's Web site for instructions.

Most users don't want to be bothered with deciphering email headers, which encourages the email software vendors to make access to it as obscure as possible. Let's look at Microsoft Outlook Express. It is a popular email program for many reasons, including the fact that it comes free with Internet Explorer and recent versions of Windows.

As shown in Figure 2-5, the header information is available in Outlook Express by clicking on File and then Properties, which displays the dialog box that looks like that shown in Figure 2-6.

The General Tab for the properties in Outlook Express displays some basics about the message such as the subject of the message, the apparent sender, and the date and time sent and received. Click on the Details tab to display the information like that shown in Figure 2-6. By examining the headers of this message, it is clear that both the From address (test@testing.org) and the Reply-To address are fake addresses (another_test@test. org). This is a real message that we sent from the Internet, but before sending the message, we first changed the From address to "HTCIA NE Chapter." The From address is completely arbitrary—it contains whatever the sender configures into their email program.

The most important tracks are found at the top of the message. In this case, the first line shows the computer that the message was originally sent from. While the name of the PC, "mypc," can easily be spoofed, the IP address that mypc was assigned when we logged on to the ISP is much more difficult to spoof. While it is not impossible to spoof an IP address, we are not aware of a case in which one has been spoofed to counterfeit email. The practical details involved in spoofing an IP address make it virtually impossible in an email transaction, which involves several round trips between the SMTP server and the connecting system. (Do be aware, though,

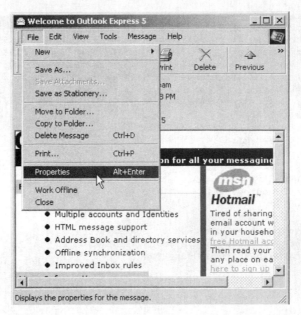

Figure 2-5 Outlook Express File menu

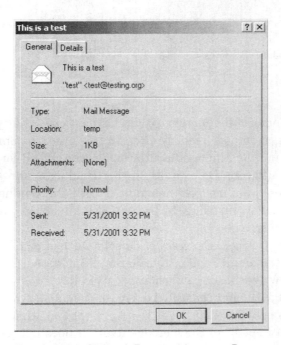

Figure 2-6 Outlook Express Message Properties window

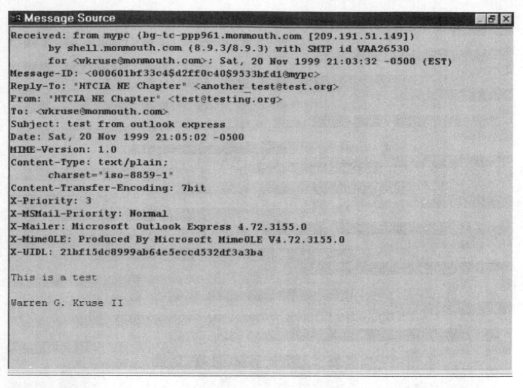

```
Received: from mypc (bg-tc-ppp961.monmouth.com [209.191.51.149])
        by shell.monmouth.com (8.9.3/8.9.3) with SMTP id VAA26530
        for <wkruse@monmouth.com>; Sat, 20 Nov 1999 21:03:32 -0500 (EST)
Message-ID: <000601bf33c4$d2ff0c40$9533bfd1@mypc>
Reply-To: "HTCIA NE Chapter" <another_test@test.org>
From: "HTCIA NE Chapter" <test@testing.org>
To: <wkruse@monmouth.com>
Subject: test from outlook express
Date: Sat, 20 Nov 1999 21:05:02 -0500
MIME-Version: 1.0
Content-Type: text/plain;
        charset="iso-8859-1"
Content-Transfer-Encoding: 7bit
X-Priority: 3
X-MSMail-Priority: Normal
X-Mailer: Microsoft Outlook Express 4.72.3155.0
X-MimeOLE: Produced By Microsoft MimeOLE V4.72.3155.0
X-UIDL: 21bf15dc8999ab64e5eccd532df3a3ba


This is a test

Warren G. Kruse II
```

Figure 2-7   Viewing the message source in Outlook Express

that the actual sender of the message could have cracked the system from which it was sent, and logged on as somebody else.) In this case, the email was sent from a computer in the same domain, monmouth.com, as the SMTP server that relayed the mail, shell.monmouth.com. Do a whois on the IP address and see if you get something that matches the purported domains of both the originating client and the relay server. Then follow up using the Dig w/AXFR advanced query, as shown in Figure 2-8, using NetscanTools.

In contrast to Outlook Express, Microsoft Outlook (included with Microsoft Office) places the full email header information in an obscure position. As shown in Figure 2-9, to view the header information, you click on View and then Options. Clicking on Message Header seems to be a more obvious way to access header information—a mistake that we make all the time—but all that does is hide the To, From, and Subject lines from the message itself. It does not show you the detailed header information that you need to track an intruder. By clicking on Options, you access the Message Options window shown in Figure 2-10.

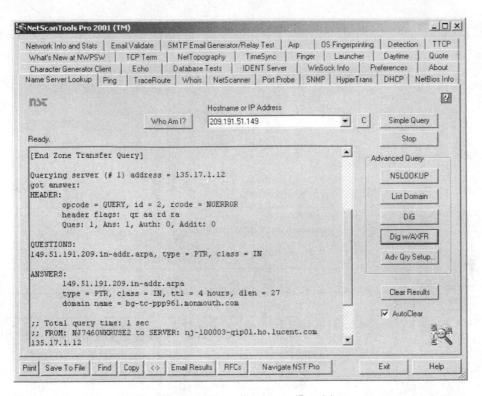

Figure 2-8   Using NetScanTools to investigate an IP address

Figure 2-9   Outlook View menu

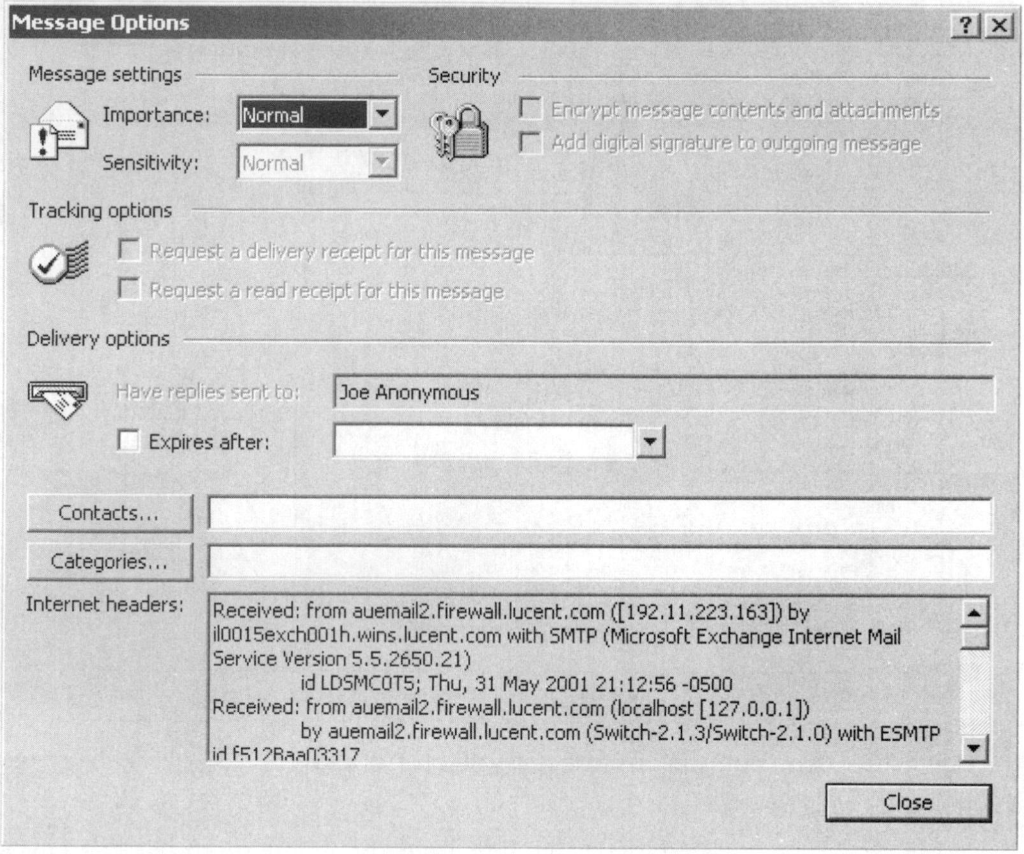

Figure 2-10   Viewing a message header in Microsoft Outlook

You've probably already noticed "Joe Anonymous" in the Have replies sent to field. We faked this deliberately to illustrate how you cannot believe everything you read. The only way to extract this information from this window is to select it all (hint: try Control-A), copy it, and then paste it into a text document, which we've done in the following:

```
Received: from hoemlsrv.firewall.lucent.com ([192.11.226.161]) by
    nj7460exch002h.wins.lucent.com with SMTP (Microsoft Exchange
    Internet Mail Service Version 5.5.2448.0) id W4VCF23A; Sat, 20
    Nov 1999 21:19:10 -0500
Received: from hoemlsrv.firewall.lucent.com (localhost [127.0.0.1]) by
    hoemlsrv.firewall.lucent.com (Pro-8.9.3/8.9.3) with ESMTP id
```

```
VAA06660 for <wgkruse@holmdel.exchange.lucent.com>; Sat, 20 Nov 1999
    21:19:10 -0500 (EST)
Received: from shell.?nmouth.com (shell.?onmouth.com [205.231.236.9])
    by hoemlsrv.firewall.lucent.com (Pro-8.9.3/8.9.3) with ESMTP id
    VAA06652 for <wgkruse@lucent.com>; Sat, 20 Nov 1999 21:19:09
    -0500 (EST)
Received: from mypc (bg-tc-ppp961.?onmouth.com [209.191.51.149]) by
    shell.?onmouth.com (8.9.3/8.9.3) with SMTP id VAA01448 for
    <wgkruse@lucent.com>; Sat, 20 Nov 1999 21:17:06 -0500 (EST)
Message-ID: <001401bf33c6$b7f214e0$9533bfd1@mypc>
Reply-To: "Joe Anonymous" <another_test@test.org>
From: "Joe Anonymous" <test@testing.org>
To: <wgkruse@lucent.com>
Subject: test from outlook express
Date: Sat, 20 Nov 1999 21:18:35 -0500
MIME-Version: 1.0
Content-Type: text/plain;
    charset="iso-8859-1"
Content-Transfer-Encoding: 7bit
X-Priority: 3
X-MSMail-Priority: Normal
X-Mailer: Microsoft Outlook Express 4.72.3155.0
X-MimeOLE: Produced By Microsoft MimeOLE V4.72.3155.0
```

This header is longer than it was in our first example. This time, the message was relayed through four different servers. Each time an SMTP server accepts a message, it places a new Received header at the top of message before forwarding it on to another server or a user mailbox. In the first message, we intentionally sent the message *from* our ISP account *to* our ISP account. The second message originated externally and then was relayed through the Lucent firewall and to the mail server used to host our mailbox. But even with the extra headers, it is still apparent that the original message was received from: "mypc," and our address at the time was: ?onmouth.com [209.191.51.149]. The lines in the header tell a story about where the email message has been, when it was there, and when it was delivered to its destination. It may be a contrived story, but it is still a story. Virtually any of the headers with the exception of the topmost one could be bogus—it is up to you to verify each one of them and determine the actual history of the message.

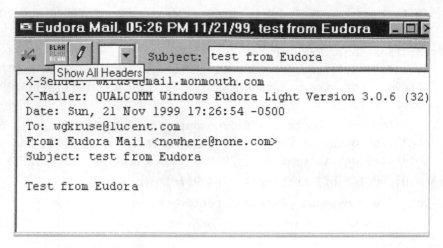

Figure 2-11   Viewing the X-Sender header on Eudora Lite

The last example that we will look at is from Eudora, another popular email client.[6] Eudora hides the header information by default, like the rest of the client programs, but as you can see from the Eudora Lite example in Figure 2-11, the full header is only a mouse-click away. A helpful piece of information is X-Sender, which shows the mail server and the account the message was sent from. One of the quirky characteristics of Eudora is that the icon is labeled "Blah, Blah, Blah." Strange label, but it provides the information we need. When you click on the Blah button, your email message changes from that shown in Figure 2-11 to something that looks like that shown in Figure 2-12.

When you are conducting an investigation involving email, even if the computer's name is bogus, you have the IP address that the user was assigned. If you trust the ISP, or the company that the address resolves to, you can ask for their assistance in identifying your suspect. They probably won't disclose the information to you immediately, but by noting that IP address, along with the exact date and time that the message was sent, you can ask the ISP to save the logs until you have a chance to get a court order. As long as the logs are still available, the ISP or other organization should be able to identify the user that was assigned that IP address at the time the message was sent.

Look at the two headers the arrows are pointing to in Figure 2-13. Compare the domain name in the Received header, "monmouth.com," to the domain in the From header, "test.org." Because they do not match, we can assume that the user configured

---

6. http://www.eudora.com

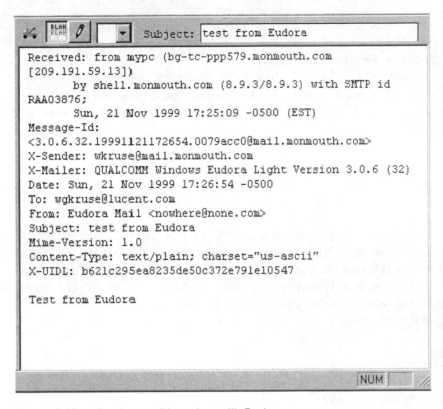

Figure 2-12   Viewing mail headers with Eudora

his or her email incorrectly or that the user is trying to hide his or her identity. A message can be injected anywhere in the chain of Received headers—you can be sure that only the topmost one is accurate. Do an nslookup against each domain—especially the purportedly original domain—and see if they exist. Do a whois against each of those domains to find out who the administrator is and contact that person. Keep in mind that if the administrator is the originator of a phony or illegal message, he or she probably won't be inclined to cooperate.

When you are investigating a case on behalf of a victim, but you can't visit the victim or otherwise obtain the original message on your own, it is possible for the victim to email you a copy of it. You must give the victim very specific instructions on the appropriate way to send the mail to you—especially if the victim usually deletes messages right after receiving them. Ask the victim to send the message as an *attachment* and not to forward the message. Forwarding replaces the suspect's information with your victim's information. You might want to ask your victim not to delete the original message until he or she hears from you.

```
Received: from hoemlsrv.firewall.lucent.com ([192.11.226.161]) by
nj7460exch002h.wins.lucent.com with SMTP (Microsoft Exchange Internet
Mail Service Version 5.5.2448.0)
        id W4VCF23A; Sat, 20 Nov 1999 21:19:10 -0500
Received: from hoemlsrv.firewall.lucent.com (localhost [127.0.0.1])
        by hoemlsrv.firewall.lucent.com (Pro-8.9.3/8.9.3) with ESMTP id
VAA06660
        for <wgkruse@holmdel.exchange.lucent.com>; Sat, 20 Nov 1999
21:19:10 -0500 (EST)
Received: from shell.monmouth.com (shell.monmouth.com [205.231.236.9])
        by hoemlsrv.firewall.lucent.com (Pro-8.9.3/8.9.3) with ESMTP id
VAA06652
        for <wgkruse@lucent.com>; Sat, 20 Nov 1999 21:19:09 -0500 (EST)
Received: from mypc (bg-tc-ppp961.monmouth.com [209.191.51.149])  ◄────
        by shell.monmouth.com (8.9.3/8.9.3) with SMTP id VAA01448
        for <wgkruse@lucent.com>; Sat, 20 Nov 1999 21:17:06 -0500 (EST)
Message-ID: <001401bf33c6$b7f214e0$9533bfd1@mypc>
Reply-To: "Joe Anonymous" <another_test@test.org>  ◄──────────────────
From: "Joe Anonymous" test@testing.org

To: <wgkruse@lucent.com>
Subject: test form outlook express
Date: Sat, 20 Nov 1999 21:18:35 -0500
MIME-Version: 1.0
Content-Type: text/plain;
        charset="iso-8859-1"
Content-Transfer-Encoding: 7bit
X-Priority: 3
X-MSMail-Priority: Normal
X-Mailer: Microsoft Outlook Express 4.72.3155.0
X-MimeOLE: Produced By Microsoft MimeOLE V4.72.3155.0
```

Figure 2-13   Extended email header with discrepancies in originator fields

SMTP Server Logs

All email servers have the ability to maintain logging information. If available, these logs are usually a more reliable source of information than the mail headers. Because of the high volume of email traffic, the ISP may not store records for very long. SMTP server logs are important tools, used by both ISPs and user organizations to troubleshoot email problems and track down the unauthorized use of mail. The only way to completely verify the path of the mail is for the administrator of each host to check the logs to find that they both sent the message to the recipient as indicated and that their host received it from a specific IP address. If you are lucky, you can follow the chain all the way back to an original IP address. Examination of the original system, which might need to be cross-referenced against RADIUS logs and phone records, is the only way to prove that a specific message existed at a specific place. Accessing this workstation usually requires a court order, but once a perpetrator is confronted with having the incriminating evidence on his or her personal computer, a confession is often not far behind.

Usenet

Usenet is a vast, distributed bulletin board, consisting of thousands of hierarchically arranged topics contributed to and read by millions of people worldwide. It was originally developed during a time in which Unix computers used modems for external connectivity. Email and even individual files could be sent between noncontiguous UNIX computers, as long as you knew the intervening series of connecting systems and chained their names within the destination mail address (such as ober! doebling!seismo!krampus!kirk). Usenet still takes advantage of this same point-to-point model, although now it uses the Internet as a transport backbone. As shown in Figure 2-14, when a post is made, it is transmitted through a chain of news servers

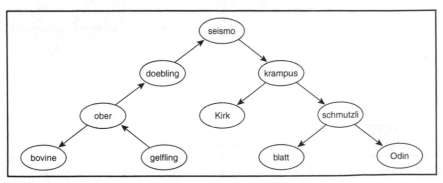

Figure 2-14 Example news server hierarchy

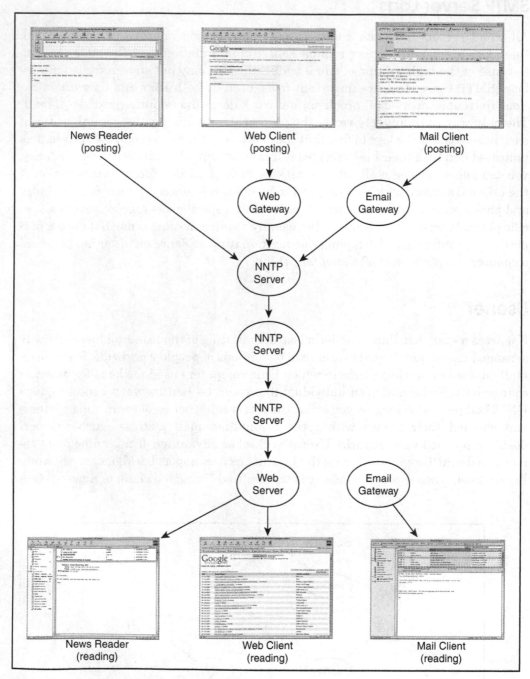

Figure 2-15 Those reading and posting news have a choice of using a traditional news reader, a web-based service, or an email gateway.

and then it is diffused back out through all of the servers in the world that subscribe to the same newsgroup.

Usenet has adapted itself well to changes in Internet technology, resulting in a nearly seamless integration of traditional news readers with email and Web interfaces. Today, Usenet users have their choice of news clients, email or Web interfaces, both for posting and for reading news messages (see Figure 2-15). Some Usenet mail gateways are also configured as email distribution listservers, enabling Internet citizens to have all the postings for a certain newsgroup delivered directly to their mailboxes, either a message at a time or collected periodically into *digests*. The implications to you as the tracker is that your attempt to research the origin of a news message may involve multiple types of servers.

If you are not familiar with Usenet, and have not configured a client to read postings, the best place to start is the original Internet archive for Usenet, the DejaNews archives provided by Google.[7] An example search is shown in Figure 2-16.

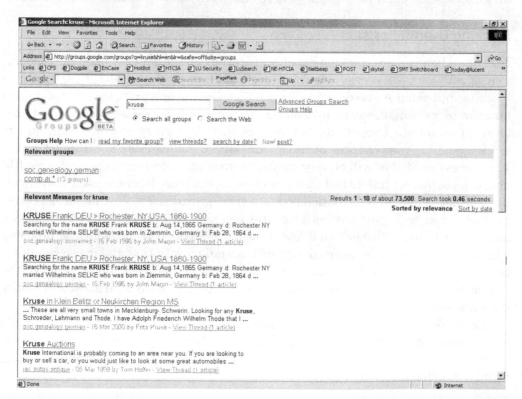

Figure 2-16   Example Google page

_____

7. http://www.deja.com/usenet

Inappropriate material is probably the most significant use of news that you are likely to encounter in an investigation. Unfortunately, huge amounts of pornographic pictures are disseminated through news, and it is common for some corporate employees to download this material, exposing their employers to the risk of sexual harassment lawsuits. Pictures, and other binaries, will be found in the uuencode format (see Chapter 4).

Usenet can provide a forum where you can publicly ask technical questions. You may also want to search archived news postings to see if you can find anything related to one of your suspects or an organization involved in your investigation. Some suspects may be active news posters. Searching for their names on a server such as Google may give you valuable clues to their activities and interests. At times, news postings are directly relevant to an investigation. It is not unheard of for disgruntled employees to try to damage the reputation of their company by making news posts containing harmful information. In some cases, it is possible to trace these inappropriate postings to IP addresses actually within the corporation.

Tracking Usenet Posts

Just like when you are tracking email, you are dependent not only upon the cooperation of all the news server administrators relevant to the message that you are tracking, but you are also dependent upon their having adequate logs. News volume tends to be very high, so the information in the logs is extremely volatile. It is not unusual for a busy Usenet site to turn over their logs every day, so if you want to track a posting, your chances of success are slim if you can't do it within 24 hours. The process you follow will be very similar to tracking a mail message, and some ISP abuse department staffers feel that news is easier to trace because, after some practice, the bogus header information is relatively easy to discern. Just like when tracking email, you work your way back from the recipient and verify each of the machine names in the path. Either you'll find a bogus connection point, which is probably where the message was inserted, or you'll actually verify that the message apparently did transit all of the hosts shown. If the origination host has a record of the poster, you can either subpoena that organization for more information or notify their abuse department.

Let's take a look at the header of a news posting. The following one is an example of a pornographic post that has spent quite a lot of time zipping around the Internet:

```
From: "YourMate" binkie1@xxx.com
Newsgroups: alt.binaries.dominion.erotica,
alt.binaries.dominion.erotica.female, alt.binaries.erotica,
alt.binaries.erotica.amateur.female, alt.binaries.erotica.blondes,
alt.binaries.erotica.centerfolds
```

```
Subject: - FREE CD !!!
Date: Sun, 5 Dec 1999 10:59:38 -0500
Lines: 2484
X-Newsreader: Microsoft Outlook Express 4.72.3110.1
X-MimeOLE: Produced By Microsoft MimeOLE V4.72.3110.3
NNTP-Posting-Host: dialup599.xxx.com
Message-ID: 384a8a4b@news.xxx.com
X-Trace: 5 Dec 1999 10:52:43 -0500, dialup599.nni.com
Path:news.rdc1.nj.home.com!newshub2.home.com!newshub1.home.com!news.ho
me.com!feeder.via.net!news.idt.net!netnews.com!newspeer1.nac.net!news.
newyork.net!ffx.uu.net!uunet!ams.uu.net!tank.news.pipex.net!pipex!news
-lond.gip.net!news.gsl.net!gip.net!nntp.news.xara.net!
xara.net!gxn.net!news.good.net!news.xxx.com!phila-dialup599.xxx.com
Xref: newshub2.home.com alt.binaries.dominion.erotica:30040448
alt.binaries.dominion.erotica.female:30252819
alt.binaries.erotica:31064499
alt.binaries.erotica.amateur.female:30199540
alt.binaries.erotica.blondes:30083027
alt.binaries.erotica.centerfolds:30058010
```

With the understanding that virtually everything on this header can be faked, each header purportedly contains the following:

- **From:** This is the name and email address of the original poster.

- **Newsgroups:** In this case, the message was cross-posted to six different news-groups.

- **NNTP-Posting-Host:** This is the machine from which the posting was sent. It is usually the same as the lower rightmost entry in the Path header.

- **Message-ID:** This is a unique serial number assigned to every post on NNTP servers. The logfile on news.xxx.com should have an entry that associates this serial number with this specific message and a specific account. This ID should be unique throughout the worldwide Usenet, and it can be used to cancel messages across all (well, most) news servers worldwide.

- **Path:** This is the meat of your investigation. In reverse chronological order, it shows every host that the message has transited. The first host, news.rdc1. nj.home.com, is the host on which this message was received, and it is the only information in this entire header that you can trust. The succeeding hostnames are the hosts that purportedly relayed this message. The next-to-last host, news.xxx.com, is apparently the news server at an ISP, while the final hostname looks like a dial-up account at that same ISP.

Note that on the preceding header, the domain name in the From field is consistent with the domain name in the NNTP-Posting-Host and Path fields. If it were not, you would know immediately that someone was attempting to cover his or her tracks. If they do match, you probably still need to verify the intermediate hosts, but you can start with the origination point. If they don't match, you need to figure out which parts of the path are real and which are bogus. It often helps to obtain other copies of the same message from other servers (either Google or servers belonging to friends of yours) and compare the paths. Whatever part of the paths is consistent among the different news hosts probably contains the actual host at which the message was inserted.

Like mail hosts, Network News Transfer Protocol (NNTP) hosts may or may not accept posts from people outside of their organization. You can test this by telneting to port 119 on that host. If you cannot connect to that host or you receive a message that posts are not accepted, odds are lower that a bogus post was made using that host as the news server. However, if you receive a message that indicates you can connect, it means that other people can connect to that host also. The chances are reduced that the administrator will really know who is using the NNTP server. Such a session may look like this:

```
C:> telnet ferkel.piglet.com 119
200 NNTP Service Microsoft® Internet Services 5.00.7515
Version: 5.0.7515 Posting Allowed
```

or this:

```
$ telnet news.isp.com 119
200 mercury2.isp.com Netscape-Collabra/3.52 17222 NNRP ready (posting
ok).
```

But if the host does not accept posts, it may look something like this:

```
$ telnet nntp.mindspring.com 119
502 You are not in my access file. Goodbye.
```

NetBios

For historical reasons, Windows computers often use a protocol called NetBIOS. Although originally used only within LANs, NetBIOS has been extended so that it can run over TCP/IP, allowing organizations to provide Windows file- and print-sharing services across a WAN. A helpful command to identify a user over a network using NetBIOS is nbtstat. nbtstat is a standard component on all current Windows platforms, and a Linux version is also available.[8]

From your remote computer you can run this command against either the suspect's IP address:

```
nbtstat -A 111.222.333.000
```

or against a specific machine name:

```
nbtstat -a suspect.computer.com
```

nbtstat displays protocol statistics and current TCP/IP connections using NBT (NetBIOS over TCP/IP). If the remote computer is reachable over the network, you can receive the following information:

```
NBTSTAT [-a RemoteName] [-A IP address] [-c] [-n] [-r] [-R] [-s] [S]
[interval]
```

-a	(adapter status)	Lists the remote machine's name table given its name
-A	(Adapter status)	Lists the remote machine's name table given its IP address.
-c	(cache)	Lists the remote name cache including the IP addresses
-n	(names)	Lists local NetBIOS names.
-r	(resolved)	Lists names resolved by broadcast and via WINS
-R	(Reload)	Purges and reloads the remote cache name table
-S	(Sessions)	Lists sessions table with the destination IP addresses
-s	(sessions)	Lists sessions table converting destination IP addresses to host names via the hosts file.
RemoteName		Remote host machine name.
IP address:		Dotted decimal representation of the IP address.

---

8. http://razor.bindview.com/tools/index.shtml

Interval: Redisplays selected statistics, pausing
                                 interval seconds between each display. Press
                                 Ctrl+C to stop redisplaying statistics.

If a user is logged into the computer, you receive output similar to that shown in Figure 2-17. As you can see, it provides the machine name, the Windows NT domain the computer is registered in (in this case, a domain named "security"), and the MAC address. Since the MAC address is unique, it is a positive method of identifying a computer after it has been seized. Unless the NIC is swapped out, you have a promising lead that this is the computer you're looking for. nbtstat is a handy command because it enables you to associate a user with an IP address and then copy and paste that information into a document that you can print.

```
Microsoft Windows 2000 [Version 5.00.2195]
(C) Copyright 1985-2000 Microsoft Corp.

C:\>date
The current date is: Sat 04/07/2001
Enter the new date: (mm-dd-yy)
C:\>time
The current time is: 22:39:54.90
Enter the new time:
C:\>nbtstat -a krusingonnt
NetBIOS Remote Machine Name Table
Name                Type        Status
---------------------------------------------------
NJ7460WGKRUSE       <00>        UNIQUE    Registered  ◄─── machine name
SECURITY            <00>        GROUP     Registered
NJ7460WGKRUSE       <20>        UNIQUE    Registered
NJ7460WGKRUSE       <03>        UNIQUE    Registered
SECURITY            <1E>        GROUP     Registered        ◄─── NT Domain
SECURITY            <1D>        UNIQUE    Registered
.._MSBROWSE__.      <01>        GROUP     Registered
WGKRUSE             <03>        UNIQUE    Registered  ◄─── Username
MAC Address = 00-60-1D-04-45-14                       ◄─── MAC
```

Figure 2-17 nbtstat output

We mostly use the nbtstat command from within our network since nbtstat issues a User Datagram Protocol (UDP) request and is blocked by default on many firewalls. Don't be surprised if you can ping the system, but an nbtstat returns "host not found" on a computer you know to be a Windows platform.

Third-Party Programs

If you have the budget, you can purchase additional programs that will do any of the previously discussed commands for you, usually with a convenient GUI. Two of the tools we use most often are Neotrace and Netscan Pro (the latter was shown previously in Figure 2-8). Both can do a traceroute for you, but Neotrace overlays a map and attempts to geographically plot the traceroute. This is a sexy feature, but its utility is questionable. It appears to map based on the zip code that the domain names are registered to. It would be more useful if the map could accurately show where the intermediate routers are located, but it should be apparent to you by now that this information is not available. Both programs are chock-full of capabilities. The NetScanTools Pro version obviously has a few more features, but for tracking purposes either will do nicely.

NetBIOS Tool

Essential NetTools (shown in Figure 2-18) is a set of network tools that are especially useful when investigating Microsoft networks. It includes

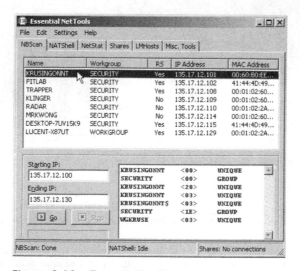

Figure 2-18   Essential NetTools

- **NBScan:** A fast multithreaded NetBIOS scanner for locating computers that are sharing resources on the network. Instead of having to manually check each system on the network individually (nbtstat –a 135.17.243.1, nbtstat –a 135.17.243.2, and so forth), simply enter a beginning address and an ending address and let NBScan run nbtstat for you.

- **NATShell:** A user-friendly interface for the popular NetBIOS Auditing Tool (NAT) network-auditing utilities.

- **NetStat:** Displays all of a computer's network connections and monitors external connections to a computer's shared resources.

You will find this handy set of utilities useful when you examine networks using Windows file-sharing or Samba on Unix.[9]

Whois Help

SmartWhois[10] automates the process of querying multiple whois databases and can retrieve information from more than 20 servers all over the world (see Figures 2-19 and 2-20).

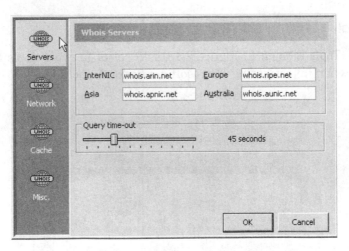

Figure 2-19   Default and user-defined whois databases

---

9. Samba is an open source software suite that provides Netbios-based file and print services on Unix systems to allow them to act as servers for Windows systems. See http://www.samba.org for more information.

10. Essential NetTools and SmartWhois are both made by TamoSoft and can be purchased from their Web site, www.tamos.com. Thirty-day evaluations are free; after that, you must purchase the programs. Their prices are reasonable.

Figure 2-20   Typical SmartWhois output

SmartWhois is designed to help inexperienced researchers find whatever information is registered on the Internet for specific IP addresses, so it comes with the most popular whois servers configured by default. Experienced users can define their own choices, making this a useful tool even for those who are accustomed to running whois from the command line.

Confirming Success

After you physically locate what you believe to be your suspect's computer, verify that its IP and machine name match that of your suspect. If the suspect computer is a Windows 9X computer, use winipcfg from either the Run box (accessible by choosing Start | Run) or from a command prompt. The initial output is shown in Figure 2-21. A drop-down window at the top of the IP configuration enables you to choose the network adapters that you want to display configuration for. In Figure 2-21, we are looking at the PPP (Point to Point Protocol) dial-up adapter, which is the default whenever PPP is configured. To access any of the other adapters, such as the network card, just drop down the list by clicking on the down arrow. Whatever you do, *do not click on the Release All button!* If the computer is using DHCP, clicking on

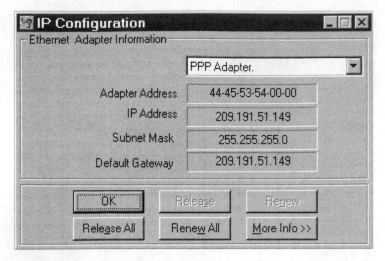

Figure 2-21   Initial winipcfg window

Release All wipes out the IP address, and depending on the network's configuration, you most likely will not get the same address back if you click on Renew All. Click the More Info button to access the information shown in Figure 2-22.

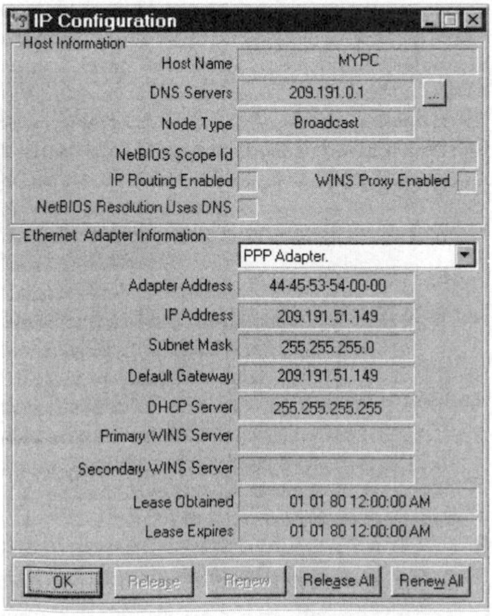

Figure 2-22   Extended winipcfg information

In the window shown in Figure 2-22, we not only see the IP address and the MAC address, but also the computer's name (in the Host Name field), and whether or not the computer is using DCHP (if static, meaning that the IP address was manually configured instead of being automatically obtained from the DHCP server, the Lease Obtained and Lease Expires fields will be blank). If there are IP addresses next to the Primary or the Secondary WINS Server fields, you can probably check them to see if the IP address was logged at the time of the incident.

Intrusion Detection Systems (IDS)

Intrusion detection systems, usually abbreviated IDS, are automated mechanisms that are intended to monitor specific subsystems, providing an alarm when a suspected unauthorized event is detected. Although IDS has many practical problems, the programs are increasingly popular, and in 2000, at least one Internet intruder was captured and brought to justice with the assistance of an IDS. At the time of this writing, IDS isn't necessarily a technology that every forensic technician needs to be familiar with, but during the next few years, it not only could become a standard tool in the detection of Internet intrusions, but could be routinely used to gather evidence used for successful prosecutions.

IDS is applied in one of two places: It is either network based or host based. Network-based systems are a specialized form of network sniffer. A network IDS sits on a network segment, viewing all traffic sent to every host on the segment, looking for evidence of unauthorized activity. It is common practice to have a single centralized intrusion detection engine that provides logging, and alarm functions based on the data provided by multiple remote sensors, each located on a different LAN segment. Even on switched networks, at least one port on the switch can usually be configured to provide all of the data being sent to each of the individual ports, which is where the sensor may be placed.

Host-based IDS places the detection capability on a single host, although the trend in host-based IDS is also to centralize the logging and alerting functions. Most business units resist having some other business unit looking over their shoulder and prefer not to have another organization place security software on their computers. Host-based IDS also tends to be more expensive because more devices have to be monitored. Although they are not as convenient to install and operate as network-based IDS, the host-based systems are generally more accurate, having fewer false positives and catching a higher percentage of actual misuses.

Intrusion detection systems are usually categorized as detecting either specific events or changes in patterns. Both types have their advantages and disadvantages. Event detection systems monitor for specific sequences of events, or sequences, that are characteristic of attempts to gain unauthorized access to a system. A simple example is a system that alerts when a specific number of failed login attempts have occurred. Commercial network-based IDS might alert when it detects a sequence of characters used to perform a buffer overflow attack against a Linux lpd daemon. These systems are dependent upon an up-to-date database of attack patterns. Although they may be able to log any arbitrary event type, they cannot alarm on events that are not in their database. Most commercial network IDS products at the time of this writing are of this type, and like the users of anti-virus software, the users of these products regularly download updated attack fingerprint databases from the publisher. Host-based IDS, such as the Tripwire product discussed in Chapter 11, work by regularly checking the consistency of system files, alerting whenever a security-relevant file has been changed. It is usually not practical to perform such a check on every host within an organization, but on those hosts that do have their files checked for consistency, intrusions are virtually always detected.

The other IDS model, the one that detects changes in patterns, is sort of an artificial intelligence thing. The theory is that instead of limiting a detection engine just to the population of known attack types, you create a system that is sufficiently sophisticated to recognize anomalous behavior and alert whenever something happens that is outside of normal parameters. For instance, say a specific person normally accessed his or her account between the hours of 9 a.m. and 7 p.m. An IDS tracks and learns this normal behavior, and if the user were to access the account in the middle of the night, the IDS would notify the security administrator that an unusual event had occurred. Obviously, such a system is more prone to false alerts than one that is based on hostile event fingerprints, but it has the significant advantage of being able to detect brand-new attack forms. Research on such systems has been ongoing for at least ten years, and most commercial products rely on fingerprint databases.

While the idea of capturing cyber criminals in the act should be an appealing one to most computer forensic types, widespread use of such products won't have a huge effect on what investigators do. The biggest advantage to the investigator is that IDS systems provide new and convenient forms of event logging. Once an attack or illegal activity is suspected, the logging or recording function on an IDS can be used to monitor and record the suspect's behavior.

Information Sources on IDS

If you are interested in doing some further research in IDS, several excellent books are available. Stephen Northcutt's, *Network Intrusion Detection* is the best hands-on guide for an analyst. In fact, it's a helpful book for a number of network security issues, and you should probably read it if you want to learn more about network protocol attacks and their analysis. Rebecca Bace's *Intrusion Detection* (Indianapolis: *Macmillan Technology Series,* 2000) is more theoretical, like a college textbook, making it a nice contrast to Northcutt's book. She describes the philosophy and architecture of IDS more comprehensively and provides a complete overview of the last ten years of relevant IDS research.

If you would like to use a network Intrusion Detection System but can't afford one of the commercial applications, you should take a look at Snort.[11]

Web Resources for Researching Internet Inhabitants

International Registries

Three international organizations are responsible for the administration of IP addresses within their region, so they should be considered definitive sources. Each of these organizations has a Web site that provides a whois interface, in addition to other information helpful in locating the owner of a specific IP address:

- **American Registry for Internet Numbers (ARIN):** Western Hemisphere, http://www.arin.net/whois/arinwhois.html

- **Asia Pacific Network Information Centre (APNIC):** Asia-Pacific, http://www.apnic.net

- **Reseaux IP Europeens (RIPE):** Europe, http://www.ripe.net

Network Diagnostic and Research Sites

- **Adhoc IP Tools:** This site is a veritable Swiss Army knife of Internet tools, providing front ends to a wide variety of research services (whois, nslookup, ping, DNS dig, and others), all accessed from a single page: http://home.ag.org/iptools.htm.

- **Sam Spade:** Also provides a wide variety of research tools, http://www.samspade.com.

- **Internet Service Provider lookup:** Enables you to search for ISPs by name, providing a summary of their business characteristics, http://www.webisplist.com.

- **Dragon Star:** Provides an index, relating IP network numbers to network names and identities. It also includes a handy explanation of the IP address numbering scheme and describes the difference between Class A, B, and C networks, http://ipindex.dragonstar.net/index.html.

---

11. Snort is available at http://www.whitehats.com, and a Windows version can be found at http://www.datanerds.net/~mike.

News and Email Abuse Information

- **The spamfaq or "Figuring out fake Email & Posts":** This site, maintained by Gandalf@digital.net, is the most comprehensive source we're aware of. It has detailed instructions on how to track both email and news, how to read the message headers in a dozen different mail clients, and how to reach the appropriate abuse contact. It also has a huge number of additional links. It isn't edited well, but it is worth your time if you really need to understand message headers, http://ddi.digital.net/~gandalf/spamfaq.html.

- **Fighting Email Spammers:** A site maintained by Todd Burgess, it is an excellent source of information on tracking email, http://eddie.cis.uoguelph.ca/~tburgess/local/spam.html.

- **Fight Spam on the Internet!:** Another site with a number of links on the subject of unsolicited email, http://spam.abuse.net/.

- **Reading EMail Headers:** A detailed explanation of the function of dozens of different email headers, http://www.stopspam.org/email/headers/headers.html.

Chapter

3

The Basics of Hard Drives
and Storage Media

We hear a lot of questions about hard drives and what to do with them. The answer is simple: Make an image copy and then restore the image to a freshly wiped hard drive for analysis (as we describe in Chapter 7). After you've restored the image, you have to mount it so that it can be recognized during your analysis—this step is different depending upon the filesystem used on the original drive. At this point, you have two different forms of evidence—the original drive and one or more exact copies of it. Remember, we are talking about evidence that may eventually wind up in either criminal or civil court, so you have to take proper precautions to ensure that the evidence is not damaged or altered while in your possession. You might become so accustomed to swapping out hard drives as part of your daily administration activities that you could forget that you are dealing with evidence. Don't make that mistake! With a little bit of training, practice, and some simple hardware, you can handle almost any type of hard drive.

What Is a Hard Drive Anyway?

Hard drives are like those Russian nesting dolls. You open them up, and inside each is another smaller one, each of which contains yet another doll. Holding a drive in your hand is like picking up one of those dolls, but instead of being able to open them by hand, you have to explore them electronically. Hard drives consist of an ever smaller set of data structures, each contained within the next larger set (see Figure 3-1). You'll be a much more effective investigator once you understand what these hardware and software layers are like, how they interrelate, and what little electronic nooks and crannies of hidden data they might contain.

Figure 3-1   A loaded hard drive contains a nested set of data structures

Controllers

Without a hardware device to interface to a computer's bus, hard drives are useless as anything but paperweights. The two most common types of interfaces are Small Computer Systems Interface (SCSI), and Integrated Drive Electronics (IDE). An IDE (more accurately called "ATA" on a PC platform) interface is cheap and easy to use, but each controller is limited to supporting only two devices (Enhanced IDE, or EIDE, allows four devices through the use of a primary and secondary channel with two devices on each channel). IDE drives connect to their controller through a ribbon cable, and when two devices are connected to a single controller, both are on the same cable. In order for the computer to tell them apart, one of them is designated as the master, and the other is the slave. Most PC IDE drives have a small jumper on the back that allows them to be set as either a slave or master, and most default to master. The only significant distinction between the two designations is that the master drive is logically first, so it appears first whenever a list of drives is created (by the BIOS, by the operating system, and so forth).

While IDE drives are the overwhelming favorite for PC workstations, SCSI drives are the workhorse drives for servers and high-performance desktops. Up to seven hard drives can be connected to a SCSI controller. If the drives are internal, they probably are on the same ribbon cable, but external drives may be "daisy chained," with each drive plugging into the output connector of a previous drive. Each SCSI device has a unique SCSI ID, which is configured through hardware. Scanners and other SCSI peripherals may have the ID configured through a push button, but hard drives normally use jumper blocks. If you are confronted with a hard drive that is not clearly marked, you can often find configuration instructions on the manufacturer's Web site.

This description is actually a gross simplification. At the time of this writing, there are at least four different ATA standards, but the interfaces are capable of using a "down-rev" drive. The latest UDMA/66 controllers on today's high-end Intel platforms can still read the ATA-2 PIO 3 drives from 1993. SCSI, which has always offered higher performance on a multidrive system, has at least eight different standards. SCSI interfaces also offer backward compatibility with the earlier standards, but in the case of SCSI, the cable standards have changed also. It is necessary to use an SCSI cable adaptor to connect an older SCSI-1 drive to today's highest speed standard, Ultra3 SCSI. Sometimes newer drives are capable of operating in a lower standard—most Ultra DMA-66 ATA drives automatically work at the slower speed when connected to an Ultra DMA-33 adaptor, but don't count on this always being the case.

Hard Drive Parameters

All hard drives, whether SCSI, IDE, or some other standard, have the same basic architecture. Within their tightly sealed casing is a vertically aligned stack of disks, sometimes called *platters,* that are covered with magnetic material. Each platter is divided into concentric rings called *tracks,* but we don't usually measure a drive in tracks; we use a three-dimensional measure called *cylinder*. Above and below each platter is an access arm with a transducer, called a *read/write head,* which operates above the magnetic media within these tracks. All of these heads are connected to a single assembly and move between the tracks as a unit. Hovering on a thin film of air, each is positioned over the same numbered track on each of their respective platters. A cylinder is the set of parallel tracks on each of the platters. The terms *cylinder* and *track* are sometimes used interchangeably, but the word *track* applies to only one side of one platter at a time, while *cylinder* applies to the entire set of platters. Each track and, of course, each cylinder are divided into an equal number of sectors. If the logical divisions on a hard drive were visible to the human eye, when viewed from above the sectors would look like cheese wedges.

When PCs first started including hard drives, it was necessary to configure the number of cylinders, heads, and sectors into the system BIOS. Without this manual configuration, the PC was unable to properly use the hard drive. This worked for a while, but the size of the drives began to exceed the configurable parameters. Even though the BIOS was updated and things started working again, the size of the drives continually got bigger and sometimes didn't work. In addition, manual configuration wasn't convenient. The upshot is that today it is seldom necessary to manually configure the BIOS to support a specific hard drive. The PC and the drive work it out between themselves. It also has become a lot less clear what the exact physical parameters of a hard drive are. Large Block Addressing (LBA), a hardware abstraction, was devised to allow drives with more than 1,024 sectors (which were not addressable by most BIOSes until recently) to remap their parameters and appear to have only 1,024 cylinders, logically increasing the number of bytes in each sector.

Soft Configuration on the Hard Drive

Opening up more layers of our Russian doll, we have one more logical layer, the partition layer, that must be understood. A hard drive can be logically divided into more than one partition, each of which can be referenced separately by the operating system. In a way, these partitions allow a single drive to appear to be multiple individual drives. There are several reasons why this is useful. First, you may wish to install multiple operating systems on a single computer. One of our lab machines has three partitions: One has the Windows 2000 operating system, one has Windows 2000 data, and the third one has Linux. If we want to reinstall Windows 2000, we can do it without disturbing either our data partition or our Linux partition. Originally, PCs allowed a maximum of only four partitions, but the hardware standard has been extended so that in addition to the four primary partitions, there can be dozens of extended partitions. At least one partition must be chosen as the boot partition, which is the one that automatically takes control when the computer is turned on. The partition information is maintained in a special area of the disk called the *partition table*. An index to the primary and extended partitions, it maps out both their locations and their types. Believe it or not, at least 66 standard partition types have been defined (see Table 3-1).

Viewing and Operating on the Partition Table

Before you start your analysis of a hard drive, you should get as much information as you can on how it is configured. A good place to start is the program fdisk (see Figure 3-2), some version of which comes with most PC operating systems. The non-Intel platforms each have their own low-level format and partition utilities, sometimes called *format*. fdisk displays the number of partitions and their respective types. If you have not used fdisk before, become intimately familiar with it on a spare, nonevidentiary computer because it is all too easy to accidentally delete a partition.

Table 3-1 Partition Types

0 Empty	17 Hidden HPFS/NTF	5c Priam Edisk	a6 OpenBSD
1 FAT12	18 AST Windows swap	61 SpeedStor	a7 NeXTSTEP
2 XENIX root	1b Hidden Win95 FA	63 GNU HURD or Sys	b7 BSDI fs
3 XENIX usr	1c Hidden Win95 FA	64 Novell Netware	b8 BSDI swap
4 FAT16 <32M	1e Hidden Win95 FA	65 Novell Netware	c1 DRDOS/sec
5 Extended	24 NEC DOS	70 DiskSecure Mult	c4 DRDOS/sec
6 FAT16	3c PartitionMagic	75 PC/IX	c6 DRDOS/sec
7 HPFS/NTFS	40 Venix 80286	80 Old Minix	c7 Syrinx
8 AIX	41 PPC PReP Boot	81 Minix / old Lin	db CP/M / CTOS / .
9 AIX bootable	42 SFS	82 Linux swap	e1 DOS access
a OS/2 Boot Manag	4d QNX4.x	83 Linux	e3 DOS R/O
b Win95 FAT32	4e QNX4.x 2nd part	84 OS/2 hidden C:	e4 SpeedStor
c Win95 FAT32 (LBA)	4f QNX4.x 3rd part	85 Linux extended	eb BeOS fs
e Win95 FAT16 (LBA)	50 OnTrack DM	86 NTFS volume set	f1 SpeedStor
f Win95 Ext'd (LBA)	51 OnTrack DM6 Aux	87 NTFS volume set	f4 SpeedStor
10 OPUS	52 CP/M	93 Amoeba	f2 DOS secondary
11 Hidden FAT12	53 OnTrack DM6 Aux	94 Amoeba BBT	fd Linux raid auto
12 Compaq diagnostic	54 OnTrackDM6	a0 IBM Thinkpad hi	fe LANstep
14 Hidden FAT16 <3	55 EZ-Drive	a5 BSD/386	ff BBT
16 Hidden FAT16	56 Golden Bow		

Whenever possible, we prefer to use a bootable copy of PowerQuest's Partition-Magic or Partinfo program (see Figure 3-3). You can use these packages to generate a report that lists the contents of the hard disk's partition table. We prefer Partinfo for forensics since it cannot change any of the partitions; it simply displays the information, which is exactly what we want. You can download Partinfo for free,[1] and it also is included with the purchase of PartitionMagic. The switch/EPC causes Partinfo to check for logical drive entries in extended partitions that are in nonstandard order.

---

1. ftp://ftp.powerquest.com/pub/utilities

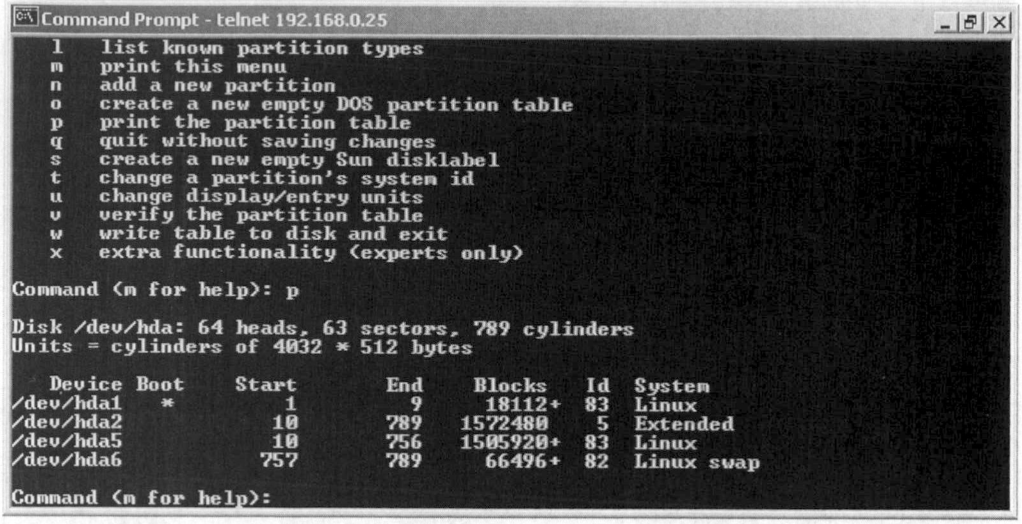

```
Command Prompt - telnet 192.168.0.25                                    _ |B| X|
    l    list known partition types
    m    print this menu
    n    add a new partition
    o    create a new empty DOS partition table
    p    print the partition table
    q    quit without saving changes
    s    create a new empty Sun disklabel
    t    change a partition's system id
    u    change display/entry units
    v    verify the partition table
    w    write table to disk and exit
    x    extra functionality (experts only)

Command (m for help): p

Disk /dev/hda: 64 heads, 63 sectors, 789 cylinders
Units = cylinders of 4032 * 512 bytes

   Device Boot    Start       End     Blocks   Id  System
/dev/hda1     *       1         9      18112+  83  Linux
/dev/hda2            10       789    1572480    5  Extended
/dev/hda5            10       756    1505920+  83  Linux
/dev/hda6           757       789      66496+  82  Linux swap

Command (m for help):
```

Figure 3-2 FDISK output on a Linux host

The advantage of these programs is that the default behavior is to display the partition information but not allow you to make any changes to the partitions. If you use PartitionMagic to change a partition as part of your normal administrative work, you'll need to go back into configuration and change it back to a view only setting so that the next time you use the program you will not be able to change the partition by accident.

Operating System Issues

The operating system sees all, but it may not tell you about it. Operating systems access the hardware using device drivers. Device drivers are written so that no matter what they may happen to encounter on the hardware side, they present a standard interface that any compliant application can use—theoretically, at least. This is why your word processor doesn't have to know if it is reading and writing to a SCSI or IDE drive, or even a network drive—the operating system and the device drivers hide this information from you through an abstraction layer called an Application Programming Interface, or API.

All operating systems provide basic input/output (I/O) for their storage devices (that is, they read and write), but some operating systems provide more capabilities than others. As discussed in Chapter 9, one of the advantages of Unix is that it treats virtually everything as a file. As far as hard drives are concerned, the device

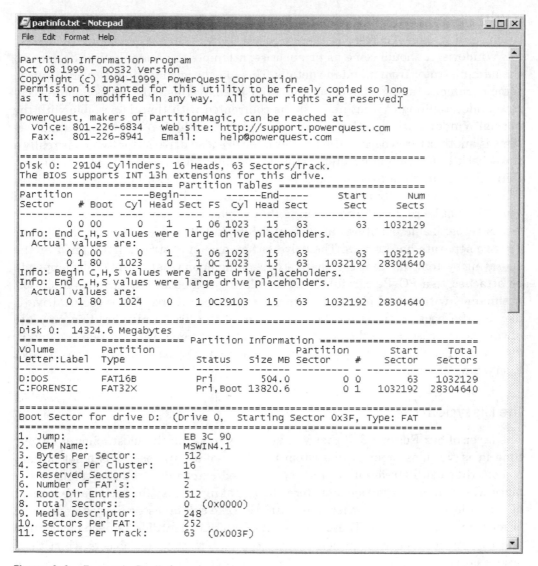

```
partinfo.txt - Notepad                                        _ □ ×
File  Edit  Format  Help

Partition Information Program
Oct 08 1999 - DOS32 Version
Copyright (c) 1994-1999, PowerQuest Corporation
Permission is granted for this utility to be freely copied so long
as it is not modified in any way.  All other rights are reserved.

PowerQuest, makers of PartitionMagic, can be reached at
  Voice: 801-226-6834   Web site: http://support.powerquest.com
  Fax:   801-226-8941   Email:   help@powerquest.com

=================================================================
Disk 0:  29104 Cylinders, 16 Heads, 63 Sectors/Track.
The BIOS supports INT 13h extensions for this drive.
====================== Partition Tables =========================
Partition      -----Begin----    ------End-----    Start      Num
Sector   # Boot Cyl Head Sect FS Cyl Head Sect     Sect      Sects
--------- - ---- ---- ---- ---- -- ---- ---- ---- --------- ---------
      0 0 00      0    1    1 06 1023   15   63        63   1032129
Info: End C,H,S values were large drive placeholders.
  Actual values are:
      0 0 00      0    1    1 06 1023   15   63        63   1032129
      0 1 80   1023    0    1 0C 1023   15   63   1032192  28304640
Info: Begin C,H,S values were large drive placeholders.
Info: End C,H,S values were large drive placeholders.
  Actual values are:
      0 1 80   1024    0    1 0C29103   15   63   1032192  28304640

=================================================================
Disk 0:  14324.6 Megabytes
===================== Partition Information =====================
Volume        Partition                    Partition     Start     Total
Letter:Label  Type          Status  Size MB Sector    #  Sector    Sectors
------------- ---------     ------- ------- --------- -- --------- ---------
D:DOS         FAT16B        Pri        504.0   0 0         63   1032129
C:FORENSIC    FAT32X        Pri,Boot 13820.6   0 1    1032192  28304640

=================================================================
Boot Sector for drive D:  (Drive 0,  Starting Sector 0x3F, Type: FAT
=================================================================
1.  Jump:                     EB 3C 90
2.  OEM Name:                 MSWIN4.1
3.  Bytes Per Sector:         512
4.  Sectors Per Cluster:      16
5.  Reserved Sectors:         1
6.  Number of FAT's:          2
7.  Root Dir Entries:         512
8.  Total Sectors:            0  (0x0000)
9.  Media Descriptor:         248
10. Sectors Per FAT:          252
11. Sectors Per Track:        63  (0x003F)
```

Figure 3-3   Example Partinfo output

drivers provided with most versions of Unix give you a choice of views. You can treat an entire hard drive as a single file, which is useful for imaging purposes, because it is the only way you can be sure that you've captured everything. You can also treat each partition as a file; so if you want, you can use a Unix system to copy an image of a single partition. In either case, when accessing a complete drive or a single partition, it matters not what operating system was used to create and store the data on that drive. At this point, the operating system is just treating the drive and the partitions as a stream of bytes.

Windows, it should come as no surprise, attempts to protect both the user and the administrator from mundane details. This may be good if you just want to write some documents and go home, but the forensic analyst usually wants a more accurate understanding of what he or she is confronted with than is possible with the normal Windows utilities. Complicating the picture with all Windows operating systems is another throwback to the DOS era, the dreaded drive letter (which is really a throwback to CP/M and beyond). Windows helpfully assigns a drive letter to anything that contains a filesystem. If you have a PC with two formatted partitions, Windows automatically refers to them as C: and D: if it understands the partition types. Do not be confused into thinking that you actually have two drives. Windows treats recognizable partitions as virtual drives, but that doesn't mean that you've got two separate hard drives. The drive letters are an abstraction assigned by the operating system, and they can change, depending upon what peripherals happen to be attached to a PC. Be careful about correlating evidence that includes Microsoft pathnames with actual physical components and partitions. While the C: drive is usually the boot partition on the first drive on the first controller, this may not always be the case. From the point of view of Microsoft operating systems, A: and B: always refer to floppy drives, and C: always refers to the partition that was booted. Everything else can change.

The Filesystem

The layer of our Russian doll that you are likely to spend the most amount of your time in is the filesystem. A filesystem is a lot like a database: it is a set of data objects that can be referenced and manipulated externally. The filesystem is the place where an operating system stores files, making it easy for you to access them by name, location, date, or other characteristic. Like a database, a filesystem has one or more indexes, or tables. These tables have a unique identifier for each object (file) and contain location information so that the system can find objects when their access is requested. Not surprisingly, these tables vary in their sophistication. The simplest filesystem in common use today is the File Allocation Table (FAT) system that was first used in Microsoft DOS and is still supported. A FAT filesystem has a flat table that lists all of the files within their filesystem and includes links to their location. We go into greater depth in Chapter 9, but for now you should know that the Unix filesystem uses two different forms of tables: the inode table contains pointers to the blocks that make up the actual files (or for longer files, pointers to pointers that point to the actual file blocks). The filenames are in a different table— a special file that is called the *directory*. Microsoft has several different versions of FAT. It introduced a new filesystem for Windows NT, NTFS, which also occurs in several variations. These newer filesystems, especially NTFS, are similar to Unix filesystems.

The process of making a computer operating environment aware of a specific file system is called *mounting*. The operating system identifies a specific partition containing a filesystem, maps that partition to a specific name or path, and then copies the file table into kernel memory so that it can be referenced and manipulated. Taking place behind the scenes on Windows, the mounting process on a Unix system is explicit and obvious. A system contains a list of filesystems that are mounted by default, and whenever a removable media is inserted, it must be mounted in order to be used. A Unix system can even mount a DOS filesystem, although most Unix implementations designed for floppy drives have utilities allowing quick access to DOS floppy disks without actually mounting them. A system may be configured to perform the mount automatically whenever a CD is inserted, but a Unix system cannot access an ISO CD-ROM without mounting it and pulling the file table into a kernel data structure.

Like a database, a filesystem operates on data in specifically sized units. These units are called *blocks* on a Unix system and *clusters* on Windows systems. These data chunks are the smallest piece of storage that an operating system can actually place data into, and every file is composed of some number of these chunks. Chunks that are not in use are just kind of hanging out, electronic benchwarmers waiting for the coach to call them back into the game. The larger the size of these data chunks, the faster data can be moved to and from the hard drive. Unfortunately, because these chunks represent the minimum size that can be referenced, if they are not filled up—which the last one almost never is—whatever storage isn't used is wasted. This excess capacity in the last block or cluster of a file is called *slack space*. Filesystems with smaller blocks have overall less wasted space, but they don't perform as well. To remedy this tradeoff between performance and efficiency, newer filesystems have introduced some flexibility into the size of blocks.

The process of turning a partition into a recognizable filesystem is called *format command*. Windows computers perform this operation with a utility of the same name, and the utility mkfs is used for most Unix systems. It basically amounts to a psyching up and organizational exercise; hence, if the drive already has data stored on it, formatting leaves most of it there. It rebuilds the tables used to reference the files, and it creates a new free list, which is the index to unallocated blocks, but it doesn't actually touch any other contents of a filesystem. In fact, unless a secure delete utility is used, the normal act of deleting a file doesn't erase it either. It just places all of the file's constituent clusters back on the bench where they aren't immediately visible to the spectators. Instead of being referenced by a directory entry (and/or inode entry), the blocks are then referenced by the free list. At this point, you've probably figured out that a lot of unsupervised data may be rattling around a hard drive. It isn't necessarily right at hand, but it isn't very far away. Let's put our

Russian doll back together and while we're doing it, we'll take a look at places that can contain useful evidence.

Mining Unallocated Space for Forensic Gold

We've devoted an entire chapter to hiding data (Chapter 5)—a lot of techniques don't necessarily involve the intimacy with the hard drive and filesystem that we're going to discuss here. In this chapter, we're going to concentrate on helping you find data that is in the unallocated spaces on a drive (summarized in Table 3-2). There usually is quite a bit of unallocated space, most of which contains some kind of data. For the most part, this data isn't deliberately hidden—it is data that the operating system left orphaned, waiting patiently to be overwritten at some indefinite time in the future.

Slack space is the space that is left over between the end of the data and the end of the last cluster or block. Every file that isn't an even multiple of the block size has some slack space associated with it. The odds are that the last block in a file has previously been used for some other purpose, and the odds are very much against any file being a size that can be evenly divided by the length of a block. The amount of slack space per file is, on average, one-half the block size, so the larger the block size (FAT32 uses 4,096 byte blocks), the more unallocated space will be found at the end of each file. When you read a file through the normal filesystem interface, you can't access the slack space because the operating system won't let you read past the end of the file. If you read a file into memory, the slack space won't come with it. If you write a file to some removable magnetic media with a different block size, the resulting file will have a different amount of slack space, and it will contain whatever data may have been left behind on the media. If you email the file to someone, or FTP it across the Internet, you won't be including the slack space. This is why a forensic copy of a hard drive cannot take place at the file level but must make an actual image of part or all of the drive.

Unallocated clusters are the blocks that are not currently in use by a file. On a system that has been busy for any length of time, chances are that all of the sectors have been written to many times. Files are constantly shuffled around a hard drive. When an application changes a file and rewrites it, the original previously changed file is deleted, unallocating all of its blocks. Until these clusters are overwritten, they contain all the data that was originally in the file. The greater the percentage of free space on a filesystem (that is, the more room it has), the longer unallocated files are present before they are overwritten. Of course, the more "empty space" there appears to be in a filesystem, the more room it has for hidden data.

Some applications have what is effectively their own internal slack space. Word 97, for instance, is notorious for vacuuming up stray data in unallocated clusters and incorporating it into Word .doc files. This data is not visible from within Word

Table 3-2 Filesystem Areas Containing Deleted Data

Data Structure Type	Description	Data Retrieval Technique
File	Application data file (especially the case with Word files) may contain stray data from filesystem.	Hex editor examination or forensic tool examination of partition or hard drive image of file.
Slack space	Last cluster of file isn't completely filled up, so data from last use of that cluster isn't overwritten.	Hex editor examination of partition or hard drive image, or forensic tool.
Unallocated blocks	Filesystem blocks (clusters) that are not currently in use usually contain deleted data.	File restore utility (unrm in The Coroner's Toolkit), hex editor examination of partition or hard drive image, or forensic tool.
Unused partitions or space on hard drive not allocated to partition	The current configuration of a computer may not use all the space on a hard drive, but previous configurations may have. Such unused space is a good place to deliberately hide data.	Hex editor examination of partition or hard drive image, or forensic tool to identify the location and type of all partitions. Use partitioning utility to identify the location and type of all partitions and to verify whether or not they use all of the available space on the drive.
Boot track	The partition table and boot information are on their own dedicated tracks that are not visible to utilities that access partitions or filesystems.	Forensic tool or hex editor examination of the image of the entire hard drive.

itself—Word is blissfully unaware that the stray data has been surreptitiously incorporated into a document, but the data can be viewed with a hex editor. From the point of view of the filesystem, the data is no longer unallocated after it has been incorporated into a Word document, so it stays with the file, even when the document is copied or emailed to someone else.

These unallocated and partially unused clusters can be examined in several ways. The most convenient way is to use a forensic software package to view the data. On a Unix system, you can view an entire partition as a single object, so a hex editor can be used to search through a partition or hard drive and examine it. Remember, this unallocated data is invisible to programs that read and write to individual files. You can run the Unix grep, or strings, command against an entire partition, treating it as a single object, but it isn't very convenient. When you try to run searches to look for keywords within the filesystem, either by doing a Windows search or a Unix grep, the program accesses individual files and can't see the data in these unallocated blocks.

When you start your examination of a hard drive, you want to find out how many partitions it has and how big they are. Make sure that the total space in all of the partitions adds up to the size of the drive. When you do this, beware that disk drive manufacturers inflate the advertised size of their drives by measuring them in powers of 10 instead of powers of 2. For a disk drive vendor, 1K is 1,000—for fdisk it is 1,024. Any tool you use to examine the partitions should tell you if the drive contains space that is not currently used for a partition. Voila! You've located unallocated space that might have data in it. The partition table itself is not a big piece of data. Even if it shares a track with some boot code, it isn't likely to fill up an entire track. This could be a great place for someone who wants to hide data in a way that a normal operating system or program cannot access or locate. Even fdisk can't see into the track that the partition table uses, but you can use a disk editor to view this area. In addition, the forensic program EnCase[2] also identifies any data in this area as "partition waste."

Unallocated space can contain anything that was written to the hard drive. On Windows, and on some Unix systems, the virtual memory, or swap space, is a file that grows and shrinks as needed. On other Unix systems, an entire partition is devoted to maintaining the ever-changing needs of the operating system's virtual memory subsystem. Virtual memory is data written to the hard drive when the system runs out of RAM, and it can contain all kinds of sensitive data, such as passwords, not normally written to a file. Remnants of email messages that were stored on a server, opened for viewing, and then deleted may be found on a hard drive. During one analysis, even though the hard drive had been reformatted and reloaded with software before it was reassigned to another employee over a year earlier, we were able to find messages from the previous employee, recovering over 1,700 pieces of data from the previous user's email. This tells us several things: First, some people send way too much email. Second, formatting is not a safe means of declassifying a hard drive. Third, no matter how difficult the analysis may seem, you never know what you will find until you try. This is important not only for forensics but also for security reviews to check for the sensitive data and also to ensure that this

---

2. http://www.encase.com

sensitive information does not leak out when a hard drive gets reused or is otherwise disposed of.

The same scenario that you hope to find on a suspect's machine may come back to haunt you—your own slack. When you open a file and then save it on your computer, you are adding your slack to the original file. If your slack gets appended to the end of your recovered files and you include those files with your evidence, some of your data may be going out with the suspect's data. This data gets picked up when you examine the files with a forensic tool or a hex editor. For this reason, you always must wipe your analysis drive clean—or start with a fresh media, such as a CD-R—whenever you are processing forensic data into another format.

Can You Really Erase a Hard Drive?

You can't really erase a hard drive. When data is written onto magnetic media, a faint image of what was previously on the drive remains. A hard drive is like the child's drawing toy, the Etch A Sketch. Well, hard drives don't leak silver powder, but we are referring to the faint traces left after you erase an Etch A Sketch. The Etch A Sketch is erased by turning it over and shaking it, allowing the silver powder to coat the inside of the clear plastic window, preparing it for more drawings. But if you've used this popular toy, you'll remember that faint traces of previous drawings are always left behind. A well-used Etch A Sketch looks very different from a brand-new one. Magnetic media—including hard drives—are similar in that every write leaves faint traces behind, even when the media have been overwritten numerous times. Special electron microscopes can be used to recover overwritten tracks, bit by bit. At one point, common wisdom held that an experienced technician with appropriate (and expensive!) equipment could recover data that had been overwritten up to seven times. This assumption is probably no longer valid, and it may well be that data can never be truly erased from magnetic media. The capabilities of sophisticated U.S. government laboratories are not common knowledge, and we can only speculate on what they can do. If you are involved in a law enforcement investigation, these sophisticated techniques may be applied to some of the evidence, but you won't have anything to do with the process.

You do have access to commercial data recovery services. They maintain laboratories with clean rooms and teams of technicians in dust-containment suits who are capable of physically opening broken hard drives and retrieving their contents. Supported and authorized by the hard drive manufacturers, they are usually hired by corporations to retrieve data from hard drives that have failed or have been subjected to some form of physical abuse, such as fire or water. The recovery firms often are capable of retrieving useful amounts of data even from broken platters. It costs a lot of money, but if you don't do backups, it may be the only way to save critical files. These firms often are used by law enforcement organizations, so they are accustomed to dealing with evidentiary rules and processes. In the United States, Europe, and Asia, recovery services can be provided by Ontrack.[3] We've visited the Norwegian laboratory of Ibas[4] and were impressed by their facility and staff.

Dealing with Laptops

Hard drives come in various shapes and sizes and with various connectors, depending on the manufacturer. The small drives in a laptop use the same logical standards as other PC platforms, but they have smaller physical connections to the drive controller. One of the handiest adapters a forensic analyst can have is a laptop converter enabling you to connect a drive from a laptop to your desktop computer. We know of two types of laptop converters. One is a small device with an IDE ribbon connector and power connector on one side for connection to a desktop machine, and a connector for the laptop drive on the other side. Desktop PCs have two separate connectors, one for the ribbon cable and one for the power, but laptops use only one cable for both the IDE and the power. This adapter can be obtained from several sources,[5] and the shipping will probably cost you more than the device itself.

If you don't encounter laptops that often, we recommend going to the manufacturer's tech support Web page to view a diagram of the laptop you are processing. You should find instructions there on where the hard drive is located and possibly how to remove it. After a while, you will become accustomed to the way most hard drives are installed—on the bottom of the laptop is room for only so many doors, covers, and so on to choose from, and accessing the hard drive is fairly easy. Figure 3-4 is a picture of the connector on top of a laptop ready to have the hard drive removed.

Carefully follow the manufacturer's instructions for removing the hard drive. When you remove it, you will notice that the drive is contained in some type of case, and the manufacturer's connector for the drive may look very different than your adapter. Unscrew the metal case (not the hard drive's cover), which enables you to remove the manufacturer's connector from the drive itself. In Figure 3-5, you can see the drive removed from the case. Notice that the manufacturer's connector is removed as well, revealing the pins to attach your connector to.

After you remove the case from the hard drive, you have to check the drive's label for the location of pin 1 on the laptop drive. Pin 1 is always the side of the hard drive with the red stripe on the ribbon cable. While ribbon orientation is usually easy to determine on a desktop computer because the IDE or SCSI connector is

---

3. http://www.ontrack.com/

4. http://www.ibas.net/

5. http://www.cablesnstuff.com

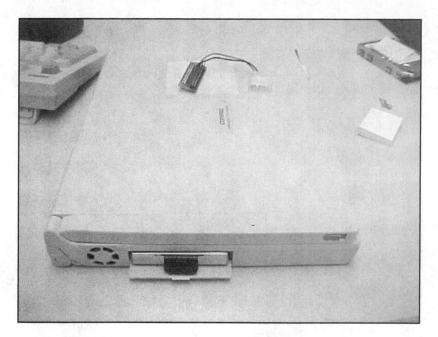

Figure 3-4   Laptop hard drive adapter

Figure 3-5   Uninstalled hard drive ready for adapter

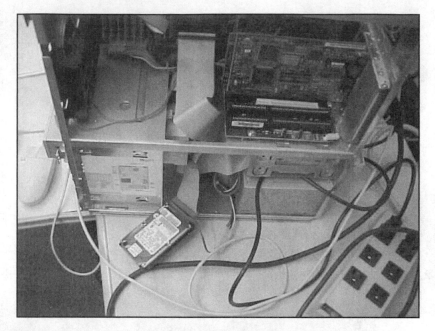

Figure 3-6 Suspect hard drive connected to forensic workstation

shaped, or notched, in such a way to allow the drive to be installed in only one way, this is not the case with a laptop drive. If you don't connect the drive properly, you run the risk of damaging the hard drive. Pin 1, the red stripe on the ribbon cable, is opposite the power connector. After you have the connector on properly, you can attach it as a slave to your desktop as depicted in Figure 3-6, and then you'll be ready to capture the drive image. If the drive has a jumper set to master, you must change the jumper to slave. Once again, you should consult the drive manufacturer's Web page for more information.

The other type of laptop adapter that we use is a little more expensive, but it is also sturdier, which is important when you are out in the field working on a case.[6] The problem with the cheaper device is the pins on the adapter are exposed, and with a lot of use, they may bend. The Forensic-Computers.com adapter does not have the pins exposed, so you won't encounter this problem.[7]

---

6. http://www.forensic-computers.com

7. http://www.ics-iq.com

Figure 3-7   Image MASSter Solo Forensics unit

After you've connected the laptop drive to your forensics computer, you should be able to connect your tape drive and make your drive images. If you are on the road and do not have the luxury of doing the forensics in your own lab, you may want to consider using the Image MASSter Solo Forensic unit (see Figure 3-7). The Solo will do an image backup when in Forensics mode. The Image MASSter is designed to make drive-to-drive bit-level copies quick and easy, and it includes adapters for laptop drives. You simply connect the image drive inside the unit and the suspect's drive to the external ribbon cable and power. After they're connected, turn on the Image MASSter, select Forensic backup and click go.

We also recommend you buy an SCSI card and a large capacity SCSI tape drive. Whatever image software you choose, it will include an option to image to tape. If you choose to image a tape, use of an SCSI drive reduces the time spent backing up a computer or waiting for it to restore. Non-SCSI tapes, especially parallel port solutions, are painfully slow. One company offering a parallel port solution claims that their device can back up a gigabyte per hour. We are able to back up a 10–12 GB drive in about 45 minutes by using an SCSI card and SCSI tape drive. A parallel port solution is the most flexible because virtually every computer has a parallel port, so it's is a good alternative. But if you have the budget, a faster tape drive on your lab machine makes a huge difference.

Conclusion

Hard drives are the storage devices that you will be examining most often in your investigations. This chapter is only a brief introduction to the subject drive hardware and some of the tools used to examine it. As you develop into an experienced forensic analyst, you will find that time spent learning more about the intricate technical details of hard drives is time well spent.

Further Resources

"A Guide to Understanding Data Remanence in Automated Information Systems," National Computer Security Center, 1992. Available at http://www.iwar.org.uk/comsec/resources/standards/rainbow/NCSC-TG-025.2.html

Chapter

4

Encryption and Forensics

Digital encryption techniques are used to protect data in two ways: to maintain privacy and to prove integrity. These are both vital concerns to the forensic analyst, and at least a basic familiarity with cryptographic techniques is mandatory for anyone responsible for analyzing or preserving digital evidence. Necessity is the mother of invention, and history has shown us that humans invent new ways to protect themselves from new risks. It's ironic, but the better we become at digital forensics, the more motivated criminals are to conceal their behavior—the threat of detection encourages the use of encryption. In our new virtual society, law-abiding citizens also have many legitimate reasons to protect their privacy. The needs of both lawbreakers and law-abiding citizens are increasingly being met by greater utilization of encryption technology. While criminals use any available tool to further their antisocial goals, the appropriate use of encryption technologies protects privacy and transactions, thereby preventing crime. Furthermore, cryptographic technology is an integral part of our burgeoning virtual economy. Increasingly, forensic analysts are confronted with encryption and other data-hiding techniques. A brief explanation of encryption concepts is necessary to prepare the investigator; however, in-depth study of this topic is recommended for serious forensic analysts. We'll provide an overview of encryption concepts first and finish with a discussion of data-hiding techniques with and without the use of encryption. On the way, we'll talk about some increasingly important cryptographic mechanisms that are used by the investigator.

The words *encryption* and *cryptography* are subtly different in scope. Encryption is the process of obscuring the content of a message. The use of *codes,* where one symbol is arbitrarily substituted for another (i.e. RAINBOW might mean "meet me at the Café Rouge at noon."), won't be dealt with in this book, although we do discuss *encoding*. This is a form of symbolic substitution that is meant to facilitate transmission, not obscure meaning. Common encoding systems include ASCII and Morse Code. We are more concerned with ciphers, which involve the use of mathematical techniques to alter data so that its meaning is not discernible unless an additional mathematical technique is applied. This is what we mean when we use the word *encryption* in this book. "Clear text" is "enciphered" with an encryption algorithm and key, resulting in "cipher text" (see Figure 4-1). Every character has been changed in

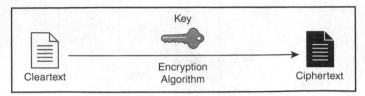

Figure 4-1   Basic encryption

such a way that the original can be retrieved only by knowledge of the appropriate formula and usually a key. *Cryptography,* which contains the Latin root meaning "secret writing," is the practice of protecting messages, and as we shall see, there are other ways to protect a message than by encrypting it. A person who practices message protection techniques is called a *cryptographer*. Government intelligence agencies, such as the National Security Agency (NSA) have specialists in *cryptanalysis,* which is the practice of attempting to determine the cleartext of a message without authorization. This is otherwise known as *breaking* or *cracking. Cryptology* is the field of knowledge that involves both the creation and analysis of encryption algorithms. *Cryptologists* are highly specialized academics who major in arcane mathematical disciplines.

There are a number of ways to attack encrypted text and provide clear text without having access to the requisite key (see Table 4-1). The easiest way, or course, is to obtain the key, either by asking someone for it or finding it written down. Cryptanalysis, or cracking, involves the exploitation of weaknesses within either the algorithm itself or the implementation of the algorithm. Successful cryptanalysis requires a thorough knowledge of cryptology and an above-average aptitude for math, so it won't be practical for most readers. When using cracking software, which is often quite successful against proprietary algorithms, you are actually using cryptanalysis, although you are effectively a *script kiddie*. A *brute force attack* is the methodical attempt to substitute every possible key until the correct one is discovered. On average, the correct key is discovered halfway through the total population of possible keys. For a 40-bit keyspace, this would be 2^{39} keys, a huge number of attempts that can be performed only by software. Educated guessing is more of a psychological exercise, and it can be quite successful because people tend to use keys that are easy to remember. They are often based on the name of a pet or family member, or something else significant to the user. Many key-cracking programs are a hybrid. The L0phtCrack password-cracking tool,[1] for example, uses cryptanalytic techniques to effectively reduce the potential keyspace (total population of usable

---

1. The L0pht organization has been merged into a firm known as @stake, and the tool is available at http://www.atstake.com.

keys) and then offers you a choice of a dictionary attack, an attack based on permutations of dictionary words, or a brute force attack. This results in the quick determination of a number of simple passwords, and the eventual cracking of virtually all human-usable passwords.

Unless you are confronted with a weak encryption system, such as the one used to protect Windows NT passwords, looking for and finding a key is the most efficient way to decrypt ciphercode without being an authorized keyholder. This is called a *compromise*. Just as some people place their house keys underneath their doormats, computer users often leave copies of their passwords lying around in email and other text. Bad implementations of encryption can leave keys in deleted files or swap space where they can be gathered by forensic techniques. Passwords are commonly passed across the Internet in cleartext, where they can be collected using a sniffer or monitor. Compromises like this are the most efficient means for a forensic examiner to gain access to plaintext. Asking the suspect to provide his or her key is the easiest method, and can be quite successful, but if the suspect is unavailable or uncooperative, skillful detective work can often find or guess a key. Most people reuse the same password over and over, so once a key has been identified, it is worth trying it on other applications used by the same suspect. The Cain tool, one of the password-cracking tools we discuss in Chapter 5, is a simple but effective GUI-based utility that runs against Windows 9X and can recover quite a number of passwords. When examining Windows 95 or 98 systems, always run it so you can collect a list of the suspect's commonly used passwords.

It may seem intuitively obvious, but the encryption algorithms that have proven to be strongest are those that are not a secret, but instead are published. Cryptologists have understood for at least 100 years that the best way to cryptographically protect information is to use a known and proven algorithm with a key that is so long that a brute force attack is impractical. Statistically, an attempt to guess a key, a brute force attack, will succeed when half of the key space has been tried. In other words, the safety of a bank vault should not be compromised just because a safe cracker manages to obtain its blueprints. A bank vault is safe because a criminal does not have time to try half of all possible combinations. The fact that the vault's blueprints were available for public scrutiny means that unforeseen flaws have probably been discovered before they could be exploited by safecrackers. In the same way, popular encryption algorithms have been the subject of intense review by experienced cryptanalysts, providing a high level of assurance that inadvertant vulnerabilities and weaknesses have been discovered and fixed. Proprietary algorithms, which are not subjected to such intense scrutiny, have invariably proven themselves as being weak. The weakness of proprietary algorithms explains why there are so many freeware cracking tools available for home finance programs, ZIP utilities, and office automation software. Some of these utilities work quite well, so proprietary

Table 4-1 Methods for Attacking Encrypted Text

Type	Techniques	Practicality
Cryptanalysis	Known plaintext Chosen plaintext Chosen ciphertext	Esoteric techniques that require specialized knowledge and skills. Not practical for most organizations, although software tools are available to crack some proprietary encryption technologies.
Password Guess (similar to known plaintext)	**Dictionary:** High percentage of passwords are based on common words. **Educated Guess:** Humans tend to use passwords based on names or terms familiar to them.	Highly effective. Dictionary attacks are normally software-enabled, and many specialized dictionaries are available for different languages and areas of interest.
	Brute Force: Methodical attempt to sequentially attempt all possible passwords.	Must be software-enabled. Very effective against any symmetric algorithm using 40-bit or less keys. 54-bit Data Encryption Standard (DES) has been cracked by amateurs using distributed platforms. Computationally infeasible against 128 bit keys.
Scavenge Password	**Physical search:** Locating written password in vicinity of workstation. **Logical Search:** Plain text password found in document or email message on workstation **Network sniff:** captures plain text password from network traffic.	Very effective. If password is not easily-guessable, it is probably written down somewhere. *(continued)*

Table 4-1 Methods for Attacking Encrypted Text (*cont.*)

Type	Techniques	Practicality
Extract password	**Logical Search:** Plain text password found in standard location, such as system registry.	Software-enabled attacks are very simple and practical. Many types of Windows passwords are stored within the registry or other configuration files in plaintext.
Obtain password	**Interview:** Suspect is asked for password. **Social Engineering:** Suspect is tricked into revealing password. **Coercion:** Force suspect to reveal password.	If the suspect is cooperative, interview is by far the easiest way to obtain the key.
Recover password	**Request:** If some form of key recovery is enabled, then it can be recovered from a cooperative administrator.	Extremely easy if recovery system is in use, but it is not yet common practice, so it is usually not an option.
Find plain text	**Keyword Search:** Locate unencrypted copies of desired data on hard drive	It is difficult to correlate the plaintext with the encrypted data, so you may never be certain that you have obtained all the evidence.

encryption techniques should be considered a gift to forensic investigators who might be confronted with data encrypted by them.

The term *computationally infeasible* refers to a key space that is so large that it is effectively impossible for current and anticipated computing devices to ever come close to trying half the possible keys. *Strong* encryption systems, using relatively large keys, have so many possible keys that today's computers couldn't exhaust the key space before the end of the world. Fortunately for the examiner, most implementations of encryption are *weak,* using short key lengths that are subject to simple brute force attacks. It is also important to note that no encryption algorithm has ever been mathematically proven as unbreakable. The potential always exists for a mathematical or computational breakthrough that would obsolete today's encryption implementations (a great deal of speculation exists that future forms of processor, such as quantum or organic computers, could perform calculations that are computationally infeasible today). The current public algorithms in widespread use are believed to be adequately robust, based on several hundred years of experience in theoretical mathematics, but absolute proof is lacking.

Before delving into specifics, let's cover a few more concepts. The most commonly recognized use of encryption is to maintain the confidentiality of information. Investigators encounter data that has been encrypted in order to hide its contents. While privacy is certainly an important issue, e-commerce brings new demands for authentication and verification. Electronic transactions require new trust mechanisms that are provided using encryption technology. The integrity of data is maintained when data has not been unexpectedly altered. Encryption technology can verify the integrity of data. Encryption technology can also be used to provide assurance as to the authorship or source of a document, message, or transaction. Key recovery[2] is an organizational requirement to provide some sort of emergency decryption capability by keeping copies of keys available to authorized administrators. If an employee encrypts the only copy of important corporate data, and that person becomes unavailable, the data will be lost unless the organization has a key recovery policy in place. As an investigator, you should always check to see if a system you are examining is supported by a key recovery system. When you find encrypted data, it makes your job much easier if you are given the correct key and don't have to guess a key or crack ciphertext.

---

2. The term *key escrow* is a euphemism that means "key recovery with a copy of the key held by the U.S. federal government." Because of the controversy surrounding the Clipper chip and its plans for key escrow, many politically inclined security experts feel that all forms of key recovery are unacceptable. While it is never necessary for transmission encryption, in most cases, it is irresponsible for an organization to allow a single individual to hold the only key to valuable corporate information. Fortunately, a forensic examiner isn't responsible for setting corporate policy and can remain impartial on this issue. From an investigative point of view, the important concept to keep in mind is that many commercial encryption products do provide some form of organizational backdoor access.

Cryptographic Integrity Services

Data can become distorted in transit or during use and even can be manipulated, so some form of accuracy testing is appropriate in a variety of circumstances. Computer memory uses parity bits, communications protocols use cyclic redundancy checks, and the Unix operating system includes a utility for creating *checksums*. Parity is a 1-bit sum—0 and 1 are the only possible values, so it isn't a very conclusive test. Checksums are longer and provide a marginally higher level of assurance. Obviously, the more resources you put into a verification test, the more accurate the results. Each of these tests has its place and is appropriately used to detect changes to data. Unfortunately, none of these tests is immune to deliberate attempts at data modification. Simple hacker utilities are available to twiddle insignificant bits inside an altered file until its checksum matches that of the original. To detect deliberate attempts at data manipulation requires a cryptographically secure form of checksum operation, called a *hash function* (don't confuse this use of the term *hash* with the database usage *hash table*). The result of applying a hash function to a data object is a *hash value,* sometimes called a *message digest,* and it is like a checksum on steroids. It is considered computationally infeasible at this time to counterfeit a robust hash algorithm such as MD5 and SHA. (Many experts anticipate that MD5 will be obsolete in a few years.)

A cryptographic hash algorithm is a one-way form of encryption, taking a variable-length input and providing a fixed-length output. As long as the size of the original object is within the operational restraints of a particular implementation, it is statistically impossible for cryptographically secure hash algorithms to allow two different source files to have intersecting values, effectively making the hash value into a fingerprint of the original file.[3] Such an algorithm is designed to be *collision free,* meaning that it is functionally impossible to create a document that has the same cryptographically secure hash value as another document. Because of this characteristic, a hash value can serve as a surrogate for the object it is derived from. A relatively small fixed-size hash value can securely represent a data object of any

---

3. Obviously, there are an infinite number of possible documents, but only 2^{160} possible SHA hash values, making it theoretically possible that collisions (that is, two documents having the same hash value) could occur. The number 2^{160} is incredibly huge, and only mathematicians, astronomers, and government budget planners can truly comprehend it. Sometimes cryptographic hash values are aptly described as being similar to DNA testing. DNA testing, which is well-accepted in court, is statistically *less* reliable than MD5 or SHA. DNA testing establishes incontrovertibly that two different samples could not have come from the same person, but even in a population the size of that in the United States, several people may appear to have virtually identical DNA. The statistical possibility of two data objects having the same hash value is so infinitesimally small as to be functionally impossible—a theoretical result that has also been tested extensively through research. All evidence is subject to some degree of doubt, but virtually no form of nondigital evidence has such a high degree of certainty as cryptographic hash values.

practical size. The MD5 algorithm from Rivest outputs a 128-bit hash value. The SHA algorithm, which is a U.S. federal standard, outputs a 160-bit hash value.

Hash functions are used by forensic examiners in two ways. First, hash functions can positively verify that a file has been altered. If you suspect that the binaries on a system may have been compromised, you have to assume that they have been so carefully compromised that their access times, sizes, and checksums have been manipulated to match the original files. A convenient and reliable way to confirm that a file has been changed is to compare its message digest with a message digest from either the original or a known good binary from the original source. The second use of hash functions is to verify that files (or their copies) are intact and have *not* changed. A computer crime investigator gathers digital evidence that needs to be preserved and verified in the future. When the examiner runs a hash utility against evidence files and saves the hash values, he or she can demonstrate that the files were not manipulated between the time of their initial collection and the trial. (Later in this chapter, we discuss time stamping, which can make hash values much more useful as evidence.)

Cryptographic Privacy Services

There are two basic types of bidirectional encryption: secret key and public key. Secret key, or conventional encryption, uses a single key for both the encryption and decryption of data, just like your car uses the same key to lock and unlock it. This is the most common form of encryption, and it is easily understood by most computer users. As shown in Figure 4-2, application of an encryption algorithm and key to cleartext data results in ciphertext. Because applying the exact same process a second time reverses it, once again providing cleartext, this process is sometimes called *symmetric encryption*. Secret key encryption, provided by algorithms such as DES, TripleDES (3DES), RC5, and Blowfish, is fast and efficient. The downside of secret key encryption is the inconvenience of maintaining the key's secrecy. If you are encrypting data for your own use, you already have a copy of your key, and decryp-

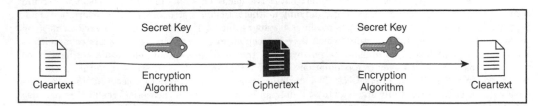

Figure 4-2   Secret key encryption

tion is not a problem. What if you want to encrypt a transaction that is being sent to someone else? You have to exchange a key ahead of time, and this may not be convenient. Many married couples share a car; it isn't a problem for each to have two keys for the vehicle, but what if a couple needed to loan the car to people they didn't already know? What if they had to loan their car to many different people, and they had to do it often? They'd keep the hardware store in business, cutting new keys. This same problem confronts e-commerce and other secure digital transactional environments. Not only do you have to manually exchange keys with your transactional partners—and you may not be personally acquainted with them—but trustworthy encryption practices (actions you take to prevent successful cryptanalysis) call for using a new key in each transaction. What if every time you ordered a book over the Web, you had to telephone the owners of the Web site and dictate a lengthy key over the telephone? You'd better hope that they can remember it, that they don't write it down, and that they subsequently forget it and don't give it to someone else. To avoid the key exchange inconvenience associated with symmetric algorithms that use a single key, another form of encryption was devised.

Public key encryption requires a bit of effort to understand, but it is time well spent because it is the basis of electronic commerce and plays an increasingly significant role in data protection. You must be familiar with it before you can understand the significance of digitally signed objects. Public key encryption is sometimes called *asymmetric encryption* because it uses two different keys. One of the keys is used to encipher data, and only the corresponding key can be used to decipher it. In practice, one key is called the *private key,* and its owner carefully protects it from disclosure to others. The other key is called the *public key,* and it is made freely available to anyone who wants to conduct transactions with the holder of the private key. The enciphering and deciphering process, as shown in Figure 4-3, is the same as the symmetric process, with the significant exception that it requires two matched keys. Possession of either key provides no information that can be used to derive the value of the other key. One of the implications of this mathematical magic is that two parties can securely share a secret without any prior coordination, which is an extraordinarily powerful concept that can be applied in dozens of ways to increase the level of trust in a transaction. The most popular form of public key encryption was developed by Rivest, Shamir, and Adleman and is referred to as RSA. Another family of

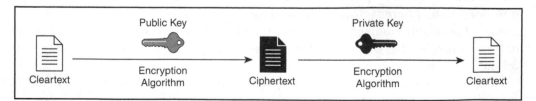

Figure 4-3 Public key encryption

asymmetric algorithms, called *elliptic curve,* is growing in popularity—especially on dedicated hardware devices with limited processing power.

Let's start with some simple examples and build our way to an understanding of a Public Key Infrastructure (PKI). Let's say that Warren has some confidential information that he wants to share with Jay, but he can provide it to Jay only by writing it down on a piece of paper and placing it in Jay's mailbox in a shared office. Fortunately, outside of both Warren and Jay's offices are locked cabinets with glass doors where they can securely post messages that can be read by anyone inside of Lucent Technologies (we'll work around this requirement for locked corkboards shortly, so bear with us for now). Warren and Jay both generate their own pair of asymmetric keys, and each posts one of his keys, which immediately becomes the public key, on their locked message board. Both have taken the time to visit the hallway and manually copy down the other's public key. When Warren wants to send a message to Jay, he encrypts it with Jay's public key and places it inside Jay's inbox. As long as Jay keeps his private key safe, only he can decrypt Warren's message.

At first, this works pretty well. Jay receives a message and decrypts it. It is apparently from Warren so he drafts a response, encrypting it with Warren's key. This goes on for a week until Warren asks Jay for the five dollars that he promised him in an encrypted message. Jay denies having sent the message, challenging Warren to prove that he actually sent it. Jay points out that everyone in the building has access to Warren's public key and could have just as easily encrypted the message. Jay is relieved that he has successfully denied a five-dollar transaction, but Warren challenges him to think up a more sophisticated protocol that enables him to trust future messages. Denying either the transmission or receipt of a message is called *repudiation,* and its prevention is a requirement of most contractual and commercial transactions. Jay suggests that if the sender encrypts the message with his or her own private key, a recipient can easily verify it by decrypting it with the sender's public key. Anything that provides a readable result when decrypted with the public key of the purported sender must actually have been encrypted by the sender's private key. Sender verification is provided, but privacy is not maintained because anybody can decrypt the message with the sender's public key. This protocol discourages denial but doesn't provide privacy. Furthermore, it is a bit awkward with some data types to verify that the decrypted contents actually represent a real message and not just gibberish. What is needed is a method that combines two different things: a message that can be decrypted only by the intended recipient, and something inextricably linked with that message that can only be provided by the purported sender. This is what a digital signature is intended to do.

A digital signature is a simple process that provides verification as to both the integrity and originator of a message. The process of creating a digital signature and

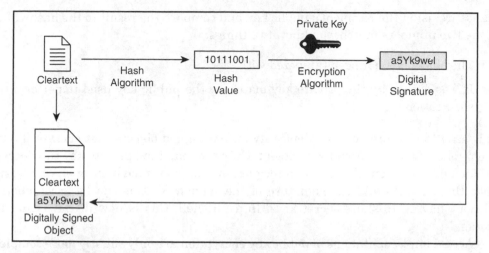

Figure 4-4 Digitally signing an object

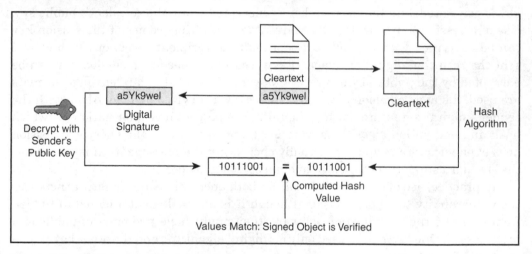

Figure 4-5 Verifying a digital signature

using it to sign an object is shown in Figure 4-4. First, the signer calculates the hash value of a message. Second, the signer encrypts the hash value with his or her own private key. The resultant encrypted message digest is the digital signature, and appending it to the original object makes that object digitally signed. Verification of the message is simple. As shown in Figure 4-5, just separate the signature from the original object, run the appropriate hash algorithm against that object, decrypt the signature using the recipient's public key, and compare the result to the hash value. If the two numbers match, you know two things:

- The object has not been tampered with.
- It was signed by the private key matching the public key used to perform the verification.

It is easy to also provide confidentiality for our signed object—just encrypt it with the public key of the intended recipient. Only the matching private key can decrypt this sealed digital envelope. After a recipient has unencrypted it, he or she can verify both the contents and the signature of the sender. All this can be accomplished without having to share secret keys. In a nutshell, this is how digital signature works.

Actual implementations of public key encryption are only slightly more complex. It turns out that public key encryption is horribly slow, so it is rarely practical to encrypt an entire message using an asymmetric algorithm. Instead, a random session key is generated, and that session key is encrypted using the recipient's public key. Use of a session key provides other advantages. Multiple copies of the session key can be encrypted with the public key of multiple recipients, each of which can be sent the resulting digital envelope. If key recovery is needed, a session key can be encrypted by the public key of a recovery agent. Several standard envelope formats are used, the most common of which, PKCS #7, was devised by RSA. Along with the sender's digital signature, such a digital envelope contains information on which hash and encryption algorithms were used, and it includes the encrypted session keys of one or more recipients. Actually encrypting the message itself is optional—the standard supports both sealed and unsealed envelopes.

In practice, use of the same key pair for both encryption and signature increases the vulnerability to cryptanalysis. Although it is an implementation detail hidden from users by their application software, they might have two pairs of public and private keys. One key pair is used only for digital signature, and the other key pair is used only for encryption.

The level of assurance in a digital signature scenario is based upon the rigor of the associated practices. If a private key is stolen, it is tantamount to stealing the owner's identity. Anyone capable of using a private key can masquerade as the owner of that key. If digital signature is important to either side in an investigation, you must determine how well protected the key was. The most common place to store private keys is the local hard drive. They are not stored in cleartext but are first encrypted with a symmetric algorithm and must be decrypted with the owner's passphrase before they can be used. RSA keys are normally 1,024 bits long, which is too long for a human being to remember, which is fine because a user never sees his or her own private key. Private keys are in cleartext only when they are being generated and when they are used in a calculation. Cleartext passwords should be found only within system processes that are in RAM. They never appear on the screen and hopefully are never placed on the hard drive. (Note that some encryption implementations might allow private keys to be written to the hard drive if the encryption process is swapped out to virtual memory.) Private key systems that are purely software-based, storing the private key on a hard drive where it can always be accessed by operating system processes, are relatively easy to subvert. The human password or passphrase used to access the private key may be sniffed by hostile software, or the encrypted key could be cryptanalyzed and broken. Be aware that digital signature can be faked in many circumstances—someday you may well be asked to help determine whether or not one is genuine. When digital signature is evidence in a case and you are an expert witness, assume that a defense attorney will attempt to create reasonable doubt by asking you if the signature key could have been stolen.

Private keys stored on some form of removable hardware device, such as a smart card, are harder to steal than software-based keys. However, be aware that such cards are usually initialized on an administrative workstation or at the manufacturer's site. On a software-based system, it is common practice to generate the keys on the end system so that no one else ever has access to the private key. If a cryptocard is not initialized by its user—and it usually is not—the private key must be generated by someone else, raising the possibility that he or she could keep a copy. There should never be a need to recover a digital signature key, and it is not considered good practice in a commercial environment to maintain copies of them. If an organization maintained extra copies of its users' signature keys, lawyers for those users would be able to argue that an identity theft could have taken place.

Let's return to the locked glass cabinets in the hallway that provide secure viewing of Warren's and Jay's public keys. Although the keys themselves can be freely distributed, a public key is useless without some sort of association with a specific sender. The trick is to find some way to securely provide this association, and physical devices such as locked cabinets don't scale well at all. The only way to really scale a PKI is to use trusted third parties. Pretty Good Privacy (PGP), once a popular freeware product and now a commercial product from Network Associates,[4] uses a transitive trust model. People who know and trust each other can share the public keys of other people they trust. If Warren trusts Jay, and Jay trusts Jody, then Warren can trust Jody without having to meet her in person and exchange keys. Warren can get a copy of Jody's keys from Jay. Because he trusts Jay, and he trusts Jay to deal only with people he trusts, Warren can assume that the key he receives from Jay with Jody's name on it actually did come from Jody. PGP works well in small work groups

---

4. http://www.nai.com

but does not necessarily scale to larger groups. This is what digital certificates are for.

A certificate authority (CA) is a trusted third party that endorses a public key and binds it to a specific identity. A CA does so by digitally signing a keyholder's public key with the private key of the CA. The digitally signed keys are placed into a compound object that includes information on the holder's identity, the identity of the CA, the algorithms that the keys support, and the certificate's expiration date. The resultant object is called a *digital certificate*. A digital certificate (*cert* for short) is a mechanism used to distribute public keys while simultaneously supporting third-party verification. Certs provide some arbitrary level of assurance that a particular public key belongs to a specific individual or organization. If Jay needs to send Warren another IOU, he can digitally sign the message and enclose his digital certificate with it. When Warren receives the message, he uses the process illustrated previously in Figure 4-5 to verify that the digitally signed document is intact and matches the public signing key contained within the accompanying digital certificate. If he wants to be certain that it was really Jay who sent the message, he can then verify the digital certificate itself using the public signing key of the CA. Having the digital certificates of the CA itself already on the workstation facilitates this additional step. Popular mail clients and Web browsers are shipped from the factory containing digital certificates from the major commercial CAs. If you use one of these products and do not change the security configuration, you trust all of the CAs whose certificates were included. Figure 4-6 shows a typical example.

Organizations that use their own CAs must come up with a secure method of distributing copies of the CA's certificate to those who will need to refer to it.

Commercial certificate authorities offer a variety of certs supporting different levels of assurance. The degree of trust appropriate to place in a digital certificate is a function of two processes: the effort used by the CA to verify the identity of the applicant before creation of his or her digital certificate, and the effort that the certificate holder uses to protect his or her private key. These different levels of rigor provide corresponding levels of assurance. No matter how secure the key issue process, it is always the responsibility of the key holder to protect his or her own private key with the appropriate amount of diligence.

Let's put this into perspective with a real-life situation. In Microsoft Outlook, when you choose Tools | Options and then click the Security tab, a screen like that in Figure 4-7 is displayed. Pressing the Get a Digital ID button launches your Web browser, pointing it to a Microsoft site with links to several commercial certificate authorities. If you decide to go to one of these sites and obtain your own digital certificate, you'll launch an automated process that locally generates a matching set of keys and then sends the public key to the CA to be digitally signed and returned to you in the form of a digital certificate.

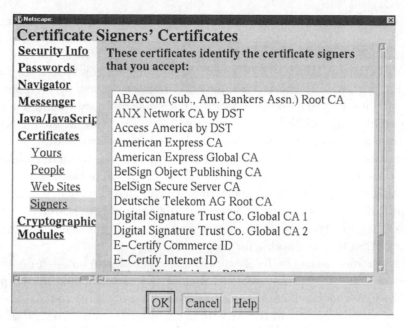

Figure 4-6 Certificate authorities trusted by Netscape on Linux RedHat 6.1 distribution

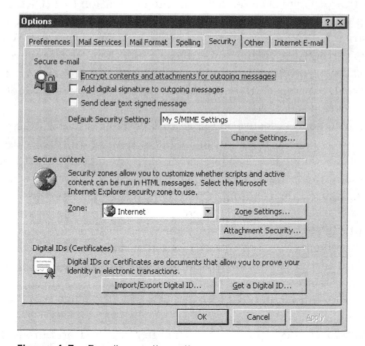

Figure 4-7 Email security options

Note that all of these sites prominently display their certification practice statements (CPS). This document describes how certificate authorities operate, and especially how they maintain the security of their infrastructures. Ideally, they also publish a Certificate Policy (CP) for each type of digital certificate they offer. The information contained in these documents is intended for use by recipients of digitally signed messages to help them decide whether or not they should trust the messages. As an investigator, this information helps you understand the purported level of rigor that a CA uses to verify someone's identity before issuing him or her a certificate. Just because a certificate exists with a certain name associated with it doesn't necessarily mean that an individual with that name is associated with that certificate. Obtaining one of the less stringently verified certificates in a false name is about as difficult as obtaining one of those rubber signature stamps. Such a signature has utility, but the ease of counterfeiting or stealing it decreases the value of transactions that it is acceptable for.

Digital certificates can be freely copied and resent by anyone—it doesn't matter where you obtain someone else's cert because it can be verified using the public key found in the CA's root certificate (assuming that you are willing to trust the CA). The downside of this model is that if a private key actually is stolen, or if the issuer of a certificate considers that certificate obsolete for any reason, he or she has no way of knowing where all the copies of the digital certificate are located. The mechanism used to solve this problem is called a Certificate Revocation List (CRL). If revocation lists are supported by a CA, they are updated regularly, and certificates associated with a revocation list include information on the location of that list. Whenever such a certificate is verified, the verifier should also check the CRL to ensure that the certificate hasn't been revoked by the issuer. The ability to use revocation lists, although it greatly increases the security of digital certificates, is not widely supported by application software.

If you wish to send a secure message to a correspondent whom you have not dealt with before, you need to get a copy of his or her digital certificate so you have access to his or her public key. The bigger the PKI, the more likely it is that you can accomplish this by querying a directory service. A directory service is merely a database that is optimized for reading. It may be a centralized service but to support large numbers of unknown potential correspondents, it is usually a distributed service with multiple servers. The directory service infrastructure is still at an early stage in its implementation, but in anticipation of widespread use of directory service most digital certificates follow a standard object format called X.509. If certificate revocation lists are supported, they may also be provided through the directory service. Public Key Infrastructures that actually provide revocation capabilities and are supported by client software are still rare.

A few timing issues complicate the reliability of a PKI and are especially relevant to the forensic investigator. After a digital certificate has expired, it may not be possible to verify it. Even if CRLs are used, it isn't practical to make them so large that they contain a complete historical list of all certificates that were revoked before their expiration—current CRLs list only unexpired certs. The root certificate of a CA has an expiration date also. After it expires, it may not be possible to verify older certificates that were signed with the obsolete CA key. These timing issues are not a problem during ongoing transactions, because certificates and signatures are verified within minutes, or at the most a few days, of their original use. Verifying transactions that took place several years in the past, however, presents serious practical difficulties. It is up to the CA to maintain historical records and to provide mechanisms for the verification of expired certificates, and it is unlikely that a CA will have financial incentive to do so for low-assurance certs. An investigator may well be confronted with digitally signed objects that are too old to be verified.

Time Stamping

The time when an object is signed affects its trustworthiness—a signature that occurred after expiration or revocation of a cert should not be considered valid. Digital signature is designed to verify the integrity of an object and the identity of its originator, but unfortunately, digital signature does not make provisions for the verification of signature time. What prevents someone from creating a back-dated signature? Actually, very little. It is easy to misrepresent the date on a digitally signed object. The problem of trusting digital signature dates is addressed by another form of trusted third party, a digital timestamping service. Sometimes called a "digital notary," it is a service that registers digital objects, providing proof from registration time onward that a specific object existed at a specific date and time. It isn't even necessary to provide the object itself to the timestamp service—only the hash value must be sent. Not only does this save bandwidth and storage space, but it means that the owner of the document never needs to risk losing control of the document's contents by transmitting it to the notary. Confidentiality and convenience are maintained.

A timestamping service can be quite useful when collecting and saving forensic evidence because it provides nearly incontestable proof that the digital evidence was in existence at a specific time and date and that it has not been changed between that date and its presentation in court as evidence. Unless the data is timestamped, the ease with which log data and hard drive contents can be changed by an unscrupulous investigator is always going to be an issue in court cases. When the original data is not only digitally signed by the investigator, but also is registered by a trusted third party, it's clear to the judge or jury that if evidence tampering occurred, it took place before it was timestamped and not at some later point after potentially conflicting evidence was gathered. Virtually any electronic files or images collected as evidence are candidates for third-party notarization. In addition to time-stamping the images of hard drives and any volatile information saved before shutting down a suspect machine, the following are also candidates for timestamping:

- Ongoing collection of suspect activities, including log files, sniffer output, and output from intrusion detection systems
- Output from any reports or searches performed on a suspect machine, including a list of all files and their associated access times
- Daily typed copies of investigator's notes

Investigators not wishing to go to the trouble of contracting with a digital notary service should still consider digitally signing copies of their evidence on a daily basis. Companies in the business of providing digital time stamp include Surety[5] and DigiStamp.[6]

Codes and Compression

In addition to encryption, other common forms of data manipulation can complicate your investigation. You need to be aware of them so that you can recognize them and extract the original data from them. You also need to know that they can defeat keyword searches, because the strings you are searching on may not be visible. Codes are systematic substitutions with a one-to-one correspondence between the original unit and its encoded form. In data-hiding terms, codes are a linguistic system. Certain words or phrases have agreed-upon meanings. The phrase "Mr. Smith is going to Washington" might actually mean something like "Roger Abernathy will be on tonight's 7 p.m. flight from Albuquerque." Such codes are inflexible and can be used to hide only a small amount of data, but it is common in a conspiracy or other team crime for the suspects to develop their own secret code. Deciphering such codes is beyond the scope of this book, but we suggest that if you find unusual or odd statements in messages, you do some keyword searches to see if you can correlate any of the messages with other communications containing the same odd or unique words.

Nonsecret codes are quite common on computers. The simplest standard representation for Roman letters in computers is ASCII, which stands for American Standard Code for Information Interchange. The original Internet email implementation, SMTP, supported only ASCII, which is inconvenient for binary data because ASCII uses only seven-bit bytes. In order to reliably shove binary data through

5. http://www.surety.com/

6. http://www.digistamp.com/trust.htm

email, the uuencoding standard was developed. The name derives from "UUCP," which is Unix to Unix Copy (note that the ISP, UUNet, also takes its name from UUCP). Uuencoded data is common on Unix systems and is sometimes found on Windows systems as part of an email message. A uuencoded file always starts with the word "begin," the file's Unix permissions in octal, and the name to use for the document after it is extracted. The lines are fixed width with a hard carriage return at the end. This can be seen as the "M" for Control-M in the following example, which is what a short uuencoded file looks like when viewed in Windows with Notepad. A uuencoded file also has the keyword "end" at the end. Many common archive utilities, such as WinZip, can extract the original from uuencoded versions.

```
begin 600 Kruseb2.c
MT,\1X*&Q&&N$```````````````````/@`#`/[_"`0`&```````````#
M```.P$$$$$$$$$$$$$\@```$```#```#`^_```````/8```^`0``/`$$/__
M($QQ42!F92$!(87)K;;F5SS<PP`>````@```#4`=3D8<<$````$$J;]!j^a
M;W):D(#&@N?[```0`````0(8D7]%B```(`)#j]1@$$$````"J$j)5"L`!
M`P```!$``````@%%`````````````````````````````````````````````
M```````````````````````````````````````````````````````````````
M```````````````````````````````````````````````````````````````
6```````````````````````````````````
`

end
```

Uuencoding obscures binary data, but not ASCII text, which is readable within the archive file and searchable.

An increasingly common form of encoding used for Internet mail is Multimedia Internet Mail Extension (MIME). Macintosh uses its own encoding format, BinHex, but many PC archive utilities, such as WinZip, can save to and extract from both of these formats. And speaking of archive utilities, it is important to understand both the concepts of *compression* and an *archive file*.

Compression is a way of reducing the size of a data object, making it easier to store and transmit. Compression is normally a reversible process. The compressed file cannot be used until it is uncompressed back into its original form. Dozens of different compression algorithms, each optimized for different data types, do the same basic task: they look for patterns, or repeating elements in a data object, and strip out redundant information. Let's take a simple example. Which of the following two lines requires more ASCII characters, A or B?

```
A. JJJJJJJJJJJJJJJJJJJJJJJJJJJJJJJJJJJJJJJJJJJJJJJJJJ
B. Write letter 'J' 50 times
```

Line B is a compressed version of line A. For another example, envision a bitmap, say a screen shot similar to the ones in this book. Such bitmaps have significant numbers of contiguous pixels that are the same color. The GIF and TIFF bitmap formats have optional compression that works well with drawings and screen shots. Because human languages, and their written expression, contain many patterns, text files usually can be compressed considerably, and some data files (Microsoft Office 97 is notorious for file bloat) are composed of huge amounts of repeating data, sometimes allowing them to be compressed to a fraction of their original size. Photographs, however, do not have the same characteristics as text or cartoons. Life is complex, and every pixel in a digital photo may be a slightly different value than its neighbors. Compressing such data with an algorithm that looks for contiguous areas of common data is rarely effective, so a different approach is taken. JPEG is an example compression algorithm for photographs, and MPEG is one for video and sound. These are called *lossy* algorithms because they cannot be fully reversed. They make minor changes to the original data, and every time the same data is recompressed with the lossy algorithm, the result becomes less like the original.

An archive is a group of related files that, as a convenience, are bundled together into a single object. Modern operating systems and applications consist of thousands of separate files, and even a simple upgrade may include dozens of files. To make it easier to distribute and install these files, they are often bundled into an archive. You are probably familiar with the Zip archive that is popular on Windows, but there are many other archive formats. Microsoft uses one called CAB—you can find .cab files on Windows installation CDs. Zip and CAB are both compressed, but not all archive formats are compressed. Unix archive formats, such as ar, shar, and tar, are often compressed after they are created, but they don't have to be compressed and frequently are not. In addition to simply putting a group of files into a common object, WinZip (and any other Zip-compatible archiver) compresses the files. This has important implications in your forensic examinations. As shown by the compression ratio column in Figure 4-8, compression can often make dramatic decreases in the size of a file, making storage devices much more efficient. This makes compression very popular, so you are likely to run into it often.

A compression algorithm is really a weak form of encryption, especially from the point of view of a forensic analyst who is attempting to run keyword searches on a hard drive. Guess what happens when your text string search encounters a compressed file? Nothing. Virtually all string searching routines blithely work their way through all the data on a hard drive. These routines have no way of knowing that some of the data they encounter, if it was just compressed, actually includes the strings that are being searched for. Although it is trivially easy to uncompress any file that was compacted into a standard format, if you don't know the file is

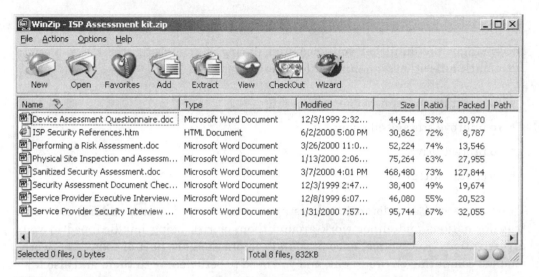

Figure 4-8   Contents of a compressed WinZip archive

compressed, you won't bother to convert it back into a form that your keyword search routine can use.

Keep in mind that any transformation performed on text data may make it difficult or impossible for you to do a batch search for keywords. Text strings will *not* be recognizable within encrypted or compressed files, and they may be hidden by non-ASCII encoding. It isn't easy to find such files. Very little research has been done in this area, and reliable tools are not available. The classic way of identifying encrypted data is to see if it can be compressed. If it cannot be compressed, it has either been compressed already or is encrypted. Why? Compression takes advantage of recognizable patterns. A particular algorithm has fully encrypted a data object when it can no longer recognize any patterns. Well-compressed data is essentially random data. Encrypted data should also appear to be totally random—it if is not, chances are good that the algorithm has allowed some clues about the original data to slip through. If encrypted data can be compressed, it is almost certainly vulnerable to cryptanalysis. This is one of the two reasons that data is often compressed before it is encrypted—because it increases the randomness of the resulting object (the second reason being that strong encryption is computationally costly and compressing the data speeds up the overall process). Encryption is just one of many techniques that someone hoping to conceal his or her activities can use to hide data files. In the next chapter, we'll take a look at all the different ways of hiding data.

Conclusion

Increasingly, the data that you encounter during your investigations is subject to systematic alteration for a number of different reasons:

- to facilitate transmission or processing
- to improve storage efficiency
- to protect privacy
- to ensure integrity

To be successful as a forensic analyst, you must recognize and understand these transformations and either work around them or risk being handicapped in your investigations. Encryption, encoding, and compression are part of today's network-enabled computing environment, and you need to both deal with them and also take advantage of them as appropriate technologies that can protect and improve the quality of the evidence that you collect.

Further Resources

Schneier, Bruce, "Why Cryptography Is Harder Than It Looks," http://www.counterpane. com/whycrypto.html. A number of useful and well-written documents are available on Schneier's site.

Chapter

5

Data Hiding

One of the most challenging aspects of a forensic analysis of a computer is the possibility of data being intentionally hidden by your suspect. Always assume that a system you are examining might contain hidden data. Even if it was not intentionally hidden to defeat analysis, data hidden by the operating system exists on all systems. With practice and the techniques we will share with you, many of your encounters with hidden data can be rewarding experiences.

As shown on Table 5-1, there are a number of different ways to hide data on a computer. We discussed encryption in the previous chapter, but it should be clear from Table 5-1 that encryption is not the only way to obscure information. Many of these techniques have no real legitimate use—the mere fact that someone attempts to hide data raises suspicions when it is discovered in conjunction with a crime or suspicious incident. During one of your investigations, if you discover that someone is trying to hide data, it is a clue that you should dig deeper. For the same reason, someone who wants his or her activities to remain secret may both hide the data and "lock" it through encryption. The techniques in Table 5-1 aren't mutually exclusive—a serious data hider may use several of them simultaneously. Note also that some of the data-hiding techniques may not be deliberate. Someone who routinely compresses data files just to save space is probably not trying to intentionally complicate your investigation, but the effect is the same. Certainly a great deal of data can end up in parts of the hard drive that aren't being stored—this isn't consciously hidden data either, but finding it may be helpful in understanding what was happening on a system. A system can have huge amounts of invisible data, and as an investigator, it is your job to find as much of it as possible—just in case it is relevant to your investigation.

Using and Cracking Encryption Applications

Hiding data through encryption is so simple that some people who do it undoubtedly don't even realize that they are using encryption. Most application suites, such as

Table 5-1 Data-Hiding Techniques

Category	Hiding Technique		Investigative Method
Obfuscating data The existence of the data is obvious to anyone who looks, but the meaning or content of the data is not discernable.		**Encryption**	Must be located first, then cracked.
		Compression Defeats keyword searches and allows data to fit in smaller spaces (think of it as a weak form of encryption).	Compressed data must be located, then uncompressed using the correct algorithm.
Hiding data The actual existence of the data is hidden.	In plain site	**Codes** Innocent-looking data has an alternate meaning.	Make guesses, or find the key to the codes.
	Within filesystem, in a file	**Steganography** Data is secreted within files that appear to be normal.	Locate first, then crack.
		Invisible names Filenames are not listed by standard OS utilities.	Search for characteristics of invisible names. Keyword search on filesystem.
		Misleading names Files may be masquerading as different files, or their suffixes may be incorrect. Unix filenames may have invisible characters in them.	Keyword search on filesystem. Look for anomalies. Use a utility that can identify a file based on its contents.
		Obscurity Files are placed in unusual places where an inexperienced administrator would not look.	Keyword search on filesystem. Look for anomalies.
		No Names Zero link files (Unix) are associated with no directory entry at all.	Must locate all zero link files before shutting down, or they will be lost.

(continued)

Table 5-1   Data-Hiding Techniques (cont.)

Category		Hiding Technique	Investigative Method
	Within filesystem, not in data file	Slack space, swap space, free space. (Swap space is a file on Windows, either a file or partition on Unix, and it may be remotely stored.)	Keyword search on complete drive. Undelete software.
	Outside computer	Data stored on removable media or other system on LAN or Internet.	Find and examine all media. Look for evidence of remote connectivity.
Blinding Investigator The data isn't hidden, but the sensory tools used to view data are surreptitiously modified so that specific data is not listed or found when using normal tools on the suspect system.		Changing behavior of system commands.	Remove data from subject computer and conduct exam on known good system. Verify integrity of system commands.
		Modifying operating system.	Remove data from subject computer and conduct exam on known good system. Verify integrity of operating system modules.

Microsoft Office (see Figure 5-1), have a built-in capability to password-protect their data files. This password protection invokes a simple form of encryption.

If you attempt to open the protected file, you receive a dialog box requesting the password (see Figure 5-2).

Of course, if you can't enter the correct password, you can't open the file. If you were to open the file with a text viewer, as we did using EnCase, you would see something similar to what is shown in Figure 5-3. Here, the text is not readable. (Figure 5-4 shows you the unencrypted version of the same file.)

An interesting "feature" in Word is the ability to automatically create a copy of a file as a backup when you are working on a document (many applications provide a similar option). This is meant to protect data, so that if you accidentally blow away a file, its predecessor still exists. As an investigator, it will be advantageous to you if your suspect has a copy of Word set up this way (in Word, choose Tools | Options | Save—always create a backup copy) because the backup copy of the file (with the file extension .wbk) is not password-protected. The backup copy is stored in plain text.

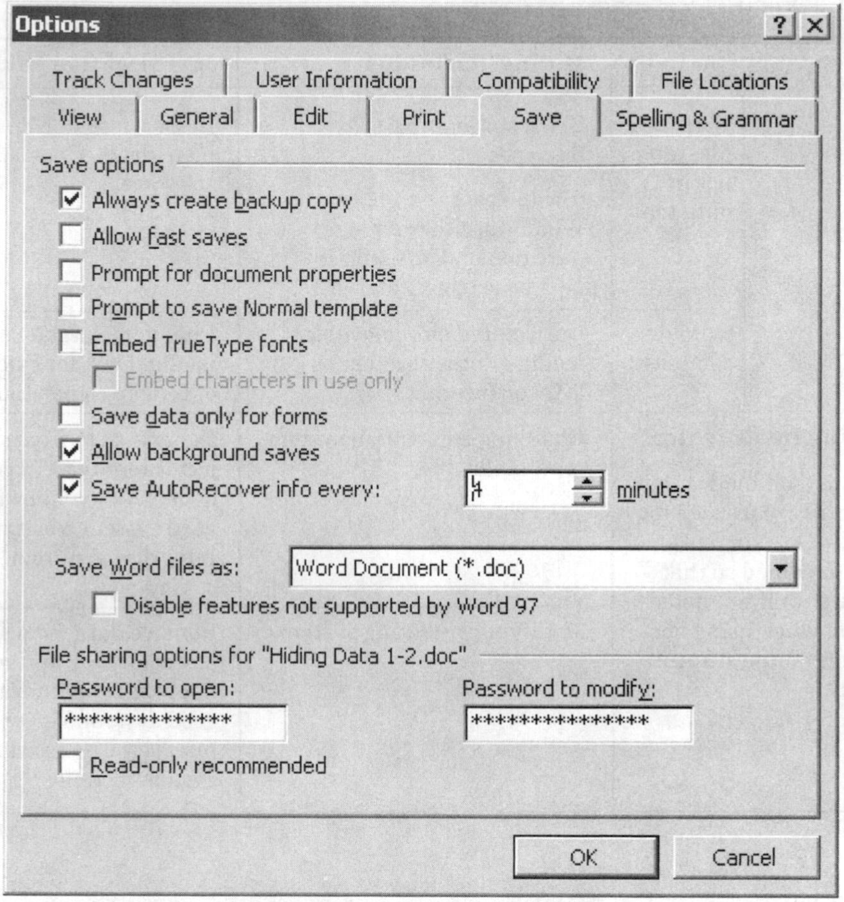

Figure 5-1   Using the Microsoft Word encryption option

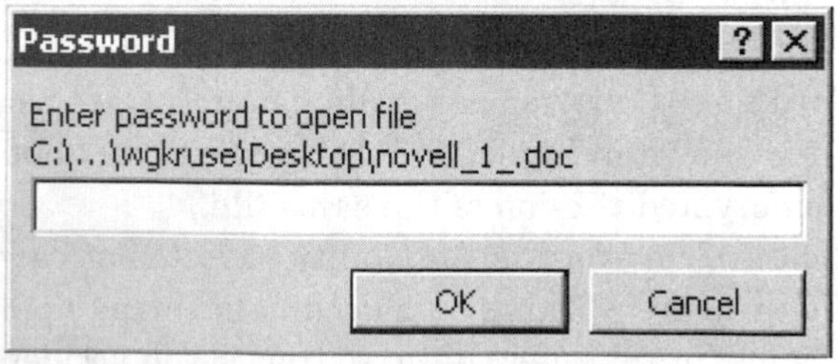

Figure 5-2   To open a protected file, you must provide a password.

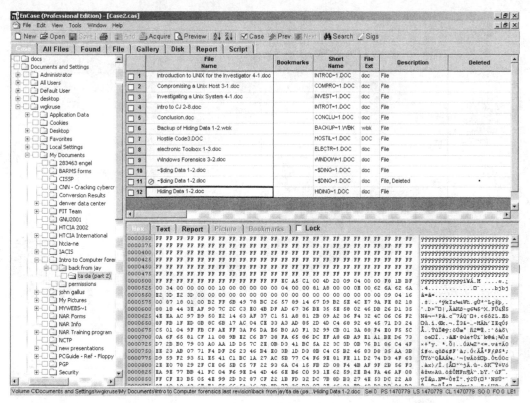

Figure 5-3   Hex view of a password-protected Word document is unreadable.

If you are not so lucky as to find cleartext versions of encrypted documents lying around, there are lots of other ways to attack the text. As discussed previously, the easiest way to crack encrypted text is to obtain the key, either by finding it or by asking someone who knows it. When you seize a computer, you should already be thinking about how the investigation will proceed. Anticipate that some data will be encrypted, so keep your eyes open for passwords. Remember to look under the keyboard, around the desk, in the Rolodex, and other places where someone would be likely to store a written password. Also, you can try guessing the password based on information that you know about the individual. An interview with the person responsible for the suspect computer is one of the most effective ways to learn relevant passwords, but you should be experienced in conducting an interview before you try to get this type of information. Conducting an interview is a lot more effective when

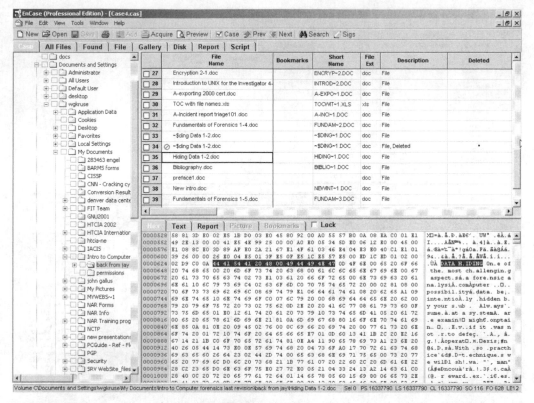

Figure 5-4 The original of that same file not encrypted

you already know most of the answers. You'll be able to control the process better, and it will be easier to evaluate the truthfulness of the subject's answers.

If you are unable to find the password or obtain it by asking the suspect, you'll probably need to use tools. Using tools to obtain user passwords is easier on some platforms than others. The nature of Microsoft Windows 9X is such that it has a tendency to store passwords in cleartext—apparently another "feature" added to improve usability. Utilities such as Cain can be run to obtain cleartext passwords that are cached by Windows for Internet dial-up accounts, email accounts, Web pages, and Microsoft networks.

Cain's ability to instantly return a list of cached passwords is impressive, but this feature isn't the only one the tool offers. It also has a lightning-fast password dictionary test, and it does a good job with brute force checks, both of which can be used to attack .pwl or .dat files that Cain automatically locates (see Figure 5-5).

Humans have a limited ability to remember passwords, so most people reuse the same simple passwords over and over again, often for years. Whenever you're confronted with an encrypted file, try decrypting it using any passwords you may

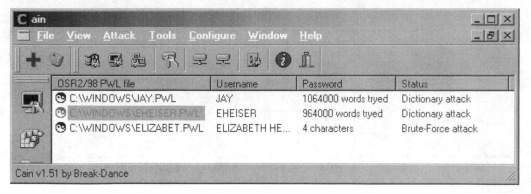

Figure 5-5 Cain can also perform dictionary and brute force attacks against encrypted passwords.

already have identified as having been used by your suspect—you'll often get lucky. If none of your password guesses open the document, you'll need to be more ambitious. Although we don't expect most readers of this book to be experienced cryptanalysts, if none of your password guesses open the document, you'll need to try breaking the code. Fortunately for the investigator, Microsoft uses fairly weak encryption that can be cracked with commercially available tools. One of the most effective is from AccessData.[1] Their password recovery tools are effective against Word, WordPerfect, Excel, and over a dozen common applications.

In addition to the standalone password crackers, AccessData also has the Distributed Network Attack (DNA) program. DNA enables you to load client software on multiple computers, distributing the encryption key attack process among them, greatly reducing the time it takes to perform a brute force attack (see Table 5-2). The client software uses spare processor time and therefore does not affect performance on the client computers. One computer is set up as the DNA Master and has a physical dongle, or key, attached to the parallel port. The master computer is the only computer that can open the file once the key is recovered so you don't have to worry about your clients receiving any of the information the document contains. If necessary, you can safely change the configuration of the DNA client software remotely, without the requirement of having any other administrative access to the client PC, using the DNA Manager. This remote configuration capability can make it much more politically acceptable for members of an organization to 'loan' some processing time on their workstations to a password cracking effort. The first time we tried the software was with a document that contained a password so strong that other programs, including AccessData's standalone software, ran for several weeks (24×7) without recovering the password. With the DNA software, the key for the same file

---

1. http://www.accessdata.com

Table 5-2   AccessData's Reported Decryption Times on 200MHz Intel Machines

Product	Maximum Time	Expected
25-client network	16 days	8 days
50-client network	8 days	4 days
100-client network	4 days	2 days
500-client network	20 hours	10 hours
1,000-client network	10 hours	5 hours

was recovered, and a copy of the file was successfully opened. While we highly recommend this software and can't wait for upcoming versions (including support for Unix clients), you should run other programs to try dictionary attacks while DNA is attacking the encryption key. This way you are attacking the document on more than one front.

If you are looking for a password cracker with fewer features and less expensive than AccessData, you may want to consider the software available from LostPassword.com.[2] They offer password recovery software for popular programs including Microsoft Office, WordPerfect, Outlook, and Quicken. Private use is free, and the price for business use is reasonable. They also offer software for Internet Explorer. Although it probably doesn't have any forensic utility, it is interesting to know that their Internet Explorer Key utility can reset the supervisor password for IE's Contents Advisor. Parents might want to check junior's computer for this program if you are trying to limit your children's Web surfing by using Internet Explorer's built-in Adult Content Advisor.

You should try to crack as many of your suspect's passwords as possible so that you can try them to open protected data. If the suspect has a Windows NT account, the password stored in the Security Account Manager (SAM)—either locally or on a domain controller—is relatively straightforward to attack. The most efficient of the Windows NT password crackers is L0phtCrack from @stake.[3] Taking advantage of weaknesses in the hash implementation used for Windows NT passwords, it can crack most passwords within a few minutes, and few passwords can withstand several days of L0phtCrack on a fast machine. The GUI version of this program includes a sniffer that captures password hashes from network login sessions. L0phtCrack 1.5, a command-line version of this program, is available for free.

You may encounter situations when you cannot pull the hard drive from a Windows NT PC and access it on another system, but instead need to access a Windows

---

2. http://www.lostpassword.com

3. http://L0phtCrack is available at http://www.atstake.com.

NT system without having the administrative password. You can use the following procedure to access the system under such circumstances:

1. Reboot the suspect system with a DOS boot disk.

2. Copy the SAM database from the server to a floppy disk.[4] The SAM is part of the registry and is usually found in \winnt\system32\config.

3. Run L0phtCrack on this SAM file on your forensic system.

4. Boot Windows NT on the suspect system.

5. Log on using one of the passwords returned by L0phtCrack.

As L0phtCrack cracks passwords, it will display them in its GUI as shown in Figure 5-6.

Changing Passwords

When you are completely stuck and must log on to a Windows NT system without recourse to any external systems, ntpassword is a boot floppy image distributed on the Web that enables you to change any password or, if you know your way around the registry, make changes to registry keys.[5] The developers of the program warn that it takes advantage of undocumented features and that damage may result from its use, so you should consider using this program only in emergencies. (Using such a program can severely compromise the use of a Windows NT system as evidence in a court case.) The tool is an interesting example of the use of Linux to examine a

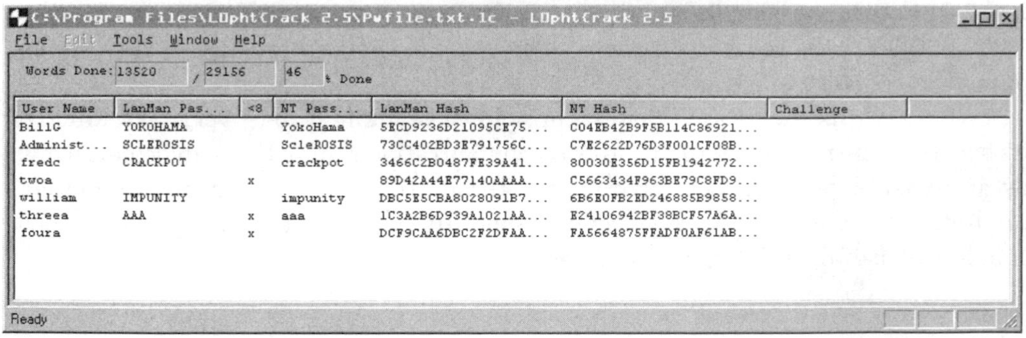

Figure 5-6 L0phCrack attacks both the LanMan password hashes and the stronger Windows NT hashes.

---

4. SAM databases can be copied using NTFSDOS from http://www.sysinternals.com.

5. http://home.eunet.no/~pnordahl/ntpasswd

Windows NT system. Fitting on a single floppy disk, it includes a small Linux kernel compiled with support for NTFS. Copy the boot image onto a floppy disk using rawrite[6] and boot it up on the system you want to crowbar. You'll access a menu-based utility enabling you to change the password on any account, make changes to the registry, and exit to a shell command line.

A single floppy disk doesn't have room for much software, but a Linux CD, such as the Bootable Business Card (discussed in Appendix F) has room for a huge amount of Unix software. tomsrtbt, which stands for "Tom's Root & Boot" is a floppy-based Linux kernel with room for lots of utilities.[7] If you are more comfortable working in a Unix environment, either a boot floppy or CD could be used to grab a SAM from an NT system that you crack on another system. You're going to continue to see new and interesting uses for Linux to examine and manipulate NTFS.

When you must change the Administrator password on a Windows NT system, AccessData (discussed previously) also offers ntaccess.[8] It is expensive, but it works like a charm. As with the other programs in this category, all you need is physical access to the machine and a DOS boot disk.

WinZip has an encryption option; Advanced ZIP Password Recovery is a Russian company that specializes in password recovery and Windows utilities. Their Advanced ZIP Password Recovery program (AZPR—see Figure 5-7)[9] is fast; they claim it can try about 2,000,000 passwords per second (on a Pentium II). The program can also work in the background, using the CPU only when it is in idle state. Advanced ZIP Password Recovery also has multilanguage support, which can come in handy when a suspect uses a password in a language you aren't familiar with.

As shown in Figure 5-8, AZPR can crack passwords consisting of simple English words in just a few seconds.

Another program for password-protected ZIP files is ZipPassword (see Figure 5-9).[10] It has a simple interface, and the company states it can "search up to 1,000,000,000 passwords per minute." The company touts it as "the world's fastest password recovery program."

Whether it is the "world's fastest" or not, we've found it to be very fast. Much of its speed can be attributed to the up-front configuration tuning that can be performed by an experienced user (see Figure 5-10). In addition to these various commercial products, lots of other software is available on the Internet at no charge—some of it is actually useful, so do some experimenting.

---

6. http://www.redhat.com

7. http://www.toms.net.

8. ntaccess is a standalone utility that is part of the Network Toolkit.

9. http://www.elcomsoft.com

10. http://soft4you.com

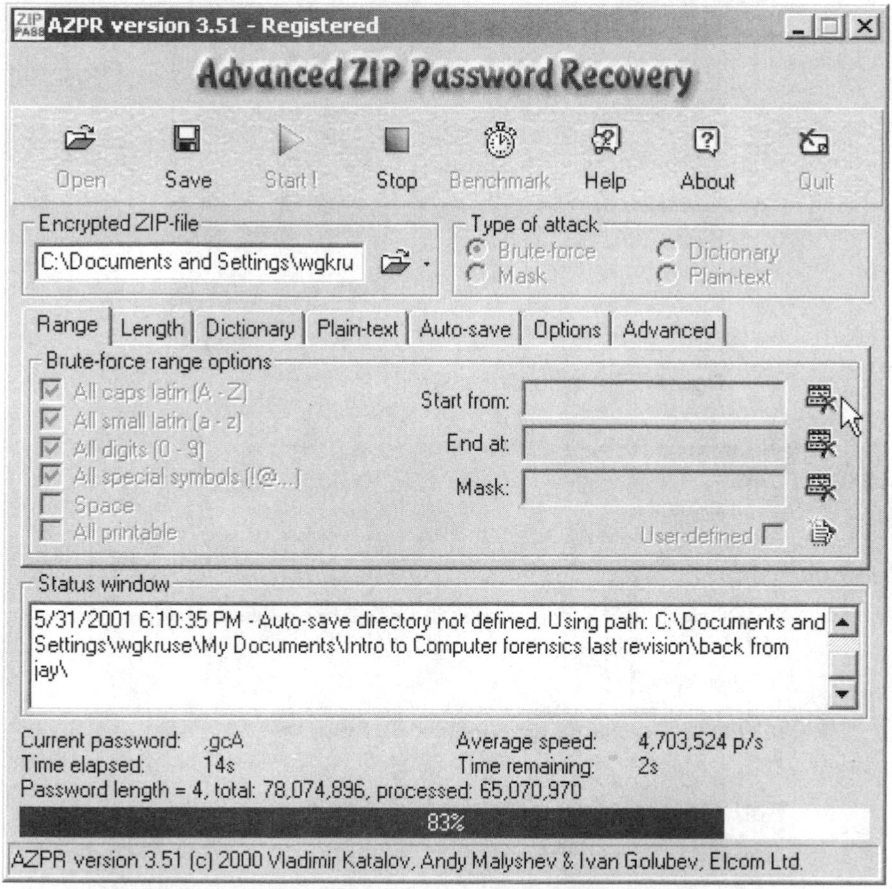

Figure 5-7   AZPR is operated through a detailed GUI.

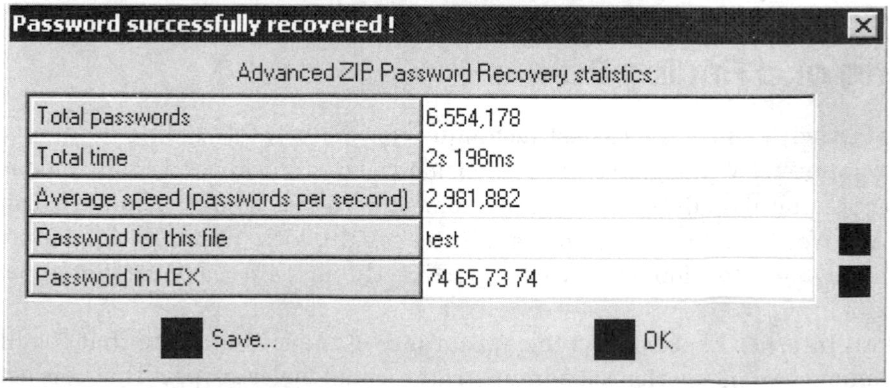

Figure 5-8   A simple ZIP password ("test") recovered in under three seconds.

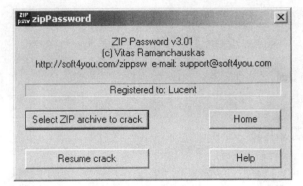

Figure 5-9   Initial ZipPassword window

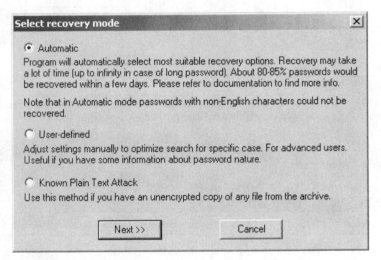

Figure 5-10   ZipPassword recovery mode choices

Hiding and Finding Data

Let's start with one of the easiest techniques for deliberately hiding data on a Windows computer. By changing a file's extension you can quickly and easily hide it from an inexperienced analyst. For example, someone who feels guilty about the contents of an MS Word file and wants to avoid being caught with incriminating data might change the file extension from .doc to .jpg. Exactly such a Word document appears in Figure 5-11.

Both Internet Explorer and the appearance of the icon indicate that the file is a JPEG image. An inexperienced administrator would never suspect that it is actually a document. Even when you double-click on this icon, Windows tries to open the file

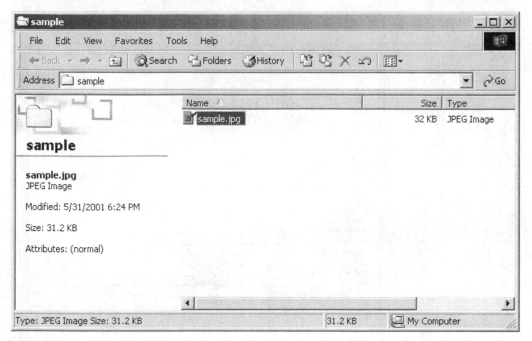

Figure 5-11   A mislabeled file

with the default viewer for a JPEG file. The simple reason for this unreliable behavior is that the Windows File Explorer uses the filename extension to identify the data type of the file—a primitive DOS behavior that is just too convenient for Microsoft to give up. Hiding data by using misleading filenames is fairly easy for an unsophisticated suspect to accomplish, but accessing the data in such hidden files is a trick that any rookie forensic technician should be able to accomplish. On Windows, you can avoid this Explorer behavior by not using File Explorer to determine the data type. If your forensic workstation is configured to always use a multifile viewer, such as INSO's Quick View Plus, you won't be dependent upon easily spoofable file extensions. Figure 5-12 shows what happens when a utility such as Quick View Plus opens this file.

Quick View Plus opens the file correctly and identifies it as a Microsoft Word 97/98 file even though it had a misleading extension. Some forensic programs, such as EnCase from Guidance Software, actually can locate files that have mismatched extensions. It is extremely helpful to have Encase search through your copy of the evidence in the background as you are conducting your analysis. The program provides a list of all files that apparently have mismatched extensions, and all you have to do is manually view each of them to see what they contain.

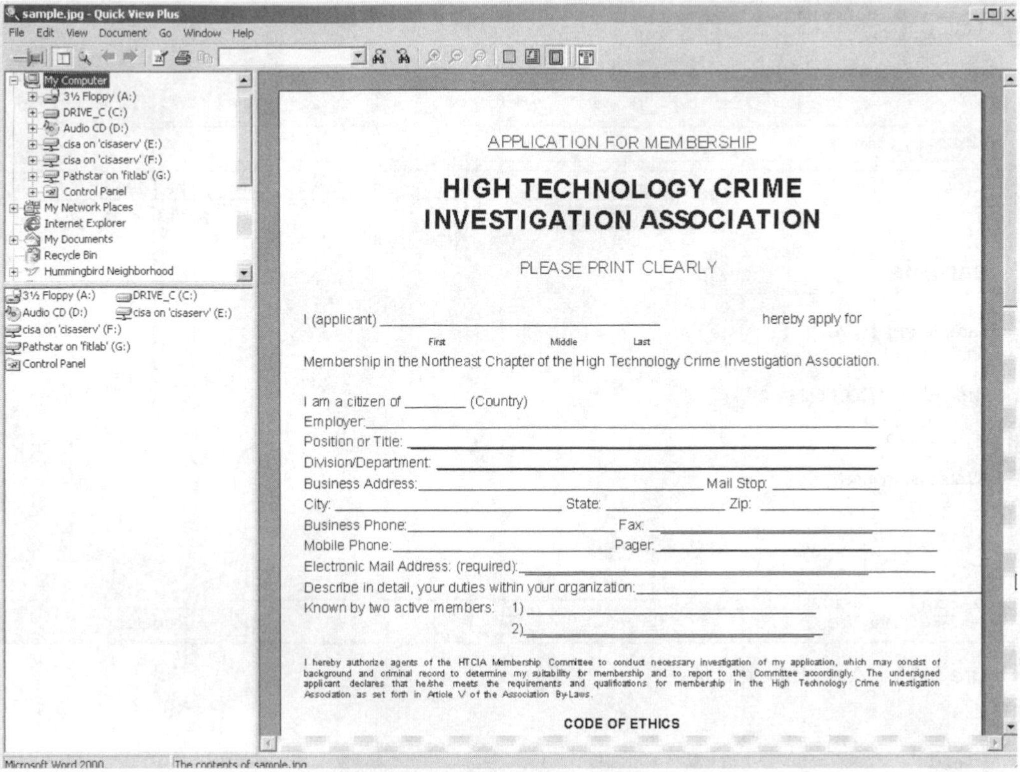

Figure 5-12   Viewing a mislabeled file with Quick View Plus

Even if you do not have one of these programs, mislabeled files are not entirely hidden from you. As long as they are not encrypted or compressed, files hidden this way still can be found by a search. For instance, if your company's documents are marked "Proprietary," you might use that word as a search term when looking for evidence of data theft. In Figure 5-13, we searched for "association" and received a hit on our JPEG file. This succeeded because the search capability doesn't care about file types (unless you explicitly configure it to search only for files with specific names or extensions). Since the file contains the text "High Technology Crime Investigation Association," the Windows 2000 search capability can find it.

When conducting a forensic analysis, you should always check file headers because they contain a hexadecimal value that can usually be correlated to file type. Use a standalone hex editor or forensic software such as EnCase. This is especially important when the initial survey of the suspect's computer leads you to believe that he or she may be intentionally hiding data. An extraordinary amount of detailed information about file formats is available at Wotsit's Format, a programmer's

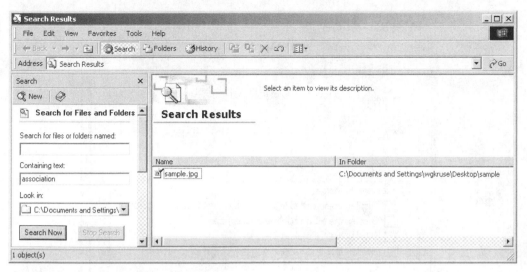

Figure 5-13   Text searches are not affected by misnamed files.

resource found on the Web.[11] You most likely will use the information found at this site for analyzing Windows systems, but it contains data on file formats for dozens of different platforms from Palm OS to the Atari ST.

On a Unix system, the file type is not determined by the name, except in very limited circumstances. As discussed in Chapter 9, the file command uses several different techniques to identify the type of data found in any particular filesystem object. Some Unix applications do use filename extensions, and an intruder may attempt to trick an administrator by using a bogus extension. It is more likely that a Unix attacker will obscure the file by starting its name with a dot character, putting it into a directory with a name that starts with one or more dots, or by putting it into a system directory where the bogus file just might blend in with all the other files. This technique is common on Windows also—those who create and plant hostile backdoor applications and worms (see Chapter 6) often stick them into the system directory with an innocent-sounding name. With thousands of binaries in the system directories, it is likely that an inexperienced administrator won't notice.

Windows still ships with a lot of DOS baggage, including the attrib command for changing file options such as the hidden attribute. The simple command line "attrib +h *directory*" sets the hidden attribute on a specified directory, making it invisible to the dir command (although dir / ah will show it). It also is invisible to Windows Explorer users who haven't set the Show All Files option. Choose

---

11. http://www.wotsit.org

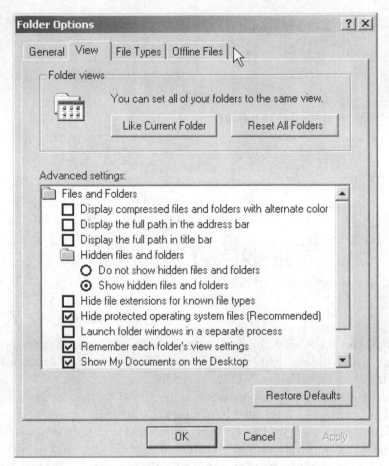

Figure 5-14   Windows 2000 Folder Options

"Start | Settings | Folder Options" to access the Folder Options window shown in Figure 5-14. In this window, you can check the Show hidden files and folders option, and while you are at it, uncheck the Hide file extensions for known file types and Hide protected operating system files options.

NT Streams

The Windows NT operating system incorporates a capability that makes it easy to attach any arbitrary data to a file, yet hides the existence of this data from normal system tools and programs. Streams are an NTFS mechanism allowing the association, or linking, of new data objects with a file. It is no secret that streams exist, although they're not really widely recognized, and they can be used to hide data. Streams were first documented publicly in 1998, and Microsoft has placed several relevant articles on its Web site.[12] If you are using NTFS, the following demonstration works on both Windows NT 4.0 and Windows 2000:

```
C:\> md test
C:\> cd test
C:\test> echo "This file will have hidden data attached" >file.txt
```

What you've just done is create a directory, and inside of it, you've created a small text file. Type **dir** to display the size of the file. Now let's stick a big chunk of data onto this file in a stream named "sneak". The syntax for referencing a stream is *filename:streamname*. Any chunk of data will do, such as the directory listing of the system directory. Try the following:

```
...
C:\test> dir c:\winnt > file.txt:sneak
```

You can even hide data in an unnamed stream like this:

```
C:\>echo "this is a test" > :test
```

Now type **dir** and see what it can tell us about the data you've just stored. You can't even see the unnamed stream, and it appears that the size of file.txt hasn't changed. Try the following and see what happens:

```
C:\test> more <file.txt:sneak
```

You saw the hidden data, right? But it wasn't visible with dir, which doesn't take into account the existence of streams. Neither does Window Explorer or any GUI-based program. You can create and edit an alternate stream from the command line, with Windows Notepad, and you can delete an alternate stream from the command line.

Executables can be hidden inside file streams, as well, and executed from those streams. Let's continue our experiment:

```
C:\test>type c:\winnt\notepad.exe > file.txt:np.exe
```

---

12. Try a search for "ntfs streams" at http://www.microsoft.com.

In their book *Hacking Exposed* (Berkeley, CA: Osborne McGraw-Hill, 2001), authors Joel Scambray, Stuart McClure, and George Kurtz discuss how the start command can be used to run executable files hidden in alternate data streams. You can verify this easily:

```
C:\test>start file.txt:np.exe
```

Other files can be executed from these hidden data streams. For example, our technical reviewer, Harlan Carvey, verified that Perl could be used to create alternate data streams, and that Perl scripts could be hidden in and executed from alternate data streams. Burgeoning Windows NT Perl programmers can demonstrate it this way:

```
C:\Perl>type myscript.pl > myfile.txt:hidden.pl
C:\Perl>perl myfile.txt:hidden.pl
```

A great deal of concern has been expressed that antivirus software can't locate executables hidden in Windows NT streams, but software vendors claim that if such malware ever appeared, code scanners could identify the visible program that invokes the one secreted away in a hidden stream.

As an investigator, you should always assume that alternate streams may exist in any NTFS filesystem, and you should include a check for their existence as part of your investigation. The best way to do so is with the SFind tool included with the free Forensic Toolkit from Foundstone[13] (see Chapter 7). Several other tools exist, including the following:

- Streams from Mark Russinovich of SysInternals[14]
- CrucialADS is a GUI-based tool from Crucial Security[15]
- Dave Roth's most recent book, *Win32 Perl Scripting: The Administrator's Handbook* (New Riders, 2001), includes Perl code for discovering alternate data streams.

Don't Forget about the Network

You might spend weeks tearing apart a computer, bit by bit, and never find the data that you know darn well is in the possession of your subject. Not all criminals are stupid—some of them try to avoid implicating themselves by placing incriminating data

---

13. http://www.foundstone.com/rdlabs/tools.php?category=Forensic

14. http://www.sysinternals.com/ntw2k/source/misc.shtml

15. http://www.crucialsecurity.com

as far from their personal workstation as possible. A file server inside the corporate LAN or WAN may be a convenient place to store hot files, but the risk of discovery is still high. As reported by the FBI, cyber criminals are increasingly taking advantage of the Internet to store data off of their systems. If you don't believe that corporate insiders are storing data outside of the WAN on Internet sites, contemplate for a moment how often you receive email from friends using one of the Web-based sites like yahoo.com or hotmail.com. Was the email sent to you during working hours—possibly while your friends were at their offices? You mean your friends are taking advantage of free Internet sites in order to circumvent their office systems? Hackers have always taken advantage of cheap Internet systems to store data, although traditionally they had to compromise the systems first. Back in the old days, home disk drives were small, and system crackers got into the habit of using hacked systems as convenient data dumping grounds. Now many Internet sites are offering free or inexpensive storage space, and criminals are taking advantage of it—sometimes with stolen or false identities. It is difficult to make a case when you can't find the evidence.

Hiding data off of the computer complicates the investigation, but it isn't totally hopeless. In our previous discussion of Windows password crackers, and later in Chapter 11, we talk about a number of places where a workstation squirrels away information about Internet activities. Check these areas thoroughly for clues about your suspect's activities on the LAN, WAN, and Internet. This information could well lead you to an off-site storage site. If the suspect system is on a LAN, also check to see what systems are listed in its Network Neighborhood—these represent systems where the suspect might have stored data.

Steganography

Steganography means "to hide in plain sight." The word *steganography* is derived from the Greek words for *covered writing,* and it refers to the practice of hiding data. It isn't a new concept. Invisible ink and microdots are two techniques, both predating the computer, for secreting data within an object without providing any visual clues that the object has a surreptitious purpose. *Cryptographic steganography,* or *stego,* secretes data within some other nonsecret data object called the *carrier*. The carrier is usually a multimedia file—either sound or a photograph—although a steganographic filesystem has recently been conceived, and an early implementation is available.

Stego utilities typically protect data in two ways. First, they make it invisible—they hide its very existence—and second, they encrypt it. This is a belt-and-suspenders approach that doesn't rely on steganography alone to protect the data. If the existence of the secreted object is discovered, it still has to be decrypted before it is useful. Stego is a concern for the forensic analyst but luckily, it's so time-consuming to use that it is not widely practiced. If you want to "stego" a file, you have to do it one file at a time. Most cases involve hundreds and even thousands of files, and it would be too time-consuming for most cyber spooks to find appropriate carriers and stego all those files into them.

If you find a stego utility on somebody's workstation, he or she is probably either the user or the recipient of stegoed files. You should download a couple of stego utilities so that you better understand how they work and what to look for. You can easily find S-Tools at http://www.Members.tripod.com/stenography/stego/s-lools4.html. Another popular stego utility is called Steganos, and it is available as shareware from the vendor.[16] When downloading software from the Web—not just security software but all forms of software—always ensure that your virus software is up to date and run a full scan after you download the software.

As shown in Figure 5-15, S-Tools[17] is simple enough for anyone to use. Dragging and dropping a file onto the S-Tools window will prompt the user for a pass phrase. After entering the passphrase, S-Tools provides a comparative view of both the original and the steganographically altered version, allowing the user to confirm that the change is not visually distinguishable. After you password-protect the file, the new image is displayed with the hidden data as depicted in Figure 5-16.

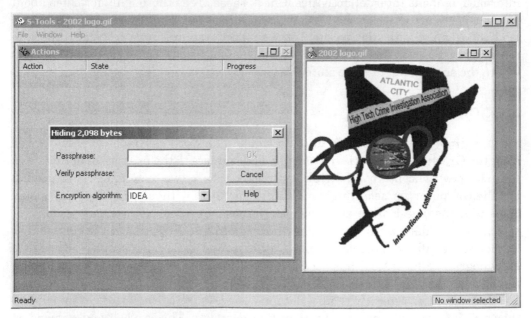

Figure 5-15   Entering a password with S-Tools

---

16. http://www.steganos.com/english

17. A commonly used steganography utility is S-Tools, and is easy to find on the web at http://members. tripod.com/steganography/stego/software.com

Figure 5-16   Comparing the original carrier image to one containing stegoed data

To retrieve the hidden data from the stegoed image, right-click on the file and select Reveal as shown in Figure 5-17. While the image with the hidden data is visually indistinguishable from the original, it took several steps and some time to get just one file, which is why this method is not popular. You have to find a carrier file that is significantly larger than the data file and has enough complexity so that the stegoed data can be hidden within it without causing a visibly discernable change in the image's appearance. It has often been suggested that the use of steganography can be detected by visually comparing the original file to the modified file, but a decent stego program won't allow you to use an unsuitable carrier. Try using Steganos and see what happens when you try to stick a 1MB document into a 500K bitmap. Don't ever count on being able to see or hear differences in a multimedia file that provide clues that the file contains secreted data. A lot of research is currently underway on the detection of steganography—not surprisingly, each algorithm has distinctive characteristics. For the time being, it isn't practical for anyone lacking the resources of a large national government to be able to detect the use of stego through file analysis.

One question we always hear when we demonstrate S-Tools is "If the program prompts you for a password after you click on Reveal, does that mean that the file has, in fact, been stegoed?" The answer is unfortunately, no. That wouldn't be a useful data-hiding tool, would it? To protect against a simple attack like that, S-Tools

Figure 5-17 Retrieving a steganographically hidden file

always prompts you for a password when you try to reveal any file, even the ones that do not have hidden data.

During your analysis, you should always look for any kind of unusual programs that can be used to hide evidence. No vendor includes a stego program as part of its standard load, and the presence of such a tool (deleted or not) should raise suspicions that perhaps somebody is trying to hide data. If you are to the point where a suspect is being interviewed, you can ask about the existence of any steganography programs you might have found. If the suspect tells you that he or she was assessing the proactive security use of stego, ask to see a file that it was tested on. If the suspect says he or she hasn't stegoed a file, you should ask yourself how someone could test the functionality of a program without actually using it.

Several commercial applications of steganography exist. *Digital watermarks* are hidden data placed on a bitmap and meant to serve as proof of its source. Data owners, such as the sellers of photographs and other original art, want to "rent" use of their intellectual property, or sell it under limited circumstances, and need a method of showing their ownership of the file. A digital watermark is a lot like a brand, except that it is invisible. Some techniques are supposed to be robust enough that the watermark can undergo manipulations to the carrier file and still be legible (remember that JPEG is a lossy format). Digital watermarks are more likely to be an issue in a civil case than a criminal case, but it is conceivable that some day a case involving felony theft of intellectual property will revolve around watermarks. Color copiers also use a similar technique. When first introduced, they were so effective at making realistic copies of original data that U.S. federal government authorities became concerned about counterfeiting. For this reason, all color copier manufacturers have agreed to include steganographically hidden data within their printed output that enables law enforcement to determine which machine made the copy. Steganography may be obscure, but it is used frequently.

Putting Blinders On

The last category of data-hiding methods consists of changing the system environment so that it provides bogus information about its contents and activities. Without actually hiding the data itself, this has the effect of making the information invisible to a user—as long as he or she is viewing the data on the crippled computer. The system environment can be changed in two ways. Either individual binaries are hacked, such as the one that lists the file directory contents (ls on Unix and dir on DOS), or the kernel is hacked, potentially affecting multiple binaries simultaneously. As we discuss in Chapter 10, hacking the system binaries on a Unix system is relatively common—so common that it is given special treatment within that chapter. It does happen on other operating environments also, although not nearly as frequently. Unfortunately, Windows NT rootkits[18] have been available for several years, and we've begun hearing reports of their use.

Increasingly, modern operating systems—including Windows NT, Windows 2000, and most versions of Unix and Linux—use dynamically linked libraries (DLLs). Commonly used code routines are not linked into individual binaries at compile time but are accessed at run time by whatever program happens to need them. This is normally a major convenience to the administrator because it removes a lot of redundant code. It also means that when a library is updated, every program that references it is updated, which is a lot easier than sending out a bunch of binaries to thousands of computers. That's the good news. The bad news is that a hostile change to a single DLL or shared library file potentially affects every executable on the system—even those that have yet to be installed. There is a certain morbid fascination to the idea of actually manipulating the kernel of an operating system to affect its behavior. Authorized changes are made to system libraries all the time, and they also affect all binaries. It is very much a question of the intent—any software introduced without the approval of the designated administrator should be considered hostile and unacceptable. Kernel attacks have been reported against Windows NT, Solaris, and Linux, and they are not straightforward to detect on any platform.

18. Rootkits, discussed in detail in Chapter 10, are sets of modified system binaries providing hackers with hidden backdoors that allow them future access to systems they have compromised.

You cannot count on antivirus software detecting them, although if the system was baselined before infection, an integrity checker such as Tripwire can detect the differences between hacked and the normal binaries.

The best way to avoid "investigator blinding" attacks is to never conduct an examination on a subject system, but to always image the data onto another trusted system where such attacks are harmless. Sometimes it is necessary to do an investigation on a suspect host, and it is because of the potential for these attacks that we recommend booting from a known good source, such as your forensic CD. Common wisdom suggests using statically linked binaries, which would be a good idea if you could get them, but their creation on some operating environments, especially Solaris, is problematic. Some volunteer groups are currently looking into the potential for creating a downloadable CD image that would contain statically linked versions of common system utilities and maybe some forensic utilities, such as The Coroner's Toolkit (TCT). This kind of CD would be appropriate for sites, such as ISPs, that are hit frequently, usually with the latest kiddie script, but don't necessarily have the budget or management support for a full-scale incident response.

Conclusion

The growing use of encryption represents both a challenge and an opportunity for the digital detective. Increasingly, suspects wishing to hide their activities are resorting to convenient and widely accessible strong encryption. Digital forensic investigators must accept that skillful criminals can hide or encrypt data in such a way that it may never be recoverable. The spy versus spy world of data hiding will continue to be driven by technology. New and clever code and techniques will be developed, and then investigators and researchers will discover practical ways to find evidence of their use. The good guys will figure out how to crack the contents of the hidden data, too, but not always right away, and sometimes the cost will be too high. Clever criminals always can come up with new methods, and given time and resources, clever investigators always can break them.

Chapter
6

Hostile Code

A friend once confided to us his concern that they had a hacker working for their company. They were observing port scanning coming from a machine whenever the user was logged on. After examining the system and interviewing the user, it seemed unlikely that he was hacking, and they didn't know what to do next. We asked them to run a full antivirus scan on the computer, and it took only a few seconds to find a hostile executable, Ataka. A quick check of the antivirus software vendor's Web page provided the helpful information that the executable was a Trojan designed to flood specific Internet servers with TCP connection requests. The site also included instructions on removing Ataka.

Possession of some types of burglar tools is a crime. Although it isn't proof of guilt when someone possesses lock picks, an investigator understands the significance. Software tools that enable electronic breaking and entering have become a significant part of computer misuse. This chapter introduces the topic of hostile code and helps you understand its implications and purpose so you'll be better prepared to recognize and deal with it in the field. Our first piece of advice is to forget anything you've read in the popular press about viruses. You'll need a more sophisticated picture in order to deal with the software creepie-crawlies you will encounter during your investigations.

Opinions differ on what exactly constitutes hostile code. For your purposes, any code you encounter that is not approved by the authorized system administrator should be considered hostile. Period! This doesn't mean that users cannot install their own software. If a user is authorized to install software at his or her discretion, the user is functionally a system administrator. If that same user is sent an email message with an innocent-looking attachment that, when double-clicked, secretly installs some kind of software that will run later without the knowledge or consent of that user, the attachment contains hostile code.

A great deal of software is created to enable some people to exercise power over others. System administration suites, access control programs, forensic utilities, and hacking tools are all designed to enable one person to exercise electronic superiority at the disadvantage of someone else. Some people are authorized to use this power, and others are not. When software is used to gain advantage or power over someone, and the person wielding it is not authorized to use it, then the software should be considered hostile code. Any code that can be used to destroy or steal information, or gain unauthorized access, must be treated as potentially hostile when found in the hands of someone who has no authorization to use it—he or she might be merely curious or might be using the software to gain power—you cannot know without additional information. People who accidentally lock themselves out of their cars expect that a parking lot attendant has access to a slim jim and can use it to open their car, but when discovered in the hands of a teenager, that same simple device can be considered incriminating. The slim jim lock picking device is analogous to software—often one powerful software tool has both positive and negative uses. Finding such a tool during an investigation is one more indication that the system you are examining might have been involved in a cyber crime—as either the victim or the source of the attack. It is reasonable to expect your parking lot attendant to have a slim jim, but should everyone within your organization have lock-picking equipment?

Hostile code is becoming increasingly significant and prevalent, and it is only a matter of time before you, as an active forensic investigator, encounter it. Digital criminals don't need direct access to a computer in order to harm it—they can do it safely and remotely using their software agents. Indeed, many virtual vandals don't even know what systems they have damaged. They cast their malware onto the cybernetic waters of the Internet and often never know where it goes and whom it attacks. Other virtual attack agents—when successful—do eventually report back to their masters. When they find a vulnerable prospect, or actually steal passwords or other data from a computer, they contact their masters with a report on what they've learned.

It isn't practical for this book to list every possible example of hostile code that you might encounter. New malware is created every day, and it continues to increase in sophistication and potency. This chapter will teach you to categorize malware, making it easier for you to recognize, research, and analyze it when you encounter it.

Categories

Malware can be internally directed, meaning that its unfriendly purpose is directed at the computer it is located on, or it can be externally directed, performing its attack function remotely through a network or telephone line. Furthermore, malware is either autonomous or manual. Manual hostile code is malware that is used interactively under the direct control of a malicious human being. Autonomous hostile code is designed to operate without human intervention, performing its function

Table 6-1   Examples of the Four Categories of Hostile Code

	Internally Directed	**Externally Directed**
Manual	Log manipulators Fix utility that can seamlessly replace a legitimate binary with a hostile version Network tools that allow unauthorized remote access (NetBus, BackOrifice, Internet relay chat [IRC] bots)	Vulnerability scanners Smurf denial-of-service Berkeley Internet Name Daemon (BIND) and LPR buffer overflow attacks
Autonomous	Melissa virus Time bombs Trojaned binaries	Distributed denial-of-service zombies (Stacheldraht and Trinoo) IRC bots

according to its programmed parameters. As shown by the examples in Table 6-1, these two distinctions can be used to assign all hostile code four different categories.

A final distinction can be made between code that is self-replicating and code that must be manually distributed. Viruses and worms are the two types of self-replicating code. Viruses do not lead a standalone existence—they are code fragments that must ride piggyback within some other program. Worms are discrete programs that copy themselves to other computers over a network. The Melissa virus and the I Love You/Lovebug worm were similar in their effects. They both spread as email attachments and when triggered, they sent copies of themselves to other victims whose email addresses were in the initial victim's Microsoft Outlook address book. However, Melissa is a virus, and I Love You/Lovebug is a worm. This distinction is important to the forensic analysis of malware because it describes the placement of the hostile code. The virus is found only in files capable of carrying it—in this case, Microsoft Word documents, which actually support a powerful programming capability. Worms are always standalone executable files.

All self-replicating code is autonomous—if nothing else, the replication process itself represents an example of its self-directedness. Not all autonomous hostile code is self-replicating, though. Many examples of hostile code are manually inserted and can function with no further direction. The spread of self-replicating code is almost completely random, so it isn't typically used for directed attacks against a specific target.

Forensic analysis of viruses and worms is best performed by skillful programmers, although the current crop of scripts written in Visual Basic can be understood by many Windows NT systems administrators. Programmers analyzing binary malware reverse-engineer it to determine its methods and purpose, and poke around with a hex editor looking for clues into the code's source or authorship. We don't anticipate that most of the readers of this book will become this specialized—it certainly isn't something that most corporate incident response teams are capable of doing. Law enforcement agencies may support the investigation and act on the results, and the FBI is increasing its capabilities in this area.

The Purpose

As previously defined, hostile code is code that is used to gain or keep unauthorized power or advantage over another person. Some of the ways it can be used to do this include

- Remote access
- Data gathering
- Sabotage
- Denial-of-service
- Eluding detection
- Resource theft
- Circumvention of access control mechanisms
- Social status
- Self-fulfillment

Self-fulfillment seems a bit abstract in this context, but computer crimes are analogous to physical crimes. Just as a perpetrator may throw a rock through a window for no apparent reason, cyber criminals engage in hostile acts that cannot possibly benefit them financially. They perform them indiscriminately, without even the excuse of revenge or political advantage. They are gaining, at someone else's expense, an inappropriate opportunity for self-expression. The types of hit-and-miss attacks carried out by self-replicating code frequently fall into this category. Perhaps it is the sheer Frankensteinian joy of creation that motivates some coders to develop and unleash software that is intended solely to destroy. Not all viruses are necessarily created to destroy, but by inserting themselves where they are neither wanted nor approved, they cross an unacceptable boundary. Some relatively benign viruses—

either through miscoding or mutation—exhibit harmful characteristics that their creators never anticipated.

During 1998, it became apparent that a new class of Windows malware was being spread—hostile remote control applications. Similar in functionality to commercial programs such as Symantec pcAnywhere, hostile code such as NetBus and Back Orifice is designed to facilitate convenient and invisible remote control of a Microsoft Windows system. The use of these programs is increasing, and while writing this book, we assisted with response efforts at several firms when Back Orifice was discovered on their internal corporate systems. Unlike Unix, which has a powerful command-line environment accessible through telnet and a windowing system (the X Window System) that is equally at home running over the console or on a network, Windows was designed to be used primarily through the console. Although telnet is possible, it isn't especially useful, and Microsoft's remote management solution, Systems Management Server (SMS), is not the same as actually logging onto a system. To gain remote access to a Windows system and run applications requires purchasing a third-party product, such as Symantec pcAnywhere or Citrix WinFrame. No doubt inspired and perhaps even challenged by the existence of these commercial programs, noncommercial programs were created that have the ability to totally control a Windows system over a network connection. What sets these noncommercial programs apart from their commercial counterparts is their built-in stealth capabilities. After they are installed on a system, they can be difficult to detect—indeed, these programs are intentionally difficult to find. Their creators have claimed that they are legitimate remote system administration tools and are not hidden from the user to any greater extent than Microsoft's own SMS remote administration tool. This may well be the case, and fortunately, it isn't an argument on which we have to take sides. Remember our definition of hostile code: if the system administrator doesn't want it and didn't authorize it, it must be considered hostile. If an instance of pcAnywhere or the SMS software is unexpectedly discovered on a system you are examining, you should consider it hostile and assume that someone is remotely accessing the system without the consent of the administrator. Furthermore, if the administrator explains that he or she prefers to remotely administer the systems using NetBus because it is cheap and efficient, it isn't your job to pass judgment on the choice of software suppliers. If the NetBus software is part of the standard distribution on the systems you are examining, you shouldn't be surprised to find it—in fact, in this case, if you *didn't* find NetBus, you should be suspicious.

Computers are created to increase efficiency, and criminals are just as interested in increasing the efficiency of their work as are forensic examiners. Both have specialized tools to facilitate gathering data without the authorization of their subjects. Data gathering is one of the marvelously efficient activities that hackers are increasingly performing through the use of automated software. As shown in Table 6-2, three basic types of hostile information-gathering software are used by

Table 6-2   Types of Hostile Information-Gathering Software

Method	Type	Characteristics
Vulnerability scanning	Externally directed Active	Maps network/locates hosts. Identifies characteristics of located hosts.
Sniffing	Externally directed Passive	Collects data visible over network segment. Hostile sniffers are usually application-specific, collecting logon/password pairs.
Data mining	Internally directed Active	Searches for specific data (often passwords) on a compromised host.

computer criminals: network scanning, network sniffing, and data mining, all of which can be either autonomous or interactive. Network-scanning software has been available since the early 1990s, although its significance wasn't really widely recognized until the release of SATAN (System Administrator's Tool for Analyzing Networks) in 1995. This category of software methodically probes a set of network addresses, determining if computers exist that use those addresses, and if so, whether they have any exploitable vulnerabilities. In contrast to vulnerability scanning, sniffing software is passive. A sniffer collects all of the network traffic visible to it on a specific network segment, which is often just what a network administrator needs to perform network diagnostics. Tcpdump is the most common sniffing software found on Unix systems, and it is often installed on Linux and BSD systems. While it is a tremendously useful diagnostic tool for the legitimate system administrator, it usually isn't an especially convenient tool for a remote attacker. Tcpdump can save huge amounts of data, but hostile sniffers are more selective, designed to filter extraneous data and save only specific types of data. An application-specific sniffer that targets a single type of private information is a more common sign of intrusion than Tcpdump. The most common form of hostile sniffer is the password sniffer, which collects logons and their associated passwords. This attack can be highly productive because the standard FTP and telnet protocols do not encrypt passwords. Passwords on Microsoft Windows networks are encrypted (using a one-way hash algorithm), but the encryption technique is easily broken, making it practical to collect information that is easy to translate into user name/password pairs.

In the fall of 1992, a notorious hacker called "Phantomd" was tired of the overhead of running password crackers and was looking for a more efficient way to exploit the newly developing Internet. A friend of his named "Jsz" came to his rescue with a new type of hacker tool—the password sniffer. Exploiting a bug in Sendmail, allowing him to gain root access, Phantomd stealthily inserted Jsz's spy code on systems that were able to access a significant part of the nascent Internet's backbone. He was eventually able to collect a 60MB collection of passwords, allowing him access to his choice of hundreds of thousands of Internet hosts.[1] Throughout the rest of the 1990s, hostile sniffers, planted on systems without the knowledge of their administrators, proved themselves to be highly effective, and they are still common on compromised systems. Table 6-3 shows a few examples of the many different sniffer programs that are available on hacker Web sites.

Internally directed data-gathering software is perhaps newer and much less prevalent, but it is more insidious. Running on a compromised host, internally directed malware methodically and invisibly searches for some specific data required by its creator. Again, like sniffing software, passwords are the most common objective. Since 1998, several examples of malware have been created that target America Online account passwords, mailing their booty out to a safe account where hackers can later retrieve it. In 1999, the Caligula MS Word virus appeared in the wild. A self-proclaimed "espionage-enabled virus," it searches for a victim's PGP key ring containing their encrypted private key, FTPing it to a virus Web site when successful. Access to other people's accounts is the most common goal of people who use

Table 6-3 Examples of Application-Specific Sniffers

Name	Purpose
PPTP sniffer	Sniffs passwords from Microsoft VPN sessions.
Readsmb Nthash	Sniffs passwords from Microsoft file- and print-sharing sessions.
Linsniff	Linux utility that collects passwords from FTP, telnet, rlogin, and email sessions.
Icq_sniff	Sniffs unencrypted passwords from ICQ sessions.
Web_sniff	Sniffs passwords from logons to password-protected Web pages.
Ebpd	eBay password daemon, sniffs eBay passwords (a more specific attack than web_sniff).

---

1. For more information, visit http://www.usnews.com/usnews/issue/970602/2crac.htm

espionage software, but malware can be used to steal many things besides passwords. Hostile software easily can be created that searches for any specific kind of data. Just like you may use your forensic software to search for every file containing specific keywords, so may an industrial espionage agent, private detective, or underage hacker in the employ of an information broker. Such directed attacks are currently rare to nonexistent but are technically feasible. Existing hostile code is often recycled for new purposes, so you should be aware of the possibility that you may someday encounter a password-stealing virus that has been modified to look for some specific form of business data, credit card numbers, or whatever else a cyber criminal thinks he or she can get away with.

Resource Theft

Cyber criminals usually don't have authorized and secure access to anything offering more processing power than a home PC. While they may have access to more powerful CPUs at work, if they have illegal purposes in mind, they may not want to run the risk of being discovered and losing their jobs. From a hacker's viewpoint, hacked computers on the Internet are the ideal place to run data-analysis tools—especially password crackers. These brute force decryption engines require huge numbers of CPU cycles to run, so clever hackers run them on someone else's system and avoid getting caught.

It isn't just CPU cycles—bandwidth is also vulnerable to theft. Computers belonging to large corporations, universities, and research centers, and especially those located at ISPs have access to high-speed Internet connections. This network connectivity is highly desirable to someone wanting to attack large numbers of computers—especially if he or she accesses the Internet through a dial-up connection. By installing the attack code on a system that has a high-speed Internet connection, a cyber attacker can perform attacks much more efficiently than from home.

Identity theft is potentially the most costly form of resource theft. CPU cycles and network access are increasingly less expensive, but electronic identities are *increasing* in value. Being able to masquerade as someone else means taking advantage of all their privileges and trust relationships. This has been dramatically illustrated to millions of people over the last several years by hostile code such as Melissa and messages with a more subtle subject than "ILOVEYOU," which arrive in your inbox with the return address of a trusted correspondent. It's no wonder that so many people double-click on the attachment and inadvertently execute these programs (the creators of this kind of malware use social engineering to exploit trust, which is a lot like what the Greeks did to the Trojans). In these cases, just originating a mail message with someone else's identity is advantageous to some attackers. In other cases, it is useful to run hostile code as if it were being run by someone else. This code then has all of that person's privileges and is able to view every file that the victim can view. Data-stealing code takes advantage of someone else's permissions. A third major advantage in stealing an identity is that it reduces the chances that the attacker will be caught. Any attempt to trace it points to an intermediate victim, not the actual attacker.

Bionic Men: Intelligent Agents

Internet bots (short for "robots") are like digital prosthetics. They are programs that provide extraordinary capabilities to human beings who are participating in virtual environments, such as online games and chat rooms. Able to respond automatically to events and "type" faster than a human being, bots can do things that a person cannot. In the context of a game, they can give a normal user "bionic" powers or can serve as a virtual team member. In an IRC chat room, bots are used to control the conversation. This is a normal function of the authorized system moderator, but a hostile moderator may prevent legitimate users from participating. Bots are very common on compromised Internet Unix systems, not only providing control over a specific application, but in many cases, providing remote control root access over their victims. If they are not owned by a legitimate chat moderator, they are probably hostile.

It is common to find that systems are hosting unauthorized bots, and sometimes complete chat rooms have been installed without the permission of the system administrator. Those who need a place to park an IRC or game bot, or need a place to run a chat room or game, may compromise a system just so they can use it for their hobby. We once helped a small software firm recover from a fatal hack. Sometime after their Unix administrator left the company, someone discovered an unauthorized chat room running on the e-commerce server that was the firm's only source of sales revenue. When the inexperienced replacement administrator tried to kick off the hacker and his chat buddies, the hacker retaliated and sabotaged the Unix configuration, making it impossible for the firm to reboot their server. Given that they no longer had any Unix talent, they completely replaced their Internet server with one running Windows NT, and placed it behind a firewall we installed.

Denial-of-Service

Aesop wrote a fable about a dog in the manger. The canine carnivore had no use for hay, but he wasn't willing to let the ox have any either. The ox was later heard to comment something along the lines of "Oh well, people often begrudge others things that they themselves cannot enjoy." Cyber denial-of-service attacks are just the latest manifestation of this human behavior wryly commented on in the ancient fable. Electronic communication mechanisms of all types have suffered under denial-of-service attacks. The government of Cuba continues to deny its citizens access to

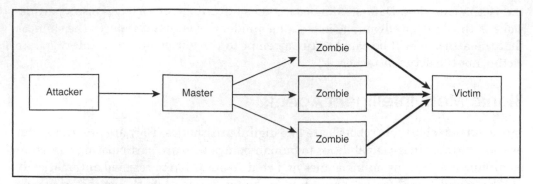

Figure 6-1   A distributed denial-of-service attack

Radio Marti broadcasts by jamming its signals, an attack similar to the smurf and fraggle denial-of-service attacks that can bring a TCP/IP-based LAN to its knees.

The Internet has been hit with many denial-of-service attacks over the last half of the 1990s, but the recent distributed denial-of-service (DDoS) attacks launched against several prominent Web sites in early 1999 are especially relevant to forensic analysts who are investigating host-based attacks because most of the hostile code required to perform the attack is found on intermediate victim hosts. DDoS attacks are coordinated hits by multiple hosts against a single target (see Figure 6-1), making it impossible for the end victim, a Web server, to accept connection requests from legitimate users.

A single attacker can perform a DDoS attack without assistance by leveraging multiple victims, called *slaves* or *zombies,* each of which runs a denial-of-service program installed by the attacker. To complicate tracing the origin of the attack (or *traceback*), the slaves are controlled by a master program running on another compromised victim. Insertion of the zombies is facilitated by running sophisticated automated attack software on the master system that searches for vulnerable hosts and automatically installs the zombie daemon on as many as several thousand machines in a day. These attacks, going by names such as Stacheldraht, Trinoo, and Tribe Flood Network (TFN), have tended to use Unix hosts as carriers for the zombies, but at least one Windows NT version has been discovered (more can be expected; vulnerable home systems with high-speed access through cable or Asymmetric Digital Subscriber Line (ADSL) are tailor-made for DDoS attacks). Detection of these agents from within the compromised hosts themselves may be exceedingly difficult for the victim. As described in Chapter 10, Unix rootkits can make it impossible for the system administrator to see hostile code—including DDoS agents—using the utilities on the compromised system. The listening network session, and certainly any outgoing sessions, normally are visible with netstat, but not if netstat has been trojanized to ignore it. Commercial network intrusion detection systems

(IDS) have been updated so that they can see control sessions from the masters to the agents, but don't count on every network-based IDS catching every new form of DDoS. Several detection utilities have been created for both Unix and Windows, and links to the most up-to-date versions of these detectors can be found on the SANS Institute Web site.[2] On Windows systems, antivirus (AV) software normally can locate malware, but if the process is actually running, it complicates identification and removal, so you should check with your AV vendor to see what the product limitations are.

Bombs Away

Logic bombs and time bombs are sabotage programs that are installed by a disgruntled insider, altering and usually destroying data. The different terms refer to the two different triggering mechanisms. A logic bomb is launched when a specific event or event sequence occurs. A time bomb is launched at a specific date and time. Typically, a system administrator installs a logic bomb as an unauthorized job protection system. The triggering mechanism periodically checks to ensure that the administrator still has an active account or is otherwise active. If the administrator is ever fired, the bomb automatically triggers without human intervention. A time bomb may be used to extract ransom, forcing a victim to pay in order to disarm the bomb.

All bombs are one-offs.[3] You won't recognize a bomb by name, nor can AV software find it. Sabotage bombs are created by trusted insiders to work in specific circumstances. They are often incorporated as hidden subroutines within custom software, and during the Y2K scare, it was commonly believed that contractors fixing creaky old COBOL accounting programs were sneaking in logic bombs. So far, no Y2K bombs have been reported. As long as the bomb didn't delete itself, one way to determine if a time-actuated bomb is being used is to turn back the system clock (on the copied image of the victim system, of course) and see if the system returns to its normal functioning. In one case we investigated, every time the client's computer clock reached the time set in a time bomb, the program started deleting files. We resolved the problem by turning back the clock and then removing the hostile code.

The term *bomb* is sometimes used to describe denial-of-service attacks, such as *pager bombs* that send large numbers of bogus messages to a specific account, or *icq bombs* that force a chat user to stop using his or her client. *Mail bomb* is a term used in the 1980s to describe hostile code imbedded in an email message that "blows up."

---

2. http://www.sans.org/newlook/resources/IDFAQ/trinoo.htm

3. One-offs are bombs custom created by the person who sets them and are normally not found on hacker bulletin boards. No two bombs look alike.

Hiding the Trail

The purpose of this book is to help you read the tracks left by computer criminals. It shouldn't be surprising that some computer criminals use specialized software to hide those tracks. Computer operating systems are designed to maintain records and logs of events that are relevant in troubleshooting and security. Those engaged in hostile or illegal activities prefer that system log entries associated with their activities didn't exist. In Chapter 5, we discussed techniques and tools used to conceal information for later retrieval. When a computer criminal uses these techniques and tools, the criminal is protecting the privacy of his or her own data. When a computer criminal covers his or her tracks, the criminal is not concealing data; he or she is removing or obscuring it to change its meaning. The hostile code used by system attackers to cover their tracks results in a loss of integrity or availability of information that belongs to the system administrator. As described in Chapter 10, many different utilities are available that selectively delete log records on Unix systems, and they are just beginning to appear for Windows NT. Such utilities really don't have a legitimate purpose, and their unexplained presence on a system is a sign that somebody is up to no good. Other activity hiding tools attack the integrity of filesystem data, allowing illegitimately substituted programs to appear to be the originals.

Horsing Around

The term *Trojan horse,* like the term *virus,* is overloaded with multiple meanings, which makes it difficult to discuss. We'll discuss several of these different meanings, so you'll be able to understand how the term is being used. It refers back to the story recorded by Homer recounting how the Greeks gained access to the besieged city of Troy through a clever deception. They built a huge wooden statue of a horse, secreted soldiers inside of it, left it sitting provocatively outside the walls of Troy, and then pretended to return to Sparta, thumbing their noses at the Trojans by making it clear to them that the Greek horse was way too big to fit into *their* city. The Trojans, undoubtedly feeling lucky at the unexpected departure of the Greeks, quickly rolled the alien horse through the gates of their city. At night, the Greek soldiers crept out of the statue and unlocked the gates, providing their triumphant army access to Troy, which has never been the same since. Several features of this classic warfare archetype are significant to the concept of a virtual Trojan horse. The Greeks used deception, tricking the Trojans into doing something that they had no real need to do. Bringing a large statue into the city was not one of their business requirements, but it was such an appealing horse that they did it anyway. The victims actually infected themselves; it wasn't the Greeks who brought the hidden payload of Greek soldiers through Troy's security perimeter. To summarize the prototype story, it was a case of an attacker tricking a victim into breaching its own security perimeter with an unnecessary artifact that had a hidden malicious capability. The term *Trojan horse* is used in at least four different ways in reference to hostile code:

Perimeter Breach

This is the classical usage of the term, describing the placement mechanism and not the payload. Many computer attacks are deliberate deceptions designed to trick the victims into infecting themselves. Autonomous attacks in this category include the Melissa virus and I Love You/Lovebug worm, two different examples of self-replicating malware that exploited the identities of their victim, automatically sending mail from that victim to subsequent victims and tricking the victim into opening the hostile attachments that apparently originated from a trusted source. AV software vendors often use the term Trojan horse to identify multipart malware that is not self-replicating, but has both a deceptive purpose and infection capability, resulting in the insertion of a payload. For example, the SubSeven.Trojan sometimes arrives in the guise of a video clip, but it is actually a remote control application. Hostile code is often concealed within video games or screen savers, and the infection occurs when the victim runs the installation script or the executable itself. Just like the prototypical case, directed attacks can also use Trojan horses. In June 2000, it was widely reported that America Online (AOL) passwords had been compromised by hostile code that had been mailed to user support representatives. When the AOL staff members opened the attachments, the hostile code was within the security perimeter of AOL, allowing the attackers access to the confidential user passwords.

Masquerade

When a hostile executable is given the same name as a legitimate executable, the result is sometimes referred to as a *Trojan horse*. This technique is usually used to gain the privileges of whoever inadvertently executes the masqueraded code. It requires access to the system in order to plant the malware. In this case, the victim may be clumsy, but unlike the classical case, they are not being tricked into performing an unusual activity.

Modified

The adjective *trojanized* is commonly used to refer to legitimate system executables that are modified to have hostile intent. To maintain consistency with the online sources we reference, this book also describes this type of malware as having been trojanized. Just as in a masquerade, the attacker breaches the security perimeter, not the victim. Also unlike the classic Trojan, the malware has a legitimate name and gives every appearance of being approved software. A successful attack depends upon the skill of the perpetrator, not the gullibility of the victim.

Nonreproducing Autonomous Malware

Using the term *Trojan horse* to refer to nonreproducing autonomous malware is an unfortunate use of the term that greatly offends our sensibilities, but sometimes, any hostile code that does not reproduce is reffered to as a *Trojan horse*. This is inexact and misleading. Hostile remote control applications, such as Back Orifice, are often referred to as *Trojans* possibly because they allow an outsider to have surreptitious internal malware access, but any other form of introduced but hidden entrance could also meet this definition. Back Orifice and NetBus are often manually bundled into a Trojan horse as the payload, but once they have been inserted, the term *Trojan* provides no insight into the malware's purpose. It doesn't make much sense to name the cargo after its vessel.

Access Exploits

Some forms of hostile code are created to automatically exploit system weaknesses, thereby circumventing access controls. Software is used either because it is convenient or because the exploit steps are not practical for a human being to perform due to length or timing. Outside of password-guessing attempts (manual and automated), the most commonly attempted type of access control circumvention today is the *buffer overflow attack*. Many programs that respond to external requests are vulnerable to malformed input. If the input is larger than the data structure available to accept it, it may be possible to insert machine code that can subvert the intended purpose of the exploited program and invoke an unexpected external program like the shell. If successful, the attacker gains whatever privileges the running application has. Windows NT programs running as "administrator" and Unix programs running as "root" are the most desirable. Because buffer overflow exploits rely on machine-specific instructions, they must be customized for each target platform and application. Malware is available to provide enhanced privileges to users who have logged onto the system as normal users, but the most popular exploits are those that attack network services visible from the Internet. If successful, such a software-enabled attack provides the equivalent of logon access. On Unix platforms, name service (such as Domain Name Service, DNS, or Sun's Network Information Service, NIS), Sendmail (which supports SMTP), the lpd print daemon (supporting the Unix LPR remote printing protocol), and Web service (supporting HTTP) are common targets. Windows NT exploits usually attack Microsoft's Internet Information Service (IIS) Web server or third-party IIS add-ons.

Buffer overflow attacks have been recognized since the mid-1960s, and they continue to be possible because of poor coding techniques and systemic problems with the C programming language. Unfortunately, C makes little or no effort to protect its programmers from themselves. The assumption that most programmers under-stand the ramifications of what they are doing ensures that forensic analysts will have plenty of system compromises to keep them busy.

Vulnerability Scanners

Vulnerability scanners are somewhat controversial because they are so commonly used for both good and evil purposes. Given that system attackers have vulnerabil-ity scanners and that nothing can be done to prevent it, our recommendation is that those responsible for securing systems also use vulnerability scanners against their own systems to ensure that no weaknesses are visible to hackers. Like the slim jim tool used to break into cars, this is a category of tools in the gray area. Anyone per-forming security consulting or management has legitimate need for such tools (and we have need for them also).

The original vulnerability scanner is called iss. The creator of this command-line utility, Christopher Klaus, went on to found the Internet Security Systems firm, which makes a slick commercial version of this product called SAFESuite.

The first vulnerability scanner to capture the imagination of the Internet commu-nity—and much of the first world—was SATAN. With its provocative name and seem-ingly mysterious powers, it was no surprise that Dan Farmer's SATAN made it to the cover of more than one national magazine. One of the first tools of any kind to make effective use of a Web browser as a front end, it was slick and useful, but it was never really powerful enough for serious hackers. The reconnaissance tool of choice today is Nmap,[4] which can perform "stealth scans" that are difficult or impossible for most system administrators to detect (see *Network Intrusion Detection* by Stephen Northcutt for a complete explanation). Useful to both hackers and security assessors is Nmap's ability to perform "TCP/IP fingerprinting." The Internet protocol stack is sufficiently complex that virtually every implementation varies slightly, responding differently to connection attempts, especially those on obscure port numbers. By sending a variety of different connection attempts to a host, Nmap often can deter-mine not only its operating system brand and version, but often even its revision number. Nmap was originally available only on Unix, but a Windows NT version was introduced in 2000.

Another vulnerability scanner used by both black-hat and white-hat hackers is Nessus.[5] This Unix-based tool is a powerful scanner, and unlike the command-line

---

4. http://www.nmap.org

5. http://www.nessus.org

Nmap, it follows SATAN's lead with a convenient Web-based GUI. Many security experts feel it is superior to any commercial products, and it is completely free for the downloading. Certainly any of the commercial vulnerability scanners can also be used for illegitimate purposes, but their limited distribution and hefty licensing fees discourage it. A cyber criminal is much more likely to have a copy of Nmap or Nessus than a commercial product.

Cracking Programs

A number of programs are available that attempt to crack encrypted data, but the ones you are most likely to encounter on a compromised host are used to crack passwords. Cracking takes a lot of CPU cycles, but some of the available tools are surprisingly efficient—especially the password crackers. The two common approaches to password cracking are a methodical brute force method that systematically tries as many combinations of characters as you have the patience to wait for and the more effective method that uses lists of common passwords. These lists are referred to as *dictionaries,* and many of them are available on the same Web sites that provide the cracking tools (see the references at the end of this chapter). As discussed in Chapter 5, L0phtCrack is a highly efficient password attack program on Windows NT (note that the second character is a zero, a typical hacker visual pun, and note also that the developers of most cracking programs squeeze the word *crack* into the program names). Created by a semi-commercial group called L0pht Heavy Industries,[6] L0phtCrack is a powerful tool for gaining access to Windows systems. L0pht-Crack actually includes two capabilities: a convenient, application-specific sniffer that snags LanMan usernames and password hashes, and a powerful password cracker that operates against both the sniffed data or, when available, the SAM password database. The last time we tried it, we cracked our boss's password in under five seconds. Fortunately, its commercial license fee discourages casual use.

Windows 9X represents an especially vulnerable password architecture, storing myriad passwords in a way that makes it easy to capture them either through remote control applications or, more commonly, through physical access. Finding any of the programs listed in Table 6-4 should be a clue that someone probably is trying to crack passwords, although these cracking utilities are also useful to forensic examiners. These tools are hostile only when they are abused—they certainly have legitimate educational, law enforcement, and data recovery uses. The Cain program

---

6. The freewheeling gray hats at L0pht, http://www.l0pht.com, were merged into a security firm called @stake, http://www.atstake.com, in 2000.

Table 6-4   Examples of Password-Cracking Software

Name	Purpose
Gammaprog	Cracks passwords of Web-based email (Yahoo, Hotmail, etc.), and POP.
Hypnopaedia	Remotely connects to POP3 mail server and attempts to guess the password of a specific account.
John the Ripper	Popular Unix-based password cracker that can attack Unix, Kerberos, AFS (Andrew File system), and Windows NT passwords.
Mssqlpwd	Cracks Microsoft SQL Server passwords.
PalmCrack	Runs on Palm PDA and can crack Unix, NT and some Cisco router passwords
PGPPASS	Cracks PGP key rings (note that the Caligula virus is designed to steal PGP key rings, FTPing them from the victim's PC to a server on the Internet).
Slurpie	Unix password cracker designed to work in a distributed mode, so the cracking task can be shared by multiple machines (same concept as the commercial cracking tool from AccessData)
Webcracker	Remote brute force tool to crack for password-protected Web sites.
Aimpw	AOL Instant Messenger Password Cracker.
!Bios	Decrypts the passwords used in common BIOSes including IBM, American Megatrends, Award, and Phoenix.
Zipcrack PkCrack	Cracks encrypted ZIP or PKZIP files.
Cain	Anyone with access to Windows 9x can use Cain to locate and retrieve cached passwords in the registry or in .pwl files. This typically recovers passwords for logon, local and remote shares, screen savers, and dial-up. An associated remote agent called ABLE, when placed on a victim's machine, can be remotely accessed to collect passwords.

is a Windows-based program that must be installed on the machine it is directed against. It is impossible to use Cain locally without leaving tracks—something to keep in mind when you examine Windows systems that you think may have been abused by an unauthorized user. Other data-collection tools can run from a floppy disk and can pull weakly protected passwords from a Windows 9X machine without leaving any trace at all. Then the passwords can be decrypted on a separate machine using Cain or some other cracking tool.

AV Software

Conveniently, AV software locates many different types of malware—in spite of the name, AV isn't limited to just viruses. On Microsoft Windows platforms, AV software locates virtually all forms of autonomous malware and most of the potentially hostile remote control applications that you are likely to encounter. This means that on Windows machines, you can locate a high percentage of malware just by running AV software. You should carry at least two different AV products with you as part of your forensic toolkit, and make sure that the definition files are up to date. The definition files contain the patterns that the AV software uses to identify specific hostile code, and AV vendors update these files at least once a month, and more often when some especially egregious bit of malware manifests itself. By default, most AV scanners skip most data files, concentrating on .exe and .doc files. It is your job to be thorough, so when you are using AV software to examine a system, change the default configuration so that all files are scanned. This process requires a long time, but you won't miss any recognizable code.

AV vendors have little to differentiate their products and have become trapped in a numbers game, each claiming to identify tens of thousands of different examples of malware. While we don't want to minimize the risk posed by hostile code, we don't have to be concerned about actually encountering this many different species. The term *in the wild* is used to describe those relatively few examples that have actually managed to infect systems belonging to real people. For the better part of a decade, Joe Wells has maintained his "Wild List" of hostile code reported as being found in the wild. In early 2000, Joe's list evolved into a Web site sponsored by the WildList Organization International.[7] Their Web site is a good place to start researching specific examples of autonomous malware. Bear in mind that the list is dependent upon a limited number of reporters. While it is reasonable to accept the list as a good indication of the relative prevalence of specific malware on a monthly and historical basis, it is not an accurate measure of the absolute number of victims of any particular virus. The annual Virus Prevalence survey from the ICSA Labs,[8] a division of TruSecure, is a statistical study providing the best estimates of the worldwide hostile code infection rate.

---

7. http://www.wildlist.org
8. http://www.trusecure.com/html/tspub/index.shtml

Further Research

The universe of hostile code is large and growing. This brief introduction can help you understand the types of code that you may find, and we encourage you to do further research. AV software can recognize and identify most Windows-based malware, and the names of the malware are listed and described on AV vendor sites. Hostile code continues to evolve rapidly, and any information in this book on filenames, registry entries, and port numbers probably has changed. You need to use the Internet sites belonging to AV vendors, CERT, SANS, and dedicated individuals for up-to-date information on current threats. Malware for Unix is not as comprehensively documented, but you can still search for it by name on Internet search engines. One of the advantages of Unix malware is that it is usually distributed in source code form, making it easier for you to determine exactly what it does. Become familiar with exploit tool sites such as PacketStorm Communications[9] and rootshell.com[10] so you can access up-to-date references aiding in the identification of unknown code.

Malware Web Sites

Computer Virus FAQs: http://www.faqs.org/faqs/computer-virus/

http://www.rootshell.com/beta/exploits.html. Large set of exploits for multiple operating environments that you can browse by date and search by platform type and name.

http://www.packetstorm.securify.com/sniffers/. Lengthy annotated list of application and general-purpose sniffers, sniffer detectors, and antisniffer utilities.

http://www.packetstorm.securify.com/dirtree.html. Topical index of most comprehensive malware archive site.

http://www.packetstorm.securify.com/Crackers/. Lengthy annotated list of crackers and dictionaries.

The WildList Organization International, http://www.wildlist.org/

Back Orifice Resource Center, http://www.skyscraper.fortunecity.com/cern/600

The Back Orifice page, http://www.nwi.net/~pchelp/bo/bo.htm

AV Vendor Sites Containing Searchable Malware References

F-Secure Virus Description database, http://www.datafellows.com/v-descs/. Comprehensive malware list with descriptions that can be searched by keyword.

McAfee Virus Information Library, http://vil.nai.com/villib/alpha.asp

---

9. http://www.packetstorm.com

10. http://www.rootshell.com

AV Product Test Sites

Virus Bulletin 100% Awards, http://www.virusbtn.com/100

Virus Test Center, http://agn-www.informatik.uni-hamburg.de/vtc

Checkmark Information, http://www.check-mark.com/

ICSA certified AV products, http://www.icsa.net/html/communities/antivirus/certification/certified_products/

Chapter

7

Your Electronic Toolkit

A forensic investigator lives and dies by the tools he or she uses to gather, save, and process evidence. To be successful in this field, you must have a lot of tools. You aren't collecting these tools to store on a shelf somewhere. This is your Batman utility belt. These are the James Bond devices that you get from Q. Maybe we shouldn't encourage you to think of yourself as a superhero, but you should think of yourself as someone whose job depends on the successful use of specialized tools that normal people usually don't need.

Because computer forensics involves the identification, extraction, preservation, and documentation of computer data, you need software and peripherals to deal with computers. In this chapter, we discuss the programs and hardware that are most practical. An important aspect of the craft of forensics is making use of programs not necessarily intended for this purpose. We start with discussions of generic programs that have many nonforensic uses, and we will work our way toward programs specifically developed for forensics. You should be aware that there are some programs only available to law enforcement or government agencies, and because they aren't available to all of our readers, we won't cover them in this book.

Not everyone can justify buying an expensive single-purpose program that may never be used. Your boss may look doubtfully at your request for a program that he or she may consider an electronic version of the Junior G-Man Fingerprint kit—we know how you feel; we've been there. To help you overcome this obstacle, we begin our discussion of forensic tools with several programs that you can sell your boss on that have everyday uses besides their forensic uses.

Be Prepared

Let's first review the difference between running forensic software locally on the suspect host or on a dedicated machine. The "forensically sound" method is to never conduct any examination on the original media. There are practical and legal reasons for not performing the examination on the suspect PC, but sometimes, you have to compromise. You're going to be presented with workstations that purportedly contain hostile code, and you're going to be asked to investigate hacked Web servers—and you're not always going to have the luxury of making a verified copy of the hard drive that you can examine from the safe environment of your forensic system. Because so many investigations are conducted under compromised circumstances, this chapter includes techniques to help you run forensic tools directly on suspect hosts. This does not mean that we recommend this practice—it is merely our recognition of the reality of forensic investigations.

Before using any program for forensics, you should first verify that the software does what you expect it to do. It is too late to learn how to use your software tools after an incident occurs. You must verify exactly what your tools do, whether the output can be trusted, and how to operate the tools. Practice, practice, practice! It is very important for you to know whether or not any of your tools are going to store data—temporarily or permanently—within the filesystems that they are examining. Testing for this behavior is a perfect opportunity for you to practice an important investigation technique. As we discuss in Chapter 4, you need to constantly verify the integrity of the data that you are examining, and the way to do so is by creating a cryptographic hash value from the media both before and after it is examined. Maresware's Disk_crc[1] can assist you in this task. Although its default behavior is to create a Cyclic Redundancy Check (CRC) value, you can use the –h option to create an MD5 hash value of the entire physical drive. New Technologies International (NTI) has two programs, DiskSig and CRCMD5, that are included with their suite of forensic programs but can be purchased separately.[2] (For those comfortable with Unix, Chapter 11 includes suggestions on free MD5 utilities.)

To verify the safe operation of a forensic tool, you need a hard drive with some data on it that is relevant to the type of tool you are testing (obviously, this drive should be one you use in your laboratory and not an evidence drive). Create an MD5 sum by running your hash utility on the entire hard drive. Save the resulting cryptographic hash sum and then use the tool that you are verifying against the data on that disk. When you are finished, run the MD5 utility again to see if the hard drive's hash value is the same. If it has changed, you know for certain that your examination utility will contaminate your data in some way. How do you determine what changes it made? The test we just did doesn't have enough granularity, so we'll have to run a different test. Use of a file level tool, such as CRCMD5, can show that no changes were made while using your tools, or it shows which, if any, files were changed.

---

1. http://www.dmares.com

2. http://www.forensics-intl.com

Hard Drive Tools

Partition-viewing utilities provide a big picture of the organization of the hard drives that are being examined. Fortunately, the default behavior on all the ones we're familiar with is to protect the user from inadvertent changes to partition information. Although fdisk is free on DOS, Windows, and Linux, this powerful but terse program makes it too easy to wipe out an entire partition. The old DOS version of fdisk isn't useful anymore because it won't identify the filesystem types that you are likely to run into, and the Windows 2000 version is so big that it won't fit on a single floppy disk. Our recommendation is to use a bootable Linux floppy disk or CD. The Bootable Business Card, which we discuss in Appendix F, can boot up just about any PC, and it has a version of fdisk that can identify dozens of different filesystems. Use of these tools requires some understanding of hard disk architecture, so we discuss the Partinfo and PartitionMagic utilities, both of which are somewhat easier tools to use for examining the partitions on a hard drive, in Chapter 3.

Viewers

A cyber investigator makes constant use of file viewers—such specialized data file-viewing utilities are more efficient than applications like Word. Their lack of editing and saving capability makes them small and fast, and you don't have to worry about them overwriting the data you are examining. One of our favorites is Quick View Plus.[3] QVP is handy for opening various files without having to import them into another application (see Figure 7-1). You might think that it's easy to open a Word file in WordPerfect, or vice versa, but imagine having a computer full of these files and having to convert each and every one of them. With Quick View Plus, which recognizes over 200 file types including PC, Unix, and some Macintosh formats, files are opened for viewing almost immediately. It is also useful for viewing various email formats such as .msg.

For Macintosh computers, Conversions Plus[4] enables you to view Macintosh application files on Windows operating systems. Although Quick View Plus can open some Mac files, Conversions Plus opens more of them. DataViz's latest suite, version 6.0, contains both MacOpener and Conversions Plus so with one suite, you have support for Mac, PC, and Unix files. Another nice feature of the DataViz suite is the ability to open email and attachments without having to copy or extract the attachment from the email message (see Figures 7-2 and 7-3).

---

3. http://www.jasc.com

4. http://www.dataviz.com

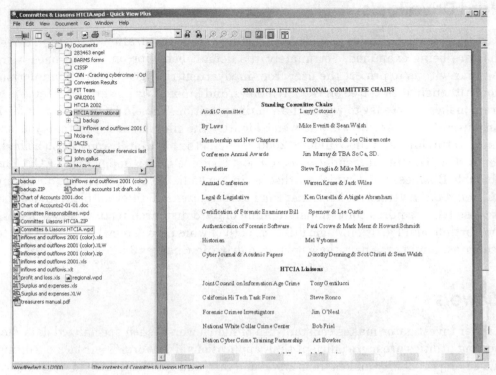

Figure 7-1 Quick View Plus

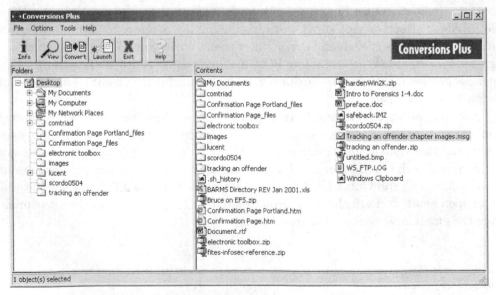

Figure 7-2 Conversions Plus opening an email message with an attachment

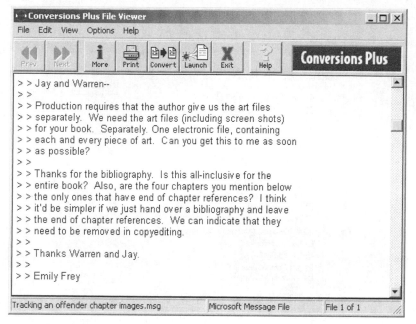

Figure 7-3   By clicking on View, both the email and the attachment (in this case, a Word document) are opened simultaneously.

ThumbsPlus

Many cases involve thumbing through stacks of images, looking for something incriminating or relevant. Most large firms complain about users who engage in unauthorized surfing of pornographic sites, and other types of cases involve graphic files—for example, when you suspect theft of intellectual property such as blueprints. Data relevant to that case might include product designs. Instead of having to go through all of the images one at a time on a large workstation or server, with ThumbsPlus,[5] you can pick a drive or directory, and the program catalogs and displays all the image files for you.

Before you use ThumbsPlus on a case, choose Options | Preferences to see the default settings. One important setting of interest is the File Types tab shown in Figure 7-4.

By default, many common formats are selected, but not every image type is selected. You may need to manually select the types of files that you want in this list, depending upon the system you are examining. You can try selecting all of them, but this often causes more harm than good because the program indexes audio files, and

---

5. Available at http://www.cerious.com, ThumbsPlus is distributed only online.

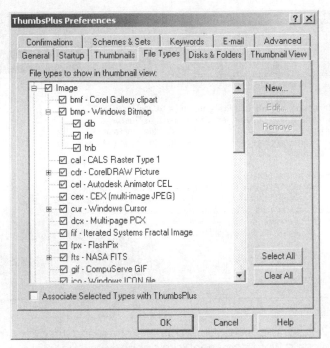

Figure 7-4 ThumbsPlus file types

every Windows PC contains quite a few .wav files. You also should be familiar with the Name Mask option on the File List tab. This option prompts for a filename mask (for example, *.gif). When you run a search, the program selects all files matching the mask and creates a ThumbsPlus database of images. If you decide to run another search, probably using a different mask, simply go to the Tools menu and create a new database. Give each search a different name, and you can quickly switch back and forth between them without having to rescan the target directory.

When you have no other choice but to perform a search on a "live" system, with some preparation you can usually run ThumbsPlus from your zip disk. To prepare a traveling version, attach your zip drive to your lab computer and install ThumbsPlus (you can't just copy the files to the zip disk—you must run the installer). When the installer asks you where you want to install the program, select the drive letter of your zip drive instead of the default C: drive (as shown in Figure 7-5).

ThumbsPlus should work just fine running from your zip drive, because it previously installed files in your Windows directory. After you've tested the installation, go to the Windows directory and sort by date to see which files were recently created. Copy them to your zip disk and try running ThumbsPlus on another machine (one that it is not loaded on already). You should be able to run it now solely from the zip disk, but if you get any error messages, write down the name of the file the program is looking for and copy that file from the machine you installed ThumbsPlus on. The files you need depend on the version of ThumbsPlus you are loading.

As you can see in Figure 7-6, ThumbsPlus displays a directory listing of the drive and you can visually scan a directory or the entire drive for relevant images.

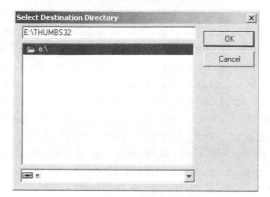

Figure 7-5   Select the location of your zip drive

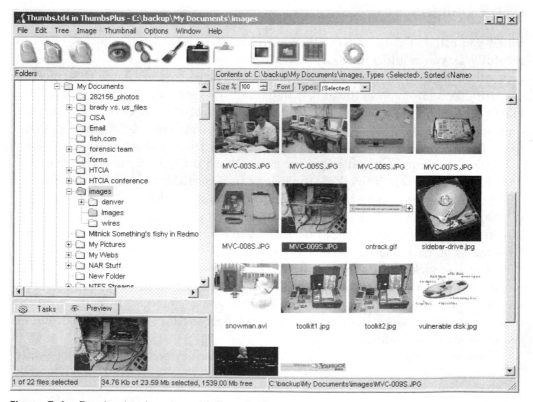

Figure 7-6   Previewing images with ThumbsPlus

Unerase Tools

Before Windows came with a Recycle Bin, a thriving market for unerase tools existed. One of the most popular of these was included with Norton Utilities, and for years, it was a staple tool for forensic analysis. A decade ago, a DOS disk with Norton Utilities Diskedit and Unerase was just about all you needed, but with today's high-capacity drives, it's no longer practical to manually thumb through every sector looking for deleted files that might contain useful evidence. Not only is it impractical for a gigabyte hard drive, but Norton Utilities does not support all the filesystems that you may encounter these days. Nevertheless, it is still a useful set of programs to bring with you because you don't know what you will encounter in the field. We still do investigations on Windows 3.x systems, and having older utilities at our disposal really comes in handy. On modern versions of Windows, and all versions of Unix, the unerase process is a bit more complex. If the file is no longer in the recycle bin, the special forensic tools we discuss later in the chapter are required. You never know what you will need, so bring everything.

CD-R Utilities

When you collect CD-Rs or CD-RWs as evidence, you must examine those CDs as carefully as you would a hard drive. Without special tools, you may not be able to view all of the data on a CD. To allow more efficient use of recordable CDs, modern operating systems support the ability to put multiple sessions on a single disk. This allows additional data—called a *new session*—to be written on CD-Rs that already have data on them. The files contained on earlier sessions may be completely invisible without the use of special software like CD-R Diagnostics.[6] Most CD writers now support a capability called *packet mode*. When a CD-R is correctly formatted and the packet driver is invoked, the drive can be written to like any other drive. Normally, special disk-mastering software is required to create a CD in a mode that is essentially batch mode. Packet mode conveniently allows any application to write directly to the CD. Such CDs can be written to over a long period of time, but the CDs may not be readable on any other drive until the packet session has been closed. If you pick up CDs during an investigation and they have unclosed packet mode sessions on them, you may not be able to read them. The developers of CD-R Diagnostics do not *guarantee* that the software can enable you to read every CD with an unclosed packet session, but they do suggest that most such CDs will be readable with their software.

If you were to look at a CD-R using Windows, you may see something like Figure 7-7, which shows session number 001002_1542 with the forms directory. When we

---

6. http://www.cdrom-prod.com/software.html

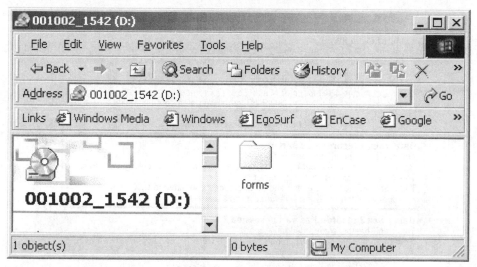

Figure 7-7   Multisession CD viewed with Windows Explorer

look at the same CD-R using CD-R Diagnostics (see Figure 7-8), we see another session, 001002_0859 with the Book directory that contains over a hundred megabytes of files (apparently an upcoming text on computer forensics). This data is hidden completely when only standard Windows or DOS features are used to view the CD's directory.

If your investigation includes information taken from writable CDs, your reports should include technical data to substantiate what you found, or what you did not find. If a CD-R or CD-RW has only one session on it, your report should document that fact also. This is easy to do with CD-R Diagnostics. It doesn't directly provide a report file, but you can cut the results of its diagnostic analysis from a window and paste it into your report (see Figure 7-9).

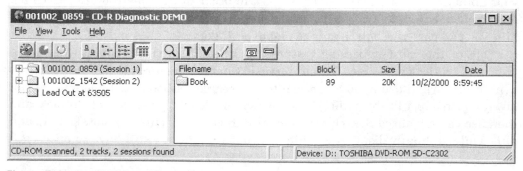

Figure 7-8   Multisession CD viewed with CD-R Diagnostics

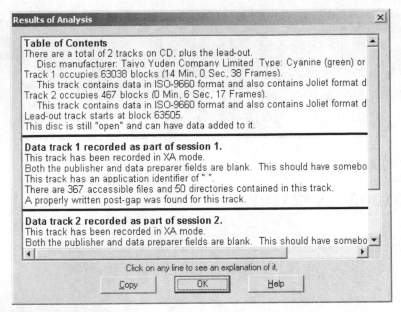

Figure 7-9   Data about the CD can be copied and pasted into your reports.

Text Searches

The developers of dtSearch[7] claim it can instantly search gigabytes of text. While this claim might be an exaggeration, after you've taken the time to allow dtSearch to create an index—and it works with all popular file types—the searches are blindingly fast. Fishing expeditions are easier with features such as fuzzy searches, which can find words even when they are misspelled, and a built-in thesaurus that can be used to automatically include synonyms in a search. Capabilities such as this make it more likely that you'll find relevant files than if you are relying solely on your ability to guess exactly which words will occur in the files you are searching. After you've entered search parameters and dtSearch has found a list of relevant hits, you can page through the files using hyperlinks.

One of the most appealing features of dtSearch is the capability to search Microsoft Outlook's .pst files. If your forensic workstation already has Outlook, you don't necessarily have to buy a special tool to search Outlook mail folders. You can always open a .pst file by adding it as a personal folder in your copy of Outlook, and then use the Advanced Search tools included in Outlook. This is a slow search, and after Outlook finally displays the hits for your search, you still have to open each

7. http://www.dtsearch.com

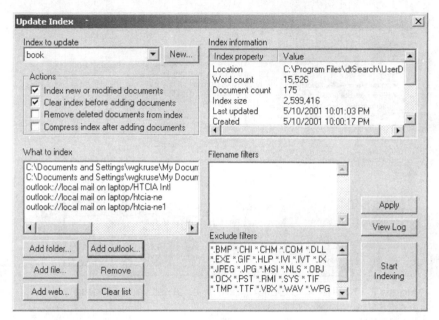

Figure 7-10   dtSearch uses a configurable word index to enhance search speed.

message and process it manually. As shown in Figure 7-10, dtSearch creates an index of every word on the hard drive. Once created, this index greatly speeds up keyword searches, and it can also be displayed for manual review. You can specify words relevant to your case, and dtSearch takes you to those words in the index. With dtSearch, the time it takes to analyze a .pst file is greatly reduced, and searches are much more likely to find the information you need.

The following steps are required, and they aren't fully documented in the version we used most recently:

1. Create an index if you do not already have one.
2. Click the Add Outlook button (see Figure 7-11).
3. Select the folder or folders contained in the .pst file (as shown in Figure 7-12).
4. Select Update Index from the menu that appears.
5. In the Update Index dialog box, click Add Other.
6. Choose Message Store in the dialog box that pops up and click Browse.
7. Select the profile for which you want to index messages.
8. Click OK and then click OK again to start indexing.

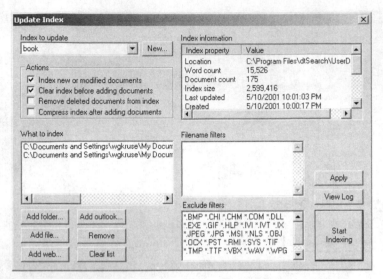

Figure 7-11   The Add Outlook button enables you to index Microsoft Outlook .pst files.

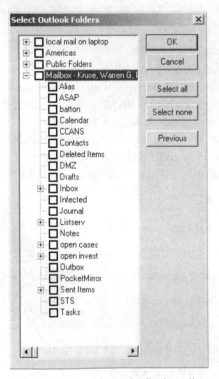

Figure 7-12   dtSearch displays the folders within the .pst file so you can select the ones you want to index.

After the index is created, you can run searches against it. Because the search is looking only in the word index and doesn't have to access each individual file, the responses are almost instantaneous. This is extremely helpful if you are looking for that proverbial needle in a haystack. You can perform several searches in a fraction of the time that the Find feature in your email program requires. You also have the advantage of being able to search for synonyms and using fuzzy logic during your search—once again, two important features not available in an email program. One of the major weaknesses of doing a keyword search with a normal email program is that you will miss synonyms and misspellings. dtSearch solves this problem by providing a built-in dictionary that optionally allows you to search automatically for synonyms of your keywords. It also has a fuzzy logic function that can find words which are similar to those that you are searching for but not spelled exactly the same way. Functioning equally well against both email folders and text files, these are very powerful and useful capabilities for an investigator. Figure 7-13 shows the results of a search against the keyword "forensic." Note that each hit is scored in the second column, and by default the results are ranked to show you which documents are most likely to contain the concept you are searching for.

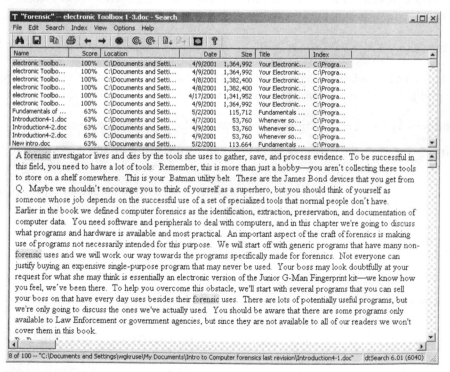

Figure 7-13 Search results for "forensic" after dtSearch created an index of My Documents.

Drive-Imaging Programs

If you create a backup of the target system with "normal" backup software, you will miss much of the hidden data located on the hard drive. Because a normal backup program backs up only individual files, it doesn't capture slack space, unallocated areas, and swap files. Only a software package capable of creating an image of the entire drive, bit for bit, can ensure that you get all the data that you are interested in processing, such as deleted and hidden files.

Once you have a good backup, you can always "go back to the tape" and restore the image on your analysis machine, and of course, several copies are required for court cases. Suitable imaging programs include

- SafeBack (http://www.forensics-intl.com)
- SnapBack(http://www.cdp.com)
- Ghost (http://www.symantec.com)
- dd (a standard utility found in every Unix distribution)[8]

To use Ghost for a forensic backup, try the following (courtesy of Mark Menz of Kroll):

```
ghostpe.exe -afile=a:\ghost.err -fro -id -z9 -ws- -autoname -split=600
```

This command sets Ghost to perform a sector-by-sector copy into 600MB image files. An explanation of each of the options follows:

-afile=a:\ghost.err	Enables creation of a log file (ghost.err) on a floppy disk.
-fro	Forces the program to continue imaging even when the source contains bad clusters.
-id	Forces Ghost to copy the boot track, extended partition tables, and unpartitioned space, all areas that must be reviewed during your forensic analysis.
-z9	Sets the compression level.
-ws	Disables disk caching on the source disk (which is critical).
-autoname	Automatically creates sequential names for the created image files.
-split=600	Splits the image file into 600MB files that can be archived to CD-R.

---

8. Instructions on the use of dd as a drive-imaging tool are found in Chapter 11.

To restore the Ghost image, type the following:

```
ghostpe.exe -fnf
```

The -fnf flag disables the creation of a fingerprint during the restoration process.

Disk Wiping

Before you restore the image to an analysis drive for forensic analysis, you must ensure that the drive doesn't contain remnants of data. Simply formatting the drive is not sufficient. Some programs are specifically designed to systemically write data to each and every sector of a hard drive. Obviously, you first need to ensure that you are wiping the correct drive. We disconnect any other drive from our forensic computer and connect only the drive we want to wipe. We then boot off a DOS floppy disk and run DiskScrub from NTI.[9]

Forensic Programs

The unique requirements of computer forensics have resulted in the creation of special software designed to either collect relevant data or to analyze that data in order to find information related to a specific case. The trend is for forensic software suites to provide utilities that can both collect and analyze data. In the following sections, we discuss several products that each provide a different approach to the automated examination of a computer crime scene. The good news for the investigator is that interest in such products is heating up the market, and in a competitive market, vendors are going to introduce more features more quickly. As an investigator, you should always approach every purported marketing "fact" with a healthy skepticism, testing the product to your own satisfaction. Given that professional attitude, you don't need us to point out that highly competitive vendors are prone to positioning their product as the optimum product for your needs. It is our experience that no single product can do everything, and that the more tools you have, the more likely you are to find that obscure bit of data that can make your case. Be skeptical about software vendor claims, and enjoy the benefits of a competitive marketplace.

Forensic Toolkit

Forensic Toolkit[10] is a set of command-line utilities helpful in reconstructing access activities in a Windows NT filesystem. Some of the programs included are

---

9. http://www.forensics-intl.com/thetools.html
10. http://www.foundstone.com/rdlabs/tools.php

AFind   Provides a list of files by their last access times, and it does not change the directory's access times.

HFind   Scans a disk for files that either have the hidden attribute set or use Windows NT's directory and system attributes to hide files.

SFind   Scans an entire disk for hidden data streams. As described in Chapter 5, data streams are a feature of Windows NT that are sometimes exploited to hide information.

FileStat   Reports all of the attributes of a single file. The following is an abbreviated example of its output:

```
C:>filestat ntobjectives.txt
Dumping ntobjectives.txt...
Extra AceFlag bits  == 0x00000010 <-This is a problem,
                                     should be all 0s

SD's SACL is Not Present
Stream name = a Size: 4608
Creation Time - 07/05/1999 21:22:26
Last Mod Time - 07/05/1999 21:22:26
Last Access Time - 03/01/2000 22:25:47
Main File Size - 4608
File Attrib Mask - Arch
```

The vendor has several other powerful command-line utilities that are not part of the Forensic Toolkit for NT. NTLast is essentially a Windows NT version of the Unix last command. To help correlate logon times with events, it provides two capabilities that are not part of the standard GUI-based event viewer. NTLast includes both the logon and logoff times for each session, and it indicates whether the logon was remote or interactive.

The Coroner's Toolkit

Designed by Dan Farmer and Wietse Venema, The Coroner's Toolkit (TCT) is designed primarily to investigate a hacked Unix host. It offers tools with useful investigative capabilities that are available nowhere else. Before beginning our discussion of TCT, it is important to point out that it wasn't designed to collect evidence that has traditionally been useful in a court of law; it was designed to help determine what happened on a compromised network host. Some of the unique capabilities it provides are difficult to explain to nonspecialists, and the fact that they must be run on the compromised host itself might be viewed as compromising the evidence. If you understand how the various TCT components work and what they do, you can determine their appropriateness for any particular investigation.

The most unusual feature of TCT is its ability to analyze activities on a live host and capture current state information that would be impractical to capture manually. As discussed in Chapter 11, a running system contains a great deal of volatile information that isn't necessarily on the hard drive and disappears in a short amount of time. Accessing this information is the best way to know what kinds of unauthorized activities are taking place and may well be the only way to find out what is happening on a particular system and where attacks are originating. The front-end tool grave-robber collects a huge amount of information on running processes, network connections, and the contents of hard drives. The data is collected roughly in the order of volatility (a concept introduced by Farmer and Venema and expanded on in Chapter 11). Collecting all that data is a slow process and can easily take several hours. If you decide to shut down an apparently compromised system, grave-robber is still useful, but the data it collects on running processes, of course, does not provide any information about what was happening before the shutdown. Before actually using it on a real investigation, compile TCT versions for your relevant environments first, and practice in your lab. Pay special attention to the numerous options for grave-robber. The optimum way to run grave-robber is to collect just the volatile data on a live system, shut down the system, image the drive, and then use grave-robber's –f option against a copy of the filesystems. Only a few of the options are invoked through the command line, but you can change the program's behavior quite a bit by editing text files. You don't have to be a Perl programming guru to do so, although it would help if you are one or know one.

The mac utility is automatically run by grave-robber, or you can run it standalone. We suggest that you keep a copy on your forensic CD. It collects a chronologically sorted list of the modify/access/change times for each inode, along with their associated filenames, which is a great analysis tool that facilitates the correlation of system activities with filesystem access. mac can be applied to any filesystem, so you don't have to run it on the suspect host—you can run it against a filesystem image in your lab.

TCT also includes a set of tools used to recover deleted Unix files. More accurately, it contains a tool to attempt to reconstruct coherent data from a stream of bits, and it includes a tool for the Unix environment to create such a stream of bits from a filesystem. The unrm utility is a Unix tool that creates a single object containing everything that is within all the unallocated space on a filesystem, which can be a *huge* amount of data. Do *not* collect the output on the same filesystem that you are analyzing—you will write over your own data. The more free space on a filesystem (the value reported under available when running df), the larger the resulting object. Plan accordingly. Once you've created this object, the lazarus tool systematically analyzes the entire object, attempting to determine whether any particular point within it is text or binary. It is a clever analysis, and it gets more detailed, eventually creating a "data map" showing the kinds of data lazarus thinks it has found. Pioneers in the use of Web browsers to create front-ends to analyze tools, Farmer and Venema have continued that pattern with lazarus, providing an option to output its results in Hypertext Markup Language (HTML) summaries that are linked to the actual recovered data. Be aware that large files are probably not contiguous, and lazarus has no way to connect the separate chunks, even if it does correctly identify them as being recovered data.

We found the beta version of lazarus simple to use and more effective than we expected when we tested it on a scavenged PC. Originally running Windows 95, the system had been repartitioned before we installed RedHat Linux to use the machine as a TCT test system. As described in Chapter 11, we used dd and netcat to copy an image of one of the filesystems over our lab LAN to our analysis machine. unrm operates on entire filesystems, so it wasn't necessary to use mount—we just ran unrm against the filesystem image, making sure that we redirected the output to a filesystem with enough room. Then we started lazarus –h and left for lunch. When we returned, we were able to use a Web browser to thumb through an astounding variety of text files (see Figure 7-14). It included email that had been exchanged

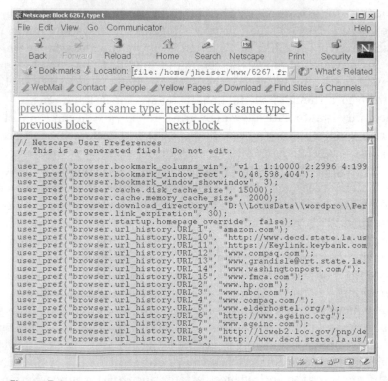

Figure 7-14 Data recovered with lazarus can be viewed with a Web browser.

several years earlier, and it provided all the clues we needed to know which applications the original Windows 95 user had been running on that old Pentium 125. As you can see from this account, lazarus doesn't necessarily have to be applied against data from a Unix filesystem. It often can make coherent any stream of bits, including kernel and memory images, or filesystems from non-Unix operating systems. Linux (or BSD) on a PC is a good laboratory environment, and lazarus is just another one of the tools that can be used effectively on a Unix variant to analyze data from other types of systems.

At the time of this writing, TCT had just ended its beta period and several minor patches for the first version had been developed. It is open source software that compiles easily on supported platforms. The makefile currently is configured only for Sun and the common open source Unix variants. While these operating systems probably constitute the majority of Unix systems used for Internet hosts, if the software becomes more popular, someone will undoubtedly tweak it so that it can be installed on other environments. The source code, documentation, and some brief tutorials are available on Dan Farmer's Web site.[11]

ForensiX

ForensiX is the best evidence we can provide that Linux is a powerful and convenient operating system for the investigation of computer-related events. Created by Dr. Fred Cohen,[12] who gained fame in the computer security world as an expert in hostile code, it is an all-purpose set of data collection and analysis tools that runs primarily on Linux. ForensiX really comes into its own on a dedicated platform with appropriate hardware—the more different types of hardware you throw at it, the more it can deal with—including specific support for hard drives, floppy drives, tapes, CD, and Jazz drives. Any supported media you feed it can be quickly imaged, MD5-checked, and logged into a case database. This is effectively a batched operation, which really facilitates the imaging of a stack of floppy drives. In addition to a wide choice of source hardware, you also have a choice of destinations to store the images including hard drive, CD, and tape.

Linux might well support a greater number of filesystems than any other OS, and ForensiX takes full advantage of this flexibility, offering the automated ability to mount images or media in dozens of different filesystems. Filesystem mounts are read-only to protect the contents against inadvertent change. Once a filesystem or image is mounted, you can perform searches for a simple string, or you can perform a more complex Boolean operation that includes proximity searches. A number of

11. http://www.fish.com/tct

12. Fred Cohen's Web site, www.all.net, not only includes information on ForensiX, but also has a number of informative and thought-provoking information security essays written by Dr. Cohen.

plugins are included that contain a dozen different search profiles for drug-related terms. A graphics file capability automatically searches images and displays bitmaps. The direct image analysis treats an entire image as one object, so it can find data in slack spaces, but it is, of course, not as convenient as the file-based search. A skilled investigator uses both types of searches. Most of the functions are accessed through a GUI, as shown in Figure 7-15.

ForensiX has several unusual capabilities, such as a function to check a Unix system for known vulnerabilities. It also has the means to build a baseline picture of a filesystem, store the hash values and filenames, and then compare the baseline to other filesystem images. This feature can be used to analyze the image of a Unix system, for example, to see if it contains trojanized binaries. Webtrace is a set of network searches that automatically research domain names on the Internet, doing some of the legwork necessary for network forensics (see Chapter 2). Other network functionality includes the ability to create and analyze TCP dumps.

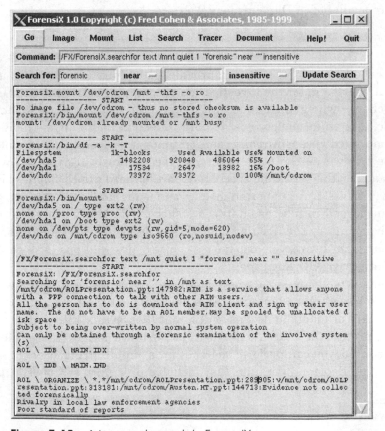

Figure 7-15   A keyword search in ForensiX

While it was not available for review at the time of this writing, a tool that Dr. Cohen is testing identifies application and data files that don't match their file types, and he is working on another utility that identifies stegoed files. As we discussed in Chapter 5, finding such files is critical in determining whether a suspect computer contains hidden data.

On the downside, Dr. Cohen's firm is relatively small, although bug fixes are returned promptly. Lacking the accoutrements of a more established software publisher, the manual for ForensiX consists of a set of slides available on the Web site. More detailed documentation would be helpful.

New Technologies Incorporated (NTI)

NTI[13] is one of the most established vendors of forensic software. They offer a popular hands-on training course that is taught by experienced forensic analysts, and class attendees are given a discount on products. A number of security service vendors have sent their staffs to NTI classes, purchased copies of their software, and hung out their shingles to provide analysis services.

Because NTI has implemented their software in the form of command-line tools, their products are fast. The individual packages are also small enough to fit on a floppy drive so that you can boot a computer into DOS and run the tools without changing or altering anything on the target system. We recommend using a zip drive, or other high-capacity removable media, when using the filelist program. The first time we used the software, we swapped floppy disks for what seemed like an eternity until the entire file list was finished. If we had used a zip drive, the long list of files would have all fit on one disk. The file list is created in dBASE III format, so it can be opened by virtually any database. NTI uses an application-based packaging scheme of sorts. You can purchase a suite of NTI utilities intended for your specific needs. The company provides custom software suites for incident response, corporate and government evidence protection, disk wiping, electronic document discovery, internal audit, and several other purposes. For example, here's the description of the tools contained in the incident response suite at the time of this writing:

- **CRCMD5:** A CRC program that validates the contents of one or more files.

- **DiskScrub:** A hard disk drive utility used to eliminate all data.

- **DiskSig:** A CRC program that validates mirror image backup accuracy.

---

13. http://www.forensics-intl.com

- **FileList:** A disk catalog tool that creates a list of the files on a system that is sorted by their last time of use, allowing an analyst to create a timeline of user activity on the system.

- **Filter_we:** An intelligent fuzzy logic filter for use with ambient data.

- **GetFree:** An ambient data-collection tool used to capture unallocated data.

- **GetSlack:** An ambient data-collection tool used to capture file slack.

- **GetTime:** A program used to document the CMOS system time and date on a computer seized as evidence.

- **Net Threat Analyzer:** Forensic Internet analysis software used to identify corporate Internet account abuses.

- **M-Sweep:** An ambient data security scrubbing utility.

- **NTI-Doc:** A documentation program for use in recording file dates, times, and attributes.

- **PTable:** A utility that is used to analyze and document hard disk drive partitions.

- **Seized:** A program used to lock and secure evidence computers.

- **ShowFL:** A program used to analyze the output of a file list.

- **TextSearch Plus:** A utility used to locate strings of text and graphic files.

These tools are intended either for gathering specific forms of evidence, such as partition tables or CMOS settings, or for the analysis of existing disk images. Some kind of image-capturing tool is also necessary, which is why NTI has purchased the company that makes SafeBack and now offers that disk-imaging tool.

EnCase

EnCase claims to be the only fully integrated, Windows-based forensic application, in contrast with NTI, whose product line consists of command-line tools. A GUI can increase your productivity, although forensic investigators can't be effective if they are limited to a single tool (or even a single family of tools). Like the NTI products, EnCase is widely used by both law enforcement and computer security professionals worldwide. EnCase requires a hardware dongle (a physical device, attached to the parallel port, that unlocks the program) to unlock the full package. Functions of this product include the following:

- Preview a volume

- Search (grep regular expressions and text searches)

- View disks

- View volumes
- Open a case
- Create an evidence file
- Save a case

EnCase uses a "case" methodology for the analysis of any and all drives or disks that relate to the same investigation. By creating an evidence file (EnCase refers to the image created with the EnCase DOS program as an *evidence file*) of all your original evidence media, you can add all the evidence files to a single electronic *case file* and conduct your searches on all the media at once. Without some sort of automated capability to search multiple images, a typical investigation involves manually searching each and every piece of evidence with the same search terms, over and over. Figure 7-16 shows the information that is filled in when a new case file is created. Such a "forensic" search may involve looking at each and every sector of the media, and an individual search can take days, depending on the speed of your computer and the size of the evidence media. Instead of waiting for one search to complete and then searching the next piece of media for the same case, you can search all the media that your case involves at once. That feature might not seem like a big deal, but consider a case that involves multiple computers and stacks of floppy disks.

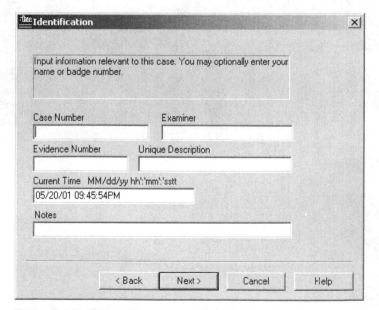

Figure 7-16   The evidence associated with each case is automatically tracked.

When you create a new case file, the program prompts you for information relevant to that case that will be included in the EnCase report. Throughout the program, you can save bookmarks to items of interest by right-clicking on the data you want to mark and then clicking on Add Bookmark. There is even a text area for your comments to remind you why you created the mark in the first place. Your bookmarks show up in the final report. In Chapter 1, we suggested that during an examination, you or a coworker document every single activity you perform during the investigation. The bookmark feature greatly reduces (but doesn't eliminate) the amount of notes you have to write. When you finish with your examination, you can right-click on the report and select Export to File. EnCase exports the report in rich text format (or RTF). You can then open the .rtf file in any word processor for additional notes and formatting.

Another useful feature of EnCase is the image viewer depicted in Figure 7-17. With most other forensic programs, you have to locate the images, recover the deleted ones, save them to external media, and then open them in yet another program for viewing. EnCase eliminates the middleman by enabling you to sort through the

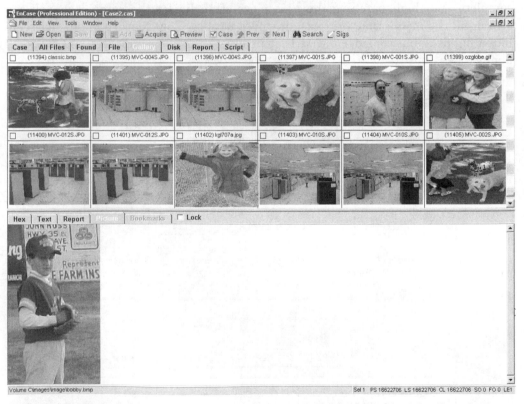

Figure 7-17 EnCase image viewer can help you quickly evaluate a subject's activities.

pictures, select the ones you want to view, and then click on preview images to actually view them.

Another convenient feature is the ability to perform regular expression searches on the evidence. This feature comes in handy especially when you are trying to locate numbers, such as phone, social security, and birth date, to identify your suspect. You can perform a regular expression search (using the same format as you use with the Unix grep command) such as ###-##-#### to find any numbers that are three digits, then a dash, then two digits, a dash, then four numbers—a social security number. The search can run in the background so that you can explore evidence while the search is running. We like to kick off our search and then manually check in the My Documents directory, the recent directory, and other directories with names such as "private," "Joe's stuff," "cool stuff," and so on. Evidently, some people think that their data is safe by putting it in directories with such names. Maybe they think we would skip those directories, but they are the first places we look. Depending on the size of the evidence, you may have some hits at this point so you can go to the Search view and look at the results thus far. We like to take a look after we get a decent number of hits to gauge the effectiveness of our search terms. If we have too many false positives and no legitimate data we might think about stopping the search, altering the search terms, and then rerunning it.

In Chapter 5, we discussed the need for identifying anomalous files, such as those with an extensions that doesn't match their actual data types (see Figure 7-18). EnCase calls this capability "File Signature Identification and Analysis," offering an automated and updateable tool that returns a list of suspicious files that appear to be attempts at hiding data.

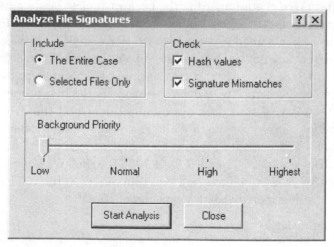

Figure 7-18   File type anomalies are automatically located in a background search.

Encase is a product of Guidance Software. In addition to a variety of forensic tools, they also offer training. Encase version 2.0 is available in two packagings: Standard and Professional. As of this writing, version 3.0 is due to be released shortly and promises faster image acquisition, faster searches, and additional Unix support.

Hardware

Along with software, you may need to purchase some hardware to conduct your forensics. When you start a forensics investigation service, you'll probably have to make do with existing equipment for awhile. This means that the cover for your computer is probably leaning against a wall and will never be screwed back onto your computer again. To make swapping hard drives easier, and to keep your computer's cover where it belongs, you may want to purchase several removable hard drive kits. A kit is mounted into a hard drive bay in the front of the computer for easy access to swap out the drives. If you don't think you need a removable tray, consider all the changes you'll make for just one investigation: you'll connect the evidence drive as a slave to boot off your operating system to acquire your image. Then you'll remove the evidence drive for safekeeping and mount your analysis drive to restore the image. You'll then remove the analysis drive for your next investigation. You can purchase a plastic kit for about fifteen dollars, but because you'll be swapping drives and pulling the tray in and out, the rails on the side of the tray wear down quite fast, and once they do, the tray may not line up properly with the connector on the removable kit. We recommend spending a few more dollars and getting a removable metal kit. You can buy metal kits on the Web.[15]

The next vital piece of equipment is the backup device. Many options are available, so when purchasing a backup device, consider the types of drives you may encounter. You most likely need to examine both IDE and SCSI drives, so a unit that only does IDE drives may not be appropriate. Don't forget that hard drives keep getting bigger. Hard drives are currently transitioning from gigabyte to terabyte size, and at the time of this writing, 10GB drives are considered inappropriately small for new PCs. A backup device that does not handle the size of the drives you will be imaging doesn't make any sense. For a while, magneto optical drives were a popular choice, but if someone tries selling you a MO solution you might want to consider how many 5.2 GB disks will be needed for a 100GB drive. We have used Exabyte[16] Mammoth drives for years, and have had great success with them. The newest drive, the Mammoth 2, while expensive, has a capacity of 150GB.

---

14. More information on version 3.0 is available at: http://www.encase.com/encase/encase_v3_features.htm

15. http://www.forensic-computers.com

16. http://www.exabyte.com

In Chapter 3, we discussed the Image MASSter from Intelligent Computer Solutions (ICS).[17] If you anticipate being on the road for most of your investigations, the Solo Forensic unit is a good choice because it is a lightweight, compact solution for duplicating drive-to-drive. If your forensics will primarily take place in a lab environment, ICS also has several desktop models to choose from.

When your forensic activity progresses from a rare occurrence to a part-time or full-time job, you can justify spending more money on tools and will want to consider dedicated forensics computers. Not only are such systems convenient, but they are rugged and impressive, too. You want to begin every investigation by gently taking control and running the data-collection process—after all, you are the expert, and it is your job to ensure that the investigation is done correctly. What better way to immediately establish your credentials than by whipping out a sophisticated, special-purpose portable system? The nosy sysadmins poking around your investigation will be suitably impressed.

The systems that we use (see Figure 7-19) are from Forensic-Computers.com.[18] The portable unit has four metal CRU hard drive trays, a CD-Recordable drive, and a floppy drive on one side of the case as shown in Figure 7-20.

Figure 7-19   Forensic-computers.com travel system is very convenient and durable

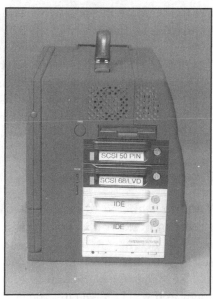

Figure 7-20   Forensic-Computers.com travel system removable IDE and SCSI drive slots and CD-R

17. http://www.ics-iq.com

18. http://www.forensic-computers.com. They can also be reached at (877) 877-4224.

Figure 7-21   Forensic-computers.com travel system external ribbon and power connector

External IDE and power connectors are included with the travel system (see Figure 7-21). Because the portable comes with two laptop adapters, this external connector makes it a snap to work with hard drives removed from laptops.

Lots of other choices are available for software and hardware; the ones discussed in this chapter are some of our favorites based on what we use and have used. Find a system that fits your needs and tastes. Consider all the possibilities and evaluate your choice in experiments that are as close to the real world as possible. The equipment is expensive, so don't make rash decisions.

Conclusion

You aren't limited to the tools we've discussed in this chapter, but they have been proven to work for us. This discussion should help you apply the tools that you end up using. Learn how to apply these tools *before* the investigation begins. Prepare yourself in your own lab. Take some time to compare similar tools and see how they differ in ease of use, speed, reliability, and output. The testing you do in your lab is time well spent and will hold you in good stead when you apply these tools in the field.

Further Resources

A growing set of tools for both Windows and Unix incident response, including statically linked Unix tools, can be found at http://www.incident-response.org/irtoolkits.htm and http://www.dmares.com/maresware/forensic_tools.htm.

Chapter

8

Investigating
Windows Computers

Since publishing its first operating system for an Intel computer, Microsoft has been
providing a steady supply of increasingly complex and sophisticated operating environments, each of which builds on its predecessor, providing backward compatibility with earlier versions. As a forensic investigator, you must be familiar with all of
them and their differences and similarities. In this chapter, we'll discuss forensic
issues relevant to all of Microsoft's environments, starting with the closely related
Windows 95 and 98 versions.[1] We assume that, by this point, you are familiar with
the fundamentals of forensics. Although we'll continue to introduce and reinforce
best forensic practices, most of this chapter consists of techniques and tricks specific
to one or more versions of Windows.

Windows

One of the keys to computer forensics is always being on the lookout for things that
can facilitate investigations. Always have the mindset that "the glass is half full." For
example, when it was discovered that Microsoft Word documents contained serial
numbers that could be used to identify the computer that created them, most people
were offended by the loss of privacy. We, on the other hand, were tickled to death,
because it represents one more arrow in the forensics quiver. Rumor has it that the
document serial number was used to track back to David Smith, the creator of the
Melissa virus, although this information has never appeared in public reports about
the case. We don't know if this number was actually used to help identify Smith,
but as long as the original Ethernet adaptor (network interface card or NIC) is
installed or available, this bit of forensics legerdemain can be helpful in associating

---

1. From a forensic point of view, Windows ME is virtually identical to Windows 98. It is intended explicitly as a home product, so few organizations large enough to need a forensic examiner are likely to have
an installed base.

a document with its source PC. Let's begin our section on Windows examinations by looking at an example of how we can use this kind of information to facilitate an investigation.

Imagine that you are investigating a theft of intellectual property case in which proprietary information was copied to a Word document and the document was saved to a floppy disk. You are handed the recovered floppy disk and asked to prove that the defendant created the disk. Examining the disk, you find that it contains a Word document. Using your forensics tool to search for PID_GUID in that document, you find a unique number that can be matched to the PID_GUID of the suspect's copy of Microsoft Office.[2]

To demonstrate this process on your computer, open Word and create a small document. Save it as a Word 97 document, which should be the default (this will not work under Office 2000). Use Quick View Plus to open the document. After you open the document, choose View | View as | Text file. Word documents are disk hogs, requiring huge amounts of overhead to accommodate formatting, revision history, the incorporation of Windows objects, and other fluff that might never be used. All this extra baggage will make your small test document larger than you would expect. Use the Find function by choosing Edit | Find. Search for "PID_GUID", and you might find something like this:

```
PID_GUID_{36FDE49B-5EFC-4DD6-A282-Abc1234567890}
```

The final 12 hexadecimal characters at the end make up a MAC address associated with the originating PC (MAC is a pretentious way of saying "Ethernet card"). All LAN adaptor vendors worldwide are assigned a unique number, and they use it along with a device-specific identifier of their own to hard-code a unique hardware address in every Ethernet card. You can easily see the MAC address on a Windows PC by running winipcfg. (You can use **ipconfig/all** from a command prompt or winmsd on Windows NT; click the Network tab and pick Transports). The MAC address appears in Adapter Address when you click More Info. Because they are used for link-level addressing on LANs, no two LAN adapter cards can share the same MAC address. This guaranteed uniqueness is obviously appealing to Microsoft engineers. Because it conveniently associates hardware and documents, it is also appealing to the forensic investigator.

To return to our hypothetical investigation, now that you have matched the suspect's PC to the PID_GUID of the document, you can prove that the floppy disk

---

2. Responding to concerns about privacy, Microsoft no longer includes a PID_GUID in documents created by the newest version of Office, Office 2000, and the application of a patch to an earlier version of Word changes the PID_GUID. But not everyone applies patches or updates software regularly, so always assume that you might get lucky.

contains a file created on the suspect's PC. Use a Hex editor, or a forensics program, to search the floppy disk and the suspect machine for the PID_GUID string. In Figure 8-1, we searched for the string using EnCase. After we received several hits, we checked for the MAC address by clicking on the File view. The MAC is displayed between the brackets right after the highlighted word "PID_GUID".

GUID stands for "Globally Unique Identifier," and as an essential component in Microsoft's COM architecture, GUIDs are pervasive in Windows. Another example of a GUID containing information potentially useful to the investigator is the information sent in when Microsoft Windows is electronically registered. If your suspect is running Windows 9X, look in the Windows directory and open the Cookies directory. Find a file ending in "microsoft.txt" and open it. It's a text file, so you can open it with any word processor or text viewer. You should see something like this:

```
MC1V=2&GUID=b0ea5322ab004da78116a0a10 microsoft.com
```

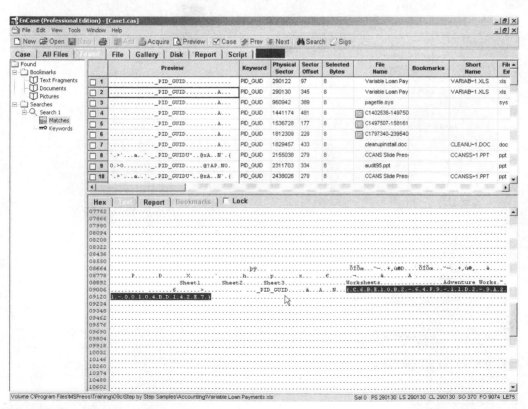

Figure 8-1   Using a forensic tool to search for the keyword "PID_GUID"

Once again, this GUID includes a MAC address. Although this is not as important for investigations as the GUID within a file, finding this GUID can be helpful if your suspect no longer has the original network card installed, or if it is a laptop computer that has a network card in a docking station which you do not have access to. If you are following recommended practice and are performing your investigation on a image copy of the original hard drive that is not in the suspect's PC, you won't have access to winipcfg and will have to rely on software evidence alone to correlate the document in question with its source PC. Another place to look is the registry—what we call the "heavenly hives"[3] for the forensic investigator. By importing the suspect's registry on your analysis machine (after first saving a copy of your registry so that you can restore it when you finish your investigation), you can search once again for "GUID", and you might find something like that shown in Figure 8-2.

Once again, the last 12 digits are from a NIC card that was loaded on the computer.

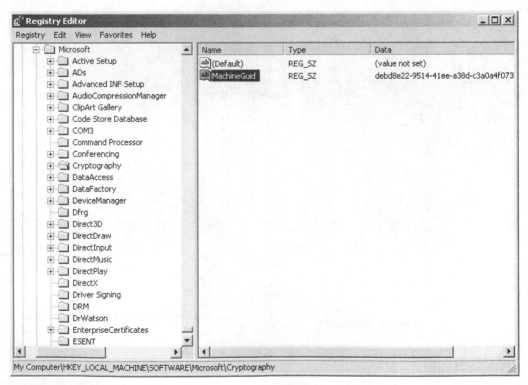

Figure 8-2 Examining registry entries

---

3. Microsoft uses the word *hive* to describe the complicated data structure that comprises the registry.

If you can boot the suspect computer with a Windows Startup disk that you created on your PC, you can select to boot the computer with network support after getting a command prompt. For Windows 9X type "winipcfg", if the Emergency Startup Disk is from NT or Windows 2000 type "**ipconfig /all**", or just install the suspect NIC card in your computer and run the commands from your computer. There is usually more than one way to accomplish your examination as long as you preserve the original evidence media.

While conducting your analysis using a Windows machine, keep in mind that Windows Explorer is configured by default to hide system files. To change this behavior on Windows 95 and Windows NT 4.0, start Explorer, click on the View menu and choose Options. Next, click on the File Types tab and make sure that Show all files is checked. Windows 98 has a more sophisticated version of Explorer with more options. To configure it optimally for investigative purposes, start Explorer, click on the View menu, and choose Folder Options. As shown in Figure 8-3, the Show all files radio button should be selected. We also recommend placing a check mark next to Hide file extensions for known file types, and next to Show file attributes in Detail View. Windows 2000 is slightly more complex, but provides essentially the same options in the same place.

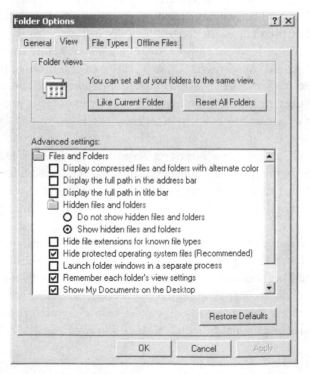

Figure 8-3   Configuring the Windows 98 Explorer

When you are sure that Windows is configured to view all files, you can start examining one of the most important system features in Windows. Go to the Windows directory on an image of the suspect's computer and scroll down to find the files with the .dat extension. If you are not familiar with Windows, here's how you locate a file on Windows by name. Click Start | Find | Search for Files and Folders and click Find Now. You should see the same file and the same path Windows displayed that we just located manually.

Windows Registry

Starting with Windows 95, all versions of Microsoft Windows have included a special data store called the *registry*. The registry contains a wealth of information for the computer and thus for the computer investigator. It is a comprehensive database containing information on every Windows-compatible program that has been installed on the computer. The registry contains information about users and their preferences, information on the hardware, and network information if the computer is or has been attached to a network. Let's look at how the registry can help investigations.

If you care to follow along on your computer, make sure that your registry is backed up *before* you start poking around. The registry consists of at least two files: System.dat and User.dat. If you have configured your system for multiple users, each user has his or her own copies of these files in Windows\Profiles*username*. Windows 98 should automatically back up your registry every time the system is booted. By default, the last five saved registries are stored in cab archive files (discussed in Chapter 4) located in Windows\Sysbckup. Double-clicking on one of these files runs Microsoft's cab editor, or if you have installed it as the default archive tool, WinZip runs. The registry can be restored by dragging the System.dat and User.dat files back into Windows. If you aren't comfortable restoring the registry manually, boot the system into DOS and type **scanreg /restore** from the DOS prompt, which launches the DOS version of the registry checker utility. It provides a list of existing registry backups and their timestamps. Highlight the one you wish to restore from and follow the instructions. The Windows 95 registry is functionally identical to the Windows 98 registry, but the newer version of Windows provides a more powerful maintenance environment. On Windows 95, a backup registry is located in two files: System.da0 and User.da0. If you accidentally delete one of the .dat files, Windows recreates the .dat file from the .da0 copy. If you really were on a deletion rampage and deleted the System.dat, System.da0, User.dat, and User.da0 files, Windows would have to recreate the entire registry from scratch, which is not what you want to have happen on the suspect machine unless you also want to practice retrieving deleted files.

Let's dive into the registry and see what it has to offer as an investigative resource. The registry is a database, and it uses a binary format that cannot be viewed with a text editor. It is optimized for computers, not people, so it isn't practical to view it with a hex editor or forensic tool either. The best way to examine the registry is with the tools provided by Microsoft. To do so, click Start | Run. Then type **regedit** (or **regedit32** on Windows NT) and click OK. Always be very careful when working with the registry. One wrong move can damage your Windows operating system. Although Windows has already created a backup, you should save a copy of your registry file before going on. To do so, click on the Registry menu and select Export Registry File. Provide a name for the file and then save it to a safe location. Don't save it anywhere in the Windows directory.

The Registry Editor works very much like Windows Explorer, and it uses a similar tree structure. Located on the left side are folder icons—these are called *keys*. Keys can contain either other keys or values. Values can be one of three types: binary, string, or DWORD (double word, 32 bit). Next to the keys are plus signs (+). Double-clicking on the key or single-clicking on the plus sign drops down the list of subkeys.

The first key we will look at is HKEY_CURRENT_USER. If the system has been configured for multiple users, or if more than one person has logged onto the computer, each has his or her own section of the registry. As an investigator, you can't afford to examine only the most recent user's history so you'll need to examine the registry carefully to see what all of the suspect system's users have been up to. As an example of the power of the registry, let's see if our "suspect" has searched for anything. Click on the plus sign and expand the list of subkeys. Find the Software key and click on its plus sign. Next, locate the Microsoft key and expand its list. Locate Windows (or Windows NT) and expand its list. Expand CurrentVersion and then Explorer. Finally, click on the folder DocFindSpecMRU. In the right window you should see the System.dat that we searched for earlier. Do you see anything else in this folder? If so, does it look familiar? Just to make sure, leave the registry open and go to the Start menu, click Find | Files or Folders. Try to position the Find window so that you can see the contents of the DocFindSpecMRU folder at the same time. Now click on the drop-down arrow next to the Name & Location field (see Figure 8-4) and notice that your search history appears in the DocFindSpecMRU folder.

As shown in Figure 8-6, Windows 2000 also has a search history function. Just like earlier versions of Windows, the search history information is stored in the registry HKEY_USERS, Microsoft, Software, Internet Explorer, Explorer Bars, FilesNamedMRU (as shown in Figure 8-5).

Another helpful type of information we can glean from the registry is the text strings used to support the functionality "AutoComplete". Starting with version 5, Internet Explorer provides an option to save data that users type into Web logons with their browsers. Remember that a user can type in his or her name, address, phone number, email address, and possibly passwords, all potentially useful information for your investigation. Once a user enters a string password on a Web page

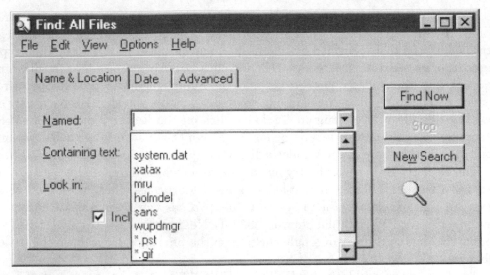

Figure 8-4 Finding the registry

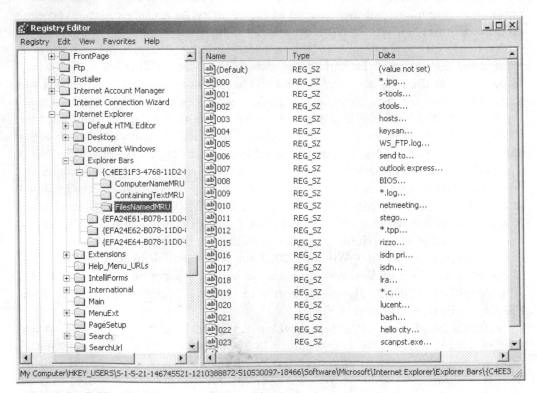

Figure 8-5 Editing the Windows 2000 registry

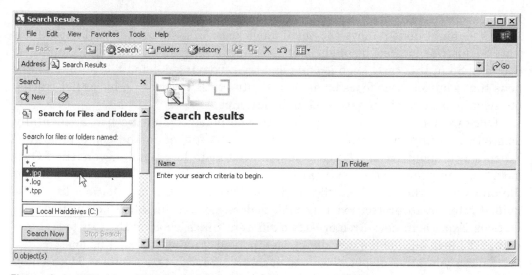

Figure 8-6 Windows 2000 Search Window with search history

with the AutoComplete feature turned on, that string is helpfully suggested to the user if they ever return to the page. (All this data that was entered by the user is stored in the registry.) Users might claim that they never visited a specific site, but you can check to see if AutoComplete saved a password for it. You cannot prove that they did not visit a specific page, but you may find convincing evidence that they actually did visit a page.

Searching the registry can help your investigations in additonal ways. Suppose you are working on a case involving harassing email purportedly originating from your suspect. Upon analysis of the suspect's computer, you do not find an email program, nor do you see any email on the computer. However, you do see in the Named field of the Find application, or in the registry, that your suspect conducted a search for *.pst. A PST file is a Personal Folder used by Microsoft Exchange and the various versions of Microsoft Outlook.[4] If you are using any of these programs, type ***.pst** in the Find application and see if you locate any PST files on your machine. If you do, make a copy of them and save the copy to a folder you create called Examples (or something similar for later use).

Finding a search by the suspect for PST files is by no means a "smoking gun," but it is a clue to the activities of whoever last used Find. If the suspect was engaged

---

4. A PST file contains stored electronic communications that are covered under U.S. Statute 18:USC 25-10. If you retrieve a PST file, you must have the authority from your company, including a clear company policy stating that the employee's email is company property, in order to read someone else's email.

in inappropriate activities and wanted to eliminate all the evidence, the first thing he or she might do is remove the email application. If a suspect didn't know where the PST file was located, he or she might conduct a search for it and after finding it, delete it. So in this case, keep looking and try retrieving deleted files. It often happens that someone who fears being investigated tries to cover up his or her tracks, but usually isn't very sophisticated in the attempt.

Once we received a call from a client who believed that he had accidentally deleted some important email files that "were no longer in the email program." When asked about recent changes, he admitted installing a newer version of Outlook. Searching for *.pst not only provided the current PST file, but also the missing file and yet another one from the original Outlook Express installation. In a misguided attempt to protect existing mail folders, he had installed new versions of Outlook Express in new directories two different times, causing Express to create a new PST file in each of the new directories instead of using the existing one.

Unless you have a special viewer such as dtSearch (see Chapter 7), the only practical way to view a PST file is to load it into Outlook or Outlook Express. Go to the Control Panel (choose Start | Settings | Control Panel) and then click Mail. Next, click Add, select Personal Folder, and then click OK. A window is displayed that is looking for a PST file. Point it to the location of the PST file you wish to open. You can also open Outlook and click Tools and then Services. Next, you click Add, select Personal Folder, and click OK as you did previously. Then open Outlook and choose View | Folders to view your email folders. Click the plus sign next to Personal Folder, which will appear in your Folder List view, and if all goes well, you see all the email from the file in question.

Explorer/RunMRU is another registry key containing useful information on user activities. It contains the most recent commands launched from the Run window (accessible from the Start button). The Run history shown in Figure 8-7 indicates that the user typed "regedit" in the Run dialog box. In addition, this information is available on the suspect computer by bringing up the Run window and clicking on the arrow to the right of the text box. When you are conducting an investigation on your forensic workstation against an image of the suspect system, the only way to see this type of suspect activity history is by importing the suspect registry file into the Registry Editor.

If Internet Explorer is loaded, its keys are also found under the Microsoft folder. Forensically useful information from these keys includes the default values for the directory into which the user last downloaded a file from the Internet, and the user's Internet Start page. The keys in the Microsoft folder also contain a list of all the URLs the user typed into the Address field. It can be accessed by clicking on the aptly named key TypedURLs. This resource is valuable for Internet investigations

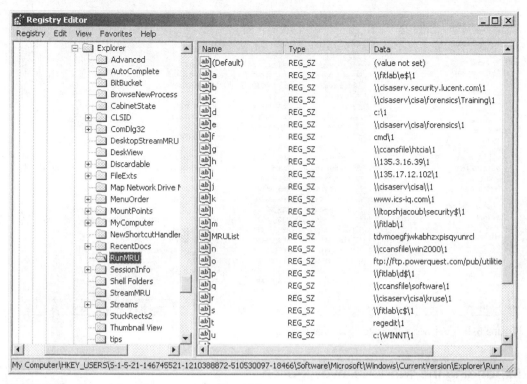

Figure 8-7   Examining the suspect's Run history

because you can see precisely what the user typed into the browser.[5] The registry can also show the user's Web browser settings. As shown in Figure 8-8, this information includes the proxy that the browser was configured to use. If you are investigating the user's surfing history, the logs on the proxy server pointed to by this key may contain helpful information on your suspect's activities.

The HKEY_LOCAL_MACHINE key stores information related to both the PC and the network. It isn't intuitively obvious that Network information is in the LOCAL_MACHINE key. The Network/Logon key contains the last username used to log onto a network, which is a good place to check if you are trying to correlate a user with a machine.

---

5. The cache directory used by Internet Explorer is normally called "Temporary Internet Files" although this is configurable and a user may change it. Within Explorer, this can be verified or changed by choosing Tools | Internet Options | General and clicking on the Settings button within the Temporary Internet Files area of the window.

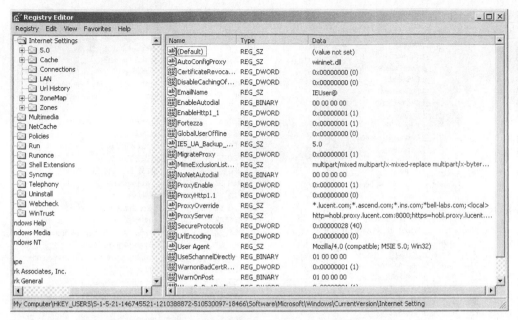

Figure 8-8   Viewing the proxy server setting

Expanding the Windows Investigation

When you boot a computer into Windows, the operating system accesses and changes files. The Federal Law Enforcement Training Center found that on a typical Windows 9X system, over 400 files are accessed, and hence their access dates are altered. A Windows NT system accesses over 500 files.

This information is important for several reasons. First, if you have to testify later that the evidence was not altered during the analysis, it can be difficult to explain that although 400 plus files were "changed" during the boot process, the system still provides acceptable evidence. Second, you'll lose the original access time on these files, and you'll lose boot messages and other information that may otherwise have been helpful to your investigation. Remember that if you boot the computer, do it in such a way so as not to alter files, by using a boot floppy disk or CD as we discuss in Chapter 1.

After you have obtained a drive as evidence, copied it, and created an inventory of its contents, notice the programs that were loaded on the drive, keeping an eye out for unusual ones, especially hacking, password-cracking, steganography, and encryption programs. We discuss these suspicious programs in Chapters 4–6. Not every program the suspect has loaded will be compliant with Microsoft's standards for installing Windows programs, so you cannot necessarily find all executables just by checking the registry or the Program Files directory.

When you have an idea of which programs are installed, look at other files on the drive. Check the My Documents directory, which is the default location for user data. If you're investigating a Windows 98 system configured for multiple users, each user has his or her own default folder, located at C:\Windows\Profiles*username*\My Documents, but nothing prevents Windows 9X users from storing files anywhere on the computer. Large drives are usually partitioned into multiple logical drives, identified by letters D:, E:, and so on. Additional partitions on the original drive and additional drives normally are used to store data, leaving the C: partition for configuration and executables. If you are using a DOS disk, the files and folders are mapped into the 8.3 naming convention (for example, My Documents is listed as mydocu~1). If you are running the DOS window on Windows 9X, both the 8.3 and the long filenames are listed when you run dir.

Good places to look for evidence include the Recycle Bin, the file Scandisk.log and scandisk lost files. Many users forget that deleted files are placed in the Recycling Bin and until it is deliberately emptied (or it fills up and begins to overwrite the oldest files), the files are still completely accessible. They are earmarked for unlinking, but files can stay in the Recycle Bin for years before being removed. The Scandisk disk maintenance utility will attempt to restore files that it believes have been inadvertently deleted. These are referred to as lost files, and their filename has the extension '.chk'. Few users are aware that these even exist. A simple search for the extension .chk will locate lost files that were saved by Scandisk. These files then can be viewed with a text viewer or a forensics program. Because scandisk files can contain pieces of files, useful data from files that may otherwise be lost is sometimes still sitting in a .chk file.

A simple way to find files is by using the Find program in Windows. We discuss additional programs for finding files in Chapter 7, but don't look a gift horse in the mouth. Be sure that you know how to take advantage of what you are given. You would be amazed at how much evidence you can find by simply doing a keyword search on titles. The Find program can be used to search for files of a certain type. For example, a search for *.jpg, *.gif, and *.jpeg shows graphics that the user may have downloaded from the Internet. By clicking on the Date tab, you can perform searches based on the date the file was modified, created, or accessed. The Advanced tab can search for files associated with specific programs (see Figure 8-9).

This pull-down list "Of Type" is based on the associations that are made between specific file extensions and specific applications. The list on your forensic system rarely is exactly like one on a suspect machine. As shown in Figure 8-10, later versions of Windows also include the ability to search for specific strings within files. The Windows 2000 search tool is especially useful when you don't have access to more sophisticated forensic utilities.

After you complete an inventory of the readily accessible material on the target computer, it's time to roll up your sleeves and start digging for the less obvious

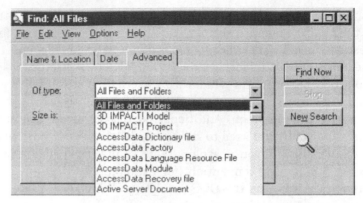

Figure 8-9   Searching for files associated with specific applications

evidence. After you've gone through the Recycle Bin, start looking for deleted files using your investigative tool of choice. Investigating digital crimes is tedious and frustrating, but it has its moments of glory. If you are lucky, the suspect will give up during the interview. Here's a little suspect psychology tip: Even if you weren't able to recover anything, make sure you bring a thick file folder with you. Just lay your hand on top of the folder and ask if you should continue the interview. Chances are you will not have to continue; you simply hand the suspect a pen to write his or her confession.

What Else to Look For

Search for the Windows password file (.pwl file). Although a password is not needed to bypass Windows 9X security, having it can help you in other ways. Locate all .pwl files by using the Find program and searching for *.pwl. You may be thinking that using the Find program is getting a little old because we could look in such-and-such folder, and you would be partly correct. You could look in the C:\Windows directory, which is where Windows is normally loaded and should be the only place where a .pwl file is located. Keep in mind that you will be analyzing suspect computers with unknown configurations, and you can't always expect to find information in the default locations. Make it a habit to be as thorough as possible.

Sometimes a search does not show a single .pwl file in the Windows directory, but a number of them, as shown in Figure 8-10. If a number of .pwl files appears in a single directory, it would be unusual and suspicious but you probably would have missed them if you had looked only in the Windows directory. When you find a directory full of password files on someone's machine, he or she may have a reasonable explanation, or the user might be cracking them for hostile reasons. Train yourself to be always on the lookout for the unusual, and when you find an anomaly, figure out why it's there.

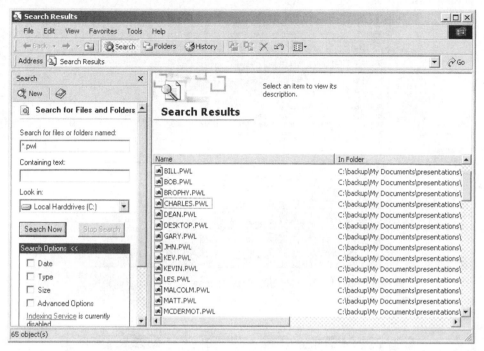

Figure 8-10   Windows 2000 search window

Suppose we're dealing with a normal system with just a single .pwl file. It can provide a list of passwords that the suspect is using, and these passwords can be a lifesaver if you encounter encryption. Instead of trying to break the encryption, try some passwords that you recovered from, or around, the user's machine (don't forget to check under the keyboard!). If your user is like most people and can't remember several passwords, he or she probably uses just one password for just about everything the user accesses, so you might be able to use it to gain access to other systems.

A password also can help you gauge the truthfulness of a suspect during an interview. When the suspect gives you his or her username and password, and it matches a password you recovered, you have reason to believe that the suspect is being cooperative. In addition, telling the subject what his or her password is before you ask any questions is one way to create the impression that resistance is futile.

Tools such as PWLTool[6] or Cain enable you to view the passwords that are cached on a specific system. As shown in figure 8-11, PWLTool also can crack password files from other computers, making it especially useful on your forensics workstation.

Chapter 5 contains a discussion on password-cracking techniques and tools.

---

6. The PWLTool allows you to find and view tools found in both Windows .pwl files and passwords that are cached. For more information visit http://www.webdon.com.

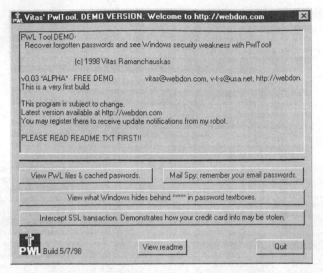

Figure 8-11 The PWLTool welcome screen highlights its capabilities

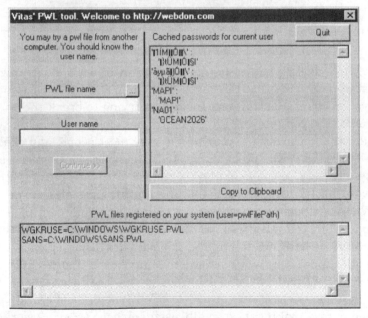

Figure 8-12 PWLTool can find passwords in several different ways

Windows Email

Email is often a rich source of information about a suspect's activities. Sometimes suspicious email is the first indication that a situation requires investigation. Unfortunately, email files in Microsoft systems are not easy to analyze. The many different email applications each have their own file formats and conventions. Even finding the email data files can be tricky. The user might download and store all email on the computer, or the user might leave it on an email server, accessing it over the network when needed. Remote email has several advantages for users, allowing them to send, receive, and store the same mail from multiple PCs, such as a laptop and a desktop machine. When stored on a server, corporate email probably is backed up regularly, which is one of the goals of storing it centrally. The suspect might well be using a personal email account remotely, especially one of the free mail services being offered by most of the major Web portals. If this is the case, the mail won't be stored on a corporate computer available for your investigation.

Think of email on the desktop as being sort of a personal database application. The individual messages are indexed in multiple ways, enabling the user to store them in multiple folders and sort them by recipient, date sent, and so on. From the user's point of view, each message is a discrete object, but from the point of view of the operating system, the complete set of mail messages and attachments may be contained within one giant file. A mail file on a Unix system is basically a text file, making searches easy to perform, but on a Windows machine, email invariably is in a proprietary binary format. In addition to the data within the mail file itself, an active mail user inevitably leaves other evidence on a PC. Mail is like any other application, in that it uses temporary files and swap space, and its data (that is, the messages) can be exported as text files. Check the hard drive for messages or check slack space for remnants of the original email. Check the suspect's Web history and see if any of the visited sites appear to be an email site. Use your forensic analysis tool to search for file fragments containing the domain name of that email provider, such as Hotmail.com.

As discussed in Chapter 7, use of a commercial forensic tool once enabled us to find 700 email messages that had been deleted over two years earlier. If you do not have access to such a forensic program, but you do have a hex editor, the same can be accomplished by using its search function. Appropriate keywords to search for include the email address, the user's name, and the domain name of the suspected email address (that is, the @name.com). If you use a hex editor, you have to search each string one at a time, whereas the special-purpose forensics tools can search multiple strings all at once, providing a convenient results summary when the tool has completed all the searches.

Email Signatures Provide Clues to Online Identities

You can learn a great deal about someone from his or her email signatures. If the user has created his or her own vCard, it is likely to contain quite a bit of identification information. If someone is frequenting chat rooms pretending to be different people, or sending out some kind of scam mail or chain mail, that person might well have different signatures for each online alias. If a user is running Windows and has loaded Internet Explorer, her or she may also have installed Outlook Express. (Microsoft Office comes with a full version of Outlook). Both Outlook Express and the "full" version enable users to create vCards. Most email users append a standard signature to messages, containing the name and perhaps additional personal information, such as phone number, employer, title, and even address. vCards can contain all this information and more, including pager numbers, mobile phone numbers, and home phone numbers. For the investigator, any form of email signature is yet another means of identifying a PC's user.

To locate signature files, search for *.vcf using the trusty Find program. If the user has created or saved any .vcf files, you should be able to find them. You also should look for the folder C:\Windows\Application Data\Microsoft\Signatures, the default location for email signatures. It may not only contain the suspect's vCard, but also the files Standard.htm, Standard.rtf, and Standard.txt. These files are the default email signatures that are appended to this user's mail even if he or she doesn't use a vCard. These signatures are in HTML, for Web-format mail; rich text format (RTF), another form of formatted text used in email; and ASCII, which is used for unformatted mail messages. If the user is really into creating signatures, he or she may have additional signatures in the Signatures directory with different names (Outlook enables a user to create as many signatures the user wishes). If you were to click on any of these files, Windows tries to open them with whatever viewer or editor is configured for that file type. When you double-click on a vCard, Windows launches Outlook so you can view it in the Contact window.

If you need to examine a vCard but don't have Outlook installed, the data can be viewed with other applications. This is how Warren's card would look using a text file viewer:

```
BEGIN:VCARD
VERSION:2.1
N:Kruse;Warren
FN:Warren Kruse
TEL;WORK;VOICE:
TEL;PREF:
ADR;WORK:Crawfords Corner Rd;Holmdel;U S
```

```
LABEL;WORK;ENCODING=QUOTED-PRINTABLE:2C-605A=0D=0A101 Crawfords Corner
Rd=0D=0AHolmdel, NJ 07733-3030=0D=0AU S
E-MAIL;PREF;EX:/o=Lucent/ou=NJ031901/cn=Recipients/cn=krusewg
REV:19990825T152831Z
END:VCARD
```

Windows NT

From an investigator's point of view, the primary difference between Windows 9X and Windows NT is the additional security built into Windows NT, especially the system access control (logon) and file access control. This section isn't a treatise on Windows NT security, but if you want to get around the security of Windows NT in order to examine a Windows NT machine, read on.

Windows NT is no different from any other operating system. If you can get physical access to a machine, you can get logical access. In Chapter 5, we provided a highly invasive procedure for hacking into a Windows NT system and gaining administrative access. It is also possible to boot from a floppy disk and access the files system directly, a more subtle technique that can allow you to examine a Windows system in place without leaving any logical tracks behind. You do this by booting the machine from a DOS floppy disk, and running a utility called NTFSDOS. This utility mounts the NTFS volume in read-only mode, which is the optimal mode for analyzing a computer. When a defense attorney challenges you for making changes to the suspect computer, you can explain that the drive was mounted read-only, which is the only option available. NTFSDOS is free and is available for download.[7] A commercial version of NTFSDOS is available, but it is not read-only. While this would be advantageous to a system administrator fixing a damaged system, for many of our purposes, the read-only version is preferred. Be sure that your notes and reports reflect that you used the read-only version.

Windows NT uses a filesystem called NTFS, which is contained within a volume. A volume can consist of a portion of a physical disk; it may be the entire physical disk, or it may span several disks. NTFS filesystem clusters differ in size according to drive capacity or the preferences of the installer, but they can be as small as 512 bytes.[8] A 1GB volume has a default cluster size of 1KB, volumes up to 2GB have a default of 2KB, and 4KB is the default cluster size for larger volumes. A 1.6GB

---

7. http://www.sysinternals.com

8. http://support.microsoft.com/support/kb/articles/Q140/3/65.asp

9. Abraham Silberschatz, Peter Baer Galvin, Greg Gagne, *Operating System Concepts, 6th Edition*. New York, NY: John Wiley & Sons, 2001.

FAT16 system loses 400MB due to fragmentation. A 1.6GB NTFS volume loses only about 17MB storing the same files. This reduction in fragmentation is a boon for the administrator, but a bane for the forensic investigator looking for deleted information that may be contained within slack space.

If the computer you are examining does not have an NTFS volume to mount, the NTFSDOS utility notifies you. After analyzing numerous Windows NT machines, we've found that many of them are loaded on top of the FAT filesystem, the primitive 16-bit system used for DOS and earlier versions of Windows 9X. While this usually means that the system was upgraded in place from one of these earlier operating systems, even Windows 2000 allows the creation of FAT filesystems, and we've seen brand-new installations with user data on a FAT partition. If NTFSDOS reports that there are no NTFS volumes to mount, you can use just about any unerase program to attack the suspect computer.

As we mentioned, a Windows NT system is secure only when it is running Windows NT. If you mount the drive (or better yet, a forensic copy of the drive) as a slave on your forensics system and boot your own operating system, you have unlimited access to all unencrypted files from the suspect hard drive (we discuss encryption later in this chapter in the section "Encrypted File System (EFS)" and also in Chapters 4 and 5).

Windows NT has a few forensically relevant differences from Windows 9X that you should be aware of. The registry is similar to that of Windows 9X but is contained in separate files that are located in WINNT/SYSTEM32/CONFIG (%SYSTEMROOT% is an environment variable which normally—but not always—has the value Winnt).

Windows NT is a multiuser system that replicates some data for each user account. You can find a C:\Winnt\Profiles*username* directory for each user that has successfully logged onto the machine locally, and it contains a user-specific registry file Ntuser.dat. It is usually not possible to copy these files while Windows NT is running because Windows NT protects them, but if you access them by booting from a floppy disk or mounting the hard drive as a slave on another PC, you should have no problem copying the files to removable media for safe storage.

Because Windows NT does not fully support plug and play, the registry contains additional information pertaining to hardware. Windows NT also comes with a different version of regedit, called regedit32. For investigative and analysis purposes, they work much the same; if you export the Windows NT hives and then you want to import them into a different system for analysis, you can import them only by using regedit32. (Remember, before experimenting on your own machine or directly accessing the registry on a machine you are examining, make sure you have a recent backup of the system or at least the registry.)

The user directories located under the Profiles directory contain more user-specific information than just their own registry. Depending on how the system is configured, the Profile directory may contain all of the user's data files. If the suspect uses Internet Explorer to access the Web, the user directory will contain a lot of data associated with the user's surfing history, including Favorites, recent history, cookie, and cached Internet files that can provide clues to the last several years of browsing history. If the suspect has administrator access to the machine in question, you should check the default user directory because the suspect may log onto the machine using another local account.

Windows 2000

Windows 2000 includes features that both aid and complicate the investigative process. Microsoft released the commercial version of Windows 2000 while this book was being written. Other than some incompatibilities with older programs, forensically speaking, there is not much difference between Windows 2000 (which was originally called Windows NT 5.0) and Windows NT 4.0.

Dynamic Disks

One change from previous versions of Windows is the new dynamic disks capability, which provides fault tolerance. It's problematic for forensic analysis, though, because other operating systems do not recognize the dynamic disk partition. Unlike other Windows partitions, which have the partitions information at the beginning of the partition, a dynamic disk has a 4MB partition table at the end of the disk. You can image a drive utilizing dynamic disks, but after you restore it, you can read it (as of this writing) only with a Windows 2000 boot disk.

System Administration Tools

If you aren't familiar with Windows 2000 administration, it might take you a while to find the User Manager and some of the other helpful tools that were previously found in Accessories, under System Tools. Microsoft has not only made some improvements to those programs, but has also put them under one hood and removed them from System Tools. You can reach the User Manager by right-clicking My Computer and then clicking Manage.

After you click Manage, you are in the Computer Management Window (see Figure 8-13), which provides administrative functionality including the following capabilities:

- Monitor system events such as logon times and application errors.
- Create and manage shares.
- View a list of users connected to a local or remote computer.
- Start and stop system services such as the Task Scheduler and the Spooler.

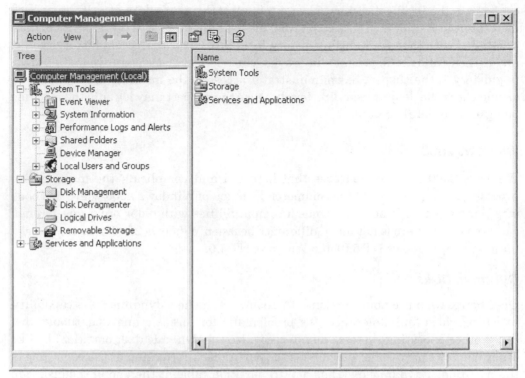

Figure 8-13   Windows 2000 Computer Management window

- Set properties for storage devices.
- View device configurations and add new device drivers.
- Manage server applications and services such as the Domain Name Service (DNS) or Dynamic Host Configuration Protocol (DHCP).

You can export the information from the Computer Management window to a text file on removable media by clicking Action and then Export. If you are forced to examine a live machine, some of the information that we recommend you routinely export for safe storage includes:

- Local Users and Groups
- Event Viewer
- Storage
- Services

One other major difference from Windows NT is the way that Windows 2000 handles parallel zip drives. Initially, Windows 2000 did not recognize our zip drive. To enable the zip drive, follow these steps:

1. Right-click on My Computer and then click Manage.

2. In the Computer Management window, click Device Manager.

3. Click Ports, right-click Printer Port (LPT1), and then select Properties.

4. Select the Port Settings tab and place a checkmark next to Enable legacy Plug and Play detection as depicted in Figure 8-14. Windows 2000 has to be rebooted in order for this change to take effect.

After you reboot the computer and you enter the password to log back on, your parallel zip drive should be recognized.

The System Information Window is another Windows 2000 feature and is usually an important place to visit during a forensic analysis. It can be reached from the

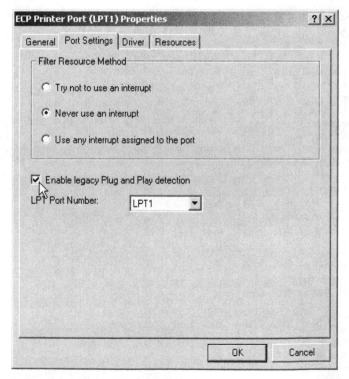

Figure 8-14   Configuring a parallel port to use a zip drive

System Tools menu by clicking Start | Programs | Accessories | System Tools. After you launch the System Information Window, you probably will want to go to the View menu first and click Advanced. From the Action menu is an option to save the System file as a text file for easier printing and later viewing without having to use the Windows 2000 System Information Window. At the risk of sounding like a broken record, we must stress the importance of saving everything you possibly can to external media before you start "looking around." You often will be confronted with situations that are less than ideal, requiring you to examine a live system, so get what evidence you can, but be careful about it.

Persistent Connections

It's always important to see if any network drives have been mapped, which can provide clues as to whether servers might also contain files belonging to your suspect. Windows 2000 lists drive mappings in the System Information applet under Software Environment (see Figure 8-15), among other places.

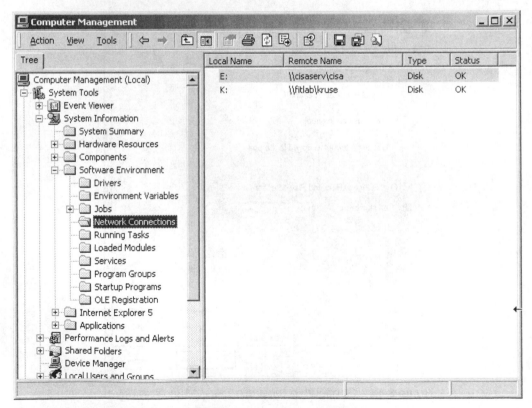

Figure 8-15   Using System Information to see mapped drives

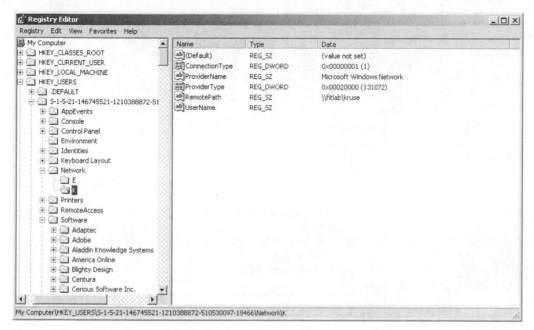

Figure 8-16   Using the Registry Editor to see mapped drives

As shown in Figure 8-16, the Registry Editor also can be used to find mapped drives, so even if you don't have direct access to the suspect system using the Registry Editor, you can find mapped drives when you are examining a Windows 2000 disk image. They are located under HKEY_CURRENT_USER, Network. In Figure 8-15, Warren has a persistent connection mapped as drive E: so that every time he logs on the network, \\cisaserv\cisa appears as drive E:.

User Home Directories

Another significant change between Windows 2000 and Windows NT is the location of user information. On a Windows NT system, the Winnt directory contains Profiles directories for user documents and other important information. On a Windows 2000 system, the default location for user-specific information is in the Documents and Settings directories, as shown in Figure 8-17.

Encrypted File System (EFS)

The use of EFS can complicate your investigation. If a computer is running Windows 2000 and is partitioned for NTFS, the user can set up subdirectories that automatically encrypt files that are stored within them. Although encryption utilities have been available for years, they are so inconvenient that their use on PCs has

Figure 8-17 The Documents and Settings Directory

been limited. This may change with the advent of EFS, which is easy to use and is included for free. In addition, the awareness of both the existence and utility of encryption is increasing. EFS is completely transparent to the user—after someone logs on to Windows 2000, any files that he or she has encrypted are available for reading. Neither an explicit decryption process nor entry of a password is required.

EFS cannot be enabled without also enabling key recovery and appointing a key recovery agent. These concepts are covered in Chapter 4. The key recovery functionality is tantamount to creating a spare key for every encrypted file. An organization has the opportunity to control encryption policy on a domainwide basis through Active Directory—those that don't run the risk of never being able to recover data on their own computers. Standalone systems use the Windows NT administrator as the key recovery administrator, but systems that are part of a domain with a recovery policy have a domainwide recovery administrator. Like the user, the recovery administrator can transparently read encrypted files (assuming that this account has read permission, which may have to be manually set during a recovery operation). If the recovery key has not been explicitly exported off the system with the encrypted files, logging on as the recovery administrator is sufficient to gain access to the recovery key. If the key has been exported, the administrator is prompted to insert a floppy disk containing the key when accessing an encrypted file.

Investigating EFS Contents

If users are logged on to Windows 2000 machines, you are confronted with a dilemma. If they happen to be using EFS, you may have convenient access to their files for only a short time period. If you log out, if the power goes off, if the system crashes, or if a password-protected screen saver starts running, you may never be able to access those users' files again. Your only comfort in this awkward situation is that no single solution is correct. Before you pull the plug, you should consider running Microsoft Management Console (MMC), if possible, and creating a key recovery certificate. This special file enables you to access any files in the corresponding EFS directory—even if those files are copied to another computer. We describe this process in Appendix D.

You might also consider changing the administrator's password, just to facilitate future access. We know some of you are saying that you would have to pull the plug first, but we must reiterate, "there are no hard-and-fast rules!" We're not saying that either decision (to pull or not to pull, that is always the question) is right or wrong. Carefully consider your options and don't start pulling power cords out of the back of the machines before you understand the implications. With the EFS, the consequences might be that the contents of the hard drive are permanently encrypted, and you'll never be able to retrieve the data. On the other hand, analyzing a computer while the suspect's operating system is running has numerous consequences, including the possibility of booby traps and defense allegations of tampering. Therefore, try to obtain as much information as you can before you attempt an office visit.

When Windows 2000 is being used, you must find out if the system is being centrally administered through Active Directory, and if so, users have been prevented from using EFS. If not, find out if there is a recovery agent for the domain and a person who knows where the recovery key is. You must have a plan of action and contingency plans before you walk into the suspect's office—don't automatically believe the information provided by local management.

You have the following options when confronted with an EFS. Always document explicitly what you did and why.

- Check to see if the computer has a domain account and then if the domain has a key recovery policy in place. Ideally, you determine this before you seize the computer. After all, if you know that the domain policy allows a domain administrator to recover the encryption key, you can pull the plug (if that is what you are comfortable doing). After you obtain a special key recovery certificate from the recovery agent, you can decrypt the corresponding EFS-encrypted files on any Windows 2000 system.

- While still logged on as the suspect, you can manually decrypt any EFS-encrypted directories. This can be accomplished by right-clicking a folder in

Explorer, choosing Properties, clicking on the General tab, and then clicking Advanced. Clear the Encrypt contents to secure data checkbox in the Advanced Attributes dialog box. When you click OK and choose the option of decrypting the folder and all its contents, all of the encrypted files are decrypted.

- If the user is cooperative, ask for his or her password. Skillful interviewing can help you convince the suspect that he or she should give you the password. We once interviewed a suspect who refused to give up his password for days, but he wanted his machine back as soon as possible. We gave him the choice of "you can pay me now or pay me later," and he gave us the password. As promised, we express-mailed the machine back to him the next day.

- Copy the files to an external medium because the files are encrypted only when they are in the encrypted folder. If a user is logged on, consider copying files before the user logs out.

- Crack the user account, or the recovery agent account (on a stand-alone system, this is the administrator account by default). As discussed in Chapter 5, a lot of tools can enable you to crack a password or change it. When you rename the SAM and reboot, the system boots up with no administrator password, enabling you to log on as the administrator. If you're working on a standalone system, the user probably has not exported the recovery key password, enabling anyone logged on as administrator to transparently access any EFS-encrypted files.

- Even when the user has exported the recovery key so that it is no longer available on the suspect PC, you may still be able to find the floppy disk that contains it.

- If the user is logged on, export the private key as described in Appendix D.

Microsoft probably made the key recovery option available so that they would not get inundated with support calls from users who encrypt data and forget their passwords or from employers who cannot get access to data on their own PCs. In most cases, you'll be able to access EFS files either by gaining local access to the administrator or user account or by getting the recovery key information from the domain administrator.

Windows 3.1

If you conduct computer investigations long enough, you will be confronted with Windows 3.1 and a host of other operating systems that you thought were long gone and that you'd never see again.

We recently worked on a case that involved what was described as a "Windows" machine. After performing a forensic backup and booting a copy of the suspect drive in our lab, we noticed that the Start button and the usual desktop icons weren't displayed. We had encountered a Windows 3.1 machine. This is what we like about computer forensics; you just don't know what you'll encounter. After reviewing some earlier cases (much earlier), we investigated the Windows 3.1 system.

This case serves as an illustration of why you shouldn't throw anything away. Good forensic analysts are usually pack rats. Fortunately, we still keep Windows 3.1 programs. We recommend carrying older programs with you as part of your traveling forensic toolkit. More often than not, we use just about every disk in our bag of tricks. As long as you recover the evidence properly and accurately without altering the original, it doesn't matter how many disks or programs it takes.

The look-and-feel of the interface was dramatically improved in Windows 9X, from the investigators' point of view. Windows 3.1 uses the FAT16 filesystem and runs on top of MS-DOS, IBM PC-DOS, or DR-DOS. Unlike later versions, Windows 3.1 creates relatively few temporary files, but it does create a swap file, 3866spart.par, found in a user-configurable location.

Windows 3.1 uses larger file allocation units, resulting in more slack space than later versions of Windows. This is a terrible waste of hard drive real estate, but it's great for the forensic analyst because it provides plenty of empty space between the files to look for evidence contained in previous files.

One of the biggest complications in dealing with a Windows 3.1 system is the use of doubleSpace or drive space, system utilities that significantly increased the usable storage space by automatically compressing all of the files in a specific filesystem. "Back in the old days," the drives were smaller than today's huge drives, so compression programs (from Microsoft and from third parties) were common. Despite the fact that this is the age of gigabyte hard drives, later versions of Windows still include disk compression, and some people are still using it. Don't forget to check the properties of every filesystem during your inventory. If you inadvertently mount a compressed hard drive during the boot process, it will be accessed, which can change a compressed filesystem and might also result in the loss of some swap or slack space.

Conclusion

Windows machines have been widely used throughout the 1990s, and you undoubtedly will encounter multiple versions during your career. If you are unfamiliar with earlier versions of Windows or Windows 2000, it is probably time for you to install it in your lab and start practicing. The good news is that you can recover a wealth of information on Windows machines. Just remember that if you decide to analyze a Windows machine while it is booted, or you boot a suspect's system into Windows, the operating system immediately overwrites your evidence. Whenever possible, you should boot from your boot disk or better yet, limit your examination to a copy of the original partitions.

Chapter
9

Introduction to Unix for Forensic Examiners

Ideally, an investigator has years of in-depth experience administering and programming an operating environment before attempting a forensic investigation on it. It is clear to us from classes and seminars that the need for skillful Unix investigators exceeds the supply. Experienced Unix users may wish to skip ahead while we provide some background information for those readers who don't have a significant background in Unix. Consider the brief introduction provided in this chapter as the minimum level of Unix knowledge required to examine a Unix system. As we've stated repeatedly in previous chapters, always do your best to preserve original evidence. The easiest way to accomplish this in the Unix environment is with the dd command, which can be used to take snapshots of huge chunks of a system at a time. We'll look at ways to use dd after reviewing some Unix essentials that a forensic investigator must be familiar with.

Unlike DOS and Windows environments, Unix comes in a bewildering variety of variations and versions. In its 30-year history, Unix has been used, abused, and diverged. Although the various versions of Unix are reconverging, you still will be confronted with many variations. Although all Unix versions have the same general set of commands, a few significant ones are different. Furthermore, the parameters or options available for these commands vary from vendor to vendor, and some of the most important commands have different syntaxes. Not only are the commands different, but the configuration information is found in different places on different Unix versions, and the structure and location of the kernel itself can be quite different depending on which Unix family a suspect's host descended from. Today's Unix systems usually belong to one of two different family trees. The original commercial version of Unix was owned by AT&T and has had several owners during the 1990s. UnixWare and Solaris are both System V variants directly descending from the AT&T commercial release. The (nonprofit) University of California at Berkeley has a long history of developing and releasing its own versions of Unix, referred to as BSD. BSD and System V have common Bell Laboratory roots, and all versions of System V Unix have been strongly influenced by BSD.

Both FreeBSD and OpenBSD are based on freely available Berkeley source code and are easily installed on PCs. Linux has characteristics of both, but its unique code was created through an open system process using volunteer developers. Although firms such as RedHat and Caldera resell their own packaged versions of Linux, both the source code and the compiled object code are freely available for anyone's use. Be aware that the administrative utilities are different on virtually every version of Unix; even when the underlying system is nearly identical, each Unix publisher attempts to differentiate itself from competing vendors by providing its own set of administrative functions. The tools used to add and maintain users and filesystems are not standardized, and the differences are most pronounced in the GUI-based administrative utilities.

In the old days, gaining hands-on experience with Unix computers sometimes required some finagling. Today, they are so prominently used on the Internet that there's no excuse for not having at least a pedestrian knowledge of Unix. Fortunately, Linux has made it much easier to gain hands-on experience. Just set up Linux on that old machine you thought was too slow for the latest Windows operating system. If you have a spare system that might not be up to the task of running the latest version of Windows, but it has at least 32MB of RAM and at least a 1GB hard drive, it probably will make a good Linux box. Even if you don't have a spare system, if you have a gig or two of space on your existing machine, you should be able to create a Linux partition, enabling you to boot into it and learn your way around the operating system.

Unix has a long history of remote hacks and subsequent takeovers. If your organization has hosts accessible from the Internet, you should expect someday to be called to investigate intrusions and intrusion attempts. In Chapter 10, we describe how such attacks take place and what the system crackers do. In Chapter 11, we discuss the techniques used to examine a Unix system to determine whether or not it has been attacked and to learn what has been done to it. Let's review some of the important features of Unix and the Unix functions that will be most important to a forensics investigator.

Unix Components

This chapter cannot provide a complete tutorial on Unix internals, but the more you know about Unix internals, the more effective you'll be as a Unix investigator.

The kernel is the heart of Unix—the operating system itself. It is the software entity that processes the system calls, a small but powerful set of functions allowing the opening, reading, writing, and closing of files; the launching of applications; communication between applications; and interactions with peripherals such as the keyboard, monitor, mouse, network, printer, and modem. Like Windows, Unix takes advantage of virtual memory. This means that when system RAM is full, the kernel writes some of the data in RAM to a special location on the hard drive, commonly referred to as *swap space*. Swap space is an important place to look for clues to what is happening on the system, and swap data can persist after a system is shut down.

Unix is a very modular environment, and it attempts to accommodate future commands and capabilities. A design element within Unix that accommodates this modularity is the use of files. In Unix, everything is a file. Not only are files treated as files, but so are most peripherals. On a Unix system, every hard drive can be treated as a single file, and so can each partition on that hard drive. The console is treated as a file, and every serial port is a file; on some versions, even the Ethernet adapter is treated as a file. Other versions of Unix treat each running process as a directory with a set of files containing context and pointing to program memory. From the investigator's point of view, this architecture is incredibly convenient. This modularity greatly facilitates forensic analysis, allowing powerful Unix tools to be applied not only to discrete files, but also to the system data structures and kernel memory space. It also allows the use of Unix permission mechanisms to provide access control over peripherals.

The command line is the primary user interface to Unix. Although all current versions of Unix provide a convenient windowing environment, serious investigations take place within the powerful command-line environment. When you boot Unix from a floppy disk, you have no choice but to use the character-based terminal environment. If you log directly into the console of either the system you are investigating or your own analysis host, you probably will start with the graphical user interface. Within that environment, though, most of your work is done using resizable windows that emulate the terminal environment. When you have logged onto Unix and are taking advantage of the command prompt, you are actually running an interactive session with a command interpreter called the *shell*. An interpreter accepts human text input and executes it directly. Unlike a compiler, it does so without creating a binary object file that can be executed in the future. (In DOS or when running a command prompt window in Microsoft Windows, the command interpreter is called *command.com*.) Depending on your point of view, Unix is either blessed or cursed with a variety of shells. If you want to be able to reconstruct the suspect's activities, you need to be aware that multiple command interpreters exist, and you must determine which one your suspect used.

Not only is the shell used interactively as the command prompt, but it is also used to run *shell scripts*. Although much more sophisticated and powerful, scripts are analogous to .bat files on DOS and Windows. On a typical Unix system, many of the programs run at startup are shell scripts. Shell scripts are run when users log on, and many administrative and maintenance utilities are actually written as shell scripts. Even mildly proficient Unix administrators are expected to be able to write and effectively apply them. Scripting is much more significant in the Unix environment than it is in the Windows environment, and even highly experienced Windows

NT administrators can be unaware of the importance played by scripting on Unix systems. If you really want to learn Unix, learn how to write and understand shell scripts.

The oldest Unix command interpreter in common use is the Bourne shell. This shell is found on every Unix system and is usually located in /bin/sh. The Bourne shell supports a unique syntax and set of keywords and has proved to be extremely flexible and useful. When launching a command from the Bourne shell prompt, it's possible to run the command noninteractively in the background by placing the ampersand character (&) at the end of the command. Once this command is launched, the only control the user has over the execution of this background process is to determine its process ID and manually stop it with the kill command.

The next shell to gain popularity is the C shell. Developed as part of the BSD distribution, csh added a powerful, albeit arcane, command history function along with job control. Job control is the ability to launch programs interactively and then suspend them, returning user access to the command prompt. Furthermore, suspended programs can be sent into the background, where they execute without disturbing the user, or they can be restarted in the foreground. A background or stopped process can be pulled back into the foreground for interactive use. In the old days, the interface to a Unix system was provided only through character-based terminals. The ability to suspend applications and have multiple running background processes, and to selectively stop and bring them back as interactive processes, was a major productivity enhancement. The C shell also has a different programming syntax, attempting to be more like the C programming language. Today, very few administrators write scripts in C shell, although those whose Unix experience dates back to the 1980s or earlier may still use the C shell as their primary command environment. Using the C shell today is the Unix equivalent of wearing a bow tie. It is a quaint anachronism that is more of a personality statement than a desire for efficiency. C shell job control set the job control conventions for Unix shells, and the use of hot keys and commands is identical or similar on virtually all shells providing job control (see Table 9-1).

Unix command-line entries can be quite lengthy, so Unix users required a mechanism to enable them to repeat and edit previously entered commands. This was provided in the C shell by using special metacharacters within commands to access a history list of previously entered commands. For example, typing the two-character sequence "!!", pronounced "bang, bang," executes the previously entered command. To perform an operation on the last word of the previous command, typically the name of a file, type the two-character sequence "!$". Metacharacter sequences are also available to selectively pull other words from within previous commands, or to choose previous commands based on their sequence number and edit or rerun them as they were originally typed. The significance of metacharacter sequences for the investigator is that a history of shell commands is saved in a file, enabling you to reconstruct a suspect's activities.

Table 9-1   Unix Hot Keys and Commands

Command or Keystroke	Default Function
Ctrl-C	Halts a running process.
Ctrl-Z	Suspends a running process.
bg	Runs the most recently suspended process in the background. Functionally equivalent to starting a process and placing an ampersand at the end of the command line.
fg	Makes a background process the foreground process.
jobs	Lists all running background jobs.

The difficulty of using C shell history commands encouraged the development of a new Unix version, tcsh. tcsh was the first shell to allow text-editing commands to be used on the command line; it supported the command conventions of the two most popular Unix editors, vi and emacs. With tcsh, Unix users can interactively review and edit previous commands using the conventions of their favorite text editor. This encouraged the development of an improved Bourne shell, developed by an AT&T programmer named David Korn. The Korn shell, ksh, provides the same interactive job control features that the C shell provides, and it also supports the same command-line editing functions as tcsh. With the Korn shell, a shell is available that supports Bourne shell scripts while providing the productivity enhancements that most users are looking for. The default shell on Linux, following a Unix tradition of puns, is called the Bourne Again Shell, or bash. bash is the functional equivalent of the Korn shell. As configured on most current Unix variants, the arrow keys are bound to the history and editing functions of bash. This means that most Unix and Linux users can expect functionality similar to the DOSKEY function available with DOS. Unless they have deliberately removed it, you will be able to find the suspect's command history file in the home directory. Whatever shell the suspect uses, the history filename starts with a dot (.) and ends with "history".

On most Unix systems, users can choose their own default shell, and nothing prevents them from starting a different shell after they have logged on. Let's take a look at some of the particulars that affect what we can learn from the shell history of the more common family of shells (sh, ksh, bash, zsh, but not csh or tcsh). Like DOS, Unix has special variables shared by all running processes (at least within a user's context) called *environment variables*. These are set by default from configuration files either within the /etc directory or within the user's home directory. The command that enables you to view these variables is env. Here's an abbreviated list of those environment variables from a Linux workstation:

```
$ env
HISTSIZE=1000
TERM=ansi
PATH=/usr/local/bin:/bin:/usr/bin:/usr/X11R6/bin:/home/jheiser/bin
SHELL=/bin/bash
PS1=\$
BASH_ENV=/home/jheiser/.bashrc
```

The variable HISTSIZE limits the maximum number of commands saved in the shell's command history array. When this limit is reached, the history commands start writing over the oldest entries. The default history file is called .bash_history. Note that the shell does not update this file on the fly—history is maintained within an array in the running bash process. When bash is exited, this file is updated. If a system is powered off without being shut down, the history of any running bash shells are lost (the next time someone tells you "always pull the plug," you'll be able to respond with a laundry list of volatile and valuable Unix system information that would be lost through a power off).

The variable PS1 configures the default prompt, one of several prompts that can be configured in Unix shells. The default user prompt for shells in the Posix family is the dollar sign ($), and to simplify our examples, we will use it as our prompt. (The default root prompt is the hash character, #.) The final variable in the preceding list, BASH_ENV, can be used by users to configure their own preferences into the bash environment. For instance, if you want more or fewer commands in your history file, you can change the HISTSIZE variable. If you are running bash as your default environment, it is the appropriate place to set environment variables, such as those affecting application parameters and other optional behaviors. Two aspects of the .bashrc filename are significant. First, any file or directory name starting with the dot character, pronounced "dot" by Unix users, is hidden when running the file list command, ls, without any special parameters. Invisibility is considered a convenience, although hackers will attempt to exploit it to make their presence less obvious (a subject that is discussed Chapter 10). Second, any filename that ends with the characters "rc" is conventionally used to set the run-time environment of an application—the application's name is usually the first part of the filename. For example, .mailrc is the file that most Unix mail programs look to for their configuration information, and .newsrc is the file that news readers use. Examination of these rc files can sometimes provide valuable clues that help locate a suspect's data or reconstruct his or her activities. Another characteristic of environment variables is that they can be manually changed. If someone attempting to hide evidence of his or her activities entered the following bash command:

```
# HISTSIZE=0
```

the shell immediately would stop keeping command history. This would be inconvenient because command history also stops working, but it also means one less thing to remember to erase later.

Let's take a look at the password file, where the user defines his or her home directory and default shell. Type **cat /etc/passwd** at a Unix command prompt. Unless the system is using NIS (see the section Unix Filesystems in this chapter), you should see something like this:

```
$ cat /etc/passwd
root:x:0:0:root:/root:/bin/bash
bin:x:1:1:bin:/bin:
daemon:x:2:2:daemon:/sbin:
adm:x:3:4:adm:/var/adm:
lp:x:4:7:lp:/var/spool/lpd:
sync:x:5:0:sync:/sbin:/bin/sync
shutdown:x:6:0:shutdown:/sbin:/sbin/shutdown
halt:x:7:0:halt:/sbin:/sbin/halt
mail:x:8:12:mail:/var/spool/mail:
news:x:9:13:news:/var/spool/news:
uucp:x:10:14:uucp:/var/spool/uucp:
operator:x:11:0:operator:/root:
games:x:12:100:games:/usr/games:
gopher:x:13:30:gopher:/usr/lib/gopher-data:
ftp:x:14:50:FTP User:/home/ftp:
nobody:x:99:99:Nobody:/:
xfs:x:100:101:X Font Server:/etc/X11/fs:/bin/false
jheiser:x:500:500:Jay Heiser:/home/jheiser:/bin/bash
sallym:x:501:501:Sally Mer:/home/sallym:/bin/csh
bobbyg:x:502:502:Bobby Geburt:/home/bobbyg:/bin/sh
```

Full name — Logon shell — Home directory — Default GID — UID — Password (if no /etc/shadow) — Username

We'll spend more time on this system file later, but for now, it's important to know that fields are delimited by a colon (:). The first field in a password entry is the username. The fifth field in a password file entry is conventionally the user's full name, although its use is totally arbitrary. The last two fields in a password file entry are the user's home directory and default shell.

You may be curious as to why a file named "password" contains no passwords. The nonpassword information in this file is considered to be useful for general viewing; removing it breaks a number of common Unix applications that refer to it. Most Unix systems offer the option of storing the encrypted password in the read-protected file /etc/shadow. As we discuss in Chapter 10, the relatively weak encryption used to protect passwords on most Unix systems can be broken with commonly-available cracking tools, encouraging system attackers to try to download copies of the password file in hopes that it contains the encrypted passwords.

Readers who are inexperienced Unix users might also be asking why the "type" command is called "cat". "cat" is actually an abbreviation for "concatenate", which provides an additional opportunity for a lesson in Unix architecture. When a Unix process is opened, three files are automatically opened: stdin, stdout, and stderr. By default, stdin is associated with the keyboard, while stdout and stderr are associated with the monitor. This association can be changed, which is a powerful and convenient feature of Unix. When you use cat followed by a filename, you are actually concatenating (appending) the contents of that file to stdout, which is normally, but not always, your monitor. This might not seem like a significant concept, but it is crucial for an understanding of how Unix works. It is a powerful abstraction that greatly increases the applicability and flexibility of Unix utilities. Remember, you are not viewing a file, you are concatenating it to the string of characters displayed on your terminal. If you desire, you can concatenate an entire filesystem to your terminal. Fortunately, Unix provides a variety of handy utilities enabling us to examine the contents of files and the filesystem without displaying the raw data on our terminals.

Unix Filesystems

If you have only a limited amount of time available to study Unix internals, the filesystem should get most of your attention. Files are accessed on Unix systems through several layers of abstraction. Every file is represented by a data structure called an *inode*, short for index node, which indexes the file's location on disk and contains information about its owner, permissions, and access times. Inodes are stored on the filesystem in an area of the disk called the *inode list*, which is not normally accessible to the user directly. When a filesystem is mounted, the inode list is read into a kernel structure called the *inode table*. The inode table is actually used by the kernel when accessing the filesystem. It periodically is synchronized with the inode list and, of course, is synchronized during an orderly shutdown. It contains volatile information that can be lost if the system were powered down before it was shut down. An inode never contains filenames—directories contain filenames and point them to specific inodes within a specific filesystem. When a directory entry points to an inode, it is called a *link,* and an inode may have multiple links. Although Windows provides a similar capability called the *shortcut,* shortcuts are more akin to what is called a *symbolic link* on a Unix system. Windows systems always have a one-to-one correspondence between individual files and the human-readable name in the directory. On Unix, this is not the case at all—when analyzing a Unix system, it is important to be aware that a single file can appear in multiple directories simultaneously and that it can have a different name in each directory. In fact, some utilities are written so that they change their behavior depending upon which name they are invoked by. Table 9-2 summarizes the contents of an inode.

Table 9-2   Contents of an Inode

Element	Description
Owner and group IDs	Permissions for Unix inodes are granted to any of three different abstractions: the owner of a file, unnamed group, or everyone who has access to the system. The inode uses numeric values for owner and group, which are indexed to names contained in /etc/passwd and /etc/group, respectively.
Type	Regular, directory, character, or block special (device drivers), named pipes (interprocess communication mechanism).
Access permissions	Read, write, and execute. Execute permission on a directory is required in order to search for a filename within it.
Times: atime mtime ctime	Last access (read) of the file, last modification to the file, last change of inode (any change to the file, or any change to owner, permission, or number of links).
Number of links	The number of directory entries pointing to this inode. Note that it is possible for this value to be out of sync with the filesystem directories.
Pointers to data blocks	Unix files are composed of blocks, and there is no requirement that the blocks be contiguous. (Several levels of indirection are used for large files.)
File size	The file size can be larger than the actual number of blocks constituting the file. This is desirable sometimes, but it can also be misleading.

The stat command provides user access to the contents of an inode. It is one of several Unix commands that are named after corresponding system calls. Let's take a look at the information it provides:

```
$ stat /etc/passwd
  File: "/etc/passwd"
  Size: 614      Filetype: Regular File
  Mode: (0644/-rw-r--r--)   Uid: (   0/   root) Gid: (   0/   root)
Device:  3,5  Inode: 98569   Links: 1
Access: Sat Apr 22 21:04:39 2000(00000.00:00:17)
Modify: Thu Apr 20 21:31:52 2000(00001.23:21:25)
Change: Thu Apr 20 21:31:52 2000(00001.23:21:25)
```

The mode of this file shows two different representations of the file's access permissions. The number 0644 is an octal value—all combinations of file permissions can be represented by a four-digit octal number. You must understand the meaning of this number in order to use the find command to search for files meeting certain characteristics that might be indicative of back doors or other hostile intent. The octal value is stored in the inode, and the characters after it, - rw - r - - r - -, are a format more intuitively obvious for humans. The letters "r," "w," and "x" stand respectively for read, write, and execute. Permission can be granted at three different granularities: the owner, the group, and everyone. In this case, read and write access are provided for the owner, read access is provided for the group, and read permission is provided to everyone.

GID and UID of zero always represent the administrative account, root, on every Unix system—this is wired into the kernel and cannot be changed. For every nonzero value, the correct logon and group names must be looked up by cross-referencing these numbers to the /etc/passwd and /etc/group files (or the equivalent Network Information System maps). If the filesystem being examined had been accessed on a different Unix host, or otherwise copied to another system, the user logon and group names associated with the UIDs and GIDs by applications such as stat and ls would be incorrect. If you are examining a file outside of its home Unix host, always use the numeric UID and GID found in the passwd and group files, manually correlating them to the logon names and group names from the original suspect's host. Be aware that some systems use a directory service to centralize the password and group files. The most common Unix directory services are Network Information System (NIS) and the newer, more secure version NIS+, although Lightweight Directory Access Protocol (LDAP) is gaining prominence. Directory services are networked databases that are optimized for lookup instead of for writing. NIS and NIS+ are used exclusively for centralizing the administration of multiple Unix systems. Look for the file /etc/nsswitch.conf, which contains configuration information for the logon routine, optionally pointing it to a directory service for some or all user accounts. Let's take a quick look at this file:

```
# more /etc/nsswitch.conf
passwd: files nis
group: files nis
```

In this example, any attempt to look up password or group file information first attempts to do so in /etc/passwd or /etc/group, and if that does not result in a hit, the system will query the Network Information System directory service.

As shown by the output of the stat command above, the last access of the inode linked to by /etc/password occurred at 21:04:39. The password file is accessed every time a password is changed or evaluated. In this case, we can correlate this time with Warren's last login by using the last command:

```
$ last wkruse | head -1
wkruse  pts/3   192.168.0.3 Sat Apr 22 21:04 still logged in
```

The password file is also accessed by many other system utilities. The shadow password file containing the encrypted passwords is accessed only when a password is compared or changed, or when a user is added or deleted. We also can use the ls command with the proper arguments to see when a file was last accessed:

```
$ ls -lu /etc/shadow
-r--------   1 root      root       573 Apr 22 21:04 /etc/shadow
```

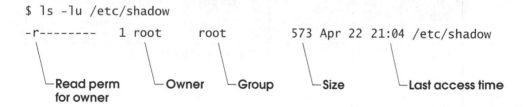

In this example, you can see that only the owner, root, has read access to this file—no other user can access it at all. (We are able to see the directory entry for this file because everyone has read and execute permission for /etc.)

No discussion of Unix file permissions would be complete without mentioning set user ID (SUID) and set group ID (SGID) files. Files that are SUID root can be run by anyone with execute permission, but when these files run, they run as if they were run by their owner. SGID files execute with the effective permissions of their group owner—even if the user executing them is not a member of that group. This capability is commonly used to access peripherals and is sometimes used to provide delegation of system administration privileges. It is also used by hackers and unscrupulous system administrators to create back doors allowing root access. When analyzing a real or suspected system hack, you must locate all SUID and SGID executables to verify their legitimacy. Let's take a quick look at the directory entry of a system executable that must access the printer:

```
$ ls -l /usr/bin/lpr
-r-sr-sr-x   1 root        lp              15768 Sep 10  1999 /usr/bin/lpr
$
```

On this system, the print command, lpr, is SUID root, which is indicated by the "s" in the owner position, and it is SGID group lp, indicated by the second "s". It is readable and executable by owner, group, and all. Be aware that different versions of Unix use the SUID and SGID bits differently, or not at all, for directories. Table 9-3 summarizes Unix filesystem permissions.

File permissions are changed with the chmod command, which can use either letter abbreviations or the octal codes. To provide more than one type of permission, add together the individual octal values. For instance, shell scripts must be executable in order to be run, and because they are interpreted at run time, they must

Table 9-3 Unix Filesystem Permissions

Abbrev	Octal	Permission over Individual Files	Permission over entire Directory
x	001 010 100	Execute	Search directory or cd to it.
w	002 020 200	Write	Remove and create files.
r	004 040 400	Read	List directory contents.
s	4000	SUID	
s	2000	SGID	Linux: files created in dir have their group set to the group owner of that dir.
T	1000	Sticky Bit (obsolete)	Prevents non-owner from deleting file.

also be readable. Read permission is 4 and execute permission is 1, so both can be assigned by changing the mode to 5. A typical shell script that is writable by the owner and executable by everyone has the mode 755.

```
$ chmod 755 sortem
$ ls -l sortem
-rwxr-xr-x   1 wkruse  wkruse          0 Apr 24 01:47 sortem
```

Remember that permissions are stored in the inode—not in the directory. Every link to the same inode indicates the same permissions and ownership.

One final piece of information associated with the inode must be explained: the device number. In the stat example run previously, the filesystem on which this inode is located has a major device number of 3 and a minor device number of 5. These numbers are used for the device special files located in the /dev directory. The major device number refers to the specific device driver used to access this type of device. The table in the kernel associates each device driver with at least one major device number. The minor device number refers to a specific device, and in many cases, a single device driver accesses multiple devices. In this case, the minor device number 5 refers to a specific filesystem on our workstation's single hard drive. This can be seen by running df, a utility that displays current filesystems:

```
$ df
Filesystem          1k-blocks      Used Available Use% Mounted on
/dev/hda5            1482208    739796    667116  53% /
/dev/hda1              17534      2647     13982  16% /boot
```

If we take a look at the inode /dev/hda5, we can see that it is not a "regular file" like /etc/passwd, but instead it is a special file of the type *block device:*

```
$ stat /dev/hda5
  File: "/dev/hda5"
  Size: 0              Filetype: Block Device
  Mode: (0660/brw-rw----)        Uid: ( 0/  root) Gid: ( 6/  disk)
Device: 3,5    Inode: 63631    Links: 1    Device type: 3,5
Access: Tue May  5 16:32:26 1998(00718.06:30:03)
Modify: Tue May  5 16:32:26 1998(00718.06:30:03)
Change: Sun Apr 16 15:53:39 2000(00006.07:08:50
```

Remember we agreed that a file consisted of blocks. A filesystem is a block device, making reads and writes more efficient by performing them in block-sized chunks instead of a bit or a byte at a time. This also means that if the system is powered off without being shut down, any data in a block that hasn't been written back to the hard drive yet is lost. All of the examples we've looked at have had only one link. The link utility, ln, allows additional directory entries to be made to an existing inode, each of which increments the number of links. It is also possible for a zero link file to exist. When a process opens a file, it refers to that file internally through the inode number, not the name. If a file's last directory link is removed while a file is open, the inode continues to exist until the process closes the file, at which point the inode list entry and all of the filesystem blocks are made available to other applications. There are both legitimate and stealth reasons for having zero link files. Because a file is deleted when a system is shut down or powered off, and it is otherwise invisible to other processes before the shutdown, processes often unlink their temporary files to prevent their being inadvertently accessed and to ensure that they won't litter the filesystem in case the process using them crashes.

A hard drive often has more than one filesystem on it, each located on its own partition. Each hardware platform has its own mechanisms for viewing and manipulating disk partitions. A variety of commercial and shareware disk partition utilities are available for PC hardware, but all PC-based operating systems should have a version of fdisk. Linux is no exception. We can use fdisk to confirm the information from df:

```
# /sbin/fdisk /dev/hda

Command (m for help): p

Disk /dev/hda: 64 heads, 63 sectors, 789 cylinders
Units = cylinders of 4032 * 512 bytes

   Device Boot    Start      End    Blocks   Id  System
/dev/hda1   *         1        9     18112+  83  Linux
/dev/hda2            10      789   1572480    5  Extended
/dev/hda5            10      756   1505920+  83  Linux
/dev/hda6           757      789     66496+  82  Linux swap

Command (m for help): q
```

Whatever you do, do not make any changes to the partitions using fdisk and especially do not save any accidental changes! We discuss hard drive partitions in Chapter 3. If you haven't reviewed that material yet, it's important to realize that partitions exist and that information about them can be accessed from within Unix in several different ways.

File Time Attributes

Every user leaves footprints throughout the filesystem. Experienced administrators and investigators can use filesystem access time data to analyze user activities (if you aren't experienced in Unix administration, bring such a person with you on Unix investigations). Access time can show what documentation someone read and can provide important clues about the purpose of the programs they compiled. Changes to inodes—without corresponding changes to the file—can be a clue that an intruder is trying to reconfigure the system. Of course, sophisticated intruders can erase these tracks. Depending upon how skillful they are, the tracks might be erased in such a way that it is obvious that tracks have been covered—a clear indication of suspicious activity. A more subtle and skillful attacker might remove those broken twigs and straighten out those bent blades of grass, making it difficult to discern that anyone ever passed that way. Inodes live on the filesystem, and anything on the filesystem can be changed by someone with root access who knows how to do it. Altering the modify and access times in an inode is simple, but not every suspect knows how to do it. The inode change time also can be altered by someone with root access and the right software.

Unix systems run their internal clocks in Universal Coordinated Time (that is, Greenwich mean time, GMT), translating time display in utilities such as ls according to a user's TZ environment variable, so be sure that you conduct your investigations in GMT or that your TZ variable is the same on every system you are examining and any forensic workstation you use. Unix tells time by counting the number of seconds that have elapsed since the "Unix epoch" (January 2, 1970).

mount

Filesystems are not born—they are made. Specifically, they are created using the mkfs command. A filesystem is essentially a database designed to store, search, and retrieve one specific type of data—files. Turning a block device or partition into a filesystem creates data structures, such as the inode list and another index called the *superblock,* and formats the blocks in preparation for file storage. The device being formatted appears as a file itself. It appears as a block special device in the /dev directory and represents a hard drive partition, tape drive, floppy drive, zip drive, or CD drive.

In order to actually use a filesystem, it must be mounted first. The mount command allows a chunk of media to be accessed as a filesystem. Certainly it is possible with Unix to dig around in the raw media itself, examining all of its bits and bytes, but if the media is formatted as a filesystem, mounting it loads the inode list into the kernel and sets up the appropriate data structures to allow access to discrete files containing logically contiguous data. The media does not have to be a hard drive. Although access time is slow, it is possible even to mount a tape and access it as a filesystem (as long as the hardware supports block addressing and random seeks). Enter **man mount** to review the options available with the mount command (see the section "Putting It All Together," later in this chapter for information on man pages). Unix systems support the ability to mount a wide variety of filesystems, and PC-based Linux systems can even mount DOS and Windows NT filesystems. Once mounted, these filesystems don't provide all the functionality of a normal Unix filesystem, but it is possible to examine them using Unix tools. Unix provides a more powerful analysis environment than Windows or DOS. An advantage of analyzing Windows filesystems on a Unix machine is that the filesystem can be mounted read-only, ensuring that you can't make any inadvertent changes to its contents. Unix filesystems can also be mounted read-only, which is an extremely convenient feature that can help in responding to defense suggestions that data was manipulated during an investigation.

Running the mount command by itself provides a list of currently mounted filesystems:

```
$ mount
/dev/hda5 on / type ext2 (rw)
none on /proc type proc (rw)
/dev/hda1 on /boot type ext2 (rw)
none on /dev/pts type devpts (rw,gid=5,mode=620)
/dev/hdc on /mnt/cdrom type iso9660 (ro,nosuid,nodev)
```

The file /etc/fstab provides clues as to what hardware devices might be available, not all of which are necessarily always mounted. It specifies all filesystems that are mounted automatically at boot time or are optionally mountable by specific users. Unix systems are invariably configured to boot into an operational state, so you should assume that any booting Unix system automatically mounts its filesystems for both reading and writing as they come up in multiuser mode. If this isn't what you want—and if you are collecting legally-defensible evidence, that is not what you want—make sure that the booting system stays in single-user mode.

Check fstab when you examine a system to see if it normally or sometimes is configured to use a remote Network File System (NFS) that may not be mounted when you are examining the system:

```
cat /etc/fstab
/dev/hda5              /                          ext2     defaults        1 1
/dev/hda1              /boot                      ext2     defaults        1 2
/dev/cdrom            /mnt/cdrom                 iso9660 noauto,owner,ro 0 0
/dev/hda6             swap                        swap     defaults        0 0
/dev/fd0             /mnt/floppy                 ext2     noauto,owner    0 0
none                  /proc                      proc     defaults        0 0
none                  /dev/pts                   devpts   gid=5,mode=620  0 0
matrix:/mnt/temp      /mnt/matrix/temp           nfs      defaults        0 0
```

In this example, neither the CD nor the floppy drive are automatically mounted at boot time, but they are ready to be mounted, and as a convenience, no auto entries are available to allow them to be mounted with a simplified mount command, such as **mount /dev/fd0.** Many PC Unix systems automatically mount the CD whenever they detect an inserted CD. Unix systems with floppy drives have commands (such as mdir and mcopy on Linux) allowing the manipulation of DOS files on a floppy drive without having to mount it. If you boot from a Unix floppy disk, or if you run forensic utilities on a suspect's computer from a floppy disk or CD, the disk has to be mounted. Just to be sure that you are familiar with the procedure, let's use a version of mkfs to format a 3.5-inch floppy disk with the default Linux filesystem and then mount it:

```
$ /sbin/mkfs.ext2 /dev/fd0
mke2fs 1.15, 18-Jul-1999 for EXT2 FS 0.5b, 95/08/09
Filesystem label=
OS type: Linux
Block size=1024 (log=0)
Fragment size=1024 (log=0)
184 inodes, 1440 blocks
72 blocks (5.00%) reserved for the super user
First data block=1
1 block group
8192 blocks per group, 8192 fragments per group
184 inodes per group
```

```
Writing inode tables: done
Writing superblocks and filesystem accounting information: done
$ mount -o ro /dev/fd0
```

We used the -o ro option for read-only (on Linux, it can be a simple -r). Get in the habit of explicitly mounting devices as read-only. When you are examining a suspect drive for evidence, you'll want to protect it from inadvertent changes, and you must be able to explain how you protected it. Mount it read-only and document this step in your notes. If you are examining a live system and have followed best practice by bringing your own disk with statically linked tools, you also should mount that disk read-only to prevent hostile code from subverting your examination utilities.

The complete mount command invocation requires specifying both the filesystem being mounted and its *mount point,* the place on an existing filesystem where it is logically attached. The complete version of the preceding command looks like this:

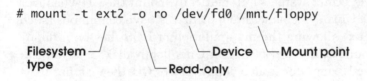

Because the floppy device is already listed in the fstab file, we don't have to be that explicit. Verify the results by using the mount command with no additional parameters:

```
$ mount
/dev/hda5 on / type ext2 (rw)
none on /proc type proc (rw)
/dev/hda1 on /boot type ext2 (rw)
none on /dev/pts type devpts (rw,gid=5,mode=620)
/dev/fd0 on /mnt/floppy type ext2 (rw,nosuid,nodev,user=wkruse)
```

The /mnt directory is called the *mount directory,* and it is conventionally used for temporarily mounting filesystems, although the root user can mount the floppy filesystem anywhere. (Different versions of Unix vary in what they allow nonroot users to do, but most have some provision enabling nonadministrators to mount specific filesystems under controlled circumstances.) The default configuration normally allows nonroot users to mount removable media only in the prescribed directories in the /mnt directory. When you're done with the floppy disk, just type **umount /dev/fd0**.

Putting It All Together

Programmers and power users are attracted to Unix because it ships with a wide variety of useful utilities. This productive environment is also appealing to system attackers, and forensic analysts should be as familiar with Unix as their adversaries are. Before diving into some of the more esoteric commands, let's be sure that you are taking full advantage of the man command used to access the online manual. The Man utility is the front-end application to a huge online database of platform-specific information about utilities, file types, and programming libraries. Each entry in the man data store uses a standard text format based on a system of commands preceded by dots. An example of one of these pages looks like this:

```
.TH GREP 1 \*(Dt "GNU Project"
.SH NAME
grep, egrep, fgrep \- print lines matching a pattern
.SH SYNOPSIS
.B grep
```

Man pages are formatted with a text-processing tool that descends from an ancient Bell Labs utility, Runoff. Depending upon the system you are examining, it either has the nroff or the groff utility, both of which are modern versions of nroff. Both security and hacker tools usually ship with the source for their associated man pages. If you encounter a file ending in a dot followed by a single-digit number, it is probably the source text for a man page, and it can be formatted by typing the command **nroff -man** *filename*. Even experienced Unix users are heavy users of man pages because nobody can remember all the options to all of the utilities. While the location of the man directory varies from system to system, each man page is a discrete file, making it easy to see when it was last accessed. As an efficiency measure, it is customary on a Unix system to save formatted versions of man pages. When a man page is requested and it doesn't already exist, the raw page is formatted, and a compressed version of the output is stored in the catman directory. On our Linux workstation, the formatted man pages are stored in numbered directories inside /var/catman. Whoever views a man page first creates the formatted page for future use and owns that file. This means that the catman directory can tell you who first looked at a man page and when, and it also can tell you when a man page was most recently visited. For example, let's look at the last five man pages to be stored in the catman hierarchy:

```
# ls -lt /var/catman/cat1 | head -5
total 364
```

```
-r--rw-r--   1 root      man            937 Apr 30 12:51 su.1.gz
-r--rw-r--   1 sallym    man           3150 Apr 28 20:14 compress.1.gz
-r--rw-r--   1 sallym    man           1934 Apr 28 19:54 od.1.gz
-r--rw-r--   1 sallym    man            899 Apr 28 01:38 touch.1.gz
```

This shows us that the user sallym was apparently the first person to look at the compress, od, and touch man pages, and that she probably did so on the evening of April 28. If the access time on these files is later than the modification time, we can't know who read them:

```
# ls -lut /var/catman/cat1 | head -5
total 364
-r--rw-r--   1 sallym    man           1934 Apr 30 13:39 od.1.gz
-r--rw-r--   1 root      man            937 Apr 30 12:51 su.1.gz
-r--rw-r--   1 bobbyg    man           2107 Apr 30 12:51 xargs.1.gz
-r--rw-r--   1 root      man          50894 Apr 30 11:59 bash.1.gz
```

You can see that the od page has been popular lately, having been accessed most recently two days after its initial use.

Man pages are contained in numbered directories, each of which contains a different type of reference. The man1 directory contains information on commands, man2 contains information on system calls, man5 contains information on file structure, and man8 contains administrative commands. These directory numbers correspond to index numbers appearing at the top of the man pages, and in some cases, you may have to specify the man section you want to read. To read instructions on the user command chmod, for changing file permissions, type **man chmod.** Type **man 1 chmod** to read the man page chmod(1). If you want to read chmod(2), which contains details on the system call used to change file ownership, type **man 2 chmod.**

The first command you should try is **man man**, which provides instructions on the man command itself. When you are on a strange Unix system, use the man pages for help with the exact invocation of commands that may vary from vendor to vendor. If you don't know the name of the command you want to run, you often can find it by searching for a keyword. For example, to learn which man pages are associated with terminals (tty), type **man -k tty** (impress your friends by typing the equivalent **apropos tty** instead). On systems supporting this capability, a list of all the man pages that reference the keyword you're searching for is displayed.

Man pages are universally available and usually are very comprehensive, but they can be terse and difficult to understand for a beginner. You have several other options available for online user documents. Check for a /usr/doc directory, try the help command, and look for FAQs on the Web.

The script command is a bit obscure, but highly useful for the forensic analyst. When you are working at a command prompt, typing **script** followed by the name of an output file results in all of your commands and their output being simultaneously sent to your screen as normal, and also sent to the file you specify. Get into the habit of using this command as a form of internal documentation and a way to store results.

One of the most powerful and useful utilities for file examination is the grep command. grep is used to search for specific strings within a file and is analogous to the Find.exe command supplied with DOS. Its name is an acronym for "global regular expression print," but it's easier just to remember grep. We use grep a lot throughout the rest of this chapter and in Chapter 11, so let's take a look at it now by finding every man page written by anyone named Hansen. The default location for the man directories on RedHat Linux is /usr/man.

```
$ cd /usr/man/man1
$ grep Hansen *
man1/cdecl.1:Wolverton, Tony Hansen, and Merlyn LeRoy.
```

It turns out that a Hansen is associated with a single man page in this directory. In most investigations, we'd probably want to look in multiple directories, and you can do so in several ways with Unix. First, let's move up a directory level and see what happens if we use the recursive option in grep:[1]

```
$ cd ..
$ grep -r Hansen *
man1/cdecl.1:Wolverton, Tony Hansen, and Merlyn LeRoy.
grep: man1/rec.1: No such file or directory
man3/libpbm.3:Copyright (C) 1989, 1991 by Tony Hansen and Jef Poskanzer.
man3/libpgm.3:Copyright (C) 1989, 1991 by Tony Hansen and Jef Poskanzer.
man3/libpnm.3:Copyright (C) 1989, 1991 by Tony Hansen and Jef Poskanzer.
man3/libppm.3:Copyright (C) 1989, 1991 by Tony Hansen and Jef Poskanzer.
```

---

1. Not all versions of Unix have a version of grep that supports recursive options. Many of the GNU versions of the standard Unix utilities do support recursive option so you'll find them in Linux and other open source platforms. UnixWare also includes a recursive option; except it uses an uppercase "R". Keep reading, and we'll show you a more portable method of doing recursive operations.

This same name appears on several pages in man3 (documentation on programming libraries). Note that this command returned an error on the second line. How is it that grep knows the name of the file rec.1, yet the file doesn't exist? Let's use the extended version of the list command and see what the directory entry for that file shows.

```
$ ls -l man1/rec.1
lrwxrwxrwx   1 root    root      37 Apr 16 16:23 man1/rec.1 -> /var/tmp/
    sox-root/usr/man/man1/play.1
```

The "l" character at the beginning of the mode string and the character sequence "->" appearing after man1/rec.1 are indications that this is a *symbolic link*. As mentioned earlier, a symbolic link is similar to a Windows shortcut. The default behavior for the link command, ln, is to create a *hard link,* which is a directory entry pointing to a specific inode within the same filesystem as the inode. This is fine as long as the file you want to link to happens to be on the same filesystem as the directory you want to put the link in. If you want to link to something in another filesystem, you can create a symbolic link using the -s flag. Not only are symlinks used between filesystems that are local to a host, but they also are used to link NFS (remote) filesystems into the local directory tree. Symbolic links are a concern to the investigator because they are broken if they're not explicitly copied. Linux is different from most Unix versions in making heavy use of symbolic links within a filesystem, as demonstrated by the broken link in the preceding example. Although this link is within a single filesystem in this case, it is exactly what would happen if you made an image of a filesystem containing a symbolic link to another filesystem and then restored only one of the filesystems on your analysis machine. Archive programs, such as tar, that copy a filesystem by operating on each file individually, have the optional ability to include symbolically linked files in the resulting archive file.

One of the most useful investigative tools is find, a command-line utility comparable to the Windows Find Files window. find is used to recursively walk a filesystem directory tree, performing evaluations on every object. find can output a list of files meeting the evaluation criteria, or it actually can operate on them. find can perform evaluations based on one of three different types of information or any combination of them:

- **Inode:** Test for any specific information contained in the inodes, including all three timestamps, owner, mode, size, and the inode number itself.
- **Filename:** Use a regular expression to search for any inode pointed to by a name meeting any specified pattern.

- **Operations:** Launch a specified command and apply it sequentially to each of the inodes meeting the specified search criteria. The return status of that command, success or fail, can be used as part of the search criteria.

The ability to perform commands on the list of files returned by the search criteria is incredibly useful. Besides operating on files as part of the search criteria, you also might want to use find as sort of a batch capability to copy, change, or otherwise manipulate a set of filesystem objects meeting your search criteria. When no command is specified, find sends the list of files meeting the criteria to stdout, it returns an error message, or worse, it just doesn't work like you expect. Linux is very user friendly and provides intelligent defaults, but don't forget to use the -print option when on non-Linux systems. It works just fine on Linux when you do include the -print option, so we recommend that you always use it, just so you don't forget when you are working on some other platform.

Let's look at a couple of examples. Suppose we're concerned about the activities on a Unix box and want to see what C source code is on it. We can use find to search for all files ending with ".c" by placing the appropriate metacharacters (a regular expression) in single quotes so the shell doesn't try to expand it first:

```
# find /home -name '*.c' -print
/home/jheiser/web_sniff.c
/home/sallym/stuff/linux_lpr.c
/home/sallym/stuff/lpr_overflow.c
/home/sallym/stuff/lprm.c
/home/sallym/stuff/lpr.c
/home/sallym/stuff/linux_httpd.c
```

Based on this output, it seems that both jheiser and sallym have some suspicious-looking source code in their directories. We don't have time right now to examine these files, but maybe if we check for just a string or two, we can determine whether any of these programs are meant as exploit code. We can do so by running the same file command and then executing grep on every file that it matches. Here's where find gets a bit arcane. The curly braces appearing after our command (in the example that follows) are a convention that means "put each of the filenames found right here as if they were all typed manually on the command line." The backslash and semicolon are the characters that end the exec string. Finally, the -print at the end of the command outputs the name of the matching object when a positive result returns from the executed command. In this case, if the string we're looking for is found in any of the files by grep, each line containing that string is output followed by the name of the file containing it.

```
#  find /home -name '*.c' -exec grep exploit {} \; -print
[20 lines of results skipped to save space]
* was unable to massage Aleph One's generic exploit enough
/home/sallym/stuff/lprm.c
  * /usr/bin/lpr buffer overflow exploit for Linux with non-executable
    stack
/home/sallym/stuff/lpr.c
```

Wow, that command returned more than we expected it to. It works well, but it is kind of slow because it has to spawn a new shell for every single file it finds. Next, we're going to do the exact same thing but in a different way. We're going to use the xargs utility that passes multiple filenames to the utility that appears after it in the command line (trust us, this method can be hugely faster). Instead of using -print with find, we'll use -print0, which, when used with the -0 option of xargs, prevents xargs from barfing on a filename with a new line contained within it. You should get in the habit of always using these options.

```
# find /home/sallym —name '*.c' —print0 | xargs -0 grep exploit
[20 lines of results skipped to save space]
/home/sallym/stuff/lprm.c:* was unable to massage Aleph One's generic
  exploit enough
/home/sallym/stuff/lpr.c: * /usr/bin/lpr buffer overflow exploit for
  Linux with non-executable stack
```

Not only does the use of xargs make this operation much quicker, but the output is better because the filenames appear before the string found by grep instead of after it. We discuss the find command further in this chapter and in Chapter 11. If you are not familiar with find, you should study it.

Several other commands provide helpful information about the contents and purpose of files. Windows uses filename extensions to determine file types. For example, when a file ends in .doc, it is considered a Microsoft Word file. When a file ends in .txt, it is considered an ASCII text file. When a file ends in .pdf, it is treated as an Adobe Acrobat file. Although Unix also uses conventions for file extensions, they're mostly for human convenience. Some commands, however, do have the default behavior of operating on files with specific extensions. A Unix user does not need an extension to determine the probable role of a file because they have access to the file command. The file command makes a best guess, but it is usually pretty accurate. When run against a file, it first checks the filesystem using the stat() system call to determine if it is a data file, an empty file, or a device special file. It then compares the first several bytes of information in the file to the magic number index, /usr/share/magic or /etc/magic, which contains a list of unique identification numbers conventionally used by specific Unix applications. Finally, the file command makes a best guess based on the contents of the file. This is especially important if the file is an ASCII text file. Many applications create ASCII files in formats easily recognizable by file. file can tell you if a file is a binary executable, what type of executable it is, what kind of archive format it uses, and a variety of other characteristics. The conventions used by file, such as the magic numbers, are shared among most versions of Unix. This means that even if you have a binary file that originated on a different version of Unix and cannot be executed on your system, the file utility on your system has a good chance of identifying its platform of origin. This is extraordinarily helpful in forensic analysis because it can help you understand either the source or the purpose of the code. First, it can help you identify foreign object code that might have been moved onto a suspect system by either a legitimate user or an an intruder. Second, if you are doing your analysis on a different platform than the one that actually created the files system being examined, the file command will help you confirm whether or not binaries you locate are native to the suspect system. Remember that distributed filesystems, such as NFS, often have directory space that is shared by multiple versions of Unix hosts running, so it would not be unusual to find executables that are native to different versions of Unix.

Let's take a look at several representative uses of file:

```
# file /bin/bash
/bin/bash: ELF 32-bit LSB executable, Intel 80386, version 1,
           dynamically linked (uses shared libs), stripped
```

This output tells us quite a bit about our executable. First, it provides us the directory name from the command line, which is helpful when combined with other commands such as the example using find later in this chapter. Next, it identifies it as an ELF 32-bit executable, one of the object file formats used on Intel-based Unix systems. The ability to determine whether or not a file is dynamically linked is important to anyone investigating hacking incidents. In order to save space, the kernel provides a set of common object code libraries with routines that can be shared by any executable that wants to use them. This is similar to the dynamically linked library (DLL) model used by Windows. Unlike Windows, Unix users normally do not have permission to create a dynamically linked library in a directory where it automatically will be used by other users. The default shared link libraries are owned by root and are found in specific locations. Only the root user can change the libraries. Hackers have been known to change these libraries, which has the disastrous effect of changing the behavior of every single utility that links to them. For this reason, when examining a potentially hacked system, utilities should be used that are statically linked. Statically linked binaries are larger, but they are not affected by hacks to shared libraries. The file command always can be used to quickly determine if a file is dynamically or statically linked.

The file command is also useful in identifying the partitions on a hard drive. On a Linux system, /dev/hda represents the boot sector of the master hard drive on the first IDE controller, with each number following the "hda" representing the partitions. (SCSI drives use /dev/sda. Use **man -k disk** to find the man pages discussing the drive naming conventions on any Unix system.) The second drive starts with /dev/hdb, and so on. The -s flag is necessary to instruct the file utility to examine device special files.

```
# file -s /dev/hda*
/dev/hda:    x86 boot sector
/dev/hda1:   Linux/i386 ext2 filesystem
/dev/hda10: empty
/dev/hda11: empty
/dev/hda12: empty
/dev/hda13: empty
/dev/hda14: empty
/dev/hda15: empty
/dev/hda16: empty
/dev/hda2:   x86 boot sector, extended partition table
/dev/hda3:   empty
/dev/hda4:   empty
/dev/hda5:   Linux/i386 ext2 filesystem
/dev/hda6:   data
/dev/hda7:   empty
/dev/hda8:   empty
/dev/hda9:   empty
```

This output confirms that our Linux filesystems are on partitions 1 and 5. Note that partition 6 appears as "data". It is actually our swap partition—one of the few things that file cannot identify.

To determine how the file utility fares against a DOS filesystem, let's mount a floppy drive and see how it appears to ls:

```
# mount -t msdos /dev/fd0 /mnt/floppy
# ls -l /mnt/floppy
total 830
-rwxrwxr-x   1 root     root        44032 Apr 25 19:30 961018.doc
-rwxrwxr-x   1 root     root        59904 Sep  4 1999 acctres.dll
-rwxrwxr-x   1 root     root        15495 May 11 1998 doskey.com
-rwxrwxr-x   1 root     root        68871 May 11 1998 drvspace.bin
drwxrwxr-x   2 root     root          512 Oct 25 1996 log
-rwxrwxr-x   1 root     root       610207 Oct 30 1996 offering.zip
drwxrwxr-x   2 root     root         1024 Oct 25 1996 tmp
-rwxrwxr-x   1 root     root        49568 Sep  1 1999 wucrtupd.exe
```

As far as the operating system is concerned, this DOS filesystem is no different than a native Unix system. Although we soon would run into limitations because the DOS directory doesn't contain as much information as an inode does, as far as Unix executables are concerned, their normal system calls work just fine against this filesystem. Let's examine this floppy disk with the file command and see how well we can identify its contents:

```
# file /mnt/floppy/*
/mnt/floppy/961018.doc:   Microsoft Office Document
/mnt/floppy/acctres.dll:  MS-DOS executable (EXE), OS/2 or MS Windows
/mnt/floppy/doskey.com:   data
/mnt/floppy/drvspace.bin: MS-DOS executable (EXE), OS/2 or MS Windows
/mnt/floppy/log:          directory
/mnt/floppy/offering.zip: Zip archive data, at least v2.0 to extract
/mnt/floppy/tmp:          directory
/mnt/floppy/wucrtupd.exe: MS-DOS executable (EXE), OS/2 or MS Windows
```

With the exception of the .com file, we are able to identify everything on the floppy disk. The file utility even provides clues about the format of the zip archive. Given that this utility can identify archive files from other operating systems, it should come as no surprise that it is able to identify all the common Unix archive formats, find's permission option, -perm, is the appropriate way to find inodes that have specific modes, but because hostile code may not be currently configured as executable, we need to examine a file's contents to determine the file's purpose. We could search an entire file directory tree, listing the type of every single file, identifying all files, but what if we realy just wanted to identify one particular type of file. We know that the file command includes the word "executable" as part of the results string whenever it encounters an executable of any kind. Thus, we can "pipe" the output from find and file through the grep command and isolate those files meeting our exact search criteria.

```
# find /home -type f -print0 |xargs -0 file |grep executable
/home/jheiser/a.out:   ELF 32-bit LSB executable, Intel 80386, version 1
/home/sallym/core:                      ELF 32-bit LSB core file,
    Intel 80386, version 1, stripped
```

Taking a quick swing through the home directories, we've found three executables (the name "a.out" is the default name that the Unix compiler uses if you don't specify a name).

Encountering this mystery executable provides an opportunity to experiment with one more file examination utility, strings. The strings command finds and outputs consecutive series of printable characters. By default, it outputs character strings that are at least four characters long. This value can be made shorter, but the number of meaningless strings returned becomes so high that it is tedious to review all of the output. It is an extraordinarily useful program for examining an unknown executable. Most binaries are chock-full of strings, including usage and error messages, default filenames, and special character sequences used by revision control software, and the first of the mystery executables discovered previously turns out to be no exception. It actually contains over 100 lines of printable strings. Because this is too much text to view conveniently on a screen, we redirect the standard output of the strings command into the standard input of the pager using a pipe. Unix has at least three different pagers in common use. The default on most systems, just like on DOS, is more, but most people prefer to use the less pager. (This is another Unix pun. less is more and more is less. Get it?) less is more convenient than more because it enables you to move forward and backward by a line or a screen at a time. Press the g key to go to the front of the output, and press the G key to go to the end of the output. It uses the Unix convention for invoking a string search within an application, which is the forward slash (/) character. When you type the slash followed by a string and press Return, that string is found within the text and every occurrence is highlighted. Now you're ready to examine this executable. Before piping the output through less, we'll number all the lines using nl. The following output is abbreviated:

```
# strings /home/jheiser/a.out | nl | less
    1  /lib/ld-linux.so.2
    2  __gmon_start__
```

```
 3  libc.so.6

 4  strcpy

 5  ioctl

 6  printf

 7  stdout

 8  sigemptyset

 9  strerror

10  geteuid

11  fgets

12  perror

13  getuid


65  couldn't open tty, assuming still okay...


77  Segmentation Violation!

78  Congratulations! You have crashed my program.

79  Please mail me: bryan@scott.net

80  describing *exactly* what you did to make this

81  program crash. Thanks and have a nice day :-)

82  *** Daemon Mode Ending at [%s] ***

83  ### Web Sniffer v1.0 by BeastMaster V ###

84            http://www.rootshell.com

85  Usage:

86  %s [-d|-v] [-p <port number>]

87  -d : run as a daemon and print output to logfile.

88  -v : run in foreground and print output to stdout.

89  -p : optionally specifies port number to sniff on.

90  You need to be root in order to run this.
```

Lines 1 and 3 refer to shared libraries. Lines 4 through 13 are the names of standard Unix library calls. Line 65 appears to be an error message. Starting at line 78, we get some excellent clues as to the purpose of this program.

Let's say that you have found some output, and you want to determine what program created it. You may very well find the needle in the haystack using grep, which can also search binaries for strings. For example, you'd be amazed at how many character-based binaries (binaries that don't have a GUI and presumably wouldn't use HTTP) contain some sort of internal reference to the Web. Try the following experiment at home:

```
# grep http /usr/bin/*
```

Unfortunately, grep doesn't provide any context. It won't return any of the text associated with the text strings you're searching for; it just tells you whether they exist. You can manually apply strings against any of the files identified by grep, but this isn't an efficient way to collect data. If we want a list of all filenames containing the string "http" that shows the textual context of that string within the files, we need a more sophistivated command invocation. This is a good opportunity to demonstrate how we can create a loop using the shell. In effect, we're writing a small program without saving it in a text file as a shell script.

```
$ for f in /usr/bin/*
> do
> strings $f | grep http && echo /usr/bin/$f
> done | less
```

This construct loops once for every object in /usr/bin, setting the value of the variable $f as the corresponding object's name. strings is run on every object, and the output is piped into grep. If grep matches the string "http", the return value is set to 0, which corresponds to true. The metacharacters "&&" mean "execute the following command if the preceding command is true." Every time strings encounters "http", it outputs the string containing "http" and the name of the file. Get into the habit of finding alternate paths to your goal—Unix almost always offers several alternatives. An option that is even better than the preceding one is to use the -f flag in strings, which places the filename at the beginning of every string it outputs:

```
$ strings -f /usr/bin/* | grep http | less
```

HP-UX is one version of Unix that does not include the filename option for strings, so on HP-UX, you'd have to use the for loop. The more comfortable you become with Unix, and the more familiar you are with the shell interface, the more effective you will be in forensic investigations involving Unix. You need as many tricks as possible to deal with unforeseen situations and environments that don't have the same capabilities as your home Unix system.

strings works equally well on binaries from other operating environments. If you've copied DOS, Windows, or Macintosh files to a Unix system, or have a filesystem from some other environment mounted on a Unix host, you can use the strings utility to analyze those files also.

Text Filters

As mentioned earlier, Unix is very much a text-oriented operating environment. Most of the log files, configuration files, and even some of the executables are in ASCII text. It is expected that system administrators will manipulate these files, so a wide variety of text filters are included with Unix distributions. Entire books have been written about text processing in Unix, so we won't go into detail on it in this chapter. The value of the text utilities listed in Table 9-4 should be evident.

We've used the man directories as a conveniently large place to demonstrate searching for files containing specific strings. To determine just how many man pages there are, we can run a command that lists all of them, and we can pipe the output from that command into the word count utility:

```
$ ls -R /usr/man | wc
   3907    3897   48629
```

The output of that command contained 3,907 lines, 3,897 separate words, and 48,629 characters. The number 3,907 is useful, but it isn't actually the number of man pages—it also includes two lines for each directory. Let's try a different approach using find, which is more portable, enables us to be more specific in our query, and doesn't insert the blank lines:

Table 9-4 Unix Text Utilities

Utility	Description
sort	Sorts text, treating each column as a field. Command-line options can specify the column delimiter and specific column to sort on.
head	Outputs the first 20 lines of text or a specified number of lines.
tail	Outputs the last 20 lines of text or a specified number of lines.
uniq	Suppresses duplicate lines. uniq is frequently preceded by sort.
pr	Formats output for a printer. Can put in headers, page numbers, and so on.
cat -v	Outputs nonprintable characters, such as control characters, by preceding them with the caret symbol (^). A simple but effective trick places control characters into directory entries, making them difficult to work with. This can also happen accidentally. Combining the output of ls with cat -v (`ls -l | cat -v`) shows these nonprintable characters.
cut	Removes sections from each line, based either on character position (envision punched cards) or by specifying a delimiter and choosing specific columns.
paste	Merges lines.

```
$ find /usr/man -type f -print0 | wc
          3793   3793  100743
```

Now we can see that there are actually 3,793 objects of type "f", which represents files. Suppose we are writing a shell script and need only the line count, and not the word or character count. Checking the man page for wc, we see that it has options for just outputting the number of characters, words, or lines:

```
$ find /usr/man -type f | wc -l
   3793
```

Unix Programming Stuff

You need to be familiar with the Unix programming environment so that you can make your own versions of publicly available tools, and so that you can understand the activities of system intruders and other suspects who can create and use their own code. Unix and most Unix utilities are written in the C programming language. The standard name for the Unix compiler is "cc". Newer open source operating environments such as Linux and OpenBSD use a free C compiler from the GNU project called "gcc", but as a convenience for older programmers, it is normally linked to cc. Administrators often install gcc on commercial systems too, so both may be available. Actually, cc and gcc are just the front ends to a set of programs that includes a precompiler, the actual compiler, and a linker. Typing "cc" followed by the name of a C source file preprocesses the source to expand any macros, compiles that text, links all resulting objects with any necessary libraries, and creates an a.out file that is ready to be executed. The file types listed in Table 9-5 are associated with the C programming environment.

A suspect may compile hostile code and then try to delete the evidence. Even if you cannot find the linked executable, finding any scrap of source or object may provide some clues as to what he or she was up to.

Large programming projects frequently include a number of .c files, all of which are compiled into .o object files and then linked. One of the advantages of splitting the source and object code across multiple files is simplified upgrades. If only one module or header file must be changed, there is no reason to recompile other objects that don't refer or link to it. The make utility acts as a project manager that determines what must be compiled and linked based upon dependencies defined in the makefile. Source code distibutions big enough to spread across multiple files invariably ship with a helpful readme file, and a makefile that contains instructions for the make utility.

Table 9-5 File Types Associated with C Programming Environment

File Type	Description
.c	C language source code.
.h	Header files containing C language data structures intended to be used by more than one program. The library directories contain a number of standard header files, and complex program builds that split code into multiple objects often use header files to ensure that all objects are using the same data structures.
.o	Object files that contain compiled code that must be linked to other objects before it can be used. The system libraries contain a number of common objects to support programs using standard system and library calls. Building a complex executable usually results in creation of a number of .o files that are linked together as the final build step.
.a	Archive files created using the ar utility. While any type of file can be incorporated into an ar archive, it is conventionally used to store .o object files.
.sh	Bourne shell script.
.csh	C shell script.
.pl .pm .perl	Perl script.

One command associated with make that is applicable in other contexts is touch. Touching a file is a simple way to set its modification time to the current time. The effect is that when make is next run, the file that was just touched probably is recompiled, because it is now newer than the objects dependent upon it that would have been created from its last compilation. Running touch is a simple way to force recompilation and relinking. touch is also the simplest way to backdate the access and modification time of a file, but it cannot affect the change time:

```
$ touch -t 199912250001.15 kringle.txt
$ stat kringle.txt
  File: "kringle.txt"
  Size: 0                Filetype: Regular File
  Mode: (0664/-rw-rw-r--)    Uid: ( 500/ jheiser) Gid: ( 500/ jheiser)
Device: 3,5  Inode: 20047  Links: 1
Access: Sat Dec 25 00:01:15 1999(00125.00:40:49)
```

```
Modify: Sat Dec 25 00:01:15 1999(00125.00:40:49)
Change: Fri Apr 28 01:40:42 2000(00000.00:01:22)
$
$ ls -l k*
-rw-rw-r--    1 jheiser jheiser         0 Dec 25 00:01 kringle.txt
```

In this example, we reset the modification time to December 25, 1999. Anyone taking a casual look at this file would assume that it last had been modified in 1999. Running ls –lc shows that the inode has been changed last in April 2000. That is a clue that maybe the file has been backdated, but it isn't conclusive.

The strip utility removes symbolic information from object files. This symbolic information facilitates debugging, but it does nothing for a completed program but increase the file size. You might have noticed that the file command earlier indicated that the binaries we had discovered were not stripped. The strings command and several programming tools have less to work on with stripped executables, making casual analysis of their purpose slightly more difficult.

Files that end in .pl are Perl scripts. Perl is an acronym for "Practical Extraction and Report Language," and facility in the powerful Perl programming language is expected for Unix programmers and administrators. It is frequently used to process the results of queries and commands, and increasingly, Perl is used as the back end to dynamic Web pages. Available as freeware on virtually all platforms, Perl really comes into its own with Unix and its text-based orientation. If you investigate systems used by programmers, you will encounter Perl scripts.

Be aware of a Unix behavior that can help you identify files that are meant to be run as scripts. The hash character (#) is used to comment out a line in shell scripts, but in one special case, it serves as an identifier. If the first two characters of a shell script are "#!", the pathname that follows is used to interpret the remainder of the script. When it is a Bourne shell script, the first line is "#!/bin/sh". When it is a Perl script the first line is "#!/usr/bin/perl".

Comparison Tools

In addition to programming, text analysis, and text manipulation, Unix provides several tools that can compare files. Running diff against a pair of files provides a list of each line that differs. It was originally suitable only for text-based files, leaving either cmp or bdiff for use on binaries. Most contemporary versions of diff are able to deal with both text and data. Although it was originally suitable only for text-based files, leaving either cmp or bdiff for use on binaries, most contemporary versions of diff are able to deal with both text and data. A slightly stronger checksum is available on some Unix versions through either the cksum command or sum -s. Two files that have the same checksum potentially are identical, but as we discussed in Chapter 4, checksums can be manipulated and spoofed. Checksums are intended to verify only that files were not inadvertently changed. They cannot verify that a file was not deliberately changed. For this reason, most Unix distributions now use hash values instead of checksums to verify the integrity of their binary distributions. The standard cryptographic hash function on Unix is MD5 (MD5sum on Linux). If this function is not installed on a particular Unix system, it is probably available from the original distribution, and source code is readily available on the Internet.

Unix Archives

Before concluding our introduction to Unix, we need to discuss one more category of tools and associated file types—archive files. We've already seen the original form of Unix archive file, the .a file used to store library objects. The idea of bundling multiple objects into a single file proved so convenient as a development system feature that other archive types were soon created for more generalized purposes. The Unix tape archiver, tar, originally was designed for storing and retrieving groups of files to and from a tape. A utility with the aesthetically pleasing moniker, dump is an administrative command that operates on entire filesystems at a time, making it appropriate only for backups. Tar is the normal Unix archive utility for groups of files, including entire directory trees. Remember that everything in Unix is a file. While the default file for the tar command is usually the tape drive—if a tape drive is configured—the output from the tar command can be redirected to a file object. The effect of this is that multiple files and their associated directory structures can be stored in a single tar archive file (sometimes called a *tarball*), enabling their easy movement between systems. The conventional identification for a tar archive is to give it a .tar extension but, of course, the file utility can recognize a tar archive without the extension. Most Unix hosts lack a tape drive, and it is likely that most invocations of tar are performed on tar files, and not on tapes. tar has a relatively straightforward set of command-line options, and most users find it the easiest archive utility to remember and use. Just remember to use the -f file option when not using a tape drive. Let's create a tar file that contains everything in the directory localdir:

```
$ tar -cf file.tar localdir
```

Now let's view its table of contents using the -t flag along with v, the verbose flag. The output looks just like the output of the ls -l command. tar maintains ownership and creation dates. (Note that we're piping the output through head to limit it to five lines, which saves space in this book. The string 'Broken pipe' indicates that further data was available but was sent to the 'bit bucket'.)

```
# tar -tvf file.tar|head -5
drwx------ sallym/501          0 2000-04-30 23:20:31 ./
-rw-r--r-- sallym/501       1422 2000-04-24 23:07:24 ./.Xdefaults
-rw-r--r-- sallym/501         24 2000-04-24 23:07:24 ./.bash_logout
-rw-r--r-- sallym/501        230 2000-04-24 23:07:24 ./.bash_profile
-rw-r--r-- sallym/501        124 2000-04-24 23:07:24 ./.bashrc
Broken pipe
```

Get in the habit of always viewing an archive like this before unarchiving it, just to ensure that tar won't do something unforeseen, like writing over files that you want to keep. To extract a tar archive, use the -x option.

```
$ tar -xf file. tar
```

Although it cannot handle device special files, making it unsuitable for a complete system restore, it does maintain most filesystem information if so instructed. For example, if you want to restore the original permissions, use the -p flag. tar is the most common format used for Unix software distribution.

In olden days, a 300MB hard drive was considered large, and networking was provided through slow analog modems. Given such a resource-poor environment, there were advantages to saving space by compressing files. pack is the original Unix compression utility. By convention, pack files end in the suffix ".z". compress is a newer Unix file size reduction utility that is much more common. Compressed files have names that end in ".Z". The most common Unix archive format is the compressed tar file, recognizable by its double suffix, ".tar.z," sometimes abbreviated to ".taz." To reverse-compress, use the uncompress command, which is just a link back to the compress binary (a symbolic link on Linux). The convention for invoking the uncompress option is to use the –d flag to the appropriate compression utility. For example, **compress –d** *filename* is the equivalent to typing **uncompress** *filename*. Individual files and tar files now are usually compressed with a Unix version of zip, gzip (also from GNU). gzip files have the extension ".gz" and are uncompressed using the command gunzip, which is linked to gzip. Or, following the Unix convention, you can use gzip with the -d option to uncompress a file archived with gzip. You can unzip a tar file and unarchive it all in one single command line like this:

```
gzip -dc tarball.tar.gz | tar -xf –
```

The Windows-based WinZip utility can unzip files created on Unix with gzip, and if they happen to be tar files, it can also untar them. Although the DOS version of Zip is both a compression file and an archive format, gzip is just a compression utility. gzipped tar files are increasingly common and often have use the extension .tgz.

Compression of any kind is tantamount to a weak form of encryption. It has the effect of hiding the contents of a file, but it is weak because anyone who knows the algorithm can access those contents. This is significant to the investigator because text-searching utilities such as strings and grep won't work on files that have been compressed. String searches are not possible on compressed files unless you uncompress them first. To be thorough in an examination of a filesystem—Unix, Windows, or Macintosh—you should identify all compressed files and uncompress them before considering the investigation complete. This is easy to do with the find command. If you are searching for the string "Stacheldraht" and want to be sure that you check all gzipped files, you can use the following invocation of find:

```
# find /home -name '*.gz' -print0 | xargs -0 gunzip | grep Stacheldraht
```

Of course, this command catches only zipped files that use the conventional file extension. The following command is more reliable way to locate all files that are in a zip format:

```
# find /home -print0 | xargs -0 file | grep zip
```

A more complete discussion on this topic can be found in Chapter 4.

Finally Back to dd

While it isn't really an archiving tool, the dd command is a powerful weapon in the forensic analyst's arsenal. It is a duplicating utility that is normally used to copy an entire filesystem or drive. Because it allows specification of the block size, it often is used to copy large amounts of data between devices. Let's show a practical example of dd by using it to duplicate a floppy disk.

First, we'll use dd to make an image of the floppy disk and store it on the hard drive. The input file, "if-," is the floppy device, and we'll redirect the standard output to a file. After that, we'll reverse the process by making that floppy image file our input file, and the floppy block special device will be our output file, designated by "of-".

```
# dd if=/dev/fd0 >floppy.image
2880+0 records in
2880+0 records out
```

```
# dd if=floppy.image of=/dev/fd0
2880+0 records in
2880+0 records out
```

If the device was a 1.44MB floppy disk, why did it show 2,880 records? Because the default for dd on PC Linux is a 512-byte block or record. Just like we stored and cloned the data on this floppy disk, dd can be used to duplicate an entire hard drive, an entire partition, or a kernel data structure. It can make an exact duplicate of almost anything accessible through a filename. In Chapter 11, we use dd frequently as an evidence-gathering tool.

10

Compromising a Unix Host

Unix systems directly connected to the Internet are often subject to hacking attempts. If you gain a reputation as being skilled in computer forensics, you'll probably have many opportunities to examine one of these Unix systems. Unix systems are not used for personal workstations as often as Windows or Macintosh systems are, although most attackers probably use Unix to launch their attacks. Technical folks tend to use Unix for their everyday workstations, but the number of people using personal productivity applications on Unix systems is fairly small compared to the more popular workstation environments. Unix is most often used for servers, including Internet Web servers, so Unix systems are often the object or victim of a crime. These crimes usually involve remote access, and the attacker usually is highly skilled or has access to attack software. To understand why investigations on Unix systems often take a different form than they do on Windows workstations, it is helpful to spend a chapter describing how and why Unix systems are compromised.

The skill level of someone attacking a Unix system may be quite high. Adolescent computer hackers often have the luxury of nearly unlimited time to spend honing their skills for breaking into Unix systems and covering their tracks. The purpose of this book is to help you become more skillful, but keep in mind that a suspect with significantly more skill than you probably can evade your attempts to detect his or her activities. System attackers vary greatly in their capability. To give you some sense of the range of abilities you may encounter, think of a spectrum roughly divided into four areas: Clueless, Script Kiddie, Guru, and Wizard (see Table 10-1).

If the suspect has more skill than you, you will probably won't be able to learn much in an investigation, but you won't know until you try.

Whatever rationale they offer to their peers or authority figures, system intruders know that they are doing something the system owner wants to prevent, and the intruders' priority is to avoid getting caught. Most Internet intruders make some attempt to cover their tracks, and a number of helpful utilities have been created to facilitate this. The mere existence of these tools means that you always must look for

Table 10-1 Hierarchy of Attacker Skills

Skill Level	Ability	Evidence
Clueless	Virtually no skills.	All activities are readily apparent.
Script Kiddie	Able to find ready-made exploit scripts on the Internet and run them following rote instructions. This code may give them root access, activity-hiding capabilities, and back doors for return visits. Unable to deal with non-standard Unix configurations. Do not write code.	May attempt to cover tracks but with limited success. Activities can be detected with minimal effort.
Guru	Equivalent to an experienced system administrator. Able to manipulate Unix systems that are not configured in the standard way. Able to program in C, Perl, and shell script. Check for existence of security programs and logging performed off-system and avoid such hosts.	Carefully clears out log files to remove evidence of original compromise. Leaves no obvious traces associated with account used to access system. May leave Trojan horses behind for future access.
Wizard	Intimate knowledge of Unix internals. Capable of programming in assembly language. Can manipulate hardware and software. Very rare!	Leaves virtually no useful evidence on the attacked host.

them. These tools are commonly used by Internet joy riders, but their existence is hardly a secret. Anyone who wants to take advantage of a Unix system without the permission of its administrator has motivation to find and use these tools.

Attack Goals

In his landmark dissertation, "An Analysis of Security Incidents on the Internet 1989–1995"[1] Carnegie-Mellon University graduate student John D. Howard analyzed several years' worth of Internet data collected by the Center for Emergency Response Teams. He discovered that the object of most attacks is to gain the Unix command prompt. While this discovery came as no surprise to those experienced

---

1. http://www.cert.org/research/JHThesis/Start.html

with Internet crime, his dissertation replaced anecdotes and common wisdom with solid evidence and methodical analysis. Howard's thesis has been widely circulated and has helped to explain the nature of Internet attacks.

We cannot repeat too often the importance of understanding the criminal mind. The more aware you are of the goals and typical process of a system attack, the better prepared you are to analyze and respond. It is rare for a compromised Unix system to be an isolated incident—most hacked hosts are just one in a series of hacked hosts. As depicted in Figure 10-1, system attackers compromise a number of systems and use them for different purposes. Although some attackers may start their attack session using a workstation at the office or at a university, most start with a dial-up session to a stolen or hacked ISP account. America Online (AOL) accounts have been notorious sources of hostile activity, but AOL has an active corporate security function, which smaller ISPs do not. Many ISPs now have dial-up routers that support caller ID, allowing them to correlate outgoing Internet sessions with the originating telephone number. ISPs that track this information keep it with their dial-up accounting records maintained by the Remote Authentication Dial-In User Service (RADIUS) servers that authenticate logon sessions. ISPs vary in how long they keep this information, but in some cases, they maintain it for months in case of questions about billing. A court order often can be used to obtain the originating telephone number associated with a specific IP address at a specific time and date (IP addresses normally are assigned dynamically to ISP dial-up accounts). To evade traceback, careful system intruders often use an intermediate telephone switch to further cover their tracks. Many phone switches offer the ability to reconnect incoming calls to a different number, and it isn't unusual for an experienced computer hacker to also be a phone phreaker.[2]

Having gained access to the Internet, an attacker needs a command prompt to start the attack from. The account on this host probably won't have root access; root access just attracts attention, and the closer to their point of origin, the more discreet attackers want to remain. This machine may be a shell server (a host providing a Unix command-line prompt) belonging to the same ISP that is being used to gain access to the Internet. It might be possible to find files on this system related to attacks, but a careful hacker tries not to leave evidence on this machine. ISP shell servers and universities are especially prone to shared accounts, and you never know who is using a particular account at any specific time. Sometimes the only evidence that a server is being exploited as the Internet source machine for an attack is simultaneous logons for the same account with different originations. The first shell host is used to establish a connection to one or more intermediary hosts.

---

2. A *phreaker* is a phone system hacker. Through manipulations of phone switches or voice mail systems, phreakers can make long distance calls for free and circumvent traps and traces that otherwise would point back to the phreaker's location through details of their calls.

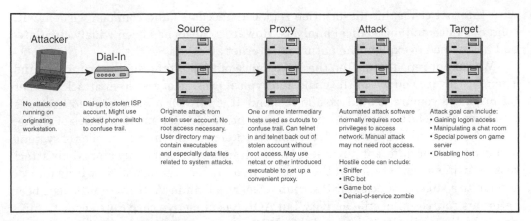

Figure 10-1 Unix host chain of attack

The intermediary hosts, or proxy hosts, exist purely to complicate any attempts at traceback, a process sometimes called *connection laundering*. Attackers try to compromise a number of hosts that are located on different continents, so the system administrator won't be on the same schedule as the other systems in the chain of attack. We once investigated a hacked Web host in Atlanta, Georgia that was being accessed from a university in Eastern Europe. This situation was ideal for the hacker because it was impossible for us to reach that system administrator through the telephone.

An attacker can take advantage of these intermediate hosts in several ways. The simplest way is to telnet in to a normal user account and then telnet back out. This method complicates traceback, but unless system binaries have been altered, it won't necessarily hide a hacker's trail. Logon records on the intermediate machine will contain the apparent source IP address, and a sloppy attacker may leave evidence of his or her destination. An attacker looking for a more automated approach may install a simple proxy enabling the session to be automatically "routed" through the intermediate host at the application level. Such a proxy easily can be configured with netcat, although it may take root access for netcat to listen on a port. (netcat is a network utility often used by hackers that is explained in Chapter 11.) Unless system binaries have been hacked, it isn't possible to hide the fact that an extra process is listening for incoming connections, although it might not be obvious either. A host used for relaying may contain little evidence of compromise. The attacker may be using a legitimate account, albeit a compromised one, and just telneting through. On the other hand, attackers may have performed some significant housekeeping on a proxy host, manipulating system binaries to hide their activities and provide access whenever they need it.

The next to last host in the chain of attack is the host actually used to launch attacks against other systems. These attacks may be both manual and autonomous (performed automatically by self-directed code) and may vary widely in their level of hostility. The host used to directly attack another host is most likely to contain evidence on its hard drive—the point of having all the intermediary hosts is to keep this evidence as far as possible from anything that can be associated with the attacker. The attack host also creates the most network disturbance. Many attack forms cause even the simplest of intrusion detection systems to alarm. A summary of some attack types and their characteristic evidence is shown in Table 10-2.

All of the systems exploited to attack a target system are victims, but the target is the primary victim, and the intermediary hosts are secondary victims. To evade detection, active hackers need a lot of intermediary systems—a careful attacker never uses a system for more than a week or two at a time. An attacker may juggle dozens of them, keeping an encrypted list on his or her home PC. When investigating

Table 10-2 Typical Attack Host Exploits

Attack Type	Target	Characteristic Evidence
Sniffer	Any host with logon sessions visible on the same LAN segment. Outgoing sessions to hosts on other networks are desirable to hackers.	• Unauthorized daemon running • Unauthorized binary • Source code for unauthorized binary • Network adaptor in promiscuous mode • Log file containing hostnames, usernames, and passwords
IRC bot	Internet Relay Chat (IRC) hosts	• Unauthorized daemon running • Unauthorized binary • Source code for unauthorized binary • Log or config files
Game bot	Game servers	• Unauthorized daemon running • Unauthorized binary • Source code for unauthorized binary • Log or config files
Distributed denial-of-service (DDoS)	Prominent Internet Web servers	• Zombie executable (unauthorized daemon) • Source code for unauthorized binary
Manual	Any hosts, local or remote	• Source or binary code for attacks • Unusual outgoing connections • Lists of hostnames or IP addresses (victims) • Password files or lists of account/password pairs

a compromised Unix host, try to determine how the system you are investigating has been used. No matter how carefully you examine a compromised system, you can never be positive that you've discovered every piece of evidence. If a system shows an apparent compromise but exhibits no other signs of ongoing hostile activity, it possibly hasn't been used yet. Perhaps the hacker lost track of it, has found another hobby, or already has enough compromised systems in use. Many compromised systems have never been actively used by their attackers—they are just spare systems being saved for future use. Assume that the attacker will return someday. All Internet citizens are responsible for ensuring that their systems are not being exploited to attack those belonging to some other organization. If you determine that a system you are investigating is either an intermediary or an attack host, you have an obligation to the organizations both upstream and downstream. You may be the only person in a position to warn their administrators that their systems have been compromised.

Target Identification

The first thing a system attacker must do is locate a potential victim. An experienced system cracker collects long lists of victims as a result of attack activities—the more systems the attackers compromise, the more information they can to gather that leads to other compromisable systems. This embarrassment of riches apparently leads some hackers to share the bounty with less-experienced system crackers, throwing them a bone or two. If someone is motivated to attack a specific organization, it isn't difficult to use the Internet's existing mechanisms to compile a list of domain names, machine names, IP addresses, and even the logon names of account holders within the organization.

Intelligence Gathering

After locating a potential victim, an attacker who doesn't already have a valid logon and password combination begins probing the system remotely to see what operating system and version it is using and what network services it is providing. Although password sniffing and guessing is often quite easy, it is even more efficient to gain access to a system by compromising a buggy network service. Network-scanning tools are used to probe and prod a target until the attacker has collected enough information to support an attack with a reasonable chance of success. The overwhelming majority of vulnerability scans are quite heavy-handed, consisting of a sequential set of connection attempts to a range of ports, all originating from a single IP address. Such an attack is immediately visible to virtually any form of network intrusion detection system. Attackers who are more patient and skillful can resort to subtleties that make it difficult to detect their scanning.[3]

Initial Compromise

It is difficult to crack even a poorly configured system without creating the digital equivalent of a sledgehammer against a steel door. A philosopher might ask if the attack still takes place, even when no one hears the attack—or when evidence of the attack is not securely logged. We can assure you, the attack is even more likely to take place when nobody is there to hear it. The initial compromise often creates a lot of smoke and noise, but if the system owners are unaware of it, the longer the attack goes on, the harder it may be for the investigator to find evidence of it. Password-guessing attempts create an unusual number of failed logon records. Attempts to compromise network applications through buffer overflows or taking advantage of undocumented behavior often result in events that the system has the ability to log—if logging is running and if it is collecting a sufficiently detailed level of application logs. Many exploits also cause applications to core dump, not only leaving core files lying around, but also causing the daemon to restart. Several attempts, each with slightly different parameters, may be required before the right chemistry occurs and access to a command prompt is gained. These attempts may cause a flurry of warning messages, although the most sophisticated attacks do not.

Privilege Escalation

When an attacker has gained a command prompt, her or she may attempt privilege escalation—assuming that the exploit didn't plop the suspect right into a root shell. If the suspect didn't gain root privileges immediately, the careful system hacker uploads exploit code to the compromised system and attempts to exploit well-known vulnerabilities that can lead to root access. Motivated and skilled attackers can usually gain root privileges after having gained access to the Unix shell, but until and unless they do so, they won't be able to hide the fact that they have logged onto a system and compromised it. The attempt to escalate privileges will be the last flurry of incriminating error messages that you can reasonably expect to see.

---

3. Northcutt, Stephen, *Network Intrusion Detection* (Indianapolis, IN: New Riders, 2000). Provides the best information on this subject.

Reconnaissance

When system crackers have the root prompt, the game suddenly changes in their favor. At this point, careful hackers perform system reconnaissance. In effect, they do their own forensic examination. They want to know how likely it is that their activities have been captured and whether it is worth their time to continue the system compromise. First, an astute hacker wants to know whether or not logging is taking place, and if so, where the logs are stored. The normal Unix logon log is easily taken care of when you have root, but the syslog daemon is a flexible service that can send logs to the console, another host, or the printer. The hacker interested in knowing where logs are being sent immediately looks at the file /etc/syslog.conf and determines what is being logged and where it is being logged. If messages are sent to the console, it is an easy matter to create a dozen bogus messages and scroll them off the screen. If messages are being sent to another host, either that host has to be cracked, too, or the attacker has to live with the possibility of discovery. If the logs are sent to a printer, they won't be convenient to read, but short of theft or fire, they won't be erasable either. If syslog files containing evidence of the attack are stored locally, or just aren't being created, it is easy for the attacker to cover his or her tracks.

Next, the attacker looks for security programs. He or she may start by doing a process status to see what is running, but a careful reconnaissance job also requires running lsof (list of open files) to get a better idea of what the currently running programs are up to. The system cracker checks for the existence of file integrity programs, such as Tripwire. Such programs might be run periodically as cron jobs (meaning that an entry has been made in a configuration file requesting scheduled execution of the program at specific times by the Unix cron daemon). It is always a good idea to look for scheduled executions to see what the administrator is doing to monitor the system and check for changes in files. Such things can be subverted. If nothing obvious appears threatening, the attacker uses Unix utilities, like find, to see what files have been changed since he or she gained entry—just to make sure that he or she has identified everything that could result in discovery. Like forensic investigators, good hackers maintain careful notes of everything they find. Hackers usually store these notes on their home PCs, and common hacker wisdom is that they should be encrypted, but keep an eye open for such notes—you might get lucky.

The final step in this initial reconnaissance stage gets personal. Hackers know the administrator will come looking for them, and they want to know who their nemesis will be. Before actually exploiting anything on a system, some attackers go to the trouble of determining just who the administrators are and where they are coming from. After they know who those people are, they can keep a lookout for them and disappear when they see them coming. The hackers may also want to monitor the administrators' email to see if they've discovered the hack and learn what they plan to do about it. The attackers methodically search the compromised system looking for clues that can provide evidence as to who the administrators are in real life. The sulog is a good starting point because it contains a list of all usernames that successfully or unsuccessfully attempted to gain root access through the substitute user (su) command (the Linux hosts in our lab log). It isn't good practice to logon directly as root, which not only implies use of su or sudo, it also means that nobody is reading the mail sent to root. The forwarding address of root's email, which usually is the address of one of the system administrators, usually can be found in the .forward file in the root account's home directory, or in an alias associated with the mail server. Users with root access also may be in the wheel or admin groups found in /etc/group, and they even may have the word "admin" associated with their logon record in /etc/password.

After the attackers have identified the system administrators, they do the same thing that you would do when attempting to analyze a user's activities. They go to the administrators' home directories and see what they have been up to. Their shell history provides an idea of their typical activities, and administrators often store their security utilities in their home directories. If they have installed security software, the PATH information in their .login or .profile files probably points to its directory. It probably wouldn't hurt to rifle through the administrators' mail, too. Maybe it contains information on their schedule and their typical activities—maybe even unencrypted passwords. By spending some time reconnoitering the administrators' home directories, methodical and careful system hackers can learn a great deal about whether they will be caught and what the response will be.

The recent trend is for intruders to use highly automated scripts that probe, compromise, and back-door hundreds or thousands of hosts in a sitting. In these cases, the intruders are not going to do any sort of forensic investigation on each of the hosts. They just run the script, which produces a list of the successfully compromised hosts for future reference. Through the use of automated software, hackers can perform both reconnaissance and subsequent compromise in one fell swoop. Although they learn less information from each host, and may potentially attract more attention, these risks are worthwhile in order to gain access to many systems so quickly and easily.

Covering The Tracks

Before or after the reconnaissance, intruders who wish to remain undetected attempt to cover their tracks. These attempts can vary in sophistication—the more care and effort put into removing the evidence of the intrusion and compromise, the more difficult it is for scouts to read the intruders' trail. Hackers often delete the log file, which does indeed remove the evidence relating to the details of their attack, but it also sends a clear "I've been attacked!" message to even the dullest system administrator. Deleting the log file is the digital equivalent to wiping the trail clean but not returning it to its natural state. Given time and motivation, skillful intruders carefully massage the log file, removing only those entries that could incriminate them and leaving behind evidence of normal system activity. Massaging the log file is the digital equivalent of restoring the trail to its natural appearance, straightening out those bent blades of grass and covering up those broken twigs that would otherwise provide a good tracker with not only evidence of the intruder's passage, but also valuable clues to the size of the party, their direction, and the time that they came through. If the attackers have created any files, they may clean them up—especially any executables that were used to compromise the system. They won't need them any longer.

Log Editors

Most Unix logs are text files, making it fairly easy for attackers to clean them out. It does take time, though, and there is always the possibility of making a mistake. Two important files containing logon data are binary, utmp and wtmp, and cannot be directly edited with a text editor. This is why smart attackers automate log cleaning with special software. Look for digital burglar tools or evidence of them. For example, some log cleaners don't do a clean job. Just as an attempt to jimmy a lock leaves visible evidence, so does a log-cleaning job. Some burglars tear a lock out of a door, while others leave only tiny scratch marks. The evidence may be subtle or it may be obvious, but there will always be some evidence.

Back Door

There's no point in going to all of this trouble unless the intruders are planning on returning. When they return, they want to be more discreet than they were the first time. Why draw attention to themselves if it can be avoided, right? And if the attack is detected, and measures are taken to prevent a repeat, it would be nice to gain access through some other mechanism. This is why attackers create back doors. Even if they do not go through all the other steps we've mentioned, most attackers at least take the time to create a few back doors that facilitate their quiet return. Once the attackers have gained administrative access, cleaned their tracks, and prepared a return path, hackers say that the system is *owned*.

   The simplest form of a back door is a hidden copy of the command shell that is SUID (set user ID) root (the file is owned by root, the SUID bit is set, and the intruder has execute permission). Anyone who can execute this binary can gain a root prompt, so it assumes that you have some form of logon to the system. When investigating a compromised Unix system, we once found two SUID Bourne shells.

It turned out that a former administrator had created one. He was working for a different firm then but retained logon privileges to "help out" at his previous job. The hacker evidently didn't find the SUID shell created by the former administrator or perhaps the hacker just felt the need to create his own. This anecdote reveals one of the weaknesses of this kind of back door. It sticks out like a wart and can be quickly discovered by someone following the steps outlined in Chapter 11.

A more subtle form of back door requires the modification or replacement of one of the standard system executables. After all, the best place to hide a tree is inside a forest. Modern hacker tools make it easy to modify a binary and its directory entry so that it has the same size, date, and checksum as the original. Unless you compare its hash value to the original, it's not obvious that the binary has been changed. Although the usage of the term is somewhat inexact, such altered binaries usually are referred to as *Trojan horses,* and a number of essays on the Internet refer to the process of substituting hostile changelings for the original executables as *trojanizing*.

Network daemons make very useful back doors because they are normally running and listening on a port anyway. Modified versions of logind or fingerd can provide the same services as the legitimate versions, but when the correct sequence or password is given, these modified versions might start a shell giving root access. Thorough attackers create several back doors so that they have multiple return paths, both as the administrator and as a normal user.

Inventory

An attacker compromises a machine because it is vulnerable—unless it is a directed attack against a specific victim, the goal is normally to see what is there. Once the evidence has been cleaned up, and the attacker has mechanisms in place facilitating an easy return, it's time to explore and see what is on the machine and what is in the readily accessible neighborhood. Finding all the .rhost files and looking through hosts.equiv provides clues as to what other systems might be trusting the compromised host. These trust relationships can be used to access additional hosts without the effort of a compromise.

Passwords can be collected from the /etc/passwd or /etc/shadow files, mail messages, and system files, and through the use of network sniffers. Password file entries have to be cracked, but because processing power is free, the cracking utility can be run on a compromised host if the hacker is willing to run the risk of attracting attention. A curious intruder may spend days thumbing through user files looking for interesting tidbits of information: source code, product plans, credit card numbers, and so forth.

Rootkits

As discussed in Chapter 8, hostile code exists and may be used to increase privileges, hide activities, or gather information. Rootkits are convenient suites of tools that usually support all three operations. Rootkits are not intended to perform the initial system compromise, but after an attacker has gained access to a system, a rootkit is an invaluable utility belt, filled with useful malware. Although Windows NT rootkits have just appeared, system intruders have used Unix rootkits for years. Whenever you are examining a compromised Unix host, assume that a rootkit was used and look for evidence of it. Be aware that a system with a properly applied kernel rootkit is impossible to detect from within the hacked system itself (see Chapter 5). Inexperienced or hasty attackers leave clues such as the source code lying around, but more experienced system crackers leave only well-disguised trojanized binaries, and you at least will have an idea which runs to look at.

Rootkits generally contain three different categories of exploit code. Cleaning tools are used to manipulate the environment and hide evidence of the intrusion itself. Data collection tools are used to find information useful in extending the attack. Careful hackers will remove evidence of both of these types of tools when they are done with them, but not all intruders are this careful. The third category of software generally found in rootkits are the trojanized binaries that we've already discussed. These are specifically made to look just like normal executables provided by the system vendor, but they have hidden hostile capabilities. Trojanized system files appear to function just like the binaries they replace, providing the desired system services, but trojanized files actually have hidden agendas. One category of trojanized utilities selectively limits the utility's normal capabilities, hiding ongoing hostile activities from the administrator. By subverting the views provided by network, process, and file status utilities, trojanized utilities manipulate the system administrators' perceptions of what is actually happening on their system. While providing a normal view of events, the trojanized utilities conveniently do not display information on some system processes and files—and nobody is the wiser. The other class of trojanized binaries adds hidden capabilities to system executables, usually to circumvent system access controls.

Rootkit Contents

New rootkits and individual exploit tools are being created all the time. Table 10-3 contains a list of the types of tools your nemesis may have installed on a system you are examining.

Rootkits are powerful burglar tools, but they don't perform magic. They must leave a password somewhere, and crippled status commands need to know what not to display. In addition, they require configuring, and the configuration information

Table 10-3   Rootkit Contents

Goal	Trojanized Binary
Subvert system applications to hide activities	
Hide logs and files	ls, du, find The utilities used to display directory contents and summarize the size of multiple directories can be replaced with versions that skip over directories serving as hacker storage depots.
Hide processes	ps, kill, and top top shows the processes using the greatest amount of system resources. It is usually the first tool used when a system bogs down. A password-cracking utility sticks out like a neon light when an intact version of top is run. Hacked versions of top or ps can allow processes to run virtually invisibly. Although specific hostile processes may be invisible to the trojanized ps and kill, systems with /proc still will have directory entries for their PIDs.
Hide scheduled jobs	crontab System administrators aren't the only ones who want to run applications periodically.
Subvert logs	syslogd and tcpd If you are going to go to the trouble to clean up a log, you might as well make sure that it stays that way. Modified versions of network daemons selectively skip certain events and do not record them.
Hide use of promiscuous mode	ifconfig To use a sniffer, the LAN adapter has to be in promiscuous mode. This is normally a clear sign of unauthorized activity, but there are few ways to actually determine whether or not a card is in promiscuous mode. The best way is through ifconfig, so it is common to replace this binary when a sniffer has been installed. Finding either sniffer code or a LAN interface in promiscious mode is a sign that further investigation is needed.
Hide connections	netstat Depending upon how a hacker wants to exploit a compromised system, there might be quite a number of unauthorized network sessions, or at least unknown daemons will be listening on unusual ports. Normally, such activity would stick out like a wart, so if intruders go to the trouble of replacing ps, they might as well take care of netstat also.

(continued)

Table 10-3 Rootkit Contents (*cont.*)

Goal	Trojanized Binary
Weaken system applications	
Prevent the administrator from stopping the running of hostile code	killall This convenient utility (mostly found on Linux) kills processes by name instead of PID. A trojanized version is available that doesn't actually kill selected processes. Even if the administrator does find the hostile activity and attempts to stop it, a weakened killall command may allow the hostile process to continue.
Establish back doors to stealthily regain system access later	
Command-line back doors (note that chfn, chsh, and passwd are all user utilities that are run SUID root)	chfn A utility that enables users to change their full names as they appear in /etc/passwd. Entering the rootkit password instead of the full name allows a normal user to gain a root shell.
	chsh A utility that enables users to change their login shells, which is also a field in the password file. Entering the root password as the new shell provides a root shell to a normal user.
	passwd The trojanized version of the utility used to change an account password grants root access when the rootkit password is entered as the current password.
logon back doors	/sbin/login A modified version of the logon routine allows a logon as any user when the rootkit password is entered. Logging on as root is a good way to attract attention. Given the existence of command-line back doors that can provide administrative privileges whenever needed, it is safer to log on as a normal user instead of logging on directly as root. The administrator may have disabled the ability to log on directly as root—especially for network connections, but this can be circumvented by logging on as "rewt".
network back doors	inetd This front-end daemon is used to launch many other Unix network services. A trojanized version of it has a root shell listening by default on port 5002. Enter the rootkit password on the first line of a session to gain root access.

(continued)

Table 10-3   Rootkit Contents (*cont.*)

Goal	Trojanized Binary
	rshd The "R" utilities are security risks because their trust model is so easily exploited. A hacked version launches a root shell when the rootkit password is entered.
	telnetd Trojanized versions of telnet provide a root shell when a particular value is set for TERM on the client side.
	bindshell Binds a root shell to port (31337 by default).
	fingerd Multipurpose back door that allows accounts to be added and deleted and logs cleaned, all by sending special strings in finger commands.
Data collection applications	
Collect logon password pairs	linsniffer Linux password sniffer.
	sniffchk Utility that checks and ensures the sniffer is still working.
Utilities	
Hide the fact that executables have been altered	fix This tool makes the altered versions of the system executables appear to be the originals. It installs the trojanized version in place of the existing version, changing its timestamp and checksum to match the original.
Log cleaners	
Hide evidence of unauthorized activity	wted wtmp editor.
	zz Erases entry from last log.
	zap/zap2 Overwrites last logon record with zeros. This covers the trail but doesn't hide it.

(continued)

Table 10-3   Rootkit Contents (*cont.*)

Goal	Trojanized Binary
	cloak2 Changes logon data (note that a DOS encryption program has the same name).
	clear Deletes logon entries.
	ACCT Handler Cleans out system accounting records.

must go somewhere. It often is stashed somewhere in /dev. This directory is a good spot because humans tend to ignore what they don't understand, and the device special directory usually contains lots of things that inexperienced administrators don't understand. Rootkits also need to be compiled, and in Chapter 11, you'll learn how to look for evidence of their having been built on a system.

Not every compromised Unix host has had a rootkit installed on it—not by any means. However, rootkits are so pervasive that it doesn't make much sense to examine a Unix system that has been compromised in any way and not check for the existence of rootkit-like activity. Chapter 11 will help you locate and analyze hostile code on systems that you are asked to examine.

Conclusion

As the rate of hacked Web servers continues to increase, the demand for skillful investigators will also increase. Unfortunately, as investigators increase their ability to locate clues about the activities of system intruders, those intruders will be encouraged to continue developing new and more obscure techniques. This is truly a spy vs. spy scenario that will continue escalating in the forseeable future. Indeed, as this book goes to press, there are more and more reports of compromised Windows Web servers that are following the same patterns that have been typical of UNIX system compromises over the last 10 years. Books stand still, but hackers do not.

Further Research

"Analysis of a fingerd replacement," SANS Global Incident Analysis Center, August 2000, http://www.sans.org/y2k/fingerd.htm

Howard, John D., "An Analysis of Security Incidents on the Internet, 1989–1995," http://www.cert.org/research/JHThesis/Start.html

Simple Nomad, "The Hacking FAQ," http://www.nmrc.org/faqs/hackfaq/hackfaq.html

Spitzner, Lance "Know your Enemy," http://project.honeynet.org/papers/. This excellent multi-part series on system intrusions, can be found on Honeypot.org, an organization devoted to the analysis and understanding of Internet attacks.

SANS Global Incident Analysis Center, http://www.sans.org/giac.htm, helpful case studies of Internet security incidents.

Phreak Accident, "How to Play Hide and Seek Unix Style," http://www.fish.com/security/hide-n-seek.html

Seifried, Kurt, "Creating and Preventing Backdoors in UNIX Systems," http://www.securityportal.com/closet/closet20000628.html

Source for sniffit: http://reptile.rug.ac.be/~coder/sniffit/sniffit.html

Chapter

11

Investigating a Unix Host

It is a sad fact of network life that the number of Unix systems successfully attacked exceeds the ability of their owners to adequately examine them. Even when sufficient human resources are available, circumstances may intrude—management may not allow a live system to be taken down in order to methodically collect the evidence of an attack. In their one-day seminar on Unix forensics,[1] Dan Farmer and Wietse Venema provided a summary of the different levels of effort that may be applied in the response to a particular incident (see Table 11-1). We certainly don't recommend that you ignore an incident and go back to work. If this was your plan, you probably wouldn't be reading this book. Many managers decide to do a simple reinstallation and hope that the problem goes away, but it usually doesn't. This chapter introduces the techniques appropriate for a "Minimum Recommended" response of one to two days, up to a "Serious Effort," lasting several weeks. Although "Fanaticism" is beyond the scope of this book, in the case of a serious crime, it always is the appropriate response. (We hope some readers will be inspired to become fanatics.) Even if no resources are currently available to examine a compromised system, at the very least, the contents of the compromised system should be saved for the future. It may not become apparent that an investigation is needed until some future time.

As we said in Chapter 10, Unix systems often are the victims of crimes, and this chapter is intended to address that situation. It is a brief tutorial on examining hacked Unix systems using just the tools available within the Unix environment. Today's reality is that system administrators are expected to be able to examine hacked Internet systems, and they usually do not have the luxury of time, budget, or extensive training in forensic techniques. While many of the techniques described in this chapter run the risk of offending the purist, we think the greater good is served by providing as many tools as possible and helping you understand their limitations.

---

1. http://www.fish.com/forensics

Table 11-1   Levels of Effort in Unix System Intrusion Response

Action	Expertise	Time
Go back to work	None	1+ hours
Minimal work	Anyone who can install system software	.5 to 1 day
Minimum recommended	Junior system administrator	1 to 2 days
Serious effort	System administrator	2+ days to 2 weeks
Fanaticism	Experienced system administrator	Weeks to months+

If the administrator has prepared for potential attack by using a filesystem integrity–checking program, your job as forensic investigator will be much easier. Prudent organizations run programs such as Tripwire on a regular basis to collect cryptographically secure hash values of system executables. The results should be saved on removable media so they cannot be manipulated by an attacker. Find out if such a program has been used and if the associated database is available. Having access to such records can reduce the level of effort by several days and increase the chance that you'll find manipulated executables.

The Manchurian Candidate, by Richard Condon, is a psycho-thriller about an American prisoner of war who is brainwashed by the Chinese. When he is released from prison, he endears himself to the presidential administration through his fervent anti-communism. This turns out to be a ruse to deflect suspicion; his hidden goal is to assassinate the president. His Chinese captors used hypnosis to create a human Trojan horse. It's an exciting story with a message that system administrators and forensic investigators should take to heart: once you've been hypnotized, you've always been hypnotized. When a system has been compromised, unless it is totally remade, it always will be a suspect system with a history of compromise that results in unknown effects. We call this *the Manchurian Candidate syndrome*. What exactly constitutes a complete remake? Does recovery require all new hardware? Actual manipulation of hardware itself is rare, but national intelligence agencies do have the ability to alter standard PC hardware. It is also becoming increasingly easy to find small, inexpensive data collection devices that may be inserted into the keyboard or the keyboard cable.

When a system has been compromised, it is impossible ever to trust it again. As we discussed in Chapter 10, compromised Unix systems are often hypnotized by their captors. The upshot is that you must treat every investigation as if the system being examined cannot be trusted. This is one reason why it is preferable to examine the data from a suspect system using a trusted second system. Any operating system can be totally compromised. Tools to do so have been widely available on Unix for years and are just now becoming available for Windows NT. Hypnotized Unix systems are common enough that you are likely to run into them—only time will tell if attacks on Windows NT systems follow the same pattern.

When you start examining a system, you or the system administrator may be able to make an educated guess as to the extent of the compromise. Although it isn't possible for you to actually know what has been done on a suspect host, you must choose an investigative methodology appropriate to the system's level of compromise. Take heart, there are no absolute correct answers in this business—use the most stringent methodology that you can. As shown in Table 11-2, the degree to which a system has been compromised can vary from the trivial to the catastrophic. Deliberately manipulated system binaries are commonly discovered on Unix hosts, and

Table 11-2 Levels of System Compromise

Level of Compromise	Ramification	Detection
Access to user account	Not difficult to continue the compromise and gain root access.	Simple to detect in logs (missing or obviously incomplete) and access times.
Application	May create bogus data.	Check hash values of all applications against hash values of known good binaries.
System application	Allows hiding of tracks.	Check hash values of all binaries in /sbin against hash values of known good binaries.
Shared libraries	Potential to subvert any binaries that are not statically linked.	Check hash values of shared library files (/lib/*.so).
Kernel	Nothing running within the kernel environment can be trusted.	Actual detection of kernel hack requires a great deal of expertise, but booting from a floppy disk or placing the data on another system isolates it from the effects of the hack.
Hardware	Nothing running on that hardware can be trusted.	Probably requires laboratory analysis by a specialist.
Forensic investigator	Test results may be manipulated.	Careful adherence to process and rules of evidence.
Violated laws of physics	Nothing can be believed.	Impossible to detect.

unfortunately, many more hacked binaries are not discovered. If an application, such as Tripwire, was run at one time providing cryptographically secure hashes of system binaries, you can verify the integrity of system files to a very high level of certainty. Be aware that if the Tripwire binaries are left on a system accessed by intruders, and especially if the hash value database is left on that system and is vulnerable to manipulation, you can't trust the results of Tripwire either. If Tripwire was run at a point when the compromised host's administrator had reason to believe that it was still intact, and if Tripwire was protected from compromise, it is relatively easy to verify the binaries. If an integrity database has never been created, it still is possible to locate corrupted executables, but it will take more effort on your part.

If you think that hacked kernels are the stuff of science fiction and are too unlikely to ever take place, think again. Take a look at the "(nearly) Complete Linux Loadable Kernel Modules Tutorial" on Hacking the Linux kernel.[2] Hacked kernels are rare, but when they do occur, they are very difficult to detect.

Unix Forensic Toolkits

At the time of this writing, two forensic toolkits are available for Unix. Discussed in Chapter 7, they are different in scope and purpose, and many investigators will be interested in both. ForensiX is a traditional capture-and-analysis tool, while TCT is designed specifically for examining hacked Unix systems.

Techniques for Collecting Evidence

No matter what level of rigor you are able to justify for the investigation, always begin with a fresh notebook. Start by recording the date and time and neatly record all of your findings. Don't trust your memory. The more professional and thorough you are in this investigation, the better the evidence will be. When you are trying to convince corporate management that your organization needs a formal incident response capability, performing your investigations as methodically and carefully as possible is the best way to make a good impression and justify a more formal response for future incidents.

When you are going to examine a system from its own console—which is mandatory if you want to collect evidence of current activity—start with the script command to ensure that everything you do is captured in a file. You must be logged on as root in order to access your tools CD and read all the files that you are going to image. Make the current time and the hostname the first two items to appear in the script file.

---

2. http://thc.pimmel.com/

```
# script > script.txt
# date
# uname -a
```

Record the reported time in your journal along with the actual time. This is your only record of discrepancies between the system clock and the real time, so be careful with this step. Mount your tool CD and set your path so that the CD is the only thing in your PATH variable; then confirm your path.

```
# mount  -t iso9660 /dev/cdrom /mnt/cdrom
# PATH=/mnt/cdrom
# echo $PATH
/mnt/cdrom
```

If you did not have the opportunity to prepare by creating a tool CD, at least protect yourself from the most obvious of Trojan horses by ensuring that the current working directory, ., is not in your search path. Alternatively, make it a habit always to type the full path of the command (/mnt/cdrom/bin/ls). You must log on as root to do some of the searching, and doing so also makes you vulnerable. One of the oldest Unix tricks in the book is creating a Trojan horse with the name of a common executable in the hopes that someone logged on as root will inadvertently execute it, creating a back door or damaging the system.

You need a place to store the data you collect. If you don't have access to a large removable storage device, you can copy your evidence to another system over a LAN. The most convenient network utility for this is the remote shell, rsh. Unfortunately, use of this capability requires opening your data collection systemwide to hacking, so it is acceptable *only* when you are on a completely isolated LAN. If you are stuck capturing data from a system connected to a modem or a network, use netcat instead. netcat is portable and requires no special configuration on the data collection host. If you are especially concerned about security, you can always use secure shell. Table 11-3 summarizes your remote data collection options.

Both rsh and netcat can accept standard output piped into their standard input. Before you try it on a real investigation, set up up a couple of Unix hosts on a LAN and experiment with the following examples. The first example requires that the data collection host, 192.168.0.2, trusts the first host.

```
# cat /etc/passwd /etc/shadow | rsh 192.168.0.2 "cat > /tmp/rsh.
  suspect.passwd_file"
```

Table 11-3 Remote Data Collection Utilities

Remote Data-Gathering Method	Advantages	Disadvantages
rsh, data collection system trusts suspect system	• Quick. • Flexible.	• Vulnerable to hacking.
nc (netcat)	• Fast. • Acceptably secure. • Binary is small enough to fit on a floppy disk and already is available on many platforms.	• Must restart on receiving end every time you want to start a new file.
scp (secure shell)	• Flexible. • Practically immune to hacking due to encryption and use of password.	• Must enter password every time you use it (or set up key pairs). Must have sshd running on collection host. • Probably not already installed on the suspect platform.

The double quotes are required. If you don't use double quotes, or you don't escape the redirect symbol with a backslash, the local shell assumes that you want to create the output file on the local host.

Using netcat

When copying data across a LAN, we prefer netcat. netcat has to be manually started on both the collection host and the suspect host, and there are a couple of tricks to using it successfully, so read this section carefully. First, start the listening process on the data collection PC (netcat works equally well on Windows NT, Windows 98, and Unix). Choose any arbitrary high-numbered port, such as 10,000:

```
$ nc -l -p 10000 > /tmp/nc.suspect.passwd_file
```

Then on the suspect host, cat a file to a netcat process like this:

```
cat /etc/passwd /etcshadow | nc 192.168.0.2 10000 -w 3
```

The nc executable on the listening host runs until it receives a connection and then the connection is broken, at which point it stops execution and the output file is closed. netcat first must be launched on the listening host and then launched on the sending host. The -w 3 option on the transmitting host means to wait 3 seconds and then time out. netcat won't automatically close when it receives the end-of-file on standard input unless you explicitly put in a timing value. If you forget the -w, it won't affect the transfer. Just press Control-C when the process being redirected to nc is finished.

Unix Information Sources

In their one-day seminar on Unix forensics, Dan Farmer and Wietse Venema introduce a concept they refer to as the *order of volatility*. It is a recognition that the lifetime of digital data varies according to where it is stored. Storage location, of course, is a function of the use that the data is being put to. The descending order of data volatility is:

- CPU storage
- System storage
- Kernel tables
- Fixed media
- Removable media
- Paper printouts

The more volatile the data is, the more difficult it is to capture, and the less time you have to do it. It is also usually the case that the more volatile the data, the more specialized the expertise required to make use of it. It is unlikely that you'll be able to use the contents of the system registers—the mere act of looking at them can change them. However, the contents of system memory and the state of the network can contain invaluable clues as to the existence, the type, and the source of an ongoing attack. Examining these data structures requires some specialized expertise. Fortunately, you don't need to actually understand Unix internals in order to safely capture this data. We'll show you how to save these volatile kernel data structures so that you can keep them for future reference. After you have captured them, you can take your time in finding an expert who can interpret them. They might even contain evidence of some new form of attack that hasn't been widely reported yet. If so, you won't know when you begin your investigation how important this data will be in the future. It's easy to save, and once you've captured this volatile data, it always is available for future reference. Table 11-4 lists the different sources of system data, their relative volatility, and their utility to your investigation.

Table 11-4 Order of Volatility

Max Life	Category	Data Storage Type	Significance to Forensic Investigator
As short as a single clock cycle	CPU storage	Registers	Infeasible to capture and of minimal utility.
		Caches	Infeasible to capture as a discrete entity but should be captured as part of system memory image.
	Video	RAM	Current screen can be captured and provides useful information if suspect was logged onto console or an X Window System terminal.
Until host is shut down	System storage	RAM	Includes information on all running processes and state of kernel. Easy to capture, but the act of capturing it changes it. Requires specialized knowledge to fully reconstruct, but it does not require special skills to search this data for keywords.
	Kernel tables	Network state	Can help determine whether a back door has been installed and is active. Should also be analyzed to determine if network activity is approved.
		Running processes	Some processes may be evidence of unauthorized activity. All running processes should be verified against known good binaries to ensure that they are not Trojan horses.
Until overwritten or erased	Fixed media (hard drive)	Swap space	When system demands exceed the capacity of RAM, some kernel data is swapped out to the hard drive. This data is just as important as the RAM in analyzing what is happening at a particular point in time.
		Queue directories	Includes information on running processes and incomplete activities. May include outgoing mail and print jobs that don't exist anywhere else on the system.
		Temp directories	/tmp (and sometimes /usr/tmp) serves as a scratch pad and working directory for the entire system. It is expected that it will be periodically cleaned out, so it is an appropriate place to leave data that won't be needed in the future. Because of this, it can be a treasure trove of data that was deliberately erased on other parts of the system.

(continued)

Table 11-4 Order of Volatility (*cont.*)

Max Life	Category	Data Storage Type	Significance to Forensic Investigator
Until overwritten or erased		Log directories	Crucial for reconstructing events. Because they would otherwise grow to infinite size, logs are maintained—older data eventually is over-written or deleted.
		User, binary, library, and configuration directories	Every part of a filesystem that isn't considered a temporary, log, or queue directory includes files that can stay indefinitely. However, anyone with write access can delete or change them at any time.
	Removable media	Floppy disks	Used less frequently in today's networked environments but may contain useful files. High-capacity floppy disks like the Jazz drive may be used for system backups.
		Tapes	Tapes are a reliable source of information about historical filesystem contents. If tapes exist from before an incident, they can be used to narrow the time period during which an incident occurred.
		CD-ROM read/write	Note that the standard for CDs is now multi-session. Be sure to examine suspect CDs on a system capable of showing all the sessions. Data cannot be overwritten, but each session creates a new directory table.
Until physically destroyed		CD-ROM write-only	Write-once media is an excellent place to store log files because they cannot be altered, yet they can still be searched electronically.
	Output	Paper printouts	Difficult to wade through lengthy printouts because they cannot be searched, but short of physical destruction, they are probably the longest lived data storage mechanism.

It is impossible to completely capture the state of a computer (although the Suspend function on a laptop can come pretty close). Just the act of examining highly volatile data changes it. For a quick demonstration of this on Linux (but not Solaris), try grepping something in the system physical memory:

```
# grep heisenberg /dev/mem
Binary file /dev/mem matches
```

No matter what string you grep, the result always is true because the act of entering a command changes the kernel data structure. In fact, when you are running a shell with history, after you run a command, it stays in the kernel memory for quite a while. Use the following command to thumb through a Linux kernel to get an idea of the amount and type of stuff it contains:

```
# strings /dev/mem | more
```

If you want to see the evidence left from your earlier grep, type **/heisenberg** at the : prompt while running strings and number on the kernel. Repeat the forward slash (/) a couple of times to repeat the search—you don't need to reinput the search string unless you want to search for a different string. You'll be surprised at how often the string appears within the kernel. /dev/mem is a device special file that allows access to the physical memory on a Unix system. The virtual memory is accessed through /dev/kmem.

Video Display

All versions of Unix have standardized on a windowing standard, X Windows System, from MIT. (It's usually referred to as "X Windows" and sometimes just as "X.") It is a networking system allowing running processes to display their windows wherever it is most convenient for a user. We run X Windows software (X Windows Server) on our Windows NT laptop and usually use it to access the Unix hosts in our LAN. With X Windows, there is no need to use a system console, so a crime in progress may not be visible on it. If you want to save a copy of the screen, you can do so in several ways (a photograph might not be a bad idea either). The X Windows dump command xwd, enables you to dump an individual window or the entire screen. When an xterm window (the X window system graphical utility that simulates a character-based terminal, providing a command prompt interface) is running, you can execute the command from there. We prefer not to disturb the screen at all, so we run xwd from another terminal.

Most PC Unix versions provide a number of virtual terminals on the console. By pressing the Control and Alt keys simultaneously with one of the F keys, you can hot-key to a character-based logon screen. On a RedHat Linux system, the default hot-key sequence is Ctrl-Alt-F2, which will provide a command prompt allowing you to log on as root (if you know the password). To identify the X Window virtual screen that you wish to capture, use the option -display localhost:0, which means the first X Windows screen on the host that you are logged onto (remember that Unix programmers start counting from 0). You can telnet from a PC or any other host and execute the same command. If you want the entire screen, it's best to use the -root option. ("root" in this context doesn't refer to the administrator, but refers to the lowest level window, which encompasses the entire screen and all of its contents.)

```
# xwd -display localhost:0 -root > screen.xwd
```

Return to the X display by pressing Ctrl-Alt-F7. For obscure reasons, the virtual terminal that is used for the default on RedHat is not F1 (which you might think is intuitively obvious) but is F7. Other PC Unixes use different F key conventions.

After you've made your screen capture, examine it to make sure that you didn't capture the screen saver. The screen capture is in a format that can be viewed with xwud:

```
# xwud -in screen.xwd
```

Several utilities, such as fbm, pbmplus, and ImageMagick, are available on Unix systems to convert XWD bitmaps to more portable formats such as TIFF and GIF.

When you want to capture an individual window with xwd, leave off the -root option. Crosshairs are displayed and you can capture the window that is under them when you press the left mouse button.

Memory

Remember that everything on Unix is treated as a file, which makes it easy to copy and save the contents of the system memory. In the following example, assume that we have a data collection system with a lot of free space in a filesystem. First, set up two listening netcat processes on the data collection system:

```
# nc -l -p 10005 > suspect.mem.image&
[1] 751
# nc -l -p 10006 > suspect.kmem.image&
[2] 752
```

Then copy the memory from the suspect machine:

```
# dd bs=1024 < /dev/mem |nc 192.168.0.2 10005 -w 3
32768+0 records in
32768+0 records out
# dd bs=1024 < /dev/kmem |nc 192.168.0.2 10005 -w 3
22+0 records in
22+0 records out
```

This technique works well on Linux, but on Solaris, dd may never reach an end-of-file, which causes it to hang. Monitor the size of the image file on the collection machine, and if it stops growing (or if the lights on your hub stop blinking), kill dd on the suspect machine by pressing Ctrl-d.

When the suspect system has a /dev/rswap file, copy it also. We cannot verify that the captured data is exactly the same as the original—as we've said previously, just the act of collecting it changes it slightly. Try this demonstration of kernel volatility on your experimental host:

```
# md5sum /dev/mem
a43b0bd94e67d46d68797eafa2656c43 /dev/kmem
# md5sum /dev/mem
64f9d825287f79f5b347dda9a253759b /dev/kmem
# md5sum /dev/mem
b43443ffaed517ab87c81105c5b7be44 /dev/kmem
```

Later in this chapter, we perform MD5 checksums on captured volatile data as protection against further alterations, but it should be clear that it is impossible to verify accuracy when copying highly volatile objects such as the system's memory. Capture whatever data you can that may help you understand the nature of the crime, even if it may be difficult to explain in court.

Network Connections

The network state provides important information on both current network connections and listening processes. When an attacker has left a network process running, you need to know about it, and when unauthorized connections are taking place either inbound or outbound, you need to know about them also. Use the netstat command to capture information on ongoing network activity. On a typical Unix workstation, most of the network connections are in place to accommodate X Windows, which uses network mechanisms even when it is only running locally. On Linux, we use the -p option to show the processes associated with specific network connections (on other platforms, "p" stands for "protocol"):

```
# netstat -p
Active Internet connections (w/o servers)
Proto Recv-Q Send-Q Local Address           Foreign Address         State       PID/Program name
tcp        1      0 localhost.localdom:1043 localhost.localdoma:www CLOSE_WAIT  797/netscape
tcp        1      0 localhost.localdom:1042 localhost.localdoma:www CLOSE_WAIT  797/netscape
tcp        0      0 192.168.0.2:1038        sleipnir.heiser.:telnet ESTABLISHED 758/telnet
tcp        0      0 192.168.0.2:1023        sleipnir.heiser.or:1022 ESTABLISHED 747/in.rshd
tcp        0      0 192.168.0.2:shell       sleipnir.heiser.or:1023 ESTABLISHED 748/bash
....
```

We didn't show the complete results here, but netstat provides detailed information on the state of X Windows and other system services. HTTP is stateless,[3] so these connections have a very short life, and their status quickly cycles to FIN_WAIT and then CLOSE_WAIT. Note also that the connecting machine names are provided. When netstat can't look up these names locally in /etc/hosts, it tries a reverse DNS lookup to determine the host name associated with the numeric address—an action that may be recorded by the DNS server of an especially alert cracker. If you are analyzing attacks in progress, try using the -n option. On NetBSD and Solaris, try the invocation netstat -an.

Although it is rare, it is possible for an attacker to mess with the routing tables and even hack the address resolution that maps Ethernet cards' MAC addresses to IP addresses (remember our discussion of the MAC address from Chapter 8). In the following example, we use netstat to display the routing tables and arp in verbose mode to capture the address resolution tables:

```
# netstat -rn
Kernel IP routing table
Destination   Gateway       Genmask         Flags  MSS Window  irtt Iface
192.168.0.0   192.168.0.1   255.255.255.0   UG       0 0          0 eth0
192.168.0.0   0.0.0.0       255.255.255.0   U        0 0          0 eth0
127.0.0.0     0.0.0.0       255.0.0.0       U        0 0          0 lo
0.0.0.0       192.168.0.1   0.0.0.0         UG       0 0          0 eth0
# arp -v
Address               HWtype   HWaddress         Flags Mask      Iface
192.168.0.4           ether    00:40:05:2C:C7:99  C             eth0
192.168.0.2           ether    00:10:4B:F1:D3:11  C             eth0
192.168.0.1           ether    00:A0:CC:25:FC:29  C             eth0
Entries: 3   Skipped: 0      Found:  3
#
```

On Solaris, use the -a option for arp:

```
solaris:
# arp -a
```

---

3. HTTP is stateless in that it doesn't maintain an active connection between the Web browser and the Web server. When you request display of a URL, it is basically a batched request. If a Web page is returned, your Web browser displays it, and the transaction is over. The Web page can display on your screen indefinitely, but the remote server has nothing further to do with it.

```
Net to Media Table
Device    IP Address              Mask        Flags   Phys Addr
------    -------------------     ---------------     ---------------
hme0      njektd.com              255.255.255.255             00:50:ba:aa:f0:da
hme0      packetwerks             255.255.255.255             00:80:c8:e7:2c:30
hme0      defaultrouter           255.255.255.255             00:d0:58:65:25:40
hme0      63.107.222.118          255.255.255.255             00:50:ba:aa:0d:5f
hme0      host909                 255.255.255.255 SP          08:00:20:87:3a:e3
hme0      BASE-ADDRESS.MCAST.NET 240.0.0.0        SM          01:00:5e:00:00:00
```

Network denial-of-service attacks, which are becoming increasingly common, might exploit ICMP (Internet control message protocol), UDP (user data protocol), TCP (transmission control protocol), or application protocols like HTTP, effectively isolating a system from the network. Only the application protocols are likely to leave traces in the system logs. Indeed, denial-of-service attacks are designed precisely to cause havoc without leaving evidence. The most reliable way to analyze such an attack is with a network sniffer located either on a nonswitched or a spanned network segment that can see the victim's traffic. Some analysis, however, is possible from within the victim. It requires viewing the process tables and network data structures in real time, during the attack itself. This data is highly volatile and when the attack is over, the only evidence left may be some of the network statistics. Unless collected immediately, that data will disappear during the next reboot or power off.[4]

Let's capture all of this data in one file on our data collection host:

```
$ nc -l -p 10007 > suspect.netstatus.txt
```

We can collect all the network information at once by running all the commands on a single line on the suspect host:

```
# (date; netstat -p; netstat -rn; arp -v) | nc 192.168.0.2 10007 -w 3
```

Because none of these utilities output a date, running the date command provides helpful documentation.

---

4. This is a good place to discuss further the concept of intrusion detection systems. An IDS, which can be either network based or host based, is designed to capture information relevant to ongoing attacks. A network IDS is a specialized form of sniffer. In the case of an ongoing attack, use of Snort or a commercial IDS may be the best way to capture information about the activities of your suspect. Another tool that is useful to TCP-aware investigators is ngrep (http://ngrep.sourceforge.net/). It's a cool tool you can use to see the payload and not just attack signatures or IP headers.

Running Processes

Unix supplies a number of utilities that provide information on the set of all running processes or provide details on a specific running process. A list of the most common utilities is provided in Table 11-5. Your next task in capturing the state of a running machine is to collect a list of all the running processes and a list of all the open files. Later, you can correlate this information with the verbose netstat you captured earlier.

You should use the process status command ps first. Confusingly, it has dozens of options, and they vary greatly among different Unix platforms. As shown in Table 11-6, System V. Unix and BSD Unix families have different invocations of the ps command.

Table 11-5   Process Information Utilities

Name	Description
uptime	Uptime Shows current processing load and 2 previous load values. Provides an understanding of current and recent activity.
w, who	Shows current logins
ps	Process Status Displays list of all running processes with details about their context and state.
top	Real-time display of most CPU-intensive processes. Useful diagnostic tool when system is running slowly. Password cracking tools will show up clearly with top.
lsof	List Open Files Provides a list of all currently open files and the processes that have opened them.
fuser	File User Identifies which processes are using a specific file or network socket.
strace	System Call Trace List all system calls being made by a running process. Ported to many Unix environments, including Linux.
truss, ktrace	Earlier versions of system call trace
ltrace	Library routine trace

Table 11-6 Process Status Commands

Unix Family	Long and Longer Versions	Results
System V	`ps -ef`	A list of running processes.
	`ps -ealf`	A bit more detail but still disappointing compared to BSD.
BSD	`ps -aux`	Most detailed list that is convenient to read on a 80-character-wide screen.
	`ps -auxeww`	Provides the complete environment. Difficult to read onscreen but helpful for later analysis.
Linux	Supports both SysV and BSD options, but we suggest following the BSD options.	Same as BSD.

All of the commands shown in Table 11-6 create lengthy output that can fill multiple screens, and so does the list of open files command, lsof (which may not be installed on every system). If you are examining a BSD or Linux system, you should take advantage of both the long and the short of it, using the first version to create a convenient human-readable status list, and the second to create detailed output that you can refer to later if you determine that hostile code is actually running on the system being examined. First, start a listening netcat process on your collection system:

```
# nc -l -p 10007 > suspect_ps_lsof.txt
```

then run the appropriate invocation of ps on the host being investigated:

On a System V host:

```
# (ps -ealf; lsof) | nc 192.168.0.2 10007 -w 3
```

On a BSDish or Linux host:

```
# (ps -aux; ps -auxeww; lsof) | nc 192.168.0.2 10007 -w 3
```

/proc

The /proc directory is a pseudo-filesystem that provides a structured interface to /dev/kmem, facilitating system diagnostics and a view into the environment of each running executable. Every process in memory has a directory in /proc associated with it named after its process ID (PID). At the time of this writing, no attacks that hide /proc entries have been reported, making /proc a more reliable guide to currently running processes than the commonly hacked ps utility. You should collect a quick list of the PID directories in /proc so that you can compare it later with the output of ps. If a process is missing from the ps output that does appear in /proc, that is a clue that ps might have been trojanned.

```
# ls -d /proc[1-9]* | nc 192.168.0.2 10008 -w 3
```

It is usually possible to tar these directories for later reference, although there can be problems with holes in memory. TCT comes with a utility, pcat, that is intended to safely capture the context of a specific running process:

```
# tar -cvf proc.tar /proc/[1-9]*
```

When the kernel has been hacked, even an unmodified copy of ps can provide misleading information. The process names in the ps output can be changed without having to modify any system binaries. ps simply reports whatever name was used to invoke a command. With these caveats in mind, Table 11-7 describes a few things to look for on systems being investigated.

Table 11-7   Signs of Hostile Processes

What to Look For	Significance
Any discrepancy between ps, top, and /proc	PIDs that appears in top or /proc but not ps may have been deliberately hidden.
Unrecognized commands, especially ones that start with a . or ./ (./app). Searching the disk for any instance of the word "eggdrop" is usually a good idea.	Clear indication that the application was started manually.
Daemons running more than once that should be running only once, such as inetd.	The only way to start two inetd processes is to have the second one start manually, which is never required. This is usually a sign of a trojanized version. Be aware that some network services, such as httpd, commonly do have multiple versions running simultaneously.
High uptimes (high system utilization) and especially a process using an unusual level of system resources.	Cryptanalysis is very processor intensive. So are bogus IRC servers, and running crack utilities stick out like warts. It isn't practical (yet) to to attempt to hide them because it would make them too slow to be useful.
High network utilization (usually discovered by network management tools external to the suspect host).	Could be a sign that one or more systems on your network are being used as zombies in a denial--of-service attack.

When you do identify a running executable that you think is bogus, you should attempt to locate the executable and copy it. Seeing the common Linux sniffer, lin-sniff, appear in ps output is a sign of two things. First, the system has almost certainly been compromised, and second, the attacker is either inept or just doesn't care.

```
# ps -ef
.....
jheiser   5426  5424  0 21:56 pts/4    00:00:00 ./linsniff
.....
```

cd to the /proc directory associated with the questionable process. In this case, the process has a PID of 5426, so its process information can be found in /proc/5426. Doing a long directory listing for this directory shows you the full path of the executable:

```
# ls -l /proc/5426
total 0
-r--r--r--   1 jheiser  jheiser  0 Jun  1 21:56 cmdline
lrwx------   1 jheiser  jheiser  0 Jun  1 21:56 cwd -> /home/jheiser
-r--------   1 jheiser  jheiser  0 Jun  1 21:56 environ
lrwx------   1 jheiser  jheiser  0 Jun  1 21:56 exe -> /home/jheiser/
                                                      linsniff (deleted)
dr-x------   2 jheiser  jheiser  0 Jun  1 21:56 fd
pr--r--r--   1 jheiser  jheiser  0 Jun  1 21:56 maps
-rw-------   1 jheiser  jheiser  0 Jun  1 21:56 mem
lrwx------   1 jheiser  jheiser  0 Jun  1 21:56 root -> /
-r--r--r--   1 jheiser  jheiser  0 Jun  1 21:56 stat
-r--r--r--   1 jheiser  jheiser  0 Jun  1 21:56 statm
-r--r--r--   1 jheiser  jheiser  0 Jun  1 21:56 status
#
```

In this case, the executable was deleted after it was executed, meaning that the inode no longer has any links to it. The file still exists and won't be deleted until the executable stops, although you can't access it with simple Unix utilities. TCT has two utilities that can be of use in this situation. ils lists inodes and has an option to list unlinked but still open inodes. icat is designed to copy a specific inode, such as one returned by ils.

```
# cat /proc/5426/maps
08048000-0809d000 r-xp 00000000 03:05 82853   /home/jheiser/linsniff
                                               (deleted stuff)
........
```

You may not want to just kill an unexplained running process, but you might want to freeze it so you can spend some time examining it. You can do so with the **kill -stop** *pid* command. If you do kill it, at least try to create a core dump, which can be done on some versions of Solaris and BSD that have the gcore command. Other Unixes create a core dump file when a running process receives the appropriate signal. On Linux, kill -5 creates a core dump. TCT includes a utility, pcat, that captures the memory of a running process and sends it to stdout. (Note that some versions of Unix have a utility called "pcat" that has nothing to do with TCT's utility.)

After you have collected all the information on running processes and network connections that you know how to collect, you can power off or shut down the system if you have been authorized to do so.

Analyzing Potentially Hostile Executables

We've already seen some methods for identifying potentially unauthorized binaries on running Unix systems. In this section, we provide several more techniques for locating hostile binaries that are not running. Confronted with code that might be malware, you first adopt the attitude that it might be a poisonous snake or the Ebola virus. Don't take mystery code lightly. Do *not* attempt to run an unknown binary—it could do anything. The only place that you should attempt to run a suspicious program is in an isolation ward—put on your respirator and don't allow any other patient to come close. Use a throwaway machine and disconnect it from the network. After you run the hostile binary, unless you can completely rule out hostile intent (proving a negative is not easy), you have to assume that the program might have damaged the test system in a way that you are unaware of. Reinstall the OS.

Table 11-8 describes a few techniques for examining hostile code. Always assume that the attacker might have made a mistake, but never count on it.

If the circumstances (name and directory) don't indicate what the code does, the strings command is the most useful tool you can use. Pipe the output through a pager:

```
$ strings -a mystery_file | more
```

Use of the all, -a, option can ensure that the entire file is being scanned.

Table 11-8 Analyzing Unknown Code

Techniques	Description
Try to read file	If the unknown code is a script, you simply can read it. If the unknown code is a binary, make sure that it is an object format the system you are examining uses. If it is not, the attacker either is ignorant or is using the suspect system as a warehouse or staging ground for attacking some other system.
Check the date	If the unknown code was installed around the time of a known incident, it is probably something that the attacker thought would be useful.
Check the name	Many attackers don't bother to change their malware's original functional name. If the unknown code is called "sniffer" or "passwordcrack," there's a good chance you've already been able to identify its function. Do a search on the Internet for the name and see if you get any hits.
Look for nearby source code	Hackers often compile their attack code on their victims. The source code might be in the same directory or in /tmp. It might be in a hidden directory, and it may have been deleted.
Use strings	Character strings within the binary can provide information on the files it accesses, its error messages, its default name, and even the name of its creator.
Use grep	If you suspect that the unknown code might be accessing specific files, or you are looking for the executable that resulted in some output that you found, you can use grep to see if those strings appear in your mystery code.
Use nm	nm is a programmer's tool that lists the symbol table. If the program has been stripped, you won't see much. **nm –Du** shows the runtime libraries it uses, which might give you some clues, such as whether the unknown code is a network-enabled binary.
Ask a programmer for assistance	If you don't have programming skills in C, Unix, and TCP/IP, you won't be able to completely evaluate unknown code. Find a skilled programmer you can trust. He or she will enjoy the challenge of analyzing mystery code.
Run the unknown code in a controlled environment	There's nothing quite like the old smoke test, but don't run the unknown code on your examination machine or the subject machine. Run it in a controlled laboratory environment that enables you trace the program's execution and limit possible damage. Put a sniffer on the LAN to see if the questionable code tries to connect back out.

In the previous chapter, we listed a number of common Unix exploits. There is no guarantee that these exploits will have the same names as we used in Chapter 10 when installed on a system that you are examining, but they might. You might also find evidence of the names of well-known malware in email messages or when using strings to examine unknown binaries. Some words, such as "warez," are typically used in hackerspeak and are clues that someone owns the system or is trying to own it. The word "sartori" is frequently associated with rootkits as a password. One trick to getting a list of the names of common hostile executables is to go to a Web site such as Rootshell,[5] display a Web page listing the names of exploits, and save a list of every name ending in a ".c."

Reverse-engineering object code is not a trivial task. If you find a binary that you believe may be significant, find someone to disassemble it and reconstruct its function.

The Filesystem

Copy the Hard Drives

In Chapter 3 we discussed how a hard drive is logically formatted with nesting units. Depending upon the circumstances of your investigation, you will be dealing with different units, including the entire hard drive, partitions, and filesystems. In the next few pages, we discuss how to deal with each of these different entities. Every standard Unix distribution provides a set of tools that enables you to capture the filesystems for examination on a safe platform when you are unable to power down the machine, or when it is impossible to remove the hard drive and create an image. If you don't have high-capacity removable storage, you can copy entire filesystems over the network. First, you need to determine which filesystems are on the hard drive. The mount command shows what is currently mounted:

```
# mount
/dev/hda5 on / type ext2 (rw)
none on /proc type proc (rw)
/dev/hda1 on /boot type ext2 (rw)
none on /dev/pts type devpts (rw,gid=5,mode=620)
```

---

5. http://www.rootshell.com

The mount command can't tell you which hard drives exist but are not currently being used, although the /etc/fstab file may contain the names of filesystems that are formatted but not currently mounted. You usually can see at boot time what hard drives are recognized by the computer. When you do take the machine down, take off the cover and see what drives it has and what controller they are connected to. fdisk is the most common disk partition utility on Intel platforms, and versions of it are available for most PC operating systems. You should run it on every hard drive and keep a list of the filesystems it reports on. If you don't know the number of hard drives on the system you are examining, and you cannot physically examine the interior of the machine, you can determine the number through trial and error or by reviewing the appropriate log file (either messages or dmesg) to see the system boot messages. The log should include a line for each hard drive that it identifies during the boot sequence. While virtually all DOS and Windows machines refer to the boot drive as "C:" but allow some flexibility with the names assigned to succeeding drives, Unix drives may not be sequentially numbered. All SCSI devices connected to a specific SCSI controller share the same set of ID numbers, 0–7. The ID numbers for modern SCSI controllers go up to 15, and multiple LUNs (logical unit numbers) could be on each ID. The boot IDE drive must always be a master drive, which is drive 1 on the BIOS, drive 0 for Unix, and drive C: for Windows. The boot SCSI drive can be any ID number from 1 to 15, with 0 the most often used boot ID.

When you are examining a PC platform, try the -l option of fdisk to list the partitions on each hard drive:

```
# fdisk -l /dev/hda
Disk /dev/hda: 64 heads, 63 sectors, 789 cylinders
Units = cylinders of 4032 * 512 bytes
```

Device Boot		Start	End	Blocks	Id	System
/dev/hda1	*	1	9	18112+	83	Linux
/dev/hda2		10	789	1572480	5	Extended
/dev/hda5		10	756	1505920+	83	Linux
/dev/hda6		757	789	66496+	82	Linux swap

If you don't have access to a version of fdisk with a list option, run it interactively, but be careful not to make any changes to the partitions. As shown in the following example, run fdisk on the boot drive of a PC Unix system, print the partition table (p), and then quit out of fdisk (q).

```
# fdisk /dev/hda

Command (m for help): p

Disk /dev/hda: 64 heads, 63 sectors, 789 cylinders
Units = cylinders of 4032 * 512 bytes

   Device Boot    Start     End    Blocks   Id  System
/dev/hda1 *           1       9     18112+  83  Linux
/dev/hda2            10     789   1572480    5  Extended
/dev/hda5            10     756   1505920+  83  Linux
/dev/hda6           757     789     66496+  82  Linux swap

Command (m for help):q
```

Repeat these commands on every hard drive until you have compiled a complete list of all partitions on every drive, including unformatted ones.

Imaging the Filesystems

After you create a list of all the filesystems on the suspect host, you can begin capturing them. There are a number of ways to capture the filesystems, depending on what device you have for storage. In the following sections, we provide instructions on using several different techniques; you should always have contingency plans because you never know what to expect when you examine a suspect system.

Imaging Utilities

The dd utility has traditionally been the tool used to create filesystem images, although in many cases, cat and cp work just as well (and faster when you forget to specify a block size for dd). The dd utility has several advantages. First, it can copy data using any specified block size, which might be a requirement of some hardware devices (especially tape). Second, when dd is finished, it reports how many blocks it processed. Third, you can keep an error log as proof of your successful backup:

```
dd if=/dev/fd0 of=/home/spinach/test/ 2>/home/smith/test/errortext
```

dd also can be used to wipe your analysis drive first to ensure no previous data still resides that could corrupt your evidence (make sure you are not wiping your boot or evidence drives):

```
dd if=/dev/zero of=/dev/fd0 2>/home/smith/test/wipedrive
```

But don't take our word for it. After you wipe your analysis drive, look at it with your favorite disk editor and confirm that the data consists of a string of zeros. You should always verify any new technique before an investigation.

By specifying a convenient block size, such as 1024, you'll know how many kilobytes of data were copied, providing a good sanity check that the operation did what you expected. Finally, dd can be used to reliably split up a large object into smaller objects that can be reassembled later. Keep this technique in mind when a filesystem is too large to store in one piece or when other methods don't work.

dd also has several disadvantages. First, when you don't specify a block size, or when you choose one that isn't optimal, dd can be substantially slower than other utilities. Second, although it is a minor issue, it is sometimes difficult to remember the complex command-line options for dd. cat's larger block size provides a faster copy process, and its command-line options are a bit easier to remember than those of dd. We include examples using both dd and cat in this chapter—they are usually interchangeable, and if you choose one that isn't compatible with the data copy you are attempting, helpful error messages should provide a clue that you should try the other method. If the "cat" barfs, dd is still your friend.

The Unix tape device usually has a name like /dev/rmt or /dev/rct (magnetic tape and cartridge tape, respectively). Find out exactly what the tape device is called on the platform you are investigating and what the recommended block size is. If you don't know the recommended block size, you can omit that option. The copy will be slow, but accuracy won't be a problem (both cat and dd stop on an error). The command to store an image of a filesystem on a tape should be similar to this:

```
dd if=/dev/hda5 of=/dev/rmt8 bs=20k
```

Copying a file system over a network—especially when you have only 10MB Ethernet adaptors instead of 100MB—can be quite slow, but it's convenient when you can't remove the hard drive and have no tape drive. Use the netcat technique from our discussion earlier in the chapter:

```
Listening host: # nc -l -p 10000 > suspect.ad0s1e.image
```

```
Suspect host: # dd bs=1024 < /dev/ad0s1e | nc 192.168.0.4 10000 -w 3
```

The dd utility has a 2GB limit on some PC platforms. If you experience fatal errors when using dd on large filesystems or drive images, a simple technique enables you to split the filesystem into smaller pieces: specify both the size of the copy and an offset. The size is the same for each section of the filesystem image that you collect, but the offset is incremented by the size during each copy. For example, suppose that a Linux filesystem on a second hard drive is 6GB in size. You can split the file into three pieces, copying each to another host with a larger filesystem. First, set up three listening netcat processes on the data collection host:

```
# nc -l -p 10001 > suspect.hdb5.image.1of3&
# nc -l -p 10002 > suspect.hdb5.image.2of3&
# nc -l -p 10003 > suspect.hdb5.image.3of3&
```

Including an ampersand after each command allows it to run in the background, so you can immediately enter another command. No sense tying up a good command line with processes that could take hours, right? Because you are running all three nc processes simultaneously, each one has to listen on a different port number. Using different port numbers for each data transfer is a good habit to get into with netcat—it decreases the chance that you'll accidentally overwrite or mislabel your data. On the suspect side, running more than one dd at a time has no advantages. It stresses the hard drive and won't increase the transfer speed (if you want to see your PC hop up and down, place ampersands after each of the following command lines):

```
# dd if=/dev/hdb5 count 2000000 bs=1024 | nc 192.168.0.4 10001 -w 3
# dd if=/dev/hdb5 skip 2000000 count 200000 bs=1024 | nc 192.168.0.4 10002 -w 3
# dd if=/dev/hdb5 skip 4000000 count 200000 bs=1024 | nc 192.168.0.4 10003 -w 3
```

These three objects can be recombined on another system, as long as it has enough room for the full 6GB.

```
# cat suspect.hdb5.image.1of3 >> suspect.hdb5.image
# cat suspect.hdb5.image.2of3 >> suspect.hdb5.image
# cat suspect.hdb5.image.3of3 >> suspect.hdb5.image
```

If nothing else works, you can always resort to tar. tar is quick, easy, and portable among all versions of Unix, and tar archives are readable by the WinZip utility. From a forensic point of view, tar contaminates the evidence because it operates on the level of the individual file, so it changes the access time (although use of the -atime option can help), and it cannot capture unallocated inodes. But if all you are allowed or able to do is to grab a couple of directory trees for later analysis, you should use tar.

For instance, when you want to review all of the logs on a particular host, you can use netcat without even having to save a tarfile on the suspect host. Logs are text files that compress well, so we can improve transfer speed by using compress. First, start a listening netcat process on your data collection host:

```
$ nc -l -p 10009 | uncompress -g > suspecthost.logs.tar
```

Then execute the following command on the remote host:

```
# cd /var/log
# tar cf - . | compress -g | nc 192.168.0.2 10009 -w 3
```

Lots of tars have compression built in these days, in which case the following works great:

```
# tar czf - . | nc 192.168.0.2 10009 -w 3
```

If you are part of a response team that has been asked to review an incident, you might ask the local administrator to tar and netcat the files to you before you decide to mobilize the response team or shut down the afflicted host. You should keep a couple of things in mind if you do so. First, check how much data is in the directory before copying this tar file across your WAN—it might be too large to be practical. Second, if your conversation with the system administrator gives you any doubts about his or her ability to collect the data on your behalf, get the root password and do it yourself remotely. Ask the administrator not to touch the machine.

Although it isn't appropriate for imaging drives or partitions, tar has several advantages. In addition to data portability, tar also can be instructed to follow symbolic links. Remember that if your suspect is using remote filesystems, the remote data can't be captured just by imaging the local drive or filesystems.

Compare MD5 of Original Device to Copy

After you've collected some data—whatever the source and whatever the method—create its hash value and record it in your notebook. You also can run a hash of the original disk drives and disk partitions. Just keep in mind that the object you are fingerprinting must be *quiescent*, which means that it cannot accept active writes. On the suspect system, use an MD5 utility from your CD. We use MD5 from TCT:

```
# /mnt/cd/bin/md5 /dev/hda1
fd7efb437dc8ba30a0956b3e824e7ead          /dev/hda1
```

On the collection host, run MD5 against the image file:

```
# md5 suspect.hda1.image
fd7efb437dc8ba30a0956b3e824e7ead          suspect.hda1.image
```

Also run MD5 against any of the volatile information that you collected previously and record the hash value in your notebook. At least you'll be able to show that the data hasn't been altered at least since you captured it.

Accessing Captured Filesystems for Examination

There are two ways to use filesystem images that have been saved from another machine. The first way is to copy the image into a partition that is the same size as the image. Wipe the partition clean using dd as described previously, and then use dd to copy the image onto the partition. A much easier and more convenient technique involves copying the image file into a filesystem large enough to contain it and then mounting the drive image file itself as a filesystem. This method takes advantage of a software abstraction called a *loopback device*. A loopback device is an abstraction for accessing filesystem images, and should not be confused with the similarly named network loopback.

RedHat Linux is configured by default with a series of loopback devices in /dev, making it convenient to mount multiple filesystem images simultaneously. To access the files within the 6GB drive image that we recombined previously, first create a directory for a mount point and then mount it *read-only* using the loopback device. On Linux, the commands look like this:

```
# mkdir /mnt/suspecthost
# mount -t ext2 -o ro,loop=/dev/loop0 suspect.hdb5.image /mnt/suspecthost
```

If you have an image from a DOS filesystem, you also can access it this way:

```
# mkdir /mnt/suspect2
# mount -t dos -o ro,loop=/dev/loop1 suspect.dos.image /mnt/suspecthost2
```

After you mount a filesystem image this way, you can treat it like any other filesystem. Change directory into it, copy it, use find within it—treat it just like any other read-only filesystem. Don't forget that we've mounted the filesystem read-only, and we encourage you always to do so when conducting an investigation. An advantage to Linux is that it supports so many different filesystem types. At the time of this writing, the following types are supported: minix, xiafs, ext, ext2, msdos, umsdos, vfat, proc, autofs, devpts, nfs, iso9660, smbfs, ncpfs, adfs, affs, coda, hfs, hpfs, ntfs, qnx4, romfs, ufs, sysv, xenix, and coherent. Several other versions of Unix have a similar capability, but Linux probably supports the widest range of filesystems. Just remember that no version of Linux supports every filesystem by default—you may have to remake the kernel in order to support a version you need, and you should wipe the filesystem clean with dd first.

Remember that the UIDs of the foreign filesystem must be manually correlated with the /etc/passwd and /etc/group files from that system, or if it is being used, from the NIS/NIS+ server. If the filesystems are mounted on an examination system, or if individual files from the suspect system have been copied to your examination system using archive options that retain the original ownership (which is what you should do), the numeric UID and GID reference a logon and a group from the suspect host—not your existing host. In other words, ls will provide misleading output. However, the root user *always* has a UID of 0, and if you are using the same operating environment, the other administrative accounts may also have the same UID. The TCT mactime utility accommodates this need by enabling you to specify which password file it should use when assigning logons to the numeric UIDs. From this point on in your examination process, the procedures we discuss in the rest of this chapter can be used to examine a copy of the original hard drive, images of the original filesystems, or if it is the only practical way to conduct your examination, the procedures can be run on the suspect host itself.

The Big mac

As long as you analyze a read-only copy of a suspect filesystem, you can collect the mac times whenever it is convenient. On a live system, inode times are highly volatile, and you must collect them before you, or some running process, inadvertently change any. You can do so on any Unix system with a combination of the ls and stat utilities:

```
$ find /mnt/suspect.root.image -type f -print0 | xargs -0 stat >
  suspect.root.statout
```

Because the output of this operation is so awkward to use, TCT includes the command mactime. It provides a convenient report with a single line for each filesystem object, sorting all the entries by inode change time. The mactime report facilitates the correlation of system events with filesystem access times. If you haven't taken the time to make mactime, you can perform time correlations using the output from ls and stat, but it is awkward.

If you know when a system intruder was active on the suspect host, refer to that section of the mactime report to see what system files were being accessed. If you don't know when a system intruder was active, but do know some of the files that were accessed, find those files on the access time report. Certain activities, such as compiling software, stand out quite clearly on a mactime report.

As you continue your examination, you constantly will find yourself referring to your mac list. Every time you encounter something suspicious, look for other file accesses that occurred in chronological proximity. This is how you build a picture of the suspect's activities.

Logs

System logs potentially are the most valuable source of information on system activities. We say "potentially" because several conditions must be met in order for logs to be useful. First, not only must logging be enabled, but it must be configured to work at a sufficient level of detail. Second, logs must be intact. The Unix syslog feature is quite flexible, and syslog-compatible processes usually allow a great deal of flexibility in the amount of information they send to syslog. When examining a Unix system, refer to /etc/syslog.conf to see how logging is configured for each system service and where it is sent. As discussed in Chapter 10, log-cleaning utilities are readily available on hacker Web sites, and it is not difficult to wipe out locally stored logs. If the syslog.conf file indicates that log entries are being sent to a different host, the odds are improved that the logging records have been protected from tampering. Be sure to get the log records from the logging host, and to be completely thorough, you should also perform a complete investigation of the logging host. This increases the level of assurance that it has not been compromised and that the log records can be trusted. If the logging host must stay up to support other hosts, see if the local system administrators can find a replacement host to take over logging while you examine the original logging host. If it isn't maintained either automatically or manually, any form of logging eventually fills up its filesystem with entries. When reviewing system logs, you must determine the log maintenance system that is in use. Log maintenance should be invoked by a cron job, so check root's crontab for information on when and how log files are moved. Relevant log files may have been copied to some other area on the system or may be found on backup media. Ask the system administrator how logs are maintained, and confirm what you are told through your personal examination of the logging system.

A major weakness of syslog is its lack of authentication services. It is easy to create bogus syslog records, which can be beneficial to a criminal in several ways. First, if an attacker doesn't have the ability to delete log records, he or she might try to bury incriminating records in a flurry of phony records. It is a common trick to scroll the relevant messages off the screen when syslog messages are being sent to the console. Second, someone might attempt to create bogus syslog records to incriminate someone else, either as a joke or as a diversion (see Table 11-9).

Table 11-9   Suspicious Logging Circumstances

What to Look For	Significance
Missing logs	If the system is configured to create logs and logs are missing, it almost invariably means that someone has deliberately tried to erase a record of his or her activities.
Logs that begin after their expected start	If you encounter a log file with a first entry that is dated much later than the expected start date (typically, logs are automatically rotated on a weekly or monthly basis), it usually means that a log file was deliberately deleted to hide activities. The timestamp of the first log entry is an important clue to what time the original log file was deleted.
Time periods without log entries	Attackers who wish to be more subtle, yet still have limited time to spend covering their tracks, may just delete sections from within the interior of a log file. You carefully have to study normal system activity within historical logs in order to identify areas that may have a gap. The smaller the gap, the more difficult it is to find and the less certain you can be in your belief that a gap exists.
Missing log entries	You can't know by looking at a log file that it is missing entries. What you can do is use other means (mac analysis, for example) to conjecture that log entries should have occurred, and then look in the relevant file to see if they actually did. Missing entries are a clue that someone may be covering his or her tracks.
Unusual activity at odd hours	Determining what is "unusual" is more than a bit subjective. The system's administrator is probably a better judge of activities that are unusual either in their nature or their time of day or the day of the week. If you are leading an incident response team and want to get the system administrators out of your hair, put them to work reviewing activity logs. It keeps them occupied, and it is an analysis activity that they are better qualified to perform than anyone else. Hackers like to perform attacks on holidays, rightly assuming that they are more likely to remain unobserved.
Logons from unusual sources	If a site does not normally have external visitors, any logon from outside of the organizational domain is suspicious. Logons originating in other countries should always be investigated. Again, the system administrator should have an idea of where user sessions typically originate.
Failed logons	It is common for users to mistype their passwords, but repeated attempts are a sign that someone may be attempting to guess a password.

(continued)

Table 11-9   Suspicious Logging Circumstances (*cont.*)

What to Look For	Significance
Failed or unauthorized use of su	Direct logons to root are often disabled, forcing both legitimate administrators and attackers to use the su command.
Attempts to access /etc/ passwd	Gaining access to the hashed passwords enables an attacker to crack them. Many remote exploits attempt to obtain a copy of the password file.
Errors from network service	Errors occurring before a compromise—especially immediately before a compromise—are clues that a certain network service, such as DNS or LPR, may have been exploited to gain system access.
Oversized records (full of gibberish)	Attempts to exploit buffer overflow vulnerabilities may leave evidence in log files. Overly long logging records full of gibberish or unusual characters are a clear indication of attempts to overflow an input buffer.

Logon Logs

The logon process on Unix maintains a record of every console logon, telnet, X session, rsh use, and FTP sessions. Unfortunately, to accommodate different purposes, the records are spread across three different files. These logon logs are used in the same way on all Unix platforms, although their locations vary. Traditionally, they were located somewhere under /etc, but the trend today is to move all log files into the /var hierarchy. Table 11-10 lists and describes each logon log.

Several Unix utilities that use these logs to report on user activity are listed in Table 11-11.

TCP Wrapper

TCP Wrapper, tcpd, is a system service created by Wietse Venema (who is also co-creator of TCT). It provides a protective layer between Internet connection attempts and the network services running on a Unix host. It installs by default on recent versions of RedHat Linux and is widely used on many Unix systems. If syslog.conf contains the line:

```
authpriv.*
```

or something similar, such as:

```
autt,authpriv.info
```

Table 11-10   Unix Logon Logs

Log	Format	Use and Characteristics
/etc/utmp /var/log/utmp	Binary	Tracks current logons. Beware that this file is world-writable by default on some older versions of Sun OS. Used by w, who, users, finger.
/etc/wtmp /var/log/wtmp /usr/adm/wtmp	Binary	Records all logons, tty, source host, logouts, reboots, and date changes. Used by last.
/usr/etc/lastlog /var/log/lastlog /usr/adm/lastlog	ASCII	Contains a list of logon times and sources. Used by lastlog.
/var/adm/loginlog	ASCII	Contains list of failed logons. Not enabled by default. System V only.

Table 11-11   Utilities that Use Unix Logon Logs

Utility	Use
last	Chronologically sorted list of all or specific user's logons since start of current wtmp file
lastlog	List of last logon of each user
who	List of currently logged on users and their terminals
w	More detailed list of logged on users that also shows what host remote users logged on from

The file /var/log/secure should contain a list of all connections to services allowed by tcpd. The files host.deny and hosts.allow provide very granular control over the circumstances in which connections are allowed. Ambitious administrators can also use these files to configure logging. Read through these files to see if any special log records are being created—their presence or absence will help determine what network activity has taken place. Activity to look for in tcpd log entries includes

- Connections from unknown sites
- Connections from specific sites known or suspected of performing attacks
- Connections from sites known or believed to be used for information gathering

- Sequence of connections from specific site
- Connections in the time frame of a suspected incident

HTTP

If you are examining a Web server, you should check the httpd logs, which can be quite lengthy on an active server. You can check a few things with grep that won't take a lot of work and can help you learn more about attacks against the system. Look for evidence of malformed URLs that could be used to gain root or shell access. Doing a grep on the string "passwd", for instance, returns a list of all attempts to capture /etc/password. A number of common Web hacks leave very clear tracks in the httpd logs.

```
# grep passwd /var/log/httpd/*
/var/log/httpd/access_log:192.168.0.4 - - [04/May/2000:00:13:31 -0400]
"GET /cgi-bin/phf?Qalias=x%0a/bin/cat%20/etc/passwd HTTP/1.1" 404 217
```

In this example, an attack was performed on May 4 attempting to exploit a bug in a CGI bin script called "phf". This exploit is an old one, and no system should have phf still installed. Script kiddies still sometimes try this attack. Many other HTTP attacks either attempt to gain a shell or to copy or manipulate /etc/passwd. Be careful—most systems automatically rotate logs and compress them. Also, examine the error and access logs separately—the error log is smaller and often more interesting for failed attempts.

System Auditing (C2)

Back in the 1970s, the U.S. military and intelligence establishment put on their collective thinking caps and tried to envision the security functionality that ideally would be available in computers used to process classified data. The resulting document, often called the "Orange Book" because of the jacket color, described a hierarchical set of security features. Many commercial versions of Unix include the C2 feature set (as does Windows NT), which is just one level up from what the intelligence establishment considered the lowest conceivable level of security functionality. A system theoretically capable of meeting the National Security Agency (NSA) C2 evaluation requirements must have an auditing system that can create a record for any security related event. In effect, this means that a C2 system should be able to record every single system call, matching each one to the real user ID.

Auditing should be a gift to the forensic examiner. Indeed, it was developed with the explicit purpose of collecting enough information at a high level of accuracy so that virtually any system event could be explained and attributed to a specific user. Every read and write, every failed access, and hundreds of other events can be logged. You can imagine that such a detailed record would take up a great deal of room. Because of the onerous storage requirements, detailed auditing is rarely turned on—not even on systems used for intelligence or defense purposes. The odds of you examining a system with a significant level of auditing already enabled are fairly slim. If you do encounter one, it should keep you busy for quite some time. More likely, auditing is enabled after an administrator becomes suspicious that unauthorized behavior is taking place. Use of auditing is so rare that we won't go into the details, but be aware that the capability does exist, and some kind of mechanism (probably an awkward and inconvenient one) will enable you to review the auditing records.

Process Accounting

You are much more likely to find process accounting running than auditing. Although it was originally used for charge back (the creation of accounting records to be used for internal billing), it is now mostly used for security purposes. This is because process accounting requires minimal system resources to run but still provides a useful record of system activities. Accounting maintains a detailed record of each invoked process, keeping track of the time, the binary name, and the user who invoked the process. Although the data volume is relatively low, it still can grow out of hand without automated tools to maintain the accounting logs, compressing them and renaming them, usually on a daily basis. You'll usually find a month's worth of accounting records.

If accounting records are being kept, you are in luck (assuming that an attacker hasn't manipulated them). On System V, the files are located in /var/adm/pact, and the command to read them is acctcom. BSD systems put accounting records in the acct directory, often /var/adm/acct, and provide the lastcomm command to read the files. The default accounting log directory on Linux is /var/log/pacct, and it also uses the lastcomm command.

File and Filesystem Contents

We're just getting started with the examination—there are many signs of criminal behavior to look for inside the filesystem in addition to the log files. One of the first things to look for is trojanized binaries, which are clear evidence of an intrusion. One quick check is to look for files in /bin, /sbin/, and /usr/bin with a modification time corresponding to the incident, which is easy to do with find. Maybe an attacker changed something but didn't run a fix utility. If you have reason to believe that the system has recently been used by an intruder, use find[6] to see all the files that have changed within the last three days. It is an easy test to run that might provide some helpful data before you conduct more methodical testing.

```
# find / -ctime -3 -type f -print0 | xargs -0 ls -l |more
```

If Tripwire or some other verification program has been run in the past, use a validated copy of that utility and a stored copy of the results to verify the integrity of the directories and files. Note any missing files or directories and any new files or directories that have been added to the areas checked by Tripwire. Such a program is normally run against the system configuration files, all executables, the kernel, and system libraries. It is not practical to use such a program on user data systems because of the constant change in contents. Several Tripwire tutorials are available online, including one at CERT.[7]

Even if an integrity checker was not run in the past, it is still possible to verify the integrity of system executables, and it is useful to do so anyway in order to identify the activities of the attacker. If you are examining a Solaris or RedHat system, their respective vendors have made MD5 fingerprints available. On a RedHat host, the command **rpm –Va** checks the consistency of installed binaries and a number of system configuration files.[8] Every object that has changed at least one of the following characteristics is listed in the output along with each of the key letters associated with the change:

- 5: changed MD5 value
- S: changed file size
- L: changed symbolic link
- T: changed modification time (mtime)
- D: changed device
- U: changed user
- G: changed group
- M: changed mode

---

6. To set an example for best practice, every invocation of find in this chapter that returns filenames uses the -print0 option. In conjunction with the xargs -0 flag, it allows the command after xargs to correctly deal with filenames containing delimiters, such as spaces and returns. The GNU utilities in Linux have these options, but many operating platforms do not. Your only choice on those systems is to watch for error messages that indicate an attempt to perform an operation on a nonexistent file—a good clue that a hacker tried to protect it by including some ill-behaved character in its name.

7. http://www.cert.org/security-improvement/implementations/i002.02.html

8. SANS has a discussion of using RPM as a recovery tool. Please visit http://www.sans.org/y2k/RPM.html

If you don't have access to either a baseline set of hash values generated onsite or one provided by the vendor, you can create one by running MD5 against verified copies of the binaries from the original distribution media, and then comparing them to the MD5 value from the same binary on the compromised system. This process is tedious but necessary. Start with the list of rootkit binaries from Chapter 10.

Examine Account Information

Password files on compromised systems frequently show signs of tampering. Check the password file and history (see Table 11-12) for inconsistencies and suspicious entries.

Unauthorized Trust Relationships

The Berkeley R utilities, remote shell (rsh), remote login (rlogin), and remote copy (rcp), are notorious for their insecurity. Just as we might use rsh to copy files from a suspect host to a data collection host, intruders often find these services convenient, too. If any of these services are enabled, intruders may try to increase the set of hosts allowed to use them. Look for unknown or inappropriate host names in any of the configuration files listed in Table 11-13. The plus sign (+) is a wildcard character in these files, allowing any host to connect remotely without authentication. A host

Table 11-12   Account-Related Discrepancies

Investigate	Relevance to Forensic Examination
Multiple accts with UID 0 in /etc/passwd	There can be legitimate reasons for having root-equivalent accounts, but all of them must be verified.
Inconsistencies in /etc/passwd	Entries with an improper number of fields or entries that look different than the other entries might have been manually entered by an intruder. Attackers often attempt to append new entries to the password file, so suspicious lines are more likely to be found toward the bottom of the file.
Account creation history	Unfortunately, Unix has no standard method of tracking this, although some versions have proprietary capabilities. The check utilities, grpck and pwck, may sometimes find improperly created accounts in either /etc/group or /etc/passwd.
Accounts with no password	If the second field of all password file entries contains an "x", some form of shadow password file is used, and it must be checked. If some entries contain an encrypted password and some are blank, the blank ones have no password.

running these services and having a plus sign in its hosts.equiv file is vulnerable to anyone who can reach it over the network.

Perform a find to locate all .rhosts and .shosts files that might be located in user directories. Pay special attention to any that are found in the home directory of an administrative account.

```
# find /home -type f -name ".?hosts" -print0 |xargs -0 ls -l
```

Table 11-13 Trust Relationship Configuration Files

Trusted Host Lists	Significance
/etc/hosts.equiv	Configures trust for all user accounts with the optional exception of root.
/etc/hosts.lpd	Contains the list of hosts that can remotely print to the local system.
.rhosts and .shosts	User-specific files located in the home directory of users choosing to allow the logon name on other hosts have equivalency with this host. .shosts is used with Secure Shell (SSH). An individual cannot use SSH unless the system administrator has already configured the local host to accept the remote host in a public key-based authentication process. If a .shosts file has been tampered with, check to see if the systemwide files have been tampered with also.

Table 11-14 Suspicious Signs in Network Configuration and Host Equivalency Files

Clues	Significance
Entries allowing access from unknown hosts	Any unauthorized hosts that are allowed access are suspicious, but finding access granted to IP addresses or host names from other organizations—especially if they are located in other countries—is usually a sign that a system is owned by an intruder.
World-writable	Intruders may have changed the permissions on the file to make it easier for them to add additional hosts to it in the future.
Modification time differs from the modification time of backed up copies.	Recent changes may be signs of unauthorized activity.

Several other files also should be examined for signs of recent or unauthorized change. When TCP Wrapper is installed, the files hosts.allow and hosts.deny determine which local services can be accessed by which remote hosts. These files, along with inetd.conf, are found in /etc and should be checked for recent changes. If SSH is configured, check the /etc/ssh/known_hosts file and search for .ssh/known_hosts in users' home directories.

Invisible Files and Directories

If you want to hide something, an invisible directory is a good place. Search for all files and especially all directories that begin with the dot character (.). Many applications, such as Gnome and KDE, which are common open system graphical user environments (see the find example that follows), use hidden directories as a convenience. These directories are found in users' home directories and are less likely to be used as a hiding place. Different permutations of dots can be very subtle and difficult to see, even when using the -a option to ls. Directory names consisting only of one, two, or three dots are usually a deliberate attempt to hide a directory from the administrator. Sometimes attackers also use control characters in directory names. The following command finds all directories with names starting with a dot. If you pipe the output to cat –A, as shown, control characters are listed as some combination of printable characters. The dollar signs represent the newline character.

```
# find . -type d -name ".*" -print0 | cat -A
.$
./jheiser/.kde$
./jheiser/.stash$
./jheiser/.netscape$
./jheiser/.xauth$
./jheiser/.secretstuff$
./jheiser/.gnome$
./jheiser/.gnome_private$
./jheiser/.enlightenment$
./jheiser/.gnome-help-browser$
./jheiser/files/...$
./jheiser/files/.../...$
./jheiser/files/.../....$
./sallym/.kde$
```

```
./sallym/.netscape$
./sallym/.. $
./bobbyg/.kde$
```

/tmp

The temp directory is the systemwide scratch pad. Because it is periodically cleaned up, it tends to be a place that attracts a lot of garbage. For the forensic examiner, garbage is good. You should take a hard look at everything in /tmp (/usr/tmp on some systems) to get an idea of what has been happening since the last routine cleanup. Sometimes intruders use /tmp as their working directory and then don't bother to clean up after themselves (see Table 11-15). You'll never know if you don't check.

Locating Hostile Code

On Windows systems, antivirus software does a good job of finding well-known hostile code. The good news is that malware is much less common on Unix, but that means that you can't buy a simple tool that locates hostile code for you. If a Unix system has been compromised by a network attacker, he or she probably has left some unauthorized code behind. When examining a system, you must use a number of different techniques to locate it—not all hostile code is going to be found in the form of a Trojan horse masquerading as a legitimate system binary. In order to do something interesting with a compromised host, an attacker frequently brings in sniffing, cracking, scanning, or bot software. You need to locate this code or rule out its existence.

Table 11-15 Signs of intrusion in /tmp

Look For	Significance
Scratch files	Any number of applications or make processes could be creating interim or temporary files in tmp. Anything created in tmp during times when intruders were believed to be active should be examined.
Executables	Executables are not normally stored in /tmp, so these may be hostile.
Intermediate files from make	The process of making and installing executables creates a lot of intermediate files. These may either be explicitly stored in /tmp, or make may be run in /tmp and some pieces may be left behind.
Complete source trees	The most extreme version of leaving something behind is to copy an entire source code tree into /tmp for some kind of malware and just leave it there. It happens. This is a good clue that something is up.

First, you need to search for SUID root and SGID root files. Unauthorized SUID programs can be located anywhere on the system, so you need to search all directories that can be accessed by unprivileged users. Any SUID root executables found outside of the normal system directories, such as the one in the following example, are unauthorized:

```
# find / -user root -perm -4000 -print0 | xargs -0 ls -l
-rwsr-xr-x   1 root     root         373176 Jun 18 22:44 /home/jheiser/.bd
```

Any SUID executables in the normal system binary directories have to be individually verified to determine whether they are legitimate. Unix versions differ in the name of the group that imparts system privileges. It might be named "root", "wheel", or "kmem". There shouldn't be any SGID programs outside of the binary directories, so it probably is easier for you simply to search for all SGID programs.

```
# find /  -perm -2000 -print0 | xargs -0 ls -l
```

You can actually use a single command to find all SUID and GID programs:

```
# find /  -perm +6000 -print0 | xargs -0 ls -l
```

System V–based versions of Unix come with the ncheck command, which among other features, conveniently locates all SUID and device special files within a specified filesystem:

```
# ncheck -s /dev/rsd0g
```

Be aware that many versions of Unix allow filesystems to be mounted with an option that prevents SUID from functioning. Taking advantage of this feature is a good system security measure, but it is not foolproof. When you are examining such a system, you still should look for SUID files. The mount options may have changed or an attacker may have created a SUID file without knowing that it wouldn't work.

cron and at jobs

Just as a system administrator might schedule security software to run one or more times in the future, so may an attacker take advantage of the crontab scheduler or the one time future invocation utility. Locate the directories containing the scheduled at jobs, and examine each job file and the file that it is invoking (see Table 11-16). Locate the crontab directory, then examine every schedule file and every executable scheduled for invocation from the individual crontab entries.

Table 11-16 Verifying crontab and at jobs

Scheduling Discrepancies	Significance
Reference to unrecognized executable or one that isn't in the normal executable directories	An attacker may be using system scheduling facilities to perform hostile activities in the future (after logging out).
Referenced executable that is world-writable	Anyone can change the executable being invoked.
crontab or at job files that are world-writable	cron and at privileges are not always granted to every user. Anyone who can change these jobs can invoke any task he or she wants. *The task is run with the privileges of the user associated with the file,* not with the privileges of the user who made the unauthorized identification.

Nonspecial Files in /dev

The /dev directory, with the exception of a few administrative housekeeping files, should never be used for anything but device special files. This directory is also laboratory to a bewildering array of obscure object names. System hackers exploit this complexity, rightly assuming that inexperienced system administrators don't know what is supposed to be in this directory and often overlook unauthorized files in it. Linux tends to throw all the devices into one directory; our home installation of Red-Hat has approximately 3,000 device special files. Other versions of Unix are a bit more organized and use one or more levels of directory to sort out all the device special entries. The fact that /dev is often the default location for rootkit configuration files and crontab files means that system intruders think it is a good place to look. Take a good hard look at any regular files located underneath /dev.

```
# find /dev -type f -print0 | xargs -0 ls -l
-rwxr-xr-x   1 root     root        26450 Sep 24  1999 /dev/MAKEDEV
-rw-r--r--   1 root     root       373176 Jun 21 19:52 /dev/booger
# file /dev/booger
/dev/booger: ELF 32-bit LSB executable, Intel 80386, version 1,
dynamically linked (uses shared libs), stripped
```

The shell script MAKEDEV is often found in /dev, although you should check to be sure that it is legitimate. The booger file, listed in the preceding example, has no business being in /dev. Running the file command on it shows that it is indeed a binary, and it requires further investigation.

Executables in User Directories

It isn't necessarily suspicious for users to have their own binaries—most system administrators and most power users probably do. However, when you are investigating a compromised system, you can't take anything for granted. Find all the binaries in the user home directories and verify what they do. A well-disguised binary may defy your attempts at identification, but many attackers make it easy by not covering their tracks. You can search to see which files are set with the executable bit, but you'll miss binaries that are not configured as executable but still provide clues on unauthorized activities. Running the file command on every file and checking to see if it is executable is slow but reliable.

```
# find /home -type f -print0 | xargs -0 file | grep executable
```

Core Dumps

Attempts at buffer overflows often cause core dumps, and a number of hacker exploits attempt to cause core dumps of executables that have password data within them. Find all the core dump files and check them out to see what programs they are dumped from. The file command usually can tell you the command that the core dump originated from and what caused it to dump.

Table 11-17   Signs that an Executable File Deserves a Closer Look

Sign	Significance
Same name as a system executable (ls, login, find, etc.) but not located in the appropriate directory	Sounds like somebody is up to something.
Same name as a known exploit	It is amazing how many binaries are discovered with names like "crack" and "sniff." Review hacker Web sites periodically, such as http://www.rootshell.com, for a list of common attack code.
Name starts with the dot character (.) or is otherwise hidden	Any attempt to hide an executable is suspicious.
Located in a directory that starts with the dot character (.) or is otherwise hidden	An inexperienced administrator is even less likely to find a binary located in a directory with a name designed to escape notice, such as "...".
Source directory might be named after known exploit	Hackers often compile their code on their victim's system. They often leave the source code lying around (as well as compilers on systems that don't have one by default, like Solaris these days).

```
# find / -type f -name core -print0 | xargs -0 ls -l
-rw-------    1 sallym                229376 Jun  8 21:42 /home/sallym/core
-rw-------    1 root      root        1228800 May 27 18:02 /root/core
-rw-------    1 root      root        1282048 May  4 01:53 /tmp/core
# file /home/sallym/core
core: ELF 32-bit LSB core file of 'top' (signal 5), Intel 80386, version 1
```

In the preceding example, the core dump originated from the system command top, which was stopped by sending it a kill –5, a signal explicitly used to create a core dump. You can also thumb through a core dump using strings, and when you really need to dig into a core dump, use the debugger, adb or gdb. On a Linux box, the command is:

```
# gdb -c /home/sallym/core
```

You might not be able to learn much more than you can with file. Try typing **info** and experimenting with the different types of information the debugger can provide. Don't hesitate to ask a programmer for assistance in analyzing a core dump if you think that it can help with your investigation.

If you've already created a list of all the files on the suspect system, using either find or macutil, you don't need to do another find for core dumps. You can simply grep the strong core in the output file from that previously collected list of files, which is much faster than searching through an entire filesystem with find.

Shell and Application History

Command-line shells that provide history capabilities have to have some place to store that history if users want to repeat commands that were performed in a prior logon session (see Table 11-18). When someone is methodically attempting to avoid detection, he or she will ensure that this file provides no clues to his or her activities. Be optimistic and assume that your quarry left tracks; you won't know if you don't check.

A fascinating example of a bash_history created by a hacker and not cleaned has been analyzed and reported on the SANS Web site.[9] Apparently the attacker hacked the password file, downloaded a rootkit, and then installed a trojanized version of the secure shell—all clearly documented by the shell history file.

9. http://www.sans.org/y2k/linux.htm

Table 11-18 Unix Shells and Their Default History Files

Shell	Default History File
sh (probably linked to bash or ksh)	.sh_history
csh	.history
ksh	.sh_history
bash	.bash_history
zsh	.history
tcsh	.history

It is easy enough to modify a shell history, and the files don't have timestamps. They are also limited because they collect commands only from the original logon shell, and they don't collect any parameters. Still, as shown in the example in the previous paragraph, they can be helpful in tracing somebody's steps, so system hacking tutorials always contain instructions on cleaning out history. Here's one method that we found on a hacker Web site that automatically cleans history on logout:

```
# mv .logout .org
# echo rm.history>.logout
# echo rm .logout>>.logout
# echo mv .org .logout >> .logout
```

Macho hackers don't use an editor—they are so sure of themselves that they can toss commands into a file from the outside, and it always works just great. These instructions echo the typed strings, concatenating them onto the end of the .logout file. This same use of echo and redirect is also useful to attackers as a convenient way to modify files remotely using netcat.

As long as you are cruising around looking for dot files, you should keep your eyes open for other common dot files that contain clues as to a user's activities (see Table 11-19).

Email

Email in Unix, unlike Microsoft Windows, is always ASCII text, and it is in a common format. You can grep it and read it with a paging utility. You usually can access suspect mail files from within an email client, even among Unix versions. Most mail clients, such as mail and pine, have an -f option that enables you to specify the file that they read.

Table 11-19   Unix Dot Files

Filename	Purpose and Relevance
.newsrc	Contains a complete list of all Usenet groups that are subscribed to or visited. If someone is suspected of downloading pornography, this file may contain the names of pornographic newsgroups.
.plan	This file is filled out by the user and is presented as part of the finger command output for logon. It may contain clues to who the user is.
.signature	Email signature for outgoing mail. Contains clues to the identity of whoever was using an account for mail. Might allow correlation between suspects and mail received on other systems.

Looking for Keywords

It is easy to find files containing a specific keyword. It's a two-step process. First, search for the occurrence of a specific keyword, treating an entire filesystem as a file. Either grep for the keyword on the image of the filesystem or on the device special file representing the file. Suppose you are looking for every file that contains the word "snow":

```
# grep snow /dev/hda*
Binary file /dev/hda5 matches
```

That grep came up positive, so we know that the string is extent on that filesystem at least once. The second step is to locate the file or files where it appears again. If we are looking for this string in files within user home directories, we can start there. This process can take a while when there are many files, but it can locate the file by name.

```
# find /home -type f -print0 | xargs -0 grep snow
/home/sallym/.stash:Look for the 'snow' in the coffee can in the kitchen.
```

In this case, we are lucky. The user sallym has a hidden file in her home directory containing this string.

Using a search like this, it is possible to identify every existing file that contains the string in clear text. If any of following conditions were true about the file containing the string, it would prevent us from finding it with this simple technique:

- Compressed
- Encrypted

- Deleted
- String deliberately obfuscated with nonprintable characters (common technique in programming to defeat strings)

There are two ways to find deleted files. Use a hex editor to examine the entire filesystem or use an unremove program. Use of the unrm utility included with TCT is discussed in Chapter 7.

Conclusion

Unix is challenging—it seems like every system we examine is different. Every version of Unix has its own way of doing things, and you probably won't have a chance to practice every technique on every version of Unix that your organization uses. You may feel ill-prepared to do incident response on Unix, but consider that you may be the best resource your firm has. Keep learning and find some trustworthy Unix administrators to assist you in your examinations.

Further Research

Web Sites

Dittrich, Dave, "Basic Steps in Forensic Analysis of Unix Systems," http://staff.washington.edu/dittrich/misc/forensics. This incredibly detailed and useful source includes instructions on the use of loopback for mounting filesystems and includes a helpful bibliography.

CERT, "Detecting Signs of Intrusion," http://www.cert.org/security-improvement/modules/m09.html. This is an excellent online guide for finding attack signatures on a Unix host.

CERT, "Steps for Recovering from a Unix or NT System Compromise," http://www.cert.org/tech_tips/root_compromise.html. This companion to "Detecting Signs of Intrusion" provides an incident response process.

CERT, "Identifying Tools that Aid in Detecting Signs of Intrusion," http://www.cert.org/security-improvement/implementations/i042.07.html. Comprehensive list of tools for real-time and forensic analysis.

Farmer, Dan, and Wietse Venema, "Computer Forensics Analysis Class Handouts," http://www.fish.com/forensics. This outline is more than a little terse, but it includes information found nowhere else and was the inspiration for the discussion of volatility in this chapter. This link also points to Farmer and Venema's forensic column in *Dr. Dobb's Journal,* where they are well on their way toward expanding in detailed prose the ideas in their class outline.

Graham, Robert, "FAQ: Firewall Forensics," http://www.robertgraham.com/pubs/firewall-seen. html. Excellent article on interpreting network logs.

Ranum, Marcus, "Artificial Ignorance: How-to Guide," http://www.nfr.net/firewall-wizards/ mail-archive/1997/Sep/0098.html. Suggested techniques on writing shell scripts to help dig through log files.

Rude, Thomas, "DD and Computer Forensics: Examples of Using DD within UNIX to Create Physical Backups," http://www.crazytrain.com/dd.html

"Linux Reverse Engineering tools," http://packetstorm.securify.com/linux/reverse-engineering. Suggested utilities for determining the purpose of an unknown binary.

Tools That Find Evidence of Sniffers

ftp://ftp.auscert.edu.au/pub/cert/tools/cpm/

ftp://coast.cs.purdue.edu/pub/tools/unix/cpm/

ifstatus works on Solaris: ftp://coast.cs.purdue.edu/pub/tools/unix/ifstatus

Chapter

12

Introduction to the Criminal Justice System

The preceding chapters of this book have dealt with finding the culprit of a computer crime. If you decide to prosecute, then what? This chapter provides an overview of the criminal justice system that will assist you in working with law enforcement agencies. Most people's only exposure to the criminal justice system is on television, either on the nightly news or a police drama. Unfortunately, television doesn't depict an accurate picture of what the criminal justice system is really like.

As you probably know, most police officers do not work on one major case after another; real detectives do not solve murders on every shift and then go home in time for dinner. Some days the most difficult decision a police officer has to make is whether to turn right or left. Most of a police officer's time is spent on calls for service, such as investigating loud noise or helping people who have locked themselves out of their cars. When an interesting call comes in, the remainder of the shift is spent doing paperwork. You should keep this in mind when you report an incident and you think that it is taking too long to get a response. Law enforcement in gereral is overworked, understaffed, and always under-budgeted. While your incident may be the most important thing in the world to you, try to remember that it is only one of the numerous cases that the law enforcement agency is working on. The court systems are even more backlogged. So while your investigator may be trying to pursue your case, he or she may be stymied by the court not having the time to hear the case.

Here's what happens during a normal case:

1. Victim notifies law enforcement that a crime has occurred.
2. Police gather evidence and develop suspects.
3. Search warrants may be executed.
4. Interviews and/or interrogations may be conducted.
5. The suspect or suspects are charged.
6. Case is turned over to prosecutors for presentation to a grand jury or for a preliminary hearing.

Notifying Law Enforcement Agencies

A victim notifying law enforcement agencies is the usual way in which a crime or request for assistance is made. This may be your first interaction with a law enforcement agency, but don't be shy and don't think that your report is not worth bringing to its attention. Law enforcement agencies always are busy, but your high tech case is worth reporting. Notice that we are using the phrase *law enforcement agency* as a generic term. We don't address which law enforcement agency you *have* to call. Although law enforcement agencies have to contend with jurisdictional issues, those issues are their concern, not yours.

When we discuss the criminal justice system in our seminars, we often hear that a report was made with a law enforcement agency and nothing came of it, or that no information was filtered back to the reporting party from that agency. It's important to understand, first, that personal relationships are key. The networking you do at organizations such as the High Technology Crime Investigation Association (HTCIA)[1] will pay off for both parties some day. Law enforcement agencies may call on you for your expertise, and you can call someone when you need assistance as well. You'll have more luck pulling a business card out of your desk drawer and calling someone directly than you will if you look in the phone book for the number of a law enforcement agency.

Second, we recommend that you be persistent. Call the agency that you are most comfortable working with and ask it to guide you through the jurisdictional boundaries. After all, the law enforcement community is a tight one, and especially in the high tech arena, most people know each other from organizations, training, or listservers. If you don't know anyone in law enforcement who may help you, keep calling until you get someone who is interested in helping you. Be mindful that the evidence won't wait for you; you have to find someone quickly, but be patient and you'll find someone to help you.

Police Gather Evidence and Develop Suspects

The more evidence that's gathered, the better the chances of developing a reliable list of suspects. Locating suspects is dependent on the nature of the case and the time delay in reporting the crime. The longer the delay, the less likely that a suspect can be located. One reason is because computer logs don't last. Decide early in your investigation whether you will turn the case over to law enforcement agencies. If you initially decide not to involve law enforcement agencies, reassess the decision when additional information comes to light.

---

1. http://htcia.org

Search Warrants May Be Executed

The Fourth Amendment to the U.S. Constitution protects us from unreasonable search and seizure. It does not protect us from searches, only from unreasonable ones and only from government actors. The Fourth Amendment states that "no warrants shall issue, but upon probable cause, supported by oath or affirmation, and particularly describing the place to be searched, and the persons or things to be seized." It requires that a search warrant "describe the things to be seized with sufficient particularity to prevent a general exploratory rummaging in a person's belongings."[2] It was adopted in response to general warrants that allowed such "exploratory rummaging."

We frequently receive questions from both victims and defendants who are waiting for law enforcement agencies to execute a search warrant or to receive a warrant from law enforcement to produce records. We often hear that a case was turned over to law enforcement and "nothing happened, they didn't even search the place." The assumption usually is that law enforcement agencies dropped the ball and decided not to pursue the case, but maybe the law enforcement agency couldn't obtain a search warrant. A search warrant is court authorization for the police to search for and to seize records, or other information, as part of a criminal investigation. The most important word in that sentence is *criminal*. Many immoral acts are not necessarily criminal, so warrants can't be issued for them. Furthermore, some states restrict issuance of a search warrant to felonies, prohibiting their use in misdemeanors or petty offenses. Therefore, officers may not be able to obtain a warrant.

If a law enforcement agency knows, after taking a report, that it won't be able to obtain a warrant, shouldn't it say so and stop the investigation? The answer clearly is no. Most cases are solved without having to resort to search warrants. For those cases in which search warrants are necessary, a substantial amount of investigation often is necessary before issuing a warrant is appropriate. Finally, a law enforcement agency may be able to build a crime out of several smaller cases, but again, it may take a while, so have patience. If you believe that you have not heard anything in an unreasonably long period of time, remind the agency that you are the victim and you are willing to help. Sometimes such a reminder will provide some enlightenment as to the investigation's status.

Probable Cause

You probably have noticed the police searching a car. The police can search without a warrant so long as the officer has probable cause that a crime was committed, which is an exception to the warrant requirement in the Fourth Amendment. A police officer also must have probable cause to obtain a search warrant. Probable cause is

---

2. *United States v. Carey,* 172 F.3d 1268, 1271 (10th Cir.1999).

more than suspicion, but less than the beyond-a-reasonable-doubt proof needed to convict. Warrants for arrest, criminal summonses, and search warrants are issued upon complaint or affidavit showing probable cause.

Interviews and/or Interrogations May Be Conducted

We strongly recommend that you attend a class in interview training. Developing good interviewing skills is critical. John E. Reid and Associates[3] has developed interview training into an art form which they call the "Reid Technique." Reid offers both introductory and advanced classes in the art of conducting a proper interview and subsequent interrogation. They teach classes all over the country, so you won't have to travel far to learn their techniques. We recommend attending the basic and advanced classes at different times. They offer a one-week class that covers both, but having some time between the two levels to try out the technique is beneficial.

About 80 percent of human communication is nonverbal, so good interviewing skills are vital to your case. Law enforcement agencies can help you in this area because they receive training and have a lot of experience in interviewing. Receiving a written statement from your subject detailing his or her activity is icing on the cake. Make sure you have a witness present to counter allegations of coercion.

Subpoena for Records

A subpoena is a court order—a demand from a judge that requires some action on the part of someone who may have information relevant to a specific case. A subpoena may simply require someone to testify, or it may require that records be produced. According to the Federal Rules of Evidence, "when the original is in the possession of a third person, inability to procure it from him by resort to process or other judicial procedure is sufficient explanation of nonproduction. Judicial procedure includes *subpoena duces tecum* as an incident to the taking of a deposition in another jurisdiction. No further showing is required." A *subpoena duces tecum* commands the recipient to be present in court and to bring certain evidence, usually documents or papers, that is requested as necessary to the successful resolution of the case. Subpoenas can come in many forms, but one that may assist you in your investigation (for those of us in private industry) is a civil subpoena as the result of a lawsuit. If you are attempting to obtain logs to identify a suspect, a "John Doe" lawsuit may fit the bill. Even though the defendant is not yet identified, subpoenas may be issued to obtain evidence that can help identify the culprit.

---

3. http://www.reid.com

Suspects Are Charged

Finally, the case is turned over to prosecutors for presentation to a grand jury or for a preliminary hearing. The difference between the two is the manner in which the case is presented. In a grand jury proceeding, the prosecutor presents the evidence to the grand jury and is the only side to present a case. By contrast, a preliminary hearing is more of a mini-trial in which both sides present their cases, call witnesses, and so forth, and the judge determines if probable cause exists to proceed to trial. While the grand jury route is usually easier, preliminary hearings have the advantage of providing an opportunity to practice your case before you have to present it to a jury. After all, practice makes perfect. The preferred, or required, charging method varies from jurisdiction to jurisdiction.

Chain of Custody

We discussed the chain of custody earlier in Chapter 1, but it is such a vital issue that it deserves mention here as well. As you may recall, chain of custody involves detailed documentation of collection, safeguarding, and analysis of evidence. The documentation should describe each person who handled the evidence, from whom he or she received it, and to whom it was transferred. While the evidence is in your control, you are responsible for its safekeeping, so you should ensure that it is locked up to permit only limited access. Again, law enforcement agencies are well versed in this activity and may assist you by safekeeping the evidence for you until trial. Keep in the back of your mind that while defense attorneys are just getting up to speed on digital evidence, motions to suppress evidence are second-nature to them.

Variation in Dollar Loss Guidelines

When Scott Charney was the head of the U.S. Justice Department's Computer Crime and Intellectual Property Section (CCIPS), he claimed that the estimated cost of damages was not an issue and that any case is investigated regardless of the dollar value. Unfortunately, the word hasn't made it out to the field, and most prosecutors ask for an estimate of the dollar loss when discussing a case or when considering sentencing guidelines. An estimate of the loss might be required ahead of time so you should have a statement of damages handy in case it is needed. In some circumstances, loss is an element of the offense and must be proven beyond a reasonable doubt as with other elements of the crime. In some offenses, dollar loss is not relevant.

Recidivism

Recidivism is a criminal justice term that means "committing a crime after being found guilty and serving time." As most people are aware, repeat offenders usually are subject to stricter sentencing—unless specific sentences are legally mandated, all courts and experienced judges have certain unwritten sentencing guidelines. Unwritten guidelines come into play on the prosecution side also. A prime example is a child pornography case, where the rule of thumb for federal cases is that possession of three images or more results in prosecution.

The Victim's Perspective

As the victim of a computer crime that is working its way through the criminal justice system, you undoubtedly have strong feelings. To help prepare you for this difficult process, you should expect the following:

- You may lose control of the investigation.

  Continually remind your law enforcement contacts that *you* are the victim. Try to be patient, but when an unreasonable amount of time passes, don't be afraid to ask about the status of the investigation.

- Cost and time involved

  Don't report a crime unless you are prepared to assist *fully* in the investigation and subsequent prosecution. If you report an offense because your insurance company required it but you have no intention to prosecute, be sure you tell the investigating officer. Law enforcement agencies are greatly overworked, and computer crimes are commonly labor intensive. No one wants the police to waste resources on cases in which the victim does not want to cooperate.

If you decide to call law enforcement for assistance, you may be asked some of the following questions:

- Has there been a delay in reporting this crime?
  If so, why?

- Who knows about the crime?
  Why?

- Has there been an internal investigation?
  If so, who conducted it and what were the results?

- Have you identified a potential suspect?
  Has anyone suspected been confronted?

If a suspect hasn't been identified, answers to the following questions may help you identify one:

- Have there been any recent layoffs or union problems?
- Has a disgruntled employee recently been terminated?
- Has the company recently taken on any new student interns?
- Have you recently canceled a vendor contract?
- Has an interoffice romance gone sour?

We heard about a situation in which an employee believed that his email was being read, but the logs didn't show any invalid attempts to log onto the mail server or other clues. The investigator asked questions similar to the preceding and discovered that the victim had recently broken up with another employee who he was dating. The other employee was unhappy with the decision and was reading the email of her former significant other. She claimed she was reading it to determine why he no longer wanted to date her. Because both parties knew each other's passwords, the logs revealed no clues. Good old-fashioned, low tech investigative skills solved this case.

The following can help you understand what may appear to be bizarre behavior when law enforcement agents arrive on the scene. Police officers are trained to

- Remove everyone from the area of the computers.
- Photograph the scene.
- Determine if the power plug should be pulled (which should not be done on servers).

If you pull the plug, remove the power at the source (at the wall outlet, uninterruptible power supply—UPS, laptop battery, and so forth). Be careful not to pull the plug from the wall without checking for a UPS. If you decide that the proper course of action is to pull the plug, you don't want to pull it and have the computer still keep chugging along.

- Place software that you are confiscating in floppy drives with evidence tape over the floppy drives.

    Police officers can purchase special software, on a floppy disk, that can be placed in the floppy drive. If the computer is accidentally booted with the floppy disk in the drive, a screen is displayed advising the user that the computer is evidence. If you don't have access to this software, a nonformatted, nonbootable floppy disk will suffice. On the floppy disk label, you can indicate that this computer (include a brief description of the computer) is evidence and that you should be contacted immediately. Place this disk in the floppy drive and cover the floppy drive with masking tape with the words "computer evidence" on the tape. This procedure assumes that your computer boots off the floppy drive by default. If you know that this is not the case, you have to make other arrangements based on the setup of the computer.

Some more tips police receive:

- Photograph and label all connections. This is vital for a complicated computer system that you may have to later reassemble.

- Seize all books, manuals, software, and disks to determine whether passwords are stored in any of the subject's books. Seizing these items also helps when the subject is using software that you are unfamiliar with.

- Transport evidence carefully. Because most digital evidence is sensitive, extra care should be taken in transporting it.

If law enforcement agents need information that can only be obtained through a subpoena, they can't just ask a private citizen to provide it either. When a company is the victim, though, law enforcement has a bit more latitude. Always keep your corporate counsel in the loop, and let them make the determination of what information is appropriate to provide without a subpoena.

Keys to Success When Dealing with Law Enforcement Agents

Don't make it too complicated. Remember the first and even the second or third person you talk to may not be the agency's technical expert, and even the expert may not know what you are talking about if you use "corp speak" or acronyms. Discuss the case as clearly as possible and be patient. The law enforcement agency may require that all crimes first be reported to a police officer before being turned over to the technical investigator or detective. The value of having personal relationships within the agency *before* you need them cannot be overstated. One advantage is that you know the agent's technical prowess ahead of time. Also, when you call to report an incident, ask the person you talk to what the policy is regarding who has to take the initial report. If the agent tells you that you first must make the initial report to a police officer, ask if it is possible to speak with a technical person as well.

Sundry Legal Stuff

If you can't tell from the cavalier title, this section is not filled with citations, briefs, and other stuff that you can find in a law book. We're going to help you attempt to do one thing: cover your assets. If you remember anything from this section, remember these three words: Do No Harm!

Criminal and civil laws vary. This section is not meant to provide legal advice, just some ideas that you can and should discuss with your legal advisors. It is good to know what laws cover the various computer crimes, but it is more important to know what you legally can or can't access. Before and after your cases, you'll have lots of time to read up on law, but during a case, don't get distracted by legal issues that are not your responsibility to solve. Work closely with your corporate legal staff and law enforcement, and let them make decisions about what is acceptable. When you're working a case, the clock is ticking, you're trying to determine where to start, and your boss wants to know what is happening, it is not the time to worry about what law covers some incident. It is the time to do what you have to do and not do anything that could get the evidence suppressed and, more importantly, get you sued.

Legal Access

Before you start any investigation in your company, you must check to make sure that you have policies in place to ensure that you are authorized to access the data that is the target of your investigation. Courts have ruled that company-owned equipment doesn't contain any "personal" information, but be sure your company has policies in place to alert employees to that fact. Most importantly, make sure you have the authority to access this "personal" data should it be there.

Searching a Personally Owned Computer

If you keep in the back of your mind that anyone can sue anybody for anything, you should also know that all it takes is a civil lawsuit in order to subpoena records, logs, computers, and so on. When writing this book, we became aware of a case involving Northwest Airlines in which the employees' computers were subpoenaed. As reported by WSJ Interactive Edition,[4] Northwest suspected that its flight attendants' union had used the Internet to run an illegal call-in-sick campaign to disrupt the airline. The airline obtained a court order to search 20 or so hard drives at flight attendants' homes and union offices.

---

4. McCarthy, Michael J., "Can Your PC Be Subpoenaed?" WSJ Interactive Edition, May 24, 2000, http://www.zdnet.com/zdnn/stories/news/0,4586,2576340,00.html

Business Records Exception

It is commonly understood that computer logs are not acceptable as evidence in court unless logging was in regular use before the incident occurred. Because they are collected by a third party, the computer itself, they can be considered as hearsay, which is inadmissible. However, the Business Records Exception allows certain forms of business records to be treated as evidence when they are an ongoing, routine part of the business process. According to Federal Rule 803, records that fall within these exemptions include "a memorandum, report, record, or data compilation, in any form, of acts, events, conditions, opinions, or diagnoses, made at or near the time by, or from information transmitted by, a person with knowledge, if kept in the course of a regularly conducted business activity, and if it was the regular practice of that business activity to make the memorandum, report, record, or data compilation, all as shown by the testimony of the custodian or other qualified witness, unless the source of information or the method or circumstances of preparation indicate lack of trustworthiness." The term "business" used in this text includes "business, institution, association, profession, occupation, and calling of every kind, whether or not conducted for profit." There is clear legal precedent for allowing computer log files to be used as evidence when they fall within the Business Records Exception. The onus is, of course, on whoever introduces the evidence to show that it was collected as part of an ongoing business process, and not in direct response to the crime in question.

While logs that are part of everyday business are allowed under the Business Records Exception to the hearsay rule, it does not mean that logs that are turned on as part of an investigation necessarily would be excluded. There "are other ways to get them in," according to Abigail Abraham.[5] Computer logs can be admitted into evidence using other rules of evidence besides the business records rules.

There are really two issues here: what do we need to know to solve the case, and what evidence is useful to us in court. Most of the evidence collected during a typical criminal case will never see the inside of a court, so questions of admissibility shouldn't discourage us from whatever legally obtainable information will help us solve the case. For example, during the course of a criminal investigation, it is expected that the police will interview people who live or work in the neighborhood of the crime scene. Most of the opinions and comments of those interview subjects would be hearsay, and would not be admissible in court, but that doesn't stop the police from collecting this information and following up on anything that offers the hope of a lead. Likewise, turning on logging after an incident occurs will create a body of data that may or may not be admissible in a court of law, but it may also contain a wealth of important clues. Admissibility is an issue, but when an incident

---

5. Abigail Abraham is the Cook County assistant state's attorney, was an Illinois state trooper, and is one of the best lawyers in this field.

occurs, we should not be so concerned about the admissibility of evidence that we avoid collecting it before the suspect is even identified.

The confusion over legal abstraction has created an unfortunate perception that it would be illegal for a system administrator to implement logging after an incident is discovered. This is just not the case. 'Inadmissibility' is a legal technicality, and must not be confused with 'illegal'. As long as the evidence is legally collected, it cannot harm your case, so do not be afraid to turn logging on at any time.

California Law

Ken Rosenblatt, an assistant district attorney in Santa Clara County, California, and author of *High-Technology Crime,*[6] wrote a California law that we think should be used as a model for other states and countries. Simply put, the law states that any electronic service provider registered as a foreign corporation in California has to accept court orders from California. The problem in most jurisdictions is that if a company, say an ISP, has customers in California but its offices are in Virginia, the court order has to be obtained in Virginia. Before this law was passed, the process of obtaining a court order through the interstate compact for ISP records was more cumbersome due to the time it would take doing it "the old way."

Testifying as an Expert Witness

You may be asked to testify as an expert about the results of your analysis. The advantage to testifying as an expert (in addition to the expert witness fees you can charge) is that you can provide your opinion on the matter as an expert whereas nonexpert witnesses are not allowed to express opinions. Be aware that if you attempt to testify as a computer expert, the other side can question you about anything regarding computers. If you have advanced computer forensics training, testify as a computer forensics expert so you can render a useful opinion while limiting the scope within which you have to qualify as an expert.

Wiretap Statute

The United States has a few well-known computer crime statutes;[7] among them is 18 U.S.C. 25–10, Wire and Electronic Communications Interception and Interception of Oral Communications, referred to as "the wiretap statute." The lengthy title indicates the scope of this statute.[8] The wiretap statute includes just about every-

---

6. ISBN 0–9648171–0–1

7. Federal computer crime statutes can be viewed at http://www.usdoj.gov/criminal/cybercrime/

8. For the complete text of any federal statute, see the Office of Law Revision Web site: http://uscode. house.gov/usc.htm

thing in computer crime, including "any transfer made in whole or in part through the use of facilities for the transmission of communications by the aid of wire, cable, or other like connection between the point of origin and the point of reception." You should become very familiar with this statute.

18 U.S.C.1029 Amended

Section 1029 covers credit cards, telephone access codes, computer passwords, and other access codes. This statute is particularly applicable to most of us in the computer security field because it makes possession of computer passwords potentially illegal. Subsection 6 of the statute states that to "knowingly and with intent to defraud traffic (as defined in section 1029) in any password or similar information through which a computer may be accessed without authorization," is a violation of this statute. The keywords for this subsection are "knowingly" and "intent." In the computer security field, we can only hope that if we are found with a computer full of passwords, law enforcement agents will understand that we possess them for security reasons and not for the intent to defraud. If you routinely check the security of your systems by attempting to crack weak passwords, protect yourself by getting written authorization from someone empowered to endorse your activity. If during an investigation you discover a user who has other people's passwords, you may have caught him or her in violation of a federal statute. Is he or she actually testing the security of corporate computers, or does he or she have these passwords for illicit reasons?

Civil Court System

The majority of this chapter, and the book for that matter, assumes the possibility of presenting your case in criminal court. While all of your processes and procedures basically are the same, the civil court system is a different venue that you may be called to testify in. The two major differences between criminal and civil courts are the sentences given out and the level of proof required. In criminal court, the penalties primarily involve the chance to go to jail without passing Go and collecting $200. In civil court, the penalties are usually monetary damages.

As far as the proof required, in criminal court the requirement is "beyond a reasonable doubt." Here again is a word that is favored by lawmakers, *reasonable*. It means that there has to be no reasonable doubt. In civil court, the proof required is the lesser standard of a "preponderance of the evidence," which sometimes is described as "more likely than not" or as "just that much evidence that makes the scales of justice tip in one party's favor." One of the major differences between sworn law enforcement forensics analysts and us in the private sector is the option of pursuing a case in civil court. If you're in law enforcement, your duty is to investigate crimes. We in the private sector have the option of pursuing the case in either or both venues. The use of computer forensics for civil cases is increasing, with attorneys for both sides of the civil process engaging the services of computer forensics specialists to process computers for evidence to prove or disprove a case. Don't let the reduced standard of proof lull you into a false sense of security and reduced processing of the evidence. Use the same methods for all your cases. Consistency is key. The defense won't ask if the procedure you used is the one you employ for a criminal case; it will ask if the procedure is the one you use for all cases.

Conclusion

The legal issues associated with computer crime are still developing, and what is held as common wisdom or appropriate practice today may change radically over the next few years. The ubiquity of the Internet, and the connectivity of virtually every workstation to this global community has ramifications that have yet to be worked out by the legislators and our legal system. Forensic investigators would be well advised to keep their eyes on developments in this area.

Chapter
13
Conclusion

This chapter may bring this book to a conclusion, but it should not be the end of your training. This book provides an introduction to computer forensics, and if you want to be proficient in this field, you should attend hands-on training, experiment with new tools and techniques, and practice, practice, practice.

We hope that while you were reading this book, you were experimenting with our tips on your noncritical machine. You also should attend a basic computer forensics class. We have compiled a list of training programs on the High Tech Crime Investigation Association Northeast Chapter's Web page.[1]

After you finish reading this book and have attended one or more formal training programs, don't stop there. Take what you have learned and experiment with new tools and techniques before you have to conduct analysis on a real case. When you are familiar with the tools, it is easier to recognize their use during your analysis. If you don't try the hacking tools on your systems, someone will do it for you.

Do you know the old saying, "you get only one chance to make a good first impression"? The same holds true for your forensic analysis: you get only one chance to make a good image. If you make a mistake and you alter the original evidence, it can have negative repercussions down the road. Remember the following:

- Take your time.
- Don't alter the original.
- Make a good bit image copy.
- Authenticate the copy.
- Conduct your analysis on the copy whenever possible.

If you take just one thing from this book, remember to safeguard the original evidence! We may all agree that an image is as good as the original, but you have to consider what the "other side" may request. If you make only a copy and don't preserve

---

1. http://www.ne-htcia.org/training.html.

the original, you can perform the best forensic analysis of your life, develop evidence, and locate your suspect. You can even offer to give the "other side" a copy of your image, but all it will take is for them to ask for the original so that they can make their own copy, and your entire case may come into question if you don't have the original. Consider all the options and consequences. Learning computer forensics is similar to defensive driving classes that tell young drivers to think about how they are driving but also be prepared for what the other driver may do. The same is true in this business: hope for the best, but make plans for the worst.

Appendix

Internet Data Incident Response Guidelines

This appendix defines a process for handling computer security incidents in Internet data centers. Because it is impossible to prevent all security incidents from occurring, your company must prepare itself. Good training and adherence to a process can provide quick resolution to security incidents while minimizing the potential damage.

This appendix applies to all hosts located in Internet data centers, including not only Web hosts, but also mail hosts, billing servers, DNS servers, and other servers visible to the Internet. Such a data center is a complex organization with many internal and external constituencies. The organizations fulfilling incident response (IR) roles change depending on the type of service they offer. Table A-1 maps the security roles used in this document into organizations, business units (BUs), and application owners.

Goals of Incident Response

Expect these goals to evolve as the organization's response process improves. The goals also may change from event to event. In every case, the IR leader should articulate the goals at the beginning of the investigation. The response goals may include

- Restore service safely
- Estimate extent and cost of incident
- Identify source of attack and their motivation
- Deter future crime
- Recover loss
- Protect public image
- Conduct due diligence
- Assume corporate responsibility
- Increase understanding of security landscape

327

Table A-1 Each data-owning organization participates in the response plan

Incident Response Role	Responsible Organization				
	Shared Host	**Core Services**	**Commercial Service**	**Managed Host**	**Co-located Host**
Application developer	Application owner	Data engineering	Business unit	Application owner	Application owner
Application owner		Operations	Business unit		
System owner	Operations		Business unit		
System administrator			Business unit or operations		
Firewall administrator (not all hosts)			Business unit or operations	Operations	Operations
Network administration			Business unit or operations		
Security consultant	None	Data Engineering (risk analysis of new applications)			None
Security investigator	Corporate SIRT				Application owner

Methodical IR should enable the organization to learn more about its threats and vulnerabilities. The organization should learn from the IR process and strengthen security measures accordingly, thereby avoiding a recurrence of similar incidents.

Not only are the goals likely to change from one event to the next, but their relative priorities often may change, depending on the nature of the incident, its source, targets, damage, and so forth.

Roles and Responsibilities

To ensure the success of corporate Internet business areas, all the involved organizations must work together as a unit. When a security incident occurs, the affected organizations may have different goals, and these different priorities may complicate a decision on when it is appropriate to place an individual host or data center system back online. However, if a security incident is not handled effectively, the cause of the incident may never be determined, and the next time that vulnerability is exploited, the damage may be worse.

To facilitate teamwork, the following sections define each organization's roles and responsibilities before and during a security incident. All organizations are required to maintain current contact information. At a minimum, a phone number has to be identified to inform the organization about the incident. For better coordination and communication, an Emergency Response Core Team (ERCT) with members from each organization should be established for the affected data center system as soon as a security incident is confirmed.

Corporate Security Incident Response Team (SIRT)

The SIRT is a corporate resource that provides full-time incident prevention and response services. The Security Investigators (SI) are members of this organization. It's mandate includes:.

- Setting response policies
- Organizing and preparing response teams
- Organizing response efforts
- Providing the initial point of contact for all suspected and actual incidents
- Tracking incident and response history
- Maintaining ongoing liaison with representatives of law enforcement

Security Investigator (SI)

This organization conducts investigations for all data center security incidents.
The SI is responsible for the following:

- Responding to the security emergency
- Leading the investigation effort and the post mortem session
- Providing guidelines to the ERCT for handling security emergencies
- Providing investigation progress updates to the ERCT
- Coordinating efforts among legal, law enforcement, outside security emergency handling agencies, and so on
- Providing investigation findings to SC to help improve system security

In addition to the roles we've identified, other people and/or organizations may be involved in incident discovery and reporting but are not directly involved in the incident-handling process.

Emergency Response Core Team (ERCT)

This team should have one representative from each of the following organizations: application owner, application administrator, system administrator, and security investigator. The ERCT's role is to facilitate information sharing and to better coordinate the security emergency handling effort.

The ERCT is responsible for the following:

- Establishing goals and setting priorities for the response

- Formulating a strategy to handle the security emergency

- Being the point of contact to disseminate information and updates to each organization

- Facilitating the investigation

- Conducting the post mortem session

Application Owner (AO)

This organization owns the application and derives revenue from it. This organization funded the development of the application; however, it may not be the organization that developed the application.

Because the revenue has a direct impact on the AO, the AO is responsible for the following:

- Establishing a channel for customers to report Web site–related problems

- Understanding the identified risks affecting the application itself

- Quantifying the risks

- Mitigating the identified application-related risks

- Accepting the identified risks and the potential revenue loss if the risks cannot be mitigated

- Determining an internal escalation procedure for an unexpected business interruption

- Determining the maximum acceptable application down time

- Determining the total actual revenue loss due to the security emergency

- Notifying the Security Incident Response Team (SIRT) when a security incident is identified

- Making the decision to expel the intruders or to monitor their activities

- Providing updated contact information to system administration organization

Application Developer/Administrator (AA)

This organization develops and maintains the application.

An application may be developed and administered by the same organization that owns it, but in many cases, these roles are split across multiple constituencies.

The AA is responsible for the following:

- Understanding the identified security risks/holes associated with the application

- Mitigating the application-related risks

- Identifying risks that cannot be mitigated and providing such information to the security consultant

- Implementing and maintaining a change management control mechanism to restrict application changes on the production system. Change management records must include information on when changes were made, what they consist of, and who performed them

- Making the change management control log available to the security investigator

- Troubleshooting application errors and documenting all actions taken

- Notifying the Security Incident Response Team when a security incident is identified

- Providing application audit trail or logging records to the security investigator

- Ensuring that application design and implementation comply with the Information Security Policy.

System Owner/Administrator (SA)

The SA organization maintains the computers running the application in the production environment. In most situations, the SA is the local data center administration staff.

The SA is responsible for the following:

- Ensuring that systems are configured and operated in compliance with the Information Security Policy

- Understanding the identified security risks/holes associated with the computing environment

- Mitigating risks

- Identifying any risks that cannot be mitigated and providing such information to the security consultant

- Keeping the latest application contact information

- Performing the regular system backup, emergency backup, and forensic backup

- Troubleshooting system errors and documenting all actions taken
- Notifying the Security Incident Response Team when a security incident is identified
- Maintaining the latest application contact information
- Providing system audit trail or logging records to the security investigator
- Ensuring a full backup tape is available immediately when needed
- Disconnecting the system from the LAN or reconnecting the system back to the LAN when directed by the security investigator
- Restoring computing environment to the pre-emergency condition

Network Administrator (NA)

This usually is run by the IS department, where different staff members are assigned to network operations and system administration.

The NA is responsible for the following:

- Providing Internet connectivity
- Providing LAN connectivity to the back-end servers of the data center applications
- Ensuring that network design and operation comply with the Information Security Policy
- Providing location of corporate-owned IP addresses
- Understanding the security risks/holes associated with the networking environment
- Mitigating risks
- Identifying any risks that cannot be mitigated and providing such information to the security consultant
- Troubleshooting network problems and recording all actions taken
- Notifying the Security Incident Response Team when a security incident is identified
- Filtering the network traffic that was identified to be attacking the application or the system at the router level if needed

Firewall Administrator (FA)

The FA usually is operations, but any Web customer—internal or external—may install its own firewall as part of a complex Web architecture. If the firewall is owned by a service provider, corporate involvement in incident response is determined by the contractual agreement, but if a firewall is owned by a corporate business unit, this process applies to that firewall.

The FA is responsible for the following:

- Providing LAN connectivity to the data center systems
- Ensuring firewall compliance with the Information Security Policy
- Understanding the identified security risks/holes associated with the networking environment
- Mitigating risks
- Identifying any risks that cannot be mitigated and providing such information to the security consultant
- Troubleshooting network problems and recording all actions taken
- Notifying the Security Incident Response Team when a security incident is identified
- Providing system activity and auditing logs to the security investigator
- Maintaining the firewall change management record and providing it to the security investigator when needed
- Filtering the network traffic that was identified to be attacking the application or the system when needed

Security Consultant (SC)

The Security Consultant conducts security risk assessments for unique data center applications and conducts intrusion detection analysis for the data center environment.

The SC is responsible for the following:

- Identifying the risks affecting the application itself and other applications in the data center
- Providing recommendations to the AO, AA, SA, and NA to mitigate the identified risks
- Presenting risk analysis results to the AO
- Classifying risks based on level of impact, such as application risks vs. corporate risks
- Gathering application profile information during the risk assessment process and providing that information to the Security Incident Response Team central repository

- Coordinating with all the AOs when a risk affects all data center applications

- Proactively detecting intrusions to data center environments and providing findings to the security investigator

- Providing the team with knowledge leadership in the realm of information security and the security policy

Data Center Application Profile

Each system located in a data center is running a specific application that is critical either to an AO, a business unit, or to the operation of the data center itself. Any incident that interrupts the normal operation of any data center host can result in a temporary loss of revenue or even a permanent loss of a business area. In cases when multiple applications or systems are affected simultaneously, they should be responded to in the order dictated by a predefined priority. System criticality is determined by the level of damage that could be caused by a compromise, both in monetary and nonmonetary terms. Web applications can be evaluated based on their projected revenue. Infrastructural applications potentially affect *all* application servers, so they have a higher priority than individual servers.

Although every data center application is reviewed by the Security Incident Response Team to estimate risk and provide recommendations on mitigation, each AO is also required to provide a profile to the Security Incident Response Team. This profile has to be updated annually or when the system's architecture is changed. The SA should be notified immediately after a personnel change takes place.

The completed profiles are stored with the computer investigation team of the Security Incident Response Team, which is responsible for leading the investigation of all computer security incidents.

Severity of Computer Security Incidents

The volume of low-level security events at an Internet Service Provider (ISP) is so high that it is impractical to conduct an investigation of events that are unlikely to result in a security failure. Table A-2 specifies the conditions under which a security event must be escalated. It also creates a priority list for events and types of servers—a low-level event on a critical server has a higher priority than a low-level event on a less significant server.

Note that in some circumstances, events may have their priority changed during the incident response process.

Table A-2 Incident Response Priorities

Level	Incident	Escalation
Highest	Electronic commerce system incident Authentication server incident Billing server incident Law enforcement subpoenas	All suspicious events must be escalated to the SIRT immediately. (An *incident* is a suspected unauthorized access or an unexplained change in the contents of a file.)
High	DNS server incident Email server incident Noncommerce Web server incident Router incident	
Medium	Requests for assistance with attacks originating outside of the normal corporate IP address space Complaints of ongoing successful attacks originating from within corporate IP address range Complaints of spam from within corporate IP address range	All suspicious events must be escalated to the SIRT, but after consultation, investigation probably is conducted by local staff.
Low	Network switch incident News server incident Shell server incident Chat server incident	Local and administrative staff may investigate first, then it must notify SIRT if a) the staff determines that a security incident took place, or b) the staff is unable to determine the source of suspicious events.
Lowest	Complaints about attack attempts apparently originating from within corporate IP address range Network probe	

Computer Security Incident-Handling Process

As depicted in Figure A-1, the computer security incident handling process consists of five steps.

All five steps are equally important to ensure that a security incident is quickly resolved with minimum impact to the business operation. Any shortfall at any stage may impact the process in the next step and ultimately make the entire process a waste of time. Every incident is unique, and the experience gained from handling

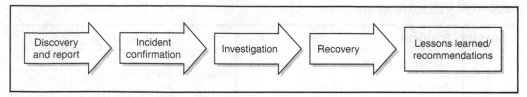

Figure A-1   Incident Response Process

one incident should provide lessons that are helpful in the future. Therefore, a post mortem session is extremely important for the team to review areas that are over-looked during the process.

Incident Discovery and Report

The flowchart in Figure A-2 depicts the process followed when an incident is sus-pected. It may not be known at first if an actual security failure has occurred—one of the purposes of this process is to make that determination.

In many Web site hacking cases, unauthorized changes to the Web sites are first discovered and reported by the users or AO. Subscriber support staff needs to respond immediately when an AO reports unauthorized changes to the Web site. Sending email to *webmaster* is not recommended for subscribers due to the potential email delay but is the only mechanism open to visitors to hosted sites. Mail sent to *webmaster* must be reviewed hourly, and any reports of potential security incidents must be promptly escalated.

To initiate an ERCT incident-handling process, the Security Incident Response Team should be contacted first. An SI will organize a core team for the system involved.

Incident Confirmation

During the early stages of incident response, it is often unknown whether or not an actual security incident has occurred. Therefore, detailed notes must be taken by all members of the ERCT—starting from the very beginning of the response. It is useful to type these notes into some electronic format periodically, but this is optional. It is mandatory that everyone participating in the response uses a bound notebook (not looseleaf or ring binder) and keeps complete handwritten notes. See the *Incident Response Form* (Appendix B) for information that must be included in these notes.

The incident confirmation process is different depending on how the incident was originally reported:

- The **User Incident Handling** process is followed when an end user or cus-tomer reports a problem.

- The **Application Incident Handling** process is followed by an AA when a problem is reported to or identified by the organization responsible for the application.

- The **System Incident Handling** process is followed by SAs whenever they become aware of a problem.

Although every corporate organization may have internal procedures that are relevant in a security incident, this corporate process must be followed to ensure a comprehensive and consistent response.

User Incident Handling

Problems typically discovered and reported by end users or subscribers include the following:

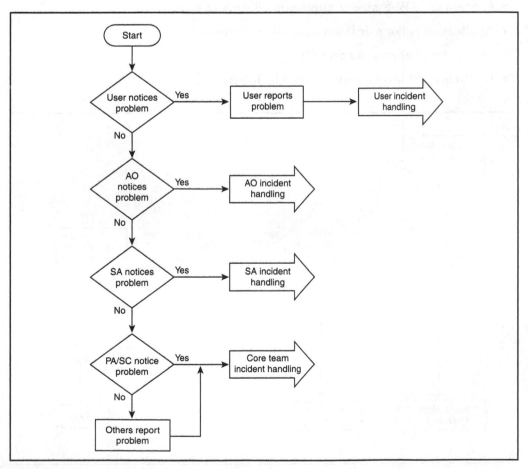

Figure A-2   Incident discovery and report

- End users cannot access the Web page or the application server from the Internet.
- Web page contents are unexpectedly changed.
- Web page or application behaves abnormally.
- A file downloaded from the Web site contains a virus.
- Web page or server is unavailable.

The flowchart in Figure A-3 shows how these problems should be handled.

Application Incident Handling

Typical problems reported to or discovered by the AA include:

- Contents of a Web page or application file are changed.
- Application is down or is not accessible via the network.
- Application behaves abnormally.
- Unauthorized access to application is detected.

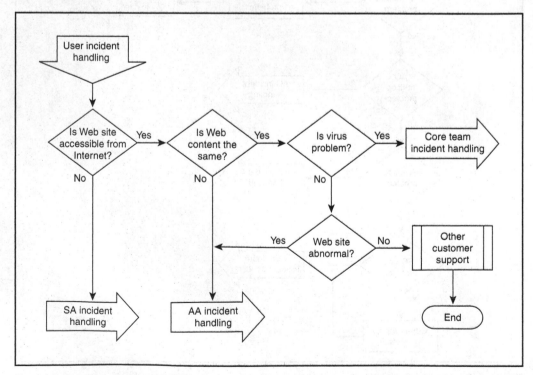

Figure A-3 User incident handling

When a problem is first noted, the application organization should conduct preliminary troubleshooting. While troubleshooting, detailed notes documenting all activities must be taken. The Incident Response Form provides a list of critical elements that are mandatory in incident investigation logs.

The flowchart in Figure A-4 shows the process for handling an application-related incident.

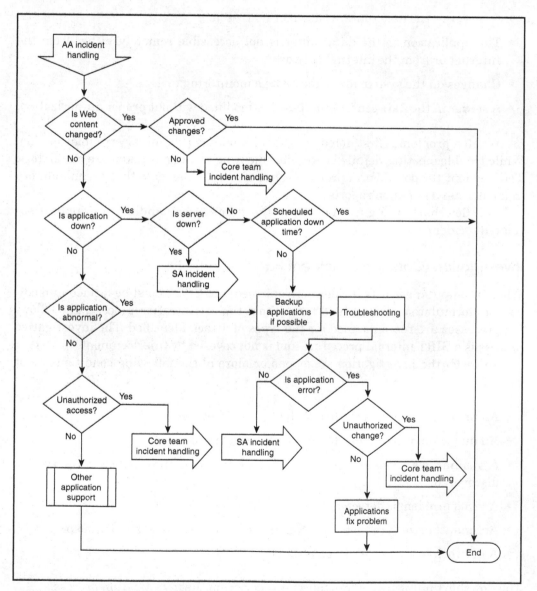

Figure A-4   Application incident handling

System Incident Handling

Problems typically reported to or discovered by the SA can include the following:

- The server is infected by a virus.
- A file distributed from the server contains a virus.
- A server in the data center is down or inaccessible.
- The application in the data center is not accessible remotely, either from the Internet or from the internal network.
- Changes on the system are detected by a monitoring tool.
- A server in the data center is accessed or modified without proper authorization.

When a problem is first noted, SAs should conduct preliminary troubleshooting. While troubleshooting, detailed notes documenting all actions taken are mandatory. The Incident Response Form provides a list of critical elements that are mandatory in incident investigation reports.

The flowchart in Figure A-5 shows the process for handling an application-related incident.

Investigation (Core Team Incident Handling)

When a computer security incident is confirmed, the ERCT must be formed immediately to formulate a strategy and to facilitate the investigation process. The following processes are recommended for the types of attack identified. The investigative process is a SIRT internal procedure and is not covered by this document.

To reach the investigation stage, one or more of the following conditions must be met:

- An undocumented change to a Web page is discovered.
- An undocumented change to a host application is discovered.
- A nonhardware-related problem that shuts down the application server is discovered.
- A virus problem is detected.
- An unauthorized access to an e-commerce application or system is suspected.
- A network intrusion or attack is detected.

The flowchart in Figure A-6 provides an overview of the investigation process.

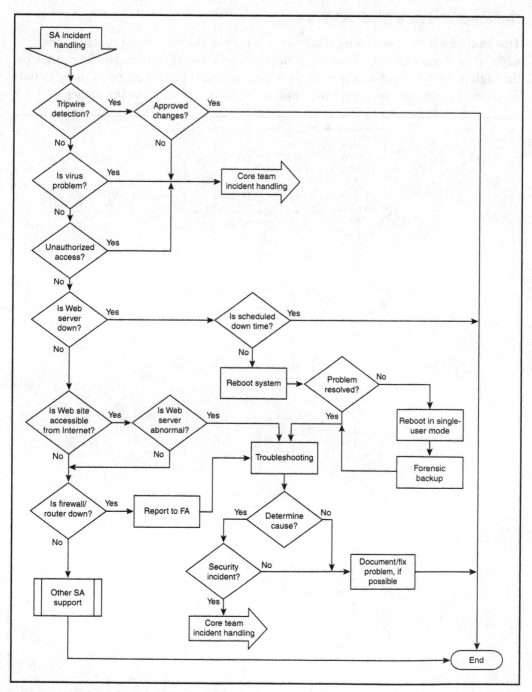

Figure A-5   System incident handling

Denial-of-Service (DoS) Attack

The goal of a denial-of-service (DoS) attack is to make the target machine inaccessible. It is done either by flooding a network so that legitimate traffic cannot get through or by overloading a service on a host so that it cannot respond to legitimate requests. Sometimes the target machine may crash as a result of the attack.

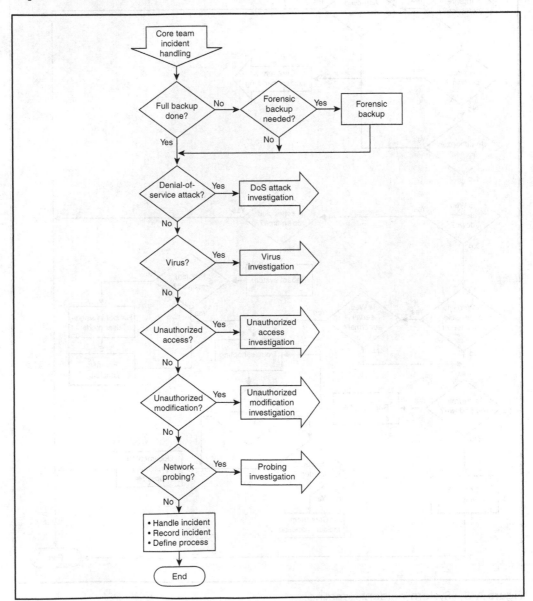

Figure A-6   Determining which response plan to follow

DoS attack packets often have spoofed source IP addresses, which complicates attempts to filter out the undesirable traffic and complicates attempts to perform a traceback (although many of the recent zombie-facilitated attacks do not bother to spoof the IP source address). The best practice for dealing with such an attack is evolving rapidly. Security team members and NAs should refer to SANS for up-to-date information on DoS response.[1] DoS attacks are increasing in frequency on the Internet, and it is very likely that data center applications will experience this type of attack. Figure A-7 depicts the process for handling a DoS attack.

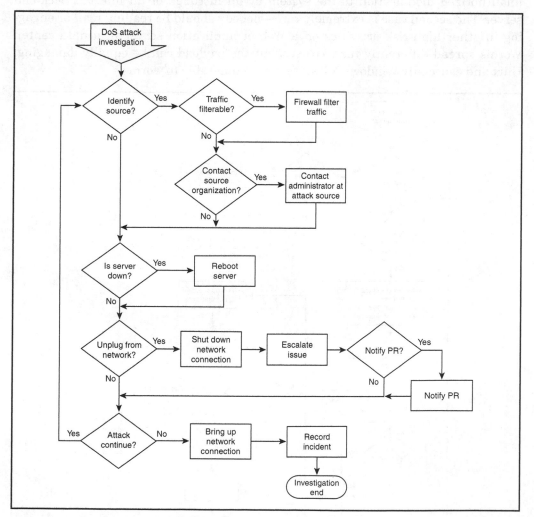

Figure A-7   Process for handling DoS attack

1. http://www.sans.org/dosstep/index.htm

Hostile Code

Malware-related incidents can fall into one of two categories:

- A document distributed at the Web site contains a virus that affects all the customers who download the file.

- The system in the data center is infected by hostile code and behaves abnormally.

The source of the malware can be a document uploaded from a back-end server, an unauthorized modification to the system by an intruder, or an infected back-end server. The second case is extremely rare—nobody should be reading mail or engaging in other high-risk activities on a Web or application server in a data center. Worms spread differently than viruses, but the payload can be equally damaging; Unix and especially Windows NT servers are vulnerable to worms.

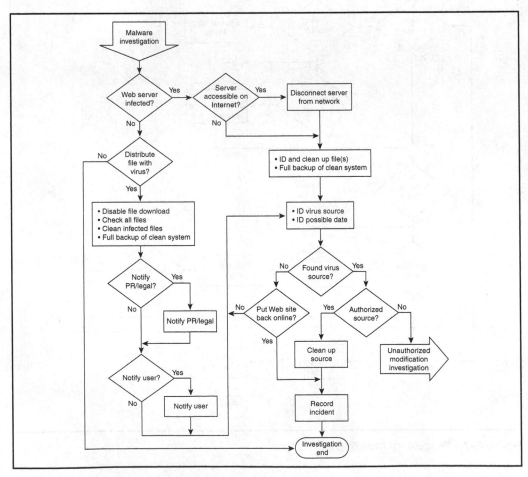

Figure A-8   Investigating a suspected malware incident

Unauthorized Access

All access to a system by an individual who does not have the proper authority on the system is considered unauthorized access, regardless of the person's employment status. To be categorized as an "unauthorized access," there must be no apparent modification. The intruder may access the system to retrieve proprietary data or, in most cases, uses the system as a springboard to access other systems. For the data center environment, the ultimate goal may be to gain access to the internal network. Back-end servers behind Web servers are vulnerable to attack through exploitation of the trust relationship between the front-end and back-end servers.

The flowchart in Figure A-9 details the procedure appropriate for this type of incident. If it is determined that the intruders are still online during the response, a decision must be made whether to keep the intruders online to better determine

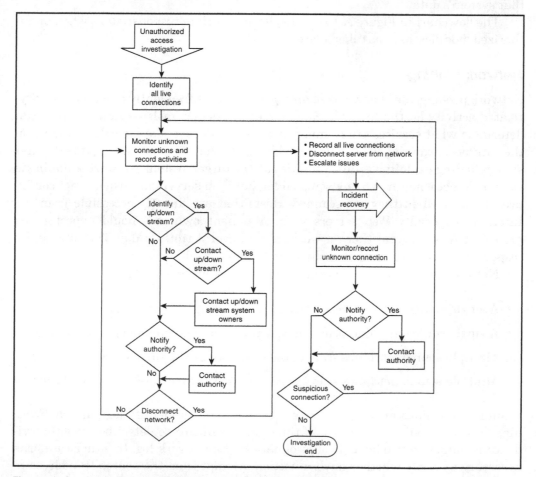

Figure A-9   Process for handling unauthorized access

what they are doing, to immediately change configuration so that the intruders cannot return, or to attempt to communicate with the intruders both to learn how they gained access and to request that they stop making unauthorized use of corporate systems. Any time intruders become aware that they have been observed, they may attempt to retaliate. If the response team has not found all of the intruders' points of entry, such as trojanized executables providing back doors, the response team will not be able to prevent the intruder from re-entering the system.

Unauthorized Modification

Any change to a system without proper authorization constitutes an unauthorized modification, regardless of the individual's employment status. A person who has authorization to access a system does not necessarily have authorization to modify that system's data.

The flowchart in Figure A-10 details the appropriate response steps when unauthorized modification has taken place.

Network Probing

Network probing, also known as *scanning,* is the most frequently observed security-related activity on the Internet. Simple reconnaissance tools—scanners—that can determine what services are running on what IP addresses are widely available on the Internet. Scanning itself causes no damage to the system; however, it is the first step in finding exploitable vulnerabilities on the target system. Network scanning is easy to detect when it is being watched for, but Web servers are usually not configured to alert when they are scanned. Hosts that are directly accessible from the Internet—especially Web servers with prominent owners—should expect to be probed at least several times a week, if not several times a day. The process for responding to network probes is shown in Figure A-11.

Network probing can be done in many different ways:

- A single source machine scans all the machines at the same time.
- A single source machine scans the machines over an extended period of time.
- Multiple source machines scan all the machines at the same time.
- Multiple source machines scan the machines over an extended period of time.

Scanning machines at the same time leaves an easy-to-identify log pattern. Scanning spreading out over a period of time can be difficult to detect because the evidence is hidden in the huge amount of data in the network log. In either case, it is necessary to verify whether any connection attempt from the source IP address to the target machine or target network has been successful.

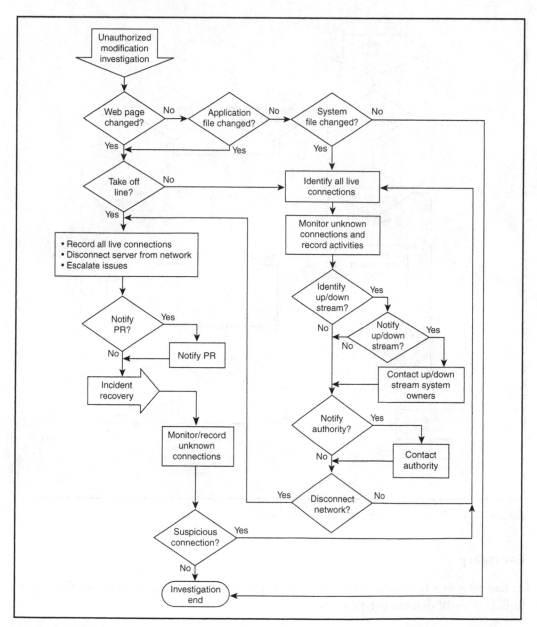

Figure A-10 Process for handling unauthorized modification

Because probing by itself does not pose any direct threat to the target machine and can be easily filtered, no special action is needed to prevent this type of incident. However, it is a good practice to record all detected probing incidents to develop some recognizable patterns as a baseline.

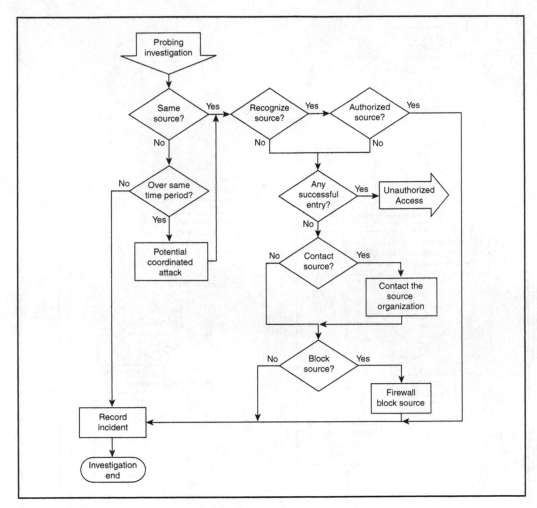

Figure A-11   Process for handling network probing

Recovery

At the recovery stage, the security incident investigation is completed. The flowchart in Figure A-12 depicts the process.

Lessons Learned and Recommendations

The ERCT is responsible for conducting a post mortem session after the system is back to normal to collect the lessons learned. The session should identify weaknesses in the process and suggest areas of improvement. Participants are not limited to the ERCT members, and the meeting is led by the SI.

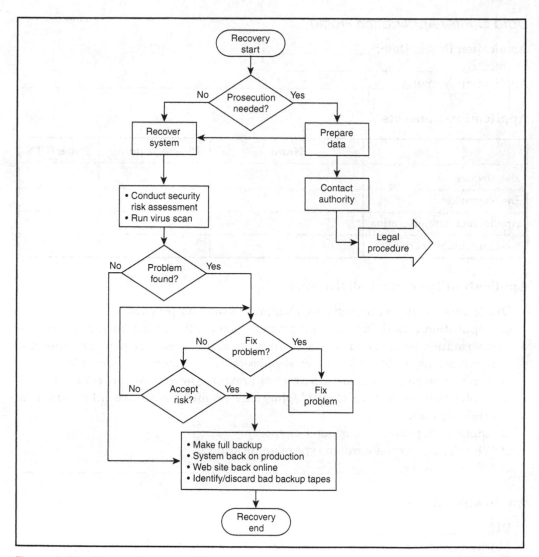

Figure A-12 Process for completing incident recovery

Conclusion

Security incidents will occur regardless of how much effort is devoted to preventing them. When an incident happens, the first priority is to limit the additional damage. The best way to achieve that goal is by preparing for incidents. This guideline must be understood and followed by all personnel involved in all data center applications and servers.

Data Center Application Profile

Application Profile Date: _____
Profiled By: _____
Application Name: _____

Application Contacts

	Name	**Phone Number**	**Pager/PIN**
Data owner			
Development			
Application administration			
System administration			

Application Type (check all that apply)

❑ e-commerce application enabling customers to order products
❑ Application containing or displaying customer information, including contact information (such as name, phone number, address, etc.) or personal information (such as credit card number, social security number, password, etc.)
❑ Application containing order history or providing order-tracking capability
❑ Application containing or displaying only product or service information in public domain
❑ Application providing customer support
❑ Whiteboard or collaboration type of application
❑ Others, specify: _____

Application Revenue

BU: _____
Marketing projected *annual* revenue from this application: _____
Potential *daily* loss if the application is offline and inaccessible from the Internet:
_____
Maximum acceptable system down time (day/hour/minute): _____

Application Overview

_____
_____
_____
_____
_____

Platform Information	
Operating system	
Machine name	
Machine IP address	
Database system used	
Machine physical location	
Security Risk Assessment Information	
Date of last assessment	
Assessment done by	
Location of the report	

What to Record

During the early stages of incident response, it is often unknown whether or not an actual security incident has occurred. Therefore, detailed notes must be taken by all members of the ERCT—starting from the very beginning of the response. It is useful to type these notes into some electronic format periodically, but this is optional. It is mandatory that everyone participating in the response uses a bound notebook (not looseleaf or ring binder) and keeps complete handwritten notes. The following information must be included with every notebook entry:

- When the action was taken, including day, month, year, hour, minute, and time zone. For example, 3/4/99 3:14pm EST or 5/20/98 16:02 MT.

- What action was taken—for example, system command or a phone call.

- Who are the people involved, including the person who took the action and the persons spoken to. Each person's full name with phone number should be included. If the person is not a corporate employee, the name of the company or organization where this person is employed should also be included.

- IP address or machine name (full name) of the machines involved.

- Why the action is needed.

- What the result is after the action was taken.

The notes will be requested and used by the SI during the investigation of a computer security incident. More importantly, the notes also will be key evidence at court if the incident results in a prosecution. Therefore, these notes should be as neat as possible and kept with care.

If prosecution is a possibility, someone should be appointed to collect the notebooks on a daily basis, make photocopies of all new information, and then maintain the notebooks in a secure place.

B

Incident Response Form

General Data Requested for All Incident Types

- ❏ Site under attack
- ❏ Incident investigation in progress
- ❏ Incident closed

What assistance do you require:
- ❏ Immediate call
- ❏ None needed at this time
- ❏ Follow-up on all affected sites
- ❏ Contact the "hacking" sites

Site involved (name and acronym): _____

Point of contact for incident:

Name _____

- • Email address _____

- • 7x24 contact information _____

Alternative point of contact for incident:

Name _____

- • Email address _____

- • 7x24 contact information _____

Type of incident (provide additional details on the appropriate form):
- ❏ Malicious code: virus, Trojan horse, worm
- ❏ Probes/scans (nonmalicious data gathering—recurring, massive, unusual)

❑ Attack (successful/unsuccessful intrusions including scanning with attack packets)

❑ Denial-of-service event

❑ High embarrassment factor

❑ Deemed significant by site

Date and time incident occurred (specify time zone): _____

A summary of what occurred: _____

_____

_____

Type of service, information, or project compromised (please provide specifics):

❑ Sensitive unclassified such as privacy, proprietary, or source selection

_____

❑ Other unclassified _____

Damage done:

- Numbers of systems affected _____

- Nature of loss, if any _____

- System down time _____

- Cost of incident (for example, unknown, none, <$10K, $10K–$50K, >$50K)

Name of other sites contacted:

Law enforcement _____

Other _____

Details for Malicious Code

Apparent source:

❑ Diskette, CD, etc.

❑ Email attachment

❑ Software download

Primary system or network involved:

- IP addresses or subnet addresses _____

- OS versions _____

- • NOS versions _____
- • Other _____

Other affected systems or networks (IPs and OSs): _____

_____

_____

Type of malicious code (include name if known):

- ❑ Virus _____
- ❑ Trojan horse _____
- ❑ Worm _____
- ❑ Joke program _____
- ❑ Other _____
- ❑ Copy sent to:

  - • _____
  - • _____
  - • _____

Method of operation (for new malicious code):
- ❑ Type—macro, boot, memory resident, polymorphic, self-encrypting, stealth
- ❑ Payload
- ❑ Software infected
- ❑ Files erased, modified, deleted, encrypted—any special significance to these files
- ❑ Self-propagating via email
- ❑ Detectable changes
- ❑ Other features

Details: _____

_____

_____

How detected: _____

_____

_____

Remediation (actions taken to return the systems to trusted operation):
- ❏ Antivirus product obtained, updated, or installed for automatic operation
- ❏ New policy established on use of email attachments
- ❏ Firewall, routers, or email servers updated to detect and scan attachments

Details: _____

_____

_____

Additional comments: _____

_____

_____

Details for Probes and Scans

Apparent source:

- IP address _____
- Host name _____
- Location of attacking host:
  - ❏ Domestic
  - ❏ Foreign
  - ❏ Insider

Primary systems/networks involved:

- IP addresses or subnet addresses _____
- OS versions _____
- NOS versions _____

Other affected systems or networks (IPs and OSs): _____

_____

_____

Method of operation:
- ❏ Ports probed/scanned
- ❏ Order of ports or IP addresses scanned
- ❏ Probing tool
- ❏ Anything that makes this probe unique

Details: _____

_____

_____

How detected:
- ❏ Another site
- ❏ Incident response team
- ❏ Log files
- ❏ Packet sniffer
- ❏ Intrusion detection system
- ❏ Anomalous behavior
- ❏ User

Details: _____

_____

_____

Log file excerpts: _____

_____

_____

Additional Comments: _____

_____

_____

Details for Unauthorized Access

Apparent source:
- IP address
- Location of host:
  - ❏ Domestic
  - ❏ Foreign
  - ❏ Insider

Primary systems involved:

- IP addresses or subnet addresses _____

- OS versions _____

- NOS versions _____

Other affected systems or networks (IPs and OSs): _____

_____

_____

Avenue of attack:
- ❏ Sniffed/guessed/cracked password
- ❏ Trusted host access
- ❏ Vulnerability exploited
- ❏ Hacker tool used
- ❏ Utility or port targeted
- ❏ Social engineering

Details: _____

_____

_____

- ❏ Level of access gained—root/administrator, user

Method of operation of the attack (more detailed description of actions taken):
- ❏ Ports or protocols attacked
- ❏ Attack tools used, if known
- ❏ Installed hacker tools such as rootkit, sniffers, L0phtCrack, zap
- ❏ Sites hacker used to download tools
- ❏ Hacker tools installed
- ❏ Established a service such as IRC
- ❏ Looked at who is logged on
- ❏ Trojanned, listed, examined, deleted, modified, created, or copied files
- ❏ Left a back door
- ❏ Names of accounts created and passwords used
- ❏ Left unusual or unauthorized processes running
- ❏ Launched attacks on other systems or sites
- ❏ Other

Details: _____

_____

_____

How detected:
- ❏ Another site
- ❏ Incident response team
- ❏ Log files
- ❏ Packet sniffer
- ❏ Intrusion detection software
- ❏ Anomalous behavior
- ❏ User
- ❏ Alarm tripped
- ❏ TCP Wrapper
- ❏ Tripwire
- ❏ Other

Details: _____

_____

_____

Log file excerpts: _____

_____

_____

Remediation (actions taken to return the systems to trusted operation):
- ❏ Patches applied
- ❏ Scanners run
- ❏ Security software installed
- ❏ Unneeded services and applications removed
- ❏ OS reloaded
- ❏ System restored from backup
- ❏ Application moved to another system
- ❏ Memory or disk space increased
- ❏ System placed behind a filtering router or firewall
- ❏ Hidden files detected and removed
- ❏ Trojan software detected and removed
- ❏ System left unchanged to monitor hacker behavior
- ❏ Other

Details: _____

_____

_____

Additional Comments: _____

_____

_____

Details for Denial-of-Service Incident

Apparent source:

- IP address _____

- Location of host:
  - ❏ Domestic
  - ❏ Foreign
  - ❏ Insider

Primary systems involved:

- IP addresses or subnet address _____

- OS versions _____

- NOS versions _____

Other affected systems or networks (IPs and OSs): _____

_____

_____

Method of operation:
- ❏ Tool used
- ❏ Packet flood
- ❏ Malicious packet
- ❏ IP spoofing
- ❏ Ports attacked
- ❏ Anything that makes this event unique

Details: _____

_____

_____

Remediation (actions taken to protect the systems):
- ❏ Application moved to another system
- ❏ Memory or disk space increased
- ❏ Shadow server installed

❏ System moved behind a filtering router or firewall
❏ Other

Details: _____

_____

_____

Log file excerpts: _____

_____

_____

Additional comments: _____

_____

_____

Appendix
C

How to Become A Unix Guru

It would be best if all forensic examiners had years of experience on the platform they will be investigating, but unfortunately, not enough people are available. If you don't know Unix well, but expect increased opportunity if you learn more about it, go for it. Devote serious study and practice time, and you quickly can learn a useful level of knowledge about Unix. Unix is an excellent learning environment. Heavily documented and with source code available for study—what you learn about operating systems in Unix is applicable to Windows NT and even future environments.

First, we suggest you use Unix on a daily basis—you can't learn it if you don't use it, and the best way to use it is to force yourself to be productive with it. Use it for your personal workstation. We're partial to Linux, but any of the PC Unix platforms is suitable (although PC Solaris is quite limited in its hardware support). You even can download RedHat for free. Run your office automation applications, such as email and word processing, on Unix so that you force yourself to use it. Try to find an office file server, processor, or maybe a Web server that you can volunteer to administer. A Web server on your intranet is ideal. Servers are likely to have more problems than workstations, so you can learn more. Try to stay away from GUI commands. It's okay to use graphical office automation applications (such as Star Office, Corel, and Applix), but do your system housekeeping chores from the command lines so that you become comfortable with it.

You should make a special effort to learn and use vi. It is ancient, and its developer, Bill Joy, has been quoted saying he never would have written it if he'd known how popular it would become. But vi is ubiquitous on Unix. If you know your way around vi, you can always count on having a full-screen editor on any Unix system you administer. Don't get sidetracked by using some text editor that isn't available on every platform.

Read a lot. You have to expect advice like this from an author, but reading really is one of the most effective ways to learn about specific technologies. Unix is well documented internally, and many supplementary FAQs and how-to documents are available on the Internet or with some installations. But don't limit yourself just to online documents. While they are usually quite helpful, they don't provide the same comprehensive approach to learning that books do. Get more books and read them.

Look for books on administering Unix, securing Unix, and read at least two books on Unix internals. The word *internals* refers to the under-the-cover functioning of the OS, and the better you understand it, the more effective you will be. Subscribe to a magazine, and make it a point to visit regularly some of the online magazines that specialize in Unix, Linux, or other open system topics.

Learn regular expressions. Regular expressions are the constructs you make out of metacharacters (such as * and ?) and are the way that you formulate a text search with Unix using grep. Metacharacters are pervasive in Unix, which is highly text oriented. (The filename wildcards, such as the splat character, *, are basically a subset of the regular expression characters.) More complex forms can be used to match more specific strings. Regular expressions are used not only as string parameters for grep, but also within a batch editor (sed) and the visual editor (vi). They are also used within shell scripts.

Speaking of shell scripts, you can't consider yourself a Unix guru without learning how to read and write within this powerful programming environment. Experienced Unix system adminstrators are expected to know how to write shell scripts, and a professionally administered system invariably contains locally written shell scripts that are in regular use. For this reason, an understanding of shell scripts is critical in understanding how a specific Unix system is configured. You should experiment and learn to write your own Bourne shell scripts. Once you are comfortable with shell scripting, branch out and learn Perl.

The C programming language is a lot like Latin, but you can actually use C, unlike a dead language. We compare it to Latin because C is at the core of everything that happens in a Unix system. The OS itself is written in C, and the command line and scripting environments are heavily influenced by it. As knowledge of Latin can help you better understand English, familiarity with C is the best way to learn how Unix functions. If you really want to learn Unix internals, do it by writing code. Work through the Rochkind or Stephens books[1] to learn about and experiment with system calls. This can teach you a lot about the filesystem and how it can be manipulated by an attacker.

Experiment with security and hacking tools. Obviously, you shouldn't experiment with hacking tools on a production system, but a couple of old 486s or 150MHz Pentiums can make a great Unix test environment. Find some machines that are too slow and small for Windows and build a Unix laboratory with them. Download exploit code from Rootshell, compile it, and see if it works. Play both the hacker and the detective, using the techniques discussed in this book to locate signs of your own "intrusion." Install security tools like Tripwire and Snort and see if they can detect your attacks.

---

1. Please refer to the Bibliography for information about Rochkind or Stephens.

Talk to Unix experts who enjoy sharing their knowledge. If you don't have people like this within your own organization, find a local users' group or some place online (a chat room, newsgroup, and so on) where you can learn how to talk the Unix talk. Develop a network of people who are willing to help you learn Unix and ask them questions when you don't understand something. If you are sincerely interested in learning Unix and make a good-faith effort to apply what you learn, you should have no problem finding gurus who will have infinite patience with you.

D

Exporting a Windows 2000 Private Key

1. Start the Microsoft Management Console (Start | Run | MMC).

2. Click Console.

3. Click Add/Remove Snap-in as shown in the following graphic:

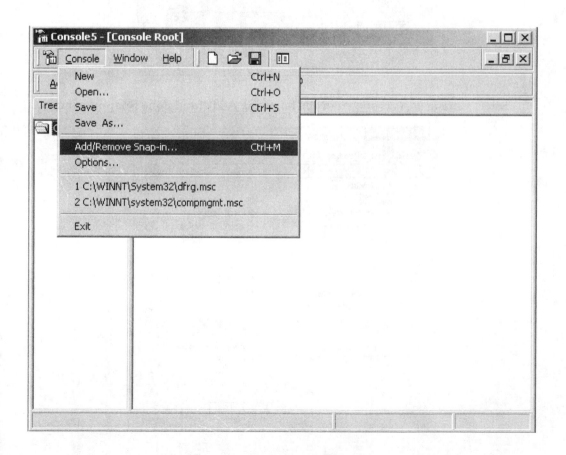

4. Click the Add button in the Add/Remove Snap-in window.

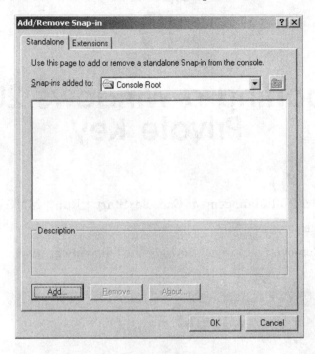

5. Select Certificates, as shown in the following Add standalone Snap-in window.

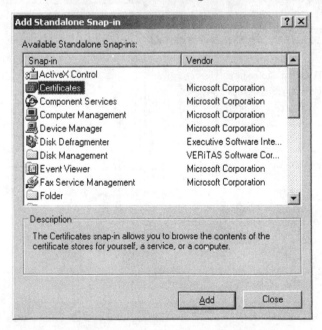

6. Select the My user account radio button as shown in the Certificates Snap-in window.

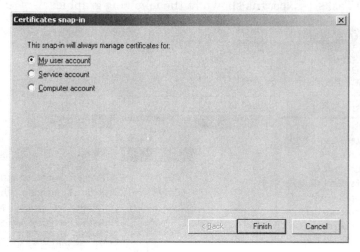

7. Click Close on Add Snap-in.

8. Click OK on Add/Remove Snap-in.

9. Drop down to Personal/Certificates.

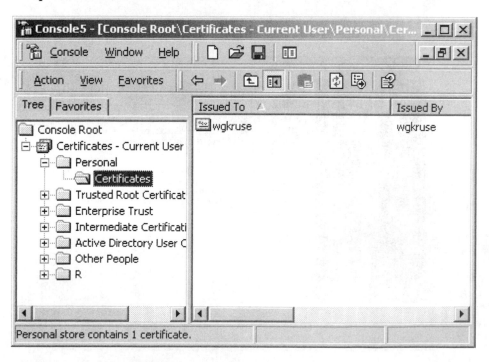

10. Right-click the user's certificate.

11. Click All Tasks | Export as shown in the following graphic:

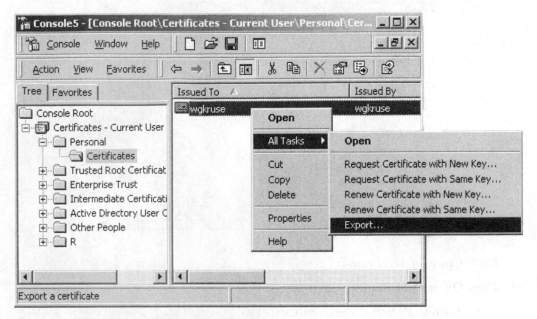

12. When the Export Wizard is displayed, click the Next button.

13. Select the Yes, export the private key radio button as shown in the following graphic:

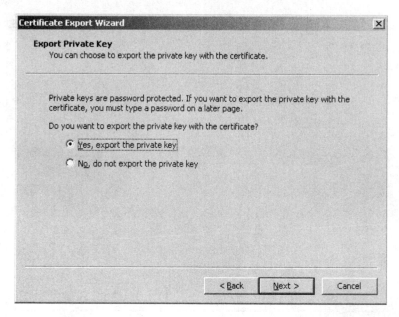

14. Make sure the Personal Information Exchange radio button is selected. (Do not select the Delete the private key checkbox.)

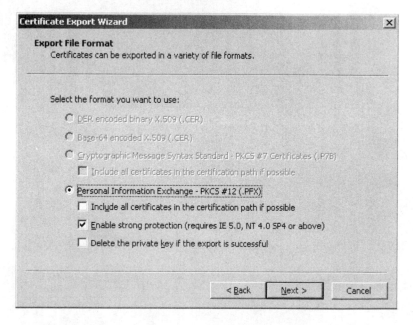

15. Enter a password to protect the key.

```
Certificate Export Wizard                                          [x]

  Password
     To maintain security, you must protect the private key by using a password.


        Type and confirm a password.

        Password:
        [ |                                              ]

        Confirm password:
        [                                                 ]




                                    < Back    Next >    Cancel
```

16. Select a path for the key.

```
Certificate Export Wizard                                          [x]

  File to Export
     Specify the name of the file you want to export


        File name:
        [ a:\warren's key|                    ]   Browse...




                                    < Back    Next >    Cancel
```

17. Verify the settings you specified.

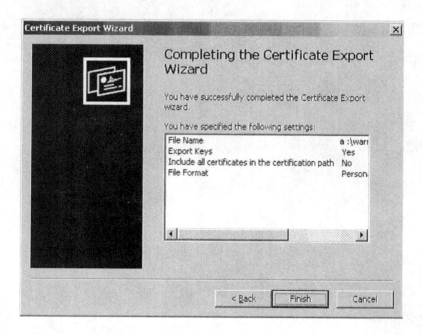

18. Click Finish to export the key.

E

How to Crowbar Unix Hosts

The term *crowbar* refers to the circumventing of a host's access control by booting it with an external medium (i.e., a floppy disk, CD, or externally attached hard drive) and then accessing the hard drives. The easiest way to do this on a Unix system is to boot from a CD, mount the root partition, and then edit either /etc/passwd or /etc/shadow to remove the password from the root account. After this process has been completed, the system can be rebooted, enabling anyone to log on as root. This trick is certainly not the preferred method of forensic investigation, but it is one that everyone doing incident response should know. If you are forced to perform a quick investigation of a Unix system and the person who has the root password is unavailable or uncooperative, this method is the fastest way to access the system.

Any computer can be broken into when you have physical access to it. If you can boot on your own terms, using your choice of platforms on removable media, then so much the better. If you cannot, your only choice may be to physically remove the drive and attach it to some other system. Intel-based systems (that is, the PC platform) are easy to crowbar because they always have bootable floppy disks and usually have bootable CDs.

Crowbarring a Linux system

Linux is fairly easy to crowbar because all the major distributions ship with bootable CDs. For instance, if you are using RedHat Linux, type **/bin/bash** at the CD's boot prompt. This gives you a root shell, and you can proceed to mount the root partition on /mnt. If you want to get more ambitious with a crowbarred system, or you don't have access to a Linux boot CD, see Appendix F: "Creating a Linux Boot CD."

Crowbarring a Solaris System

Non-PC platforms can be slightly harder to crowbar, but many of them support some form of bootable CD. Follow these steps to crowbar Solaris:

1. Boot from the Solaris CD. An ok> prompt is displayed.
2. Type **boot cdrom –S** which puts you into single-user mode.

3. Type **fsck -F ufs /dev/rdsk/c0t0d0s0** (or whatever the rawdisk device for your root partition is).

4. Create a mount point by typing **mkdir /tmp/a**.

5. Mount the root partition by typing **mount /dev/dsk/c0t0d0s0 /tmp/a**.

Appendix

E

Creating a Linux Boot CD

Several open source initiatives are underway today with the purpose of developing kits for the creation of bootable Unix CDs.[1] The one we like is the *Linuxcare Bootable Business Card*.[2] It took about two hours to download the file at dial-up speed. It comes in the form of an iso image, which is a standard format for bootable CD images. We created the CD on a Windows machine, popped it into the CD drive of a system with a Linux hard drive, booted up the CD, and within minutes had a Unix prompt. All the filesystems on the hard drive automatically were mounted read-only.

Not only does the Linuxcare Bootable Business Card include hundreds of useful Unix utilities, it also has network support. We had to know what type of card was installed in the PC, and it took two guesses to come up with the correct memory address it was strapped for. Then the network module loaded right into the Linux kernel, and we were able to start the network right up. We used Dynamic Host Configuration Protocol (DHCP) to obtain a local address, but we also could have done it manually. The CD image does not contain Secure Socket Shell (SSH) because of export issues, but the program asks if you want to download it. We said yes and had SSH running within minutes, downloading it from the Internet. The image also comes with netcat, so we were quickly able to start copying filesystem images from our "suspect" host over to our collection host.

For local investigation, the Bootable Business Card includes vi, grep, find, strings, file, and even a low-level disk editor. This CD image is a gift for the busy part-time forensic examiner. Spend just a couple minutes of your time, and you can create a CD that enables you to safely capture data from a compromised PC and perform simple investigations on both DOS and Linux filesystems.

If you are looking for a lean-and-mean solution, you might also want to try tomsrbt,[3] which is a root and boot Linux floppy. This kernel is as compact as it gets.

---

1. http://www.redhat.com/mirrors/LDP/HOWTO/Bootdisk-HOWTO/index.html

2. http://www.linuxcare.com/bootable_cd/

3. http://metalab.unc.edu/pub/micro/pc-stuff/Linux/system/recovery

If you do decide to use some form of floppy-based Unix, be aware that it might try to swap to the hard drive, which may be counterproductive to your examination. Any time you use removable media—either a CD or a floppy disk—to boot a system, be sure that you understand where it is doing swapping and configure it so that it does not swap to your hard drive.

Appendix

G

Contents of a Forensic Unix CD

You should create CDs containing the binaries you'll need for conducting your investigation. If you do get stuck doing incident response on a host (that is, you don't have the luxury of imaging the drives for examination on a trusted forensic workstation), at least use trusted binaries. The best way to carry them around is to put them on an ISO 9660 CD, which virtually every Unix platform can mount. Because you need a different set of binaries for each platform that you'll encounter, we suggest that you create a different directory for each platform. It is common wisdom that everything must be statically linked to avoid problems with compromised kernels. This is good work if you can get it, but it is virtually impossible to do on some platforms (Solaris, for example, is notoriously difficult). At the time of this writing, several volunteer initiatives were underway to create a binary set that is appropriate for an incident response CD. The binaries on this CD would be statically linked, or the CD would include safe copies of the link libraries.

Because there's plenty of room on a CD, we suggest you include copies of the following utilities:

dd	to	grep	ifconfig
cp	lsof	less	kill
cat	strings	vi (editor)	nc (netcat)
ls	find	perl	tcpdump
ps	bash file	TCT: pcat, mactime, Md5	

It won't hurt for you to include the source code also—especially the utilities that you won't find on a standard Unix distribution, such as the TCT utilities. If you have the source code, you always can make and run your most useful utilities, even when you are investigating a Unix platform that you were not able to prepare binaries for ahead of time.

Finding all the pieces needed to create statically linked binaries can be something of a scavenger hunt. While it might be a useful exercise in forensic search techniques, some readers probably will appreciate a source of ready-made statically linked binaries. Such a set of binaries for use in incident response can be found at www.incident-response.org.[4] Not only does it include standard Unix utilities for several platforms, but the site also contains a growing set of tools useful for forensic purposes on both Unix and Windows. MAC Daddy, for instance, is a modified version of several TCT utilities designed to be a more practical way to collect file time attributes when doing incident response.

---

4. http://www.incident-response.org

Annotated Bibliography

Anderson, Ross. "Why Cryptosystems Fail," http://www.cl.cam.ac.uk

Anonymous. *Maximum Linux Security: A Hacker's Guide to Protecting Your Linux Server and Workstation,* Indianapolis: SAMS, 1999. This is a detailed source of information on specific attacks. It includes links to attack code, signs of attack, and countermeasures.

Bach, Maurice J. *Design of the Unix Operating System,* Englewood Cliffs, N.J.: Prentice-Hall, 1986. Although it is showing its age and doesn't include many new developments such as /proc or Linux, a forensic technician is well-advised to have as detailed an understanding of Unix internals as presented in this classic.

Boyle, Phillip. "Intrusion Detection FAQ," http://www.sans.org/newlook/resources/IDFAQ/trinoo.htm. Helpful document on both preventing and detecting distributed denial-of-service attacks. Includes links to software that can detect DDoS code on either Unix or Windows.

Casey, Eoghan. *Digital Evidence and Computer Crime, Forensic Science, Computers and the Internet,* San Diego: Academic Press, 2000.

Cheswick, William, and Steve Bellovin. "Repelling the Wily Hacker," in *Firewalls and Internet Security* Reading, MA.: Addison-Wesley, 1994.

Cohen, Fredrick B. *A Short Course on Computer Viruses,* New York: Wiley, 1994. This informative and well-written textbook on viruses was written before the appearance of Word macro viruses.

Denning, Dorothy E., and William E. Baugh, Jr. "Hiding Crimes in Cyberspace," http://cryptome.org/hiding-db.htm. This is an essay on the subject of hiding data for criminal purposes.

Fish, Bryan, and Jim Tiller. "Packet Sniffers and Network Monitors," *Information Security Management Handbook,* 4th Edition, Volume 2 Boca Raton, FL: Auerbach, 2000.

Garfinkel, Simpson, and Gene Spafford. *Practical Unix Security,* Cambridge: O'Reilly & Associates, 1996. This thorough and detailed generic guide to administering Unix securely provides a discussion of security-related log files (including TCP Wrapper) that is especially useful to the examiner.

Graham, Robert. "Sniffing (network wiretap, sniffer) FAQ," http://packetstorm.secu-rify.com/sniffers/sniffing-faq.htm. Informative introduction to the concept and technology of sniffers by a former employee of Network General, the firm that created the first commercial sniffer. Graham categorizes hostile sniffers as *underground* and nonhostile sniffers as *diagnostic.*

Gutmann, Peter. "Secure Deletion of Data from Magnetic and Solid-State Memory," http://www.fish.com/security/secure_del.html.

Heiser, Jay. "An Introduction to Hostile Code and Its Control," *Information Security Management Handbook,* 4th Edition, Volume 2, Boca Raton, FL: Auerbach, 2000.

Honeycutt, Gerald, Jr., Jerry Honeycutt Jr., and Chriss Will, *Teach Yourself the Windows Registry in 24 Hours,* Indianapolis: SAMS, 1999.

Johnson, Neil F. "An Introduction to Watermark Recovery from Images," in *Proceedings of the SANS Intrusion Detection and Response (IDR '99) Conference,* San Diego: SANS Institute, 1999. A PDF version of this paper is available at http://www.jjtc.com/pub/nfjidr99.pdf

Johnson, Neil F., and Sushil Jajodian. "Steganalysis of Image Created Using Current Stenography Software," http://link.springer.de/link/service/series/0558/bibs/1525/15250273.htm (Other links by Neil Johnson are available at http://www.ise.gmu.edu/~johnson)

Kahn, David. *The Codebreakers: The Comprehensive History of Secret Communication from Ancient Times to the Internet,* New York: Scribner, 1996. This book is an exhaustive history of encryption and secret writing.

Krsul, Ivan. "Authorship Analysis: Identifying the Author of a Program," COAST Technical Report CSD-TR-94-030, May 1994. (To download a PDF of this report, see http://www.cerias.purdue.edu/homes/spaf/tech-reps/9430.pdf.)

Levy, Stephen. *Crypto,* New York: Viking, 2001. This book provides a highly readable account of the recent history of encryption and the conflicts between encryption advocates and law enforcement policy makers.

Maes, Maurice. "Twin Peaks: The Histogram Attack to Fixed Depth Image Watermarks." If you want to dig up more of the concepts of digital watermarks, go to http://www.informatik.unitrier.de/~leg/db/indices/atree/m/Maes:Maurice.html

Marks, Leo. *Between Silk and Cyanide: A Codemaker's War 1941–1945,* New York: Free Press, 1999. A personal biography of a World War II British cryptographer, this entertaining book should make crystal clear the importance of following proper procedures and maintaining good hygiene.

McClure, Stuart, Joel Scambray, and George Kurtz. *Hacking Exposed,* Berkeley, CA: Osborne McGraw-Hill, 1999. The best overall source of information on the use of hostile code to gain and retain unauthorized access to systems.

McDonald, Andrew D., and Markus G. Kuhn. "StegFS: A Steganographic File System for Linux." You may someday run into a steganographic filesystem although implementations are currently rare. http://www.cl.cam.ac.uk/~mgk25/ih99-stegfs. pdf.

Nemeth, Snyder, Seebass, and Hein. *Unix System Administration Handbook,* Upper Saddle River, N.J.: Prentice Hall, 1997.

Northcutt, Stephen. "Computer Security Incident Handling: Step by Step," the SANS Institute, 1998. This short document can be adapted whole or in part as a process for responding to attacks on Unix systems.

Northcutt, Stephen. *Network Intrusion Detection: An Analyst's Handbook,* Indianapolis, IN: New Riders, 2000. Excellent source of information on the use of network scanners, such as Nmap. This book should be in the library of anyone interested in network forensics.

Rochkind, Marc. *Advanced UNIX Programming,* Englewood Cliffs, N.J., Prentice-Hall, 1985. This is an excellent hands-on book for learning how Unix works from the inside out.

Rosenblatt, Kenneth S. *High-Technology Crime: Investigating Cases Involving Computers,* San Jose: KSK Publications, 1995.

Roth, David. *Win32 Perl Scripting: The Administrator's Handbook,* Indianapolis, IN: New Riders, 2001.

Scambray, Joel, Stuart McClure, and George Kurtz. *Hacking Exposed,* Berkeley: Osborne/McGraw-Hill, 2001. This book-length guide to understanding specific system attack activities covers virtually all platforms, including Unix, Windows, Web servers, and NetWare.

Schneier, Bruce. *Applied Cryptography,* New York: John Wiley & Sons, 1996. This book is widely considered the most comprehensive practical approach to cryptography and is highly recommended to anyone who wants to go into more depth.

Schnier, Bruce. "Security Pitfalls in Cryptography," http://www.counterpane.com/ pitfalls.html

Schneier, Bruce. "Why Cryptography Is Harder Than It Looks." A number of well-written documents are available on Schneier's site at: http://www.counterpane.com/ whycrypto.html.

Skoudis, Ed. "Hacker Tools and Techniques," *Information Security Management Handbook,* 4th Edition, Volume 2. Boca Raton, FL: Auerbach, 2000.

Stevens, W. Richard. *TCP/IP Illustrated,* Volume 1, Reading, MA.: Addison-Wesley, 1994. This book is perhaps the most well-recognized one on Internet protocols.

Thompson, Ken. "Reflections on Trusting Trust," September 1995, http://www.acm. org/classics/sep95. (Reprint of article from *Communication of the ACM* 27, no. 8 [1984]: 761–63). Warning against the dangers of using unreviewed code that uses an example of a trojaned compiler that removes all traces of itself after creating a modified version of /bin/login.

Whalley, Ian. "Testing Times for Trojans," presented at the Virus Bulletin Conference, October 1999, http://www.aresearch.ibm.com/antivirus/SciPapers/Whalley/inwVB99.html.

Wood, Patrick H., and Stephen G. Kochan. *Unix System Security,* Hayden Books, 1985. Now out of print, this classic text is still the best source for understanding the Unix password file and file permissions.

Zeltser, Lenny. "The Evolution of Malicious Agents," April 2000, http://www.zeltser.com/agents. A lucid 20-page discussion of autonomous malware that includes a comprehensive reference list.

INDEX